Strategies of
North and South

ALSO BY GERALD L. EARLEY

The Second United States Sharpshooters in the Civil War: A History and Roster (McFarland, 2009; paperback 2014)

Strategies of North and South

A Comparative Analysis of the Union and Confederate Campaigns

GERALD L. EARLEY

McFarland & Company, Inc., Publishers
Jefferson, North Carolina

All photographs are by the author unless otherwise noted.

LIBRARY OF CONGRESS CATALOGUING-IN-PUBLICATION DATA

Names: Earley, Gerald L., author.
Title: Strategies of North and South : a comparative analysis of the Union and Confederate campaigns / Gerald L. Earley.
Description: Jefferson, North Carolina : McFarland & Company, Inc., Publishers, 2021 | Includes bibliographical references and index.
Identifiers: LCCN 2021025256 | ISBN 9781476685663 (paperback : acid free paper) ∞
ISBN 9781476643168 (ebook)
Subjects: LCSH: United States—History—Civil War, 1861-1865—Campaigns. | Confederate States of America—History, Military. | Generals—Confederate States of America. | Confederate States of America. Army—History. | Generals—United States—History—19th century. | United States. Army—History—19th century. | Operational art (Military science)—History—19th century. | Strategy—History—19th century. | Command of troops—History—19th century.
Classification: LCC E470 .E129 2021 | DDC 973.7/3—dc23
LC record available at https://lccn.loc.gov/2021025256

BRITISH LIBRARY CATALOGUING DATA ARE AVAILABLE

ISBN (print) 978-1-4766-8566-3
ISBN (ebook) 978-1-4766-4316-8

© 2021 Gerald L. Earley. All rights reserved

No part of this book may be reproduced or transmitted in any form or by any means, electronic or mechanical, including photocopying or recording, or by any information storage and retrieval system, without permission in writing from the publisher.

Front cover image: "Gettysburg. Repulse of Longstreet's Assault" painted by James Walker; engraved by H.B. Hall, Jr. circa 1876 (Library of Congress)

Printed in the United States of America

*McFarland & Company, Inc., Publishers
Box 611, Jefferson, North Carolina 28640
www.mcfarlandpub.com*

Table of Contents

Preface   1

1. American Antebellum Martial Perceptions   5
2. 1860: Pre-War Motivation and Morale   12
3. 1861: America Stumbles into Civil War   19
4. 1861: The North Initiates Comprehensive Warfare   45
5. 1862: A Disastrous Year for the Confederacy   65
6. 1863: The Year of Northern Ascendency   138
7. 1864: The Decisive Year   185
8. 1865: The Confederacy Collapses   268
9. Comparisons and Conclusions   280

Chapter Notes   289
Bibliography   297
Index   301

Preface

For over 150 years the American Civil War has been an extraordinarily popular subject for books, magazines and literature. Civil War theme writing accounts for more than enough surviving material to fill a great library and continues to reach interested readers not only in America but worldwide. Interpretive writing about the Civil War has produced some rectified perspective in recent decades. As new information is introduced with evolving perspective, it becomes increasingly apparent that much of the writing from the century following the war requires reexamination, and additional insight is necessary to construct a more exact and impartial rendering of the conflict.

With a multitude of compelling personalities and momentous historical and social issues involved, the Civil War will probably continue to be America's single most documented and studied historical topic. However, for some Americans the Civil War remains a subject of fascination because it touches us on a personal basis. It's in our DNA.

Politicians, talking heads, pundits and the media constantly remind us that America is and has always been a nation of immigrants. While this cannot be denied, as evidence indicates that humans were not native to and originally migrated to the Americas from elsewhere, some Americans see things differently. Actor Charlton Heston expressed this viewpoint well when he wrote that he was a "native American" by virtue of birth and the birth of his parents. He also mentioned, for example, that his son Fraser could trace his maternal ancestors in America back twelve generations to 1633.[1] And so it is for Americans like me. Nearly all of my ancestors that I have traced arrived on this continent well before the American Revolution. They were not simply immigrants: they were mostly settlers, frontiersmen and pioneers. There is a difference. When most of my ancestors arrived on this continent there was no United States, and there was little or no infrastructure to nurture them. Life was dangerous and harsh in the frontier areas where they settled. Then generations later when the American Civil War erupted, all of my then living ancestors were here and were caught up in it.

Since much of the writing about the Civil War was authored by those who, like me, had ancestors involved or otherwise had something of a personal stake in how the Civil War is remembered, a tendency to give weight to the "myth of the lost cause" has persisted. Southern veterans after the war fabricated a myth that the South did not fight to sustain slavery and lost only because of superior Northern resources. Some recent writing has addressed this bias by documenting and debunking the distortion generated by the post-war myth of the lost cause interpretation and by presenting an alternative viewpoint. Unfortunately, some of this otherwise useful and accurate revisionist writing is presented much like a lawyer working a trial case. As a result valid analysis found in previous writing is seemingly ignored or diminished in an apparent zeal to discredit the myth. An impartial and balanced comparison of the overall military record with a focus on how and why outcomes were affected is still needed. The task here is to examine the subject with objectivity. Getting at the truth is not likely to please everyone, especially in this time of overbearing constraints and irrational criticisms of historical figures.

Despite a weariness of seemingly endless conflict, most Americans retain respect for and take pride in our nation's martial history. This isn't unusual or unseemly; it is common throughout the world and evident in human history. Examples of this custom are thousands of years old and are found even in the Bible. Almost an entire chapter in the Bible, II Samuel 23, records the names and deeds of King David's mighty men. How well a nation's warriors acquit themselves in battle was and remains weighty.

It seems reasonable through research to assume that the Southern states bred a more militaristic society than the rest of the nation before the Civil War. This topic has been examined and attributed to ethnic and cultural differences within the antebellum northern and southern United States. Antebellum writing reveals that Southerners, especially elites, absolutely viewed their region as martially superior in the years leading up to the Civil War. As with most generalizations this assessment was and remains somewhat exaggerated. Nevertheless, Southerners and even many Northerners obviously believed it and acknowledged it in their writing before and during the war. Given then that Southerners viewed their region as martially superior to their ultimate conquerors, some mitigating explanation for their defeat was incumbent. Consequently, much Civil War writing, past and recent, has consciously or unconsciously resembled the assessments so familiar in the myth of the lost cause school.

This book investigates the validity of the perception of Southern martial superiority that has influenced military studies of the Civil War. It is not intended to disprove any of the beliefs attributed to the myth of the lost cause, as this has been previously examined convincingly enough. Instead it is an account of Federal and Confederate military operations and battles with a view of delivering a non-biased assessment of performance as well as outcomes. This assessment takes into account the challenges and circumstances encountered during the course of the war.

It requires an encyclopedic series of volumes to examine and narrate even the somewhat significant operations of the war. The objective of this book, rather, is to condense the study of a multitude of reports, correspondence, books, articles and insight into a concise analysis of Federal and Confederate combat performance and military competence. The text will follow selected events in chronological order. The operations and battles included will be selected based on their relevance to the book's objective.

Unfortunately this type of analysis is inherently subjective. Civil War combat veteran William Humphrey defined the failings of interpretative historical writing when he noted in a post-war letter, "I have never read history yet where they had every thing correct—just as it happened. You must remember no to (two) men or 100 men can go to the Worlds Fair and come back and tell the same story of what they have seen, but that is no sign there is no such thing as the Worlds Fair."[2]

As Captain Humphrey observed, history is not an exact science. Getting historical narrative writing correct is difficult enough. To interpret and project conclusions from the narrative that satisfies everyone is impossible. No one will ever set the record absolutely straight until a time machine is invented. That is no sign that the Civil War didn't happen, only that not everyone will agree about how and why it happened. This is especially true in an age when historical morals and mores are often judged according to customs accepted in our own time.

Even great military minds disagree in evaluating the combat performance of military units. Inevitably some corps, divisions, brigades and regiments are praised beyond their merit while others are unfairly cast in an unfavorable light by commanders and historians. The U.S. 32nd Infantry Division in World War II provides a useful example. This division was comprised of the regimental descendants of the famous Civil War Iron Brigade. One of my uncles served as a rifleman in one of its regiments and remained with the 32nd during its entire service in the Pacific. General Douglas MacArthur had a somewhat low opinion of the 32nd Division, once telling a fellow general that the 32nd "never had been any good." Japanese Army Commander Tomoyuki Yamashita had a different opinion. When asked which U.S. troops were the best he encountered in two Philippine campaigns, he named the 32nd Division. The 32nd "earned the highest tribute" of Japan's "ablest ground commander," but its own area commander held a different opinion. Each general had a different perspective and appreciation of the challenges on the same battlefields and drew different conclusions as to the division's fighting abilities. It must be remembered that even an expert historical participant's account is subject to and influenced by perspective and stance, just as Captain Humphrey observed.[3]

This book will begin with a look at antebellum martial perceptions and expectations for the ensuing war. Southern morale and motivation will be examined next and compared with the same for Northerners. The text will then be devoted to an account and evaluation of operations and battles throughout the war emphasizing events with particular suitability and relevance to this study. The final chapter will provide a series of observations and conclusions derived from the comparisons of the campaigns and operations included in the main text.

Yale professor David Brion Davis in his study of the history of slavery in the Americas noted that the aging Civil War veterans themselves focused their attention upon "minute details" of the battles rather than the issues and meanings of the war. Davis observed that few wars have generated "such a strange fascination" with tactics or what one might call military minutia. Perhaps Davis presented a particularly adept analogy when he compared the war to a tremendous "athletic contest" between sections of the country, at least as it is remembered by many.[4] What Davis overlooked is that this war which changed the course and destiny of our nation, and the world, is directly linked to so many Americans through their heritage. Today a great many Americans have a not-so-strange fascination with their ancestry. The objective here is to provide a non-biased comparative analysis of the military performance of our Civil War ancestors, free of the influence of their partisanship and of our sentiments regarding their propriety.

1

American Antebellum Martial Perceptions

As a boy growing up during the Civil War centennial in southeast Kansas, I often visited my grandmothers who lived in the same town. They were both daughters of Civil War veterans. Even as a boy, I could tell that my maternal Grandmother Clara was very proud of her father. She was an erstwhile president of the local daughters of veterans fraternity. Both of my grandmothers were well aged to have a grandson so young then. My Grandmother Clara was born on a Kansas homestead in January of 1880, probably in a log cabin. She had been a bright, athletic lady in her youth, but by then she was crippled with arthritis, yet still very mentally sharp. She was a gold star mother and honored her family's tradition of military service.

Like many seniors of that time were wont, Grandmother Clara enjoyed telling stories from the past. One of her favorite topics was her father's Civil War service. She knew which regiment he had served with, that he had sometimes been called upon to be a sharpshooter and a number of stories including that his hearing had been permanently damaged during the Battle of Stones River. The most important thing she told me was his regimental information. That information launched a quest to learn all I could about him and the historical war that was receiving so much attention then. As the years passed, I have often reflected upon the mores and concepts of her generation, *passed down* from the Civil War generation, and wondered about their origins.

It had been 100 years since the momentous events of the Civil War unfolded, yet those long-past episodes were then being reintroduced in ubiquitous magazine articles, television programs and boy's toys. *National Geographic* ran a series of articles with photographs of the battlefields, maps and period art. *Life Magazine* also marked the centennial in a similar fashion. Youngsters nationwide were captivated by the images and portrayals fashioned during the centennial observation. For many of us the Civil War became a life-long fascination, especially for those of us who had heard about our ancestors and their many relatives involved in it.[1]

Much of the writing about the Civil War up to that time had been dominated or at least strongly influenced by Southerners.[2] Immediately after the war's conclusion, Confederate veterans began writing their version which was incorporated into many textbooks and histories. But even before the war began, Southern writers influenced how the Civil War would be remembered by disparaging the character and fighting abilities of Yankees.

Perhaps the most succinct and authentic portrayal of the antebellum Southern perception of Yankees comes from a scene in the depression-era movie *Gone with the Wind*.

In that scene Georgia plantation gentlemen confidently and buoyantly agreed that the Yankees couldn't fight, and, if war came, that they and their kind could fight and would win. The viewpoint recalled in this scene wasn't confined to southern gentlemen before the Civil War; it was widespread in the South and echoed in Southern newspapers.

This contempt for Yankees was so ingrained in some Confederate volunteers that it sometimes caused problems during training when the war commenced. It was reported that recruits wouldn't drill seriously because they already anticipated that one southerner could thrash ten Yankees.[3] Southern recruits felt so superior that they believed the usual instruction wouldn't be needed, if indeed the Yankees showed up to fight at all. Some rebels were bragging in April 1861 that they could whip the Yankees using "popguns and cornstalks"; apparently how they were to be armed for battle mattered but little.[4]

Many Old South cultural factors contributed to this Southern perception of complete martial superiority. Southerners believed themselves to be better marksmen and horsemen, tougher and simply more militant than Northerners. Their opinion was encouraged by literature and writing that stressed the differences between New England and the Virginia Tidewater region dating from the colonial days.

The importance of the Jamestown and Plymouth colonies may have been overstated in a theme that compared Southerners as Cavaliers to Yankees as Puritans, but this generality had enough validity to help define the origin of the differences between the regions. Puritans displeased with English politics or seeking religious freedom were the main settlers and developers of New England while English aristocrats and gentry participated in the plantation culture of the Virginia Tidewater.[5] The aristocratic, agrarian, slave-intensive system introduced in Virginia contrasted vividly with the capitalistic, egalitarian, Puritan-dominated New England.

It is necessary here to take a brief look at who the true Yankees were before accounting for the reasons why Southerners felt martially superior to them. It has been the custom since the outbreak of the Civil War to group all of the troops and sailors who fought for the Union, regardless of their state origins, under the label "the Yankees." Thus, the blanket designation of Yankees applied to troops from Missouri, Kentucky, Tennessee, Virginia and other states who served in the Federal Army, regardless of the fact that these men were not Yankees by any definition except that like the American troops of World Wars I & II they were Americans. Indeed, even before the Civil War, Americans—Northerners and Southerners—were known in London and Paris as Yankees.[6] In America the label Yankee was relative but had evolved into a blanket designation for all Northerners. In actuality a large percentage of the Federal forces were no more culturally Yankee than Robert E. Lee.

The exact origin of the word Yankee is unknown; however, it could have derived from the name Jan Kaes or John Cheese by which the Dutch referred to New Englanders before the American Revolution.[7] It is also thought to possibly be a mistaken pronunciation of the Algonquin word for English.[8] Whatever its origin, before the American Revolution the word already signified a distinct culture linked to the Puritan diaspora that had spread through Massachusetts, Connecticut, Rhode Island and portions of New Hampshire, Vermont and Maine.[9]

Just as religion has been vital in shaping the destiny of nations, Puritanism is vital in defining the character, proclivities and idiosyncrasies of Yankees. Puritan settlers, particularly those from England's East Anglia region, brought cultural traits, trades and political values familiar and common enough to create a stereotype that would characterize

New Englanders. Cultural traits attributed to these Puritan settlers included a proclivity for education, freedom, civic mindedness and town hall meetings.[10] Later in America the Yankee stereotype would be associated with capitalism, acquisitiveness and materialism.

Southern politicians, writers and editors had by the onset of the war created a depiction of Yankees as the descendants of English Saxons while Southerners were depicted as descendants of the gallant, warlike Norman barons of William the Conqueror. This generalization was clearly overstated and was not even discerned or important to many Southerners. However, a widespread perception of regional differences, particularly cultural differences, existed; the Cavalier and Yankee thesis provided a handy explanation for why the Southerner was superior. Further disdain for Yankees was rooted in encounters with traders from New England known to Southerners as Yankee peddlers, and these encounters had helped to reinforce the image of Yankees as shrewd manipulators concerned only with profit. To many in the South, the perception of Yankees was one of simple tradesmen, peddlers, and mechanics, not gentlemen and certainly not the equals of the Southern planter aristocracy.[11]

By the 1830s, when conflict over admitting new states as slave or free intensified the prospect of secession, the need for Southerners to view themselves as a separate race or at least a different nationality came into its own. The Cavalier and Yankee thesis of Southern superiority became a fashionable theme in literature until by the late 1850s the Yankee became a "figure of ridicule and contempt." After John Brown's Harper's Ferry raid in 1859, practically all Northerners were regarded as Yankees; they were despised and generally unwelcome in the South. The most important outgrowth of this loathing was to justify Southern independence and to tout Southern superiority. Increasingly scorned, the Yankees, unlike Southern Cavaliers, were seen as a race of conspirators, hypocrites, and cowards. According to the popular perception, they wouldn't fight, and even if they did, Yankees could never win.[12]

Having thus briefly described the origin of the genuine Yankee culture, it is now necessary to touch on the demographics of the Northern states that remained in the Union during the Civil War. As previously mentioned, a large percentage of the Federal troops weren't Yankees in the cultural sense. By 1860 there were three distinct cultural categories inhabiting the Northern states. Kevin Phillips in his panoramic work *The Cousins' Wars* divided the loyal Northern states into three subdivisions based on ethnic settlement and political loyalties. The largest of these subdivisions, designated as Greater New England, was composed of New England, upper New York, northern Pennsylvania, Michigan, Wisconsin, Minnesota, and most of Iowa. Greater New England was largely settled by Yankees of Puritan descent as they moved west and was dominated by Yankee culture. This area was Lincoln's strongest core of support in the elections of 1860 and 1864. Another subdivision populated by non–Yankee ethnic groups scattered in enclaves from eastern New York, the Ohio Valley, central Ohio, Illinois and portions of Greater New England was comprised of German, New York, New Jersey and Pennsylvania Dutch settlers. Settlers from Southern states and other non–Yankees populated the final lower North subdivision which included the southern halves of Pennsylvania, Ohio, Indiana and Illinois. Large numbers of Scots-Irish had settled southern Pennsylvania, especially around Pittsburgh and eastern Ohio, and the other states of the lower North contained a large population of pioneers from Virginia, Kentucky and other Southern states.[13]

From this concise description of the North it is obvious that while a large portion was dominated by Yankee values and shared a preference for the politics of Abraham

Lincoln, much of the North was also largely settled by Germans, Scots-Irish, and by non-Yankee pioneers with Southern roots. The residents of these ethnic and non-Yankee regions of the lower North and even enclaves within Greater New England itself largely disliked Yankees almost as much as they disliked slave owners and the institution of slavery. And unlike Eastern abolitionists, these Northerners did not welcome the prospect of freed slaves moving into their counties. The North was not a homologous pan-Yankee state. It was more of a conglomerate of differing ethnic and religious groups with variegated political loyalties. The abundance of political parties in the antebellum North included Democrat, Free Soil, American (Know-Nothing), Republican and Whig. Unlike the South, which was dominated by Democrats, the North would lack consensus and would depend on coalition to face the ordeal of Civil War.

Southern antebellum literature, as we have seen, provides a reflection of Southern attitudes towards Yankees. It should be noted here that Westerners, those who were pioneering in the new Northern states, were accounted greater respect than East Coast Northerners in antebellum Southern literature and perspective. Even so, the soldiers from the West would be included in the epithet "Yankee" once the fighting commenced.

Often repeated in antebellum literature, the Cavalier and Yankee thesis was a sort of literary fable, with a grain of truth, employed by Southern elites to substantiate or justify an aura of superiority over Northerners. It supplied a figurative racial or ethnic explanation for what were basically cultural differences between the nation's sections. One of these cultural differences involved each section's relationship to the military. The Old South was agrarian with a functioning slavocracy requiring regimentation dependent upon discipline, not unlike the military. Southerners, therefore, naturally valued the qualities of the soldier and those with a career in the profession of arms. The slave-based economy and slavocracy depended upon similar methods and aptitudes that were also necessary for a functioning and disciplined military.

Indeed, a military career was deemed in the South as one of a few occupations worthy of a gentleman. This had a practical application: a dependable militia was vital for maintaining the slave system and protecting whites from slave insurrections and violence. By contrast, the military was widely viewed as a refuge for idlers in the North. Ulysses Grant provided an example of this perception with a story about his experience upon donning the uniform for the first time after graduating West Point. While on leave before reporting to Jefferson Barracks, Missouri, Grant wore his new lieutenant's uniform for a ride into Cincinnati. He was quite proud of his tailor-made uniform until he encountered a barefooted, ragged "little urchin" whose shirt "had not seen a wash tub for weeks." The boy faced Grant and yelled, "Soldier! Will you work? No sir-ee; I'll sell my shirt first!" Grant admitted that he never again cared much for the uniform, as evidenced by what he wore on campaign and even for the surrender meeting at Appomattox.[14]

In addition to having a greater appreciation for the profession of arms, Southerners viewed themselves as manly in comparison to Yankees. Ralph Waldo Emerson, the American philosopher who died in 1882, once noted that Northerners asked about a man, "What can he do?" The Southerner, he observed, asked, "How does he fight?"[15] Southerners carried a reputation for sensitivity to questions of personal honor and for fighting duels over incidents as petty as insults or even differences of opinion. This penchant for resorting to violence was naturally perceived in the South as an indicator of courage, an important soldierly quality. From a Southern perspective, Northerners were much less likely to defend their honor than what was required of men, giving an impression that Yankees were effete and even cowardly. To New Englanders, duels and violence over quarrels exemplified irrationality and recklessness; nevertheless, the violent reputation of Southerners reinforced the impression that Southerners were potentially better soldier material.

One additional characteristic should be included here as relevant to the perception of Southern martial superiority. With a large complement of slaves and a tradition of indentured servitude in the Old South, Southerners were accustomed to the "habit of command" and thus assumed leadership as a natural function of everyday life.[16] Of course not all Southerners owned slaves or kept indentured servants, but many Southerners did. Assigning and supervising tasks on a daily basis was routine for a great many Southerners. Thus, it seemed logical that Southerners on the whole were better prepared than Northerners for leadership roles and the transition to military service.

The outstanding performance of Southern military leaders and volunteers during the Mexican War gave an encouraging indicator of military prowess bred in the South. In the years before the Civil War the South had produced the most famous military leaders in the country. George Washington, Andrew Jackson, Winfield Scott and Zachary Taylor were all Southern born, for example, and the South produced a long list of young and gifted officers proven in the Mexican War. This veritable example of Southern military competence naturally bolstered an impression of martial superiority.

Having considered some of the principal reasons for the antebellum perception of Southern martial superiority, a brief overview of the Northern outlook preceding the Civil War follows. In the years preceding the war, most Northerners did not seem to favor or even anticipate violence to end slavery in the South; nevertheless, a great many opposed its expansion. Two Southern slave-owning presidents had already threatened military action against secession. Following the Mexican War, President Zachary Taylor said he would lead an invasion of any state attempting to secede from the Union. President Andrew Jackson had threatened to send 50,000 Federal troops to South Carolina in 1832 in response to the Ordinance of Nullification and possible disunion. He also ordered Winfield Scott to Charleston to watch the situation. Once there Scott readied a Federal garrison as a precaution. In his second inaugural address, President Jackson said, "...of incalculable, importance is the union of these States, and the sacred duty of all to contribute to its preservation by a liberal support of the General Government in the exercise of its just powers." But the two Democratic presidents preceding Abraham Lincoln, Franklin Pierce and James Buchanan, though both Northerners, virtually collaborated with pro-slavery politics. President Pierce said in his inaugural address, "I believe that involuntary servitude, as it exists in different States of this Confederacy, is recognized by the Constitution." President Buchanan in his inaugural stated his position on the slave controversy by saying that popular sovereignty should decide which new states would be free or slave. He stressed that slavery was "beyond the reach of any human power" except the states where it already existed.[17]

The effect of the two administrations preceding President Lincoln was to embolden agitators and extremists favoring Southern secession. Pierce from New Hampshire and Buchanan from Pennsylvania followed a policy of appeasement in hopes of lessening sectional conflict over slavery. Since the time of President Thomas Jefferson the issue of secession had threatened the Union. Though all were Southerners, Presidents Jefferson, Jackson and Taylor almost certainly would have sent military force against any state or region attempting to leave the Union. Pro-slavery secessionists had little to fear from either Pierce or Buchanan. The supine response of the Buchanan administration to secession in 1860 seemed to validate the antebellum impression that Yankees wouldn't fight.

As war loomed in the spring of 1861, the South was confident in its ability to fight, if needed, for secession. Northerners, seeing that conflict appeared inevitable, faced the prospect of war with some anxiety but sufficient confidence. Examples of concern for Southern military prowess appeared in newspaper articles that spring. Veterans recalled this phenomenon years after the war in their memoirs and writing. William Y.W. Ripley, an erstwhile lieutenant colonel of the First U.S. Sharpshooters, echoed this impression in a post-war narrative. Ripley noted that at beginning of the war the rebels were superior "man for man ... in the use of arms" to the Federals. He attributed this superiority to the fact that the rebel army was mainly recruited from rural areas where men were accustomed to hunting and using a rifle. Northerners, he wrote, were drawn from farms, workshops and offices; their occupations kept them too busy to learn the skills of hunting and shooting. Indeed, he wrote, there were many Northern regiments comprised of soldiers "who had never even fired a gun ... at the time of their enlistment." Time and again descriptions of superior Southern military aptitude appear in Civil War narratives, even to this day. An example of this tendency appears in the updated American Heritage Civil War book reprinted in 2009. Its chapter describing the military branches echoed Ripley's assessment. The South was better with the rifle, it noted, because "a higher percentage of its men had lived under frontier conditions." Confederate cavalry was "infinitely superior" because of better mounts and having country boys in the saddle while the Federals were "city boys" and such. This assessment overlooks the fact that as much or more of the North was still frontier settlement as compared to the South in the 1860s.[18]

General Henry Hunt, chief of artillery for the Army of the Potomac during the war, shared this impression. According to General Hunt, the South brought men with better aptitude "for infantry and cavalry" into the war at the beginning. He had one exception to the perceived Southern martial advantage, however. In Hunt's expert opinion, "No country furnishes better men for the artillery proper than our Northern, and particularly our New England, states." Hunt reasoned that this was true because so many Northerners were shop hands, mechanics, and technicians who basically were handymen. He explained that artillery requires men with mechanical skills to function efficiently. The North, with its factories, shops and industry was clearly better able to supply such men than the agrarian South.[19]

Concern over the South's supposed pool of superior marksmen was probably greatest in the Northeast. A New York newspaper article from May 1861 gives a good example of this outlook:

> Especially should attention be paid to Sharp-shooting.... At the South, skill in sharp-shooting is almost universal. At the North it is extremely uncommon. If our raw recruits ... will consume every hour in target practice, they will be able to give a better account of themselves.[20]

Another example is found in a letter from a Northern volunteer to a New York magazine in 1861 mentioning this same subject. He observed that "some importance" was being given to the belief that generally Southern men were better marksmen than Federal soldiers. In his opinion this was not "the case to any great extent." The soldier was sufficiently prescient to predict that the looming war would not be "a contest of mere marksmen or evolution."[21] Even so, as his letter indicated, concern over Southern military capabilities troubled the North.

Southern antebellum literature fostered an impression that the South bred a society that was martially superior to the North and New England in particular. While Southern writers portrayed Southern culture as descended from Norman Cavaliers, the reality is that the South was predominately Celtic in ethnicity and culture. Examination of the first U.S. Census from 1790 reveals that the Carolinas were overwhelmingly populated by people of Celtic ancestry. By 1860 the majority of white Southerners were of Irish, Scots, Scots-Irish and Welsh ancestry, and Celtic culture had come to dominate throughout the South. While wealthy planters of the Tidewater model may have continued in the role of elites, the Celtic lifestyle with its warrior ethic, frontier adaptability and outlook was copied by other ethnic groups. The Scots-Irish helped establish this cultural hegemony by largely settling the Appalachian region from Pennsylvania to Georgia, and westward to Alabama and Mississippi.[22]

Despite the fact that the vast majority of Southerners had little or no connection to gentry, Normans or Cavaliers, indeed a great many were descended from indentured servants and convicts sent to America during the colonial period, the impression of Southern martial superiority burnished by the Cavalier and Yankee theme has persisted through the years. Even more significant in sustaining this perception was the post-war writing of Confederate veterans and other disciples of the myth of the lost cause. To this day an old adage is repeated to simplify the time-honored perception of Southern martial superiority: "The Yankees never could fight anyhow."[23] Though the South lost the war and hasn't yet rose again, it clearly projected on the collective American sentence a high regard for its fighting men.

2

1860

Pre-War Motivation and Morale

Motivation and morale played a crucial role in the combat performance of Civil War soldiers. Indeed, while motivation has been a subject of study by some historians, its impact on the conduct of the war is somewhat understated in the war's collective study. The object of this chapter is not to reexamine the causes of the Civil War or to examine the reasons men chose to fight in it. This chapter rather is a concise examination of what the soldiers were actually willing to risk their lives for, the visceral concerns and principles that compelled men to sacrifice their lives for a cause. It may be difficult in this age to sympathize with or even truly comprehend the mores and mindsets of antebellum America, but those social mores and beliefs strongly influenced motivation and ultimately combat performance throughout the war.

From the colonial days until the Civil War the South lived in a world apart from what Americans know today. It was a world where survival and self-interest were tantamount by necessity. At least it was so to those who lived in that era. From colonial times Americans ventured westward into a hostile frontier; once there they were sometimes compelled by circumstances to resort to violence in order to exist. Violence was a dreadful necessity, and to Southerners so was the unjustness of slavery. The realities of that world tempered perceptions of morality. By the 1830s Southerners knew well that they lived in a world where self-interest ruled their lives.

To most Southerners slavery was a natural, proper and ordinary fact of life in antebellum America. More importantly, Southerners also accepted slavery on a moral and religious basis. Enslaving enemies and obtaining slaves for personal benefit had been a practice of human behavior since the dawn of recorded history. European involvement with the African slave trade began to thrive with the advent of Portuguese seagoing expeditions in the 1400s. At that time "indigenous slavery and slave trading were very widespread in West Africa," as had been ongoing for "many preceding centuries."[1] Slavery and slave mongering then had been a long-established practice by Africans centuries before American colonists began resorting to the trade to obtain labor. This truth was not lost on pro-slavery Southerners.

As early as 1619 a Dutch sea captain sold twenty Africans as slaves to English colonists at the Jamestown, Virginia, colony. Colonist John Rolfe and others thus "tapped a source of labor" utilized by some Europeans since the 1400s.[2] The practice of slavery quickly spread to other North American English colonies, but slavery had already been firmly established in the Caribbean Islands and Central and South American by the Spanish and Portuguese. Statistically, British North America received less than 4 percent of the total number of African slaves brought to the New World, despite the fact that millions of slaves populated the South by 1860 as a result of natural population growth. For example, a total of approximately 256,807 of the 12,409,563 African slaves deported from Africa were sent to what became the United States. Over 4.3 million African slaves were sent to Brazil alone.[3] The Spanish and Portuguese slave-intensive colonies required continued importation of large numbers of Africans because of high mortality rates due to severe, often malignant, working conditions.

Given then that slavery was widespread in Africa and the Americas and that Southern slaves fared much better than those of other colonies, pro-slavery Southerners had some grounds for their perspective. The political and social hegemony of slaveholding elites enabled them to configure a society in support of slavery. Eventually Southern society was shaped and inculcated to collaborate with the interests of slaveholders. Well before the Civil War Southerners living in slave-intensive areas had been conditioned to accept, support and defend the slaveholder's interests and to believe their lives depended upon that support.

Chapter one of Clifford Dowdey's work on the South published in 1955 delivered an insightful overview of the most important factor in the phenomenon of support for slavery in antebellum America. Dowdey's writing portrayed the gory details of Nat Turner's Rebellion, wherein more than fifty whites, mostly women and children, were brutally and horrifically murdered by slaves in Southampton County, Virginia, in 1831. Along with the slave insurrection in Haiti and its associated greater massacre of whites, antebellum white Southerners were imprinted by the Turner massacre with a "dread reminder of what could happen to them." This terrible dread was so intense that "a fear of the Negro" was one of the basic pillars of Southern support for slavery and the call for secession.[4]

Another consequence of the Turner massacre was to "strengthen the conviction of slaveholders that abolitionism would incite insurrections."[5] Southern elites, already angry as a result of Northern trade practices they perceived as unfair and exploitative, sensed that their lives mattered little in the ongoing rift over slavery. The somewhat callous views and actions of Northern abolitionist, with an extreme example in John Brown's activities, contributed greatly to Southern resentment and anxiety. Faced with an ongoing fear of massacre by slaves, Southerners perceived abolitionism as a threat no only to their livelihood but their very lives. As war commenced at Fort Sumter, South Carolina, noted Southern diarist Mary Boykin Chestnut admitted her anxiety and mentioned that with the Yankees in front and slaves in the rear Southerners could expect a servile revolt or insurrection.[6] The importance of this perception as a motivating factor for Southern troops cannot be overstated.

Indeed, abolitionists had grown increasingly radical in their stance concerning violence by the 1850s and began calling for slave uprisings. Accepting violence as inevitable on Southern whites, abolitionists predicted that some cataclysm with an accompanying large-scale bloodbath would be necessary to purge slavery from the land.[7] Apparently white lives didn't matter provided that the end result destroyed slavery forever. White Southerners of all social classes obviously resented and despised abolitionists for the simple fact that their lives meant so little compared to the cause of ending their peculiar institution. Once the war commenced, many Southerners cast their odium on all Northern troops as if they were intentionally enabling another slave massacre. Most Southerners simply could not understand Northern war motives.

Given then that Southerners lived in a society where slavery was perceived as an accepted, proper institution, other than fear of slave insurrection and the obvious pecuniary matters, why was slavery otherwise so strongly supported in the South? An equally important reason was that African slavery was sanctioned by religious faith in the South. While the religious stance on slavery in the North had gradually progressed towards opposition, in the South Christians and Jews upheld it as Biblically sanctioned.

In the first book of the Bible, Noah cursed the son of Ham with slavery. A number of scriptures were quoted by abolitionists and other Christian sects in opposition to slavery as well. That fact did not diminish the legitimacy of the slaveholder's belief in the propriety of slavery. As anyone knows, religion is supreme in relation to morale and motivation. To Southerners, if their peculiar institution wasn't viewed as completely righteous by outsiders, it was proper and ordained by their faith. Like anyone, Southerners resented challenges and criticism of their religious beliefs, and this strengthened both motivation and morale in the face of Northern condemnation.

Although about half of the free families of South Carolina and Mississippi owned slaves, the majority of free Southerners didn't own slaves or even have a family connection to slave owners. Nevertheless, most Southerners felt compelled to defend the slave system. In addition to fear of slave revolt and belief in the propriety of slavery were a number of personal-interest reasons why Southerners backed slavery. White Southerners were led to believe that freed slaves would compete for work with resulting lower wages and degraded working and social conditions for the working class. Indeed, a great concern for ordinary white Southerners was that freeing the slaves would degrade the social status of working whites to the same level as the freed slaves and expose white families to unanticipated "horrors" and shame.[8]

One additional often-neglected factor impacting white Southerners' perception of slavery was the attitude of the slaves themselves toward non-slaveholders and other slaves. Like most people, slaves were sensitive to status, and they were wont to ascribe social distinctions to whites as well as other slaves. There was a hierarchy of occupations for slaves just as with freemen. Although slaves were required by the slave code to make a show of respect to all whites, they ridiculed whites who owned no slaves and scornfully referred to poor whites as "white trash and po' buckra." Frederick Douglass, himself a former slave, recalled that slaves considered it a disgrace to be owned by a poor man.[9] This reality simply added to the mundane aspect of slavery in the antebellum South.

Poor Southern whites were also conscious of status, and although they were at the bottom of the social strata, they were always one layer above the highest slave. The dignity of being a free white was a powerful incentive for Southerners to support the slave system and should be considered as an important morale-influencing factor for all Confederate soldiers. Southern whites were highly motivated to support slavery in order to preserve their social status, securing their place in a caste system with legal equality to slaveholders and the possibility to move up in social standing to the planter class.

In addition to motivation for fighting for their homes, property and lifestyle, Southern soldiers were motivated by reasons similar to their Revolutionary War forebearers. In fact they were motivated to fight for patriotic and ideological convictions just as Northern soldiers were, though enlisted Northerners were probably more familiar with the ideological issues as a result of greater political awareness and educational background on the whole.[10] Southerners believed they were fighting for liberty and personal rights against an oppressive government, not unlike American Revolutionary soldiers. From a modern perspective it appears that Southerners were fighting to preserve oppression and deny freedom from a hypocritical standpoint. But as we have seen, Southerners believed in the justness of their culture, and they were strongly motivated to preserve and protect it.

References of Confederate soldiers' motivation for ideological and moral reasons have been documented from an abundance of surviving wartime letters. Honor for Southerners was linked to liberty, slaveholding, self-determination and defense of home, family and property. Many Confederates viewed themselves as Christian warriors fighting oppression and upholding their personal honor in a just cause. Southerners' writing compared Northern opposition to secession to Yankee subjugation, and Southern honor demanded resistance. One Texan's letter provided a quintessential example of the rebel mindset: he wrote that it was better to be a dead freeman than to be a living slave.[11] To this Texan, remaining in the Union was tantamount to accepting Yankee domination, or virtual slavery to the Union. As any Southerner knew, slaves had no honor. To a great many Southerners, their personal freedom was conceptually linked to revolution and secession; freedom was a cause they, like American warriors of all eras, willingly died for.

As we have seen, Confederate soldiers set out in 1861 to protect their homes and families, property, personal status, lifestyle and personal liberty or rights. One can say that some of these motives are of an ideological nature, but on the whole Confederates went to war for reasons that could largely be considered as of self-interest at the core. Conversely, Northern soldiers were motivated by patriotic and ideological concerns that did not directly affect their personal daily lives to the same extent as Southerners' motivations. Comparatively, Northerners were motivated by nobler but less visceral grounds than Southerners. Noble motives often erode in the face of adversity while by nature self-interest remains supreme.

Even so, Federal soldiers had very profound motivations for going to war. They had to, or else the Federals could not have endured the ordeal of fighting in the enemy's territory for years against a highly motivated, equally trained and prepared adversary. The principal motivation for Federal volunteers was America itself: that is, the American political system.

Today Americans have a jaded, frustrated perception of politics, but in 1861 the United States was only eighty-five years old. American democracy was still viewed as an experiment then. Even to immigrant soldiers, America represented liberty, opportunity and a new form of free government. Northern volunteers believed that should the American democracy fail as a result of secession, the tyrants and aristocrats of Europe would then be entitled to boast that "such is the common lot of all republics." Northerners believed the United States served as an example of the best and freest government in the world; it could not be allowed to fail, and Northern volunteers rallied in large numbers to this cause in 1861.[12]

Civil War soldiers were the most literate soldiers ever to that point in history. Over ninety percent of white Federal soldiers were at least marginally literate.[13] Unlike in previous wars, even volunteers from the lower economic stratum could read the newspapers and grasp the issues and ideals related to the conflict. The men who rallied to the flag realized that the seemingly far-away issues that were leading to secession ultimately would affect them and their future. Many Northerners believed that secession would result in anarchy and destroy the "maintenance of law and order." Some soldiers were concerned that "constitutional liberty cannot survive the loss of unity in government." They feared a downfall of what remained of the Union and a descent in to despotism.[14] The law and order issue was an important motivating factor for Northern volunteers, especially after the attack on Fort Sumter. Upholding American democracy was synonymous with preserving the Union to Northern soldiers.

While Northerners feared a collapse of the American political system resulting from Southern secession, they also resented the virtual theft of nearly half of the country and all its related public property to sectional usurpation. Federal funds had obviously helped to improve harbors, build forts, roads and infrastructure in the South. Northern soldiers had fought in the Mexican War to protect Texas and in other military operations that had benefited the South. There was an intense, righteous backlash against the South for turning her back on the Union and rejecting compromise. Northerners believed it was their patriotic duty to defend the Union forged by the deeds and sacrifices of their ancestors in the American Revolution.

Economic concerns also had a part in motivating Northerners to fight. Western rivers, particularly the Mississippi, were important shipping routes for Northern and Western grain and farm products. The new Confederate nation posed an immediate and potential long-term threat to Northern farmers because the Mississippi River was controlled by the rebels after Arkansas, Tennessee, Louisiana and Mississippi seceded. The effect of closing the Western shipping routes was a grave concern for Northern agriculture in the 1860s. Farmers eventually provided about half of the soldiers for the Federal armies.[15] Southern control of the cotton supply for Northern textile factories was also an economic concern for the North. This issue was two-sided. On one hand there was a worry that the cotton supply would be interrupted in the short-term and thus harm the textile industry. On the other was the potential for indefinite cotton supply control by the Confederacy.

The initial Federal call for troops in April 1861 was expressly for the purpose of putting down the rebellion and, from the Northern perspective, treason. The rage inspired by the firing upon the United States flag beginning at Fort Sumter in April 1861 was akin to what Americans felt when Pearl Harbor was attacked in 1941 and was just as intense. An example of what Union veterans felt about Americans firing upon the Stars and Stripes was spoken by a color bearer of the 116th Ohio: "…I would send them all to hell for it yet if it were in my power. Talk of unpardonable sins—firing on that flag must not, shall not, be forgiven in this world nor the next, let sentimentalists … who were not where I stood say what they may."

James Dalzell, another veteran from the 116th Ohio, revealed his sentiment about secessionists in a speech years after the war: "…I knew one man, a noble fellow … that fellow was one of the best rebels I ever saw. But he was wrong, always wrong—as every rebel was wrong.… There never was any rebel right. Every rebel was wrong. Every pulsation of the fiendish, dastardly, cowardly, traitorous heart of Jeff. Davis, from beginning to end, was wrong, and it is wrong to-night."[16]

Loyal Americans found no justification for the treasonous acts of the secessionists in 1861. Southern aggression provided the prime motivation for Northerners to join the fight and sustain the war to its conclusion. To Northern volunteers the seizure of Federal forts, arsenals, and property represented an insulting betrayal and an obvious injustice that demanded rectification.

The exact percentage of Northerners who went to war for to abolish slavery cannot be determined; however, a reasonable estimate would be about 30 percent of the volunteers of 1861 supported emancipation.[17] If anyone doubts the commitment of some

Northerners to abolition, they need only to study the "Bleeding Kansas" violence of the 1850s. Hundreds of New Englanders and families from Northern states moved to the Kansas Territory for the sole purpose of preventing the territory from entering the Union as a slave state. Many of these antislavery Yankees were as tough and committed to their cause as any rebels. Their deeds in the Border War in Kansas and Missouri leave little doubt of this fact. While it has been a common misapprehension to ignore the importance of abolitionist sentiment by some, ridding slavery was absolutely a motivating factor for many Northern volunteers in 1861.

As we have seen, Northerners and Southerners had compelling motivations to fight following the attack on Fort Sumter, South Carolina. Yet somehow Southern soldiers could not quite grasp why Northerners would fight to defend the Union. Seeing that few Northerners were devoted abolitionist, Confederates initially didn't apprehend their devotion to the Union or anticipate the rage generated by firing upon the Stars and Stripes. After all, Confederate volunteers were eager to leave the United States. Many Confederates could fathom no legitimate cause for ordinary Northerners to "undergo the hardships of war" except to deprive Southerners of their rights. Northern volunteers were therefore assumed to be motivated by mercenary reasons. Federal soldiers were compared to the Hessians of the American Revolution and viewed as "hirelings" without a valid motive to fight besides payment.[18] Many of the regiments and military units organized immediately after Lincoln's call for volunteers were manned by immigrants, often Germans who were easily recognized as foreigners. By comparison, the Confederate volunteers for the eastern army in 1861 were ninety-five percent native born, and by the following year ninety-nine percent were native born.[19] The simple fact that so many Northern soldiers were immigrants bolstered the hireling-mercenary image of the Federal army from the Southern perspective. Succinctly, Confederate soldiers initially didn't believe their enemies could match their motivation and determination, and quite possibly they were correct.

The foregoing pithy examination of war motivations prompts the question: Which side brought the strongest motivation for the war and thereby gained that advantage? David Hackett Fischer in his expansive study of British folkways in America, which of course was applicable to both the North and South, maintained that the South held an advantage in the "intensity of its warrior ethic." He also made a very pertinent observation that applies to this study. Fischer noted that qualitative differences in the combat performance of the Federal and Confederate armies cannot be defined by material resources or even strategy.[20]

A quote from Confederate General Thomas J. Jackson confirms one source of motivation affecting the intensity of the Southern "warrior ethic." Jackson informed his nephew in early 1861 that if Northerners were to "endeavor to subjugate us, and thus excite our slaves to servile insurrection in which our families will be murdered without quarter or mercy, it becomes us to wage such a war," meaning showing no quarter for Federal soldiers.[21] This somewhat paranoid concern that Northerners would wish to cause the murder of the wives and children of Southerners, as would surely apply only to a few fanatics, reveals some indication of the mindset that motivated Confederate soldiers to fight with greater determination and ferocity than their Union counterparts.

Research has yielded some statistics that help define the role of slavery in motivating Southerners to fight with greater resolution. A higher percentage of Confederate volunteers serving in the Army of Northern Virginia were slave owners or resided with slave owners than the overall Southern white population. These slavery-associated soldiers suffered higher casualties and were more loyal to the Confederacy despite the fact that Southerners from all social strata supported slavery for racial, social and economic reasons. Army of Northern Virginia soldiers with a personal association to slavery were 20 percent more likely to be killed or wounded in action. Also soldiers with a slave-ownership association deserted at a significantly lower rate than other soldiers.[22]

While maintaining the slavocracy clearly was a crucial motivating factor for many Confederate soldiers, another circumstance was of even greater importance. Confederate soldiers fought with impressive tenacity because from their perspective they had been provoked, intimidated, and most importantly, invaded. Colonel J.H. Baxter the chief medical officer of the Federal Provost Marshall General's Bureau observed in a post-war report: "It has been frequently asserted (and not without foundation for the history of the remark) that *ceteris paribus*, all first-class nations excel their enemies upon their own soil." All things otherwise equal, fighting upon one's home turf is a tremendous advantage, especially in terms of motivation and morale. To use a sports analogy: any basketball team playing at home has an immediate advantage worth at least a few points, and teams usually win most often at home. Likewise, being on the defensive, fighting on their "own soil," provided a powerful advantage in motivation to the Confederates.[23]

West Point graduate and Confederate General Joseph Johnston studied military affairs diligently. In fact he may have been the most knowledgeable officer in the prewar Regular Army besides General Winfield Scott. Naturally he believed in the supremacy of Confederate soldiers. Interestingly, he did not attribute this belief, as many Southerners did, to ethnological factors or an alleged superiority of Southern breeding. Instead, Johnston opined that Confederates were better "due solely to the spirit with which they fight, a spirit excited by ... consciousness of the magnitude of the stake." This Confederate commander, steeped in Southern culture, realized that motivation to "drive back invasion" provided the key advantage to his men.[24] Johnston's opinion helps account for the qualitative and quantitative differences in the combat performance of the Federal and Confederate armies that cannot be otherwise explained.

This concise comparison of wartime motivations may favor the Confederacy by virtue of the fact that the Federal Army was the invader; however, many other factors remain to be considered in accounting for the perceived differences in the military conduct of the war. In a few instances during the war, as we will see, the motivational advantage favored the North. Late in the war, with Federal soldiers marching across much of the South, the Southern motivational advantage became irrelevant, and many Confederates deserted to attend to their families. In the years between the five Aprils of the Confederacy, the issues examined above sustained the impressive tenacity of the contending armies and contributed significantly to the war's virulence.

3

1861

America Stumbles into Civil War

On December 20, 1860, delegates from all parts of South Carolina met in Charleston and *unanimously* voted to approve that state's secession from the United States. It was a very fitting reaction to be anticipated from the one state that had for decades led or at least represented the faction calling for disunion. For the previous eight years two Federal administrations had managed to mollify Southern extremists, thereby preserving the Union. The November election of Abraham Lincoln as president was the catalyst for sectional conflict; Lincoln's election signaled a departure from past appeasement. President James Buchanan, nearing the close of his term, would take no action to prevent the contagion of secession from spreading through most of the slaveholding states.

By January 19, 1861, four other Deep South states, Mississippi, Florida, Alabama, and Georgia, in that order, had followed South Carolina in secession from the Union. Louisiana and Texas soon followed, and delegates from these seven states gathered in Montgomery, Alabama, in February to form a Southern proslavery nation.[1] Four other slave states, Virginia, Tennessee, Arkansas and North Carolina, would join to form the eleven states of the Confederate States of America by the end of spring 1861.

The object of this book is to examine and compare the military performance and competence of the Confederate and Federal armies. In order to evaluate the performance of the Confederate army it is helpful to understand the motives for Southern secession and the establishment of the Confederacy. Motivation bolsters morale and morale greatly influences performance. A lengthy and detailed letter from Alabama Commissioner S.F. Hale to Kentucky Governor Beriah Magoffin dated December 27, 1860, is an excellent example of secessionist doctrine, the actual Southern motivation for war. The following excerpts from Hale's missive provide concise insight into the mind of those willing and anxious to fight for Southern secession:

> I have the honor of placing in your hands herewith a commission from the Governor of the State of Alabama, accrediting me as a commissioner of that State to the sovereign State of Kentucky, to consult in reference to the momentous issues now pending between the Northern and Southern States of this Confederacy.
>
> At the time of the adoption of the Federal Constitution African slavery existed in twelve of the thirteen States. Slaves are recognized both as property and as a basis of political power by the Federal compact, and special provisions are made by that instrument for their protection as property. Under the influences of climate and other causes, slavery has been banished from the Northern States; the slaves themselves have been sent to the Southern States and there sold, and their price gone into the pockets of their former owners at the North. And in the meantime African slavery has not only become one of the fixed domestic institutions of

the Southern States, but forms an important element of their political power, and constitutes the most valuable species of their property, worth, according to recent estimates, not less than $4,000,000,000; forming, in fact, the basis upon which rests the prosperity and wealth of most of these States.... It is upon this gigantic interest, this peculiar institution of the South, that Northern States and their people have been waging an unrelenting and fanatical war for the last quarter of a century.... They attack us through their literature, in their schools, from the hustings, in their legislative halls, through the public press, and even their courts of justice forget the purity of their judicial ermine to strike down the rights of the Southern slave-holder and override every barrier which the Constitution has erected for his protection; and the sacred desk is desecrated to this unholy crusade against our lives, our property, and the constitutional rights guaranteed to us by the compact of our fathers.

As the last and crowning insult and outrage upon the people of the South, the citizens of the Northern States, by overwhelming majorities, on the 6th day of November last, elected Abraham Lincoln and Hannibal Hamlin President and Vice-President of the United States. Whilst it may be admitted that the mere election of any man to the Presidency is not *per se* a sufficient cause for a dissolution of the Union, yet when the issues upon and circumstances under which he was elected are properly appreciated and understood, the question arises whether a due regard to the interest, honor, and safety of their citizens, in view of this and all the other antecedent wrongs and outrages, do not render it the imperative duty of the Southern States to resume the powers they have delegated to the Federal Government and interpose their sovereignty for the protection of their citizens....

Shall we wait until our enemies shall possess themselves of all the powers of Government; until abolition judges are on the Supreme Court bench, abolition collectors at every port, and abolition postmasters in every town; secret mail agents traversing the whole land, and a subsidized press established in our midst to demoralize our people? Will we be stronger then or better prepared to meet the struggle, if a struggle must come? ...prompt, bold, and decided action is demanded alike by prudence, patriotism, and the safety of their citizens.[2]

And so the Confederate States of America was established on February 8, 1861, by delegates from the seceding states with a provisional constitution to address the issues pertinent to Commissioner Hale's letter. Mississippian Jefferson Davis was chosen president of the nascent realm and Alexander Stephens of Georgia vice president. Mr. Davis rightfully considered himself a military man; indeed, his second wife Varina believed "his genius was military."[3] His future adversary Abraham Lincoln was much less a military man and more of a natural genius. There is no consensus as to which president was the better commander in chief, but Jefferson Davis was obviously the better schooled and prepared of the two.

Davis reported to West Point in September 1824 where he was an average cadet and not particularly esteemed by Sylvanus Thayer, the superintendent and figurative father of the academy. Although Davis was dismissed after being court-martialed, he was reinstated and managed to graduate twenty-third of a class of thirty-three in 1828.[4]

While serving at a frontier fort, Davis sought to marry Sara Knox Taylor, the daughter of Colonel Zachary Taylor, his commanding officer and future president of the United States. The marriage was against Zachary Taylor's wishes, so Davis gave up his Army career, resigned his commission and returned to plantation life in Mississippi. He married Sara after leaving the Army, but soon both were stricken with a serious illness. Davis recovered but within three months his bride was dead, probably from malaria.

Following his bride's death Davis became thoroughly immersed in the plantation system and its slavocracy. After several years as a planter and with the encouragement of his successful brother Joseph, Davis was elected as a Mississippi representative in 1845.

He married Varina Howell, the much younger and vivacious daughter of an upper-class family, that year.

Davis soon resigned his House seat to lead a regiment of Mississippi Volunteers in the Mexican War. He came away from the war with a favorable reputation and experience as a combat commander. His war experience would follow him in his subsequent career to validate his reputation as something of a military expert.

Returning to politics, Davis was back in Washington by 1847 serving as a Mississippi senator and later as President Franklin Pierce's Secretary of War in 1853. During his term as Secretary of War Davis supported expansionism, as favored by most Southerners seeking new areas to introduce slavery. Although Davis seemed pleased with his military-related assignment, he returned to the Senate until the advent of Southern secession.

When Southern delegates met in Montgomery, Alabama, Davis was chosen provisional president and inaugurated on February 18, 1861. As was in the case of Abraham Lincoln when he was chosen as presidential candidate for the Republican Party, Davis was not an overwhelming favorite for the office. Davis himself probably would have preferred to assume command of the Southern armies, an assignment he later conferred upon Robert E. Lee.[5]

As early as January 3, 1861, about a month before the seceding states gathered to form the Confederacy, Southern states began seizing Federal property, forts and arsenals, in an overt act of war. While the newly-elected President Abraham Lincoln yet held hopes that the secession crisis would not inaugurate war, the states leaving the Union were preparing for it. The interval between December 1860 and Lincoln's inaugural on

The Lincoln home at Springfield, Illinois. This was Lincoln's residence when he was elected president in 1860.

March 4, 1861, gave the fledgling Confederacy an opportunity to militarize while the Federal forces lost valuable assets. Actions by the seceding states leave little doubt their leaders anticipated and prepared for an immediate conflict with the United States.

Why did the Southern leadership immediately resort to the drastic measure of war? Southerners and their leaders believed the new Confederacy would win its independence from the United States despite the obvious superiority of the North in nearly every comparison of strength and warfare potential. As examined in chapter one, Southerners had long disdained the North as martially inferior. Events in the beginning of 1861 as the cotton states left the Union reinforced the perception that Northerners would not take action to protect Federal property, much less to oppose secession. Army officers were allowed to resign their commissions and travel to the South without challenge. Northern leaders and politicians were divided in their response to the secession crisis. Many Northern Democrats called for peace, even if it meant dividing the country. Indeed, General Winfield Scott, the Federal general in chief and a former Whig, wrote to Secretary Seward informing him that he preferred that the rebellious states be left alone: Scott wanted to let the "departing sisters leave in peace."

Pro-secession Southerners believed that even if Lincoln attempted to take action against secession the majority of Northerners would not support him. The old stereotypical Yankee, as regarded by many Southerners, was too concerned with trade, profit and the pursuit of gain to fight for the Union. Some confident secessionists declared that they would "drink every drop of blood" shed to save the Union.[6]

Even those Southerners who knew from military experience that Northerners would meet the ordeal of combat on equal terms were discounted. Southerners believed their soldiers, fighting for their homes and way of life, would prevail just as their revolutionary ancestors had prevailed over the English. A Tennessee Congressman referred to the cost, "Thirty millions," to the government for the campaign against the Seminoles in Florida as a tiny comparison of the cost of subduing the South. "When you talk of conquering States, the whole arithmetic fails of figures to count the cost," he noted. Certainly the Southern leadership understood that the incoming Lincoln Administration faced a Herculean task in restoring the Union.

Many Southern leaders, especially from the Deep South, were deluded by the belief that Europe was inextricably dependent on cotton imported from the South. The doctrine of "King Cotton" was preached in the South, convincing many Southerners that textile mills, especially in Great Britain, were forced to rely upon a steady supply of cotton from the South. An interruption of the cotton supply to Europe, many believed, would create havoc or even revolution, as workers would be idled and factories shut down. To the adherents of this smug theory, the Confederacy could soon force Great Britain and France to recognize its independence and perhaps even extort an alliance against the United States.[7]

From a strictly military standpoint the South held some important advantages in the advent of war. The mass defection of professional military officers to the South, many of the ablest leaders in the Regular Army, also fostered confidence in the fledgling Confederacy. First the Federals would have to invade a vast region and blockade a shoreline stretching from Virginia to Texas. Confederate armies would have interior lines of communication and supply while the invading Federals would be forced to rely on long, vulnerable supply routes. An advantage of nearly three to one would be necessary for an attacking army, and a significant number of Federal soldiers would be needed to service and protect supply lines and garrison vital captured transportation hubs.[8] Thus the population and manpower advantage held by the North would be largely extenuated. Southern leaders also expected to utilize large numbers of slaves to replace white farmers and workers who would serve in the army. Another advantage, often understated in Civil War studies, is that the South would rely almost exclusively on a core of native-born, highly motivated soldiers defending against invasion, often fighting near their own homes.

Although the seceding states had relied on militia until the Confederacy took shape, the Confederate Congress quickly passed an act establishing a provisional army. The act approved on February 28, 1861, authorized the government to receive those "...who may volunteer ... for any time not less than twelve months, unless sooner discharged." The United States Government had not yet even called for volunteers. The Confederate leadership had shown foresight in requiring at least one year of service from recruits.

On March 4, 1861, President Abraham Lincoln made his first inaugural address, promising not "to interfere with the institution of slavery in the States where it exists." Lincoln urged restraint and said the government wouldn't "assail" his dissatisfied countrymen. He noted that there would be no conflict "without being yourselves the aggressors." He ended his speech with the sublime words: "The mystic chords of memory ... will yet swell the chorus of the Union, when again touched, as surely they will be, by the better angels of our nature."

Two days later, on March 6, the Confederate Congress authorized President Davis to "accept the services" of 100,000 volunteers for "cavalry, mounted riflemen, artillery, or infantry." Another lengthy act containing thirty-one sections passed that day, establishing the Army of the Confederate States of America. The legislation addressed pay, selection of officers, configuration of the units of the various branches, clothing, rations, etc. The South was now preparing for war, perhaps planning it, while the North remained indecisive.[9]

By March 1861 most or all United States property and military posts had been seized in the seceding states with the exception of Fort Pickens in Florida and Fort Sumter near Charleston, South Carolina. The merchant ship *Star of the West* contracted to supply Fort Sumter was fired upon and retreated without reaching the fort in January. Fort Sumter had become an outsized conundrum for the Davis and Lincoln administrations. Most of Davis's cabinet favored opening fire on the fort and forcing its surrender. There were two major considerations that supported the stance of the Confederate cabinet. South Carolina viewed the fort as an affront to its sovereignty, and there was concern that South Carolina would attack the fort without consulting the Confederate government. South Carolina had long since assumed the lead in the secession movement that had created the Confederacy. She also assumed the lead in demanding an attack on Fort Sumter.

Fort Sumter became the focal point for the new Confederacy to assert itself as a sovereign nation. Continued Federal occupation of the fort "mocked" Southern independence, undermining the prestige of the Confederate Government. Some fervent secessionists argued that blood would have to spill or else inertia would eventually restore the Union. Discounting the likelihood of a costly war and confident of an easy victory, Southern zealots demanded a military response to the Fort Sumter crisis. Southern leaders also assumed, correctly, that attacking the fort would provoke a response from the Federal Government that would rally the whole South to the Confederate cause.

Only one member of the Davis cabinet opposed firing on Fort Sumter. Secretary of State Robert Toombs, a man with a reputation for frequent quarreling, argued that attacking the fort was tantamount to suicide. "You will wantonly strike a hornet's nest," he warned. Toombs alone in the cabinet admitted that the attack was unnecessary, wrong, and would prove fatal to the Southern cause.[10]

As for the military situation at Fort Sumter, the commander, Major Robert Anderson, was nearly out of rations, had too few men, and would soon be forced to abandon his post which was being subjected to a siege. In fact, Major Anderson told Confederate envoys that he would evacuate the fort on April 15, if nothing changed. Nevertheless, President Davis decided to bombard the fort. At 4:30 a.m. on April 12, 1861, Southern batteries at various points around Charleston Harbor opened fire on Fort Sumter.

The "battle" at Fort Sumter lasted a little over a single day before Major Anderson was compelled to surrender his isolated command. Only four Federal soldiers were injured by pieces of brick or mortar thrown by impacting rounds. Only four rebels at Fort Moultrie were injured.[11]

President Lincoln reacted quickly to the attack on Fort Sumter, realizing the secessionist had stumbled and now bore the onus for war. On April 15, 1861, the president issued a proclamation calling forth "the militia of the several states of the Union, to the number of 75,000, in order ... to cause the laws to be duly executed" in the seven Southern states that had seceded by that date. Lincoln appealed "to all loyal citizens to favor, facilitate, and aid this effort to maintain the honor, the integrity, and the existence of our National Union, and the perpetuity of popular government, and to redress wrongs already long enough endured." Secretary of War Cameron that same day referred to a 1795 Congressional Act for calling upon the militia to suppress insurrections and issued a statement calling for quotas of troops to be supplied by each state remaining within the Union, including Arkansas, Kentucky, Maryland, Missouri, North Carolina, Tennessee and Virginia.

Secretary Cameron received that same day replies from several state governors, mostly from Northern states agreeing to promptly respond and supply the troops prescribed by Cameron's quota. Kentucky Governor Beriah Magoffin responded somewhat differently: "Your dispatch is received. In answer I say emphatically Kentucky will furnish no troops for the wicked purpose of subduing her sister Southern States." North Carolina Governor John Ellis also responded on the 15th: "I can be no party to this wicked violation of the laws of the country and to this war upon the liberties of a free people. You can get no troops from North Carolina."[12]

Historian Allan Nevins referred to the attack on Fort Sumter as "an act of rash emotionalism." The weakly-held fort "offered neither impediment nor threat to the Confederacy." It would have been more advantageous for the Confederacy to entice the Federals to initiate the war by some inevitable overt act elsewhere. The attack on Fort Sumter provoked an immediate response, as predicted by Secretary Toombs, from the North. The Confederacy would have benefited by delaying the onset of open war.[13]

After President Lincoln's proclamation of April 15, both the North and South began preparing for war in earnest. The Confederacy by the summer of 1861 was ahead of the North in war preparation and militarization. When Lincoln issued his call for 75,000 volunteers for ninety days, four slave states yet remained in the Union. The attack on Fort Sumter did not change the status of Arkansas, North Carolina, Tennessee and Virginia, but the president's call for volunteers to enforce Federal laws in the seceded states did soon lead these four slave states to join the Confederacy. Three Border slave states remained as potential additions to the Confederacy—Kentucky, Maryland and Missouri.

These three Border States were vitally important, strategically and materially, to each side of the conflict. The effort to retain the Border States within the Union would become a key facet of Federal strategic planning.

President Jefferson Davis held the key role in determining Southern planning at the strategic level: that is, the level where national war aims are determined as well as how resources will be employed to those ends. His fundamental objective was to defend the Confederacy from Federal invasion. The Confederacy was founded on the idea of protecting Southerners' property from Northern meddling. If Davis and the Confederacy could not repel Northern intrusion, the whole Southern mindset of martial superiority would be dispelled and Southern independence would appear futile.

Initially President Davis employed his forces in an operationally defensive posture. However, Davis never did develop a comprehensive plan to defend the Confederacy. He preferred offensive warfare and later incorporated offensive plans in his overall strategy. Over the course of the war the Confederacy suffered from a lack of central direction in its war effort. One key subordinate in the Bureau of War observed that the president "was not a comprehensive man," he had no grand scheme for the war or even a broad war policy.[14]

In the weeks immediately following the attack on Fort Sumter, neither side was in any way prepared to assume an offensive stance. Yet from the outset of the war Southerners overwhelmingly favored an invasion of the North. Secretary of War Toombs, who had opposed the attack on Fort Sumter, now urged taking the initiative. Toombs opined that the South "must invade or be invaded." President Davis would have to wait for the proper time to assume the offensive, and he stood by a policy he called defensive-offensive. Rather than attempting the impossible—conquering the North—Davis planned to punish invading Federal forces with severe losses in hopes that the cost for restoring the Union would become too great to bear. To defend the South President Davis divided his forces into departments assigned to garrison important places and to act as field armies protecting regions of the Confederacy. The plan assumed that the Confederate departmental commanders would cooperate to send reinforcements to any area threatened by a major Federal offensive. By concentrating forces against a threatened point, the Confederates expected be able to drive back invading forces. After defeating each incursion, the Confederates forces would return to their assigned departments and await another Federal offensive or assume an offensive operation of their own. If the plan worked according to theory, the Federals would eventually despair of conquering the South and accept its independence.[15]

While the Confederacy faced significant challenges in forming a new government and preparing for its defense, the Lincoln Administration and the North confronted a task of far greater proportion and difficulty. This fact is often overlooked in Civil War studies. Instead, many Civil War histories focus largely on the considerable advantages of the North, particularly in population and manufacturing.

Very few anticipated the mammoth challenge awaiting the Lincoln Administration following Fort Sumter. The level of difficulty was ultimately determined by the South, and victory over the Confederacy was made arduous indeed. The Confederacy had basically been allowed to form and announce its independence without Federal interference, making the task of restoring the Union infinitely more difficult. The Federals would have to invade and occupy an immense territory. It would require a huge navy to support invasion operations and patrol a vast coastline and numerous navigable rivers. The Federals would also have to force a rebellious population to submit to laws and conditions it obviously despised. This would be no easy task, as the British learned of Americans during the Revolutionary War.

Colonel Edward R.S. Canby's reports from the New Mexico Territory early in the war give some insight into the difficulties faced by the Federals in the Southwest. Canby, a West Point graduate and veteran of the Seminole and Mexican wars, had been appointed colonel of the newly organized 19th U.S. Infantry and then as commander of the Department of New Mexico. Canby soon faced an invasion of New Mexico from Texas, as anticipated by Confederate Secretary of War Walker. Along with a litany of troubles, he reported continuing "depredations" by the Apaches and that "the Comanches are openly at war with us." He observed that the inhabitants of the territory were "apathetic in disposition." "I question very much," Canby wrote, "whether a sufficient force for the defense of the Territory can be raised within its limits, and I place no reliance upon any volunteer force that can be raised, unless strongly supported by regular troops."[16]

Adding to his troubles, Canby later heard that funds to pay his troops and volunteers would be delayed for months. Canby's report on this matter reveals much about the situation in the Southwest:

> The Mexican people have no affection for the institutions of the United States; they have a strong, but hitherto restrained, hatred for Americans as a race, and there are not wanting persons who, from the commencement of their troubles, have secretly but industriously endeavored to keep alive all the elements of discontent and fan them into flames. The long-deferred payment of the volunteers has given so much plausibility and coloring to their representation as to have produced a marked and pernicious influence upon these ignorant and impulsive people.
>
> Without crediting these reports, I think it proper to state that, unless measures are taken at an early period to remove these causes of dissatisfaction, the consequences wilt be in the highest degree injurious to the interests of the Government.[17]

The incoming Lincoln Administration was facing troubles just about everywhere except the Northeastern and most Midwestern States. From the Nebraska Territory word came that the territory could only tender volunteers sufficient to garrison two forts because regular troops had already been withdrawn. The withdrawal of troops from the forts was causing "much alarm among our people of trouble from the Indians," reported John Thayer, commanding militia in absence of the governor.[18]

President Lincoln turned to Lieutenant General Winfield Scott, one of America's all-time greatest generals, for advice and direction. General Scott was a native Virginian, born on his father's farm in Dinwiddie County, Virginia, in 1786. In his youth he studied at William and Mary and also studied law in Petersburg, Virginia. Appointed to the army by President Jefferson in 1808, Scott earned international fame for his actions at Lundy Lane during the War of 1812. In 1841 he became commander-in-chief of the army and then masterminded the invasion of Mexico. Though somewhat under appreciated by historians, perhaps due to the unfavorable impression of the Mexican War, his campaign in Mexico was brilliant and remarkably successful. In 1847 Winfield Scott became only the second American appointed to the rank of Lieutenant General and was doubtless the most able soldier of his time. He shared Whig Party political affiliation with Abraham Lincoln and ran as the Whig nominee in the 1852 presidential election, losing to Franklin Pierce. But by 1861 General Scott was seventy-five and suffering from excessive weight, pain from an old wound, dropsy and aging. Despite concerns that he might favor his home state and the South, he remained loyal to the Union and served President Lincoln well.[19]

Perhaps General Scott's greatest, and doubtless his best-known, contribution to the Union cause during his brief service to President Lincoln was a strategic plan he envisioned to subdue the Confederacy. Unfortunately there is no comprehensive record of the plan, and thus it has been questioned whether General Scott ever submitted something known to history as the "Anaconda Plan" to President Lincoln and his cabinet. Still, it is widely believed that the general-in-chief did discuss and offer to the president a strategic plan relying on a blockade of Southern ports and control of the Mississippi River. Evidence of Scott's authorship of such a plan is found in his comments criticizing a plan suggested by Major General George B. McClellan. He did actually refer to his strategic thinking in a letter addressed to General McClellan dated May 3, 1861. Scott's strategic views were soon leaked to the press and then critiqued in newspapers, which in turn revealed the plans to the Confederacy. The plan was compared to a constricting anaconda snake in its intended affect upon the South, and it became known to history as the Anaconda Plan.[20]

General Scott's campaign plan was never implemented, at least as he envisioned it. There were far too many voices crying for a move into Virginia to capture Richmond, which in late May had become the new capital of the Confederacy. Scott's plan made strategic sense and eventually became an important facet of the Federal war effort. It no doubt could never have played out as the general had forecast, ending the war within a year. But there is no way the old general could have known in May 1861 how massive the Confederate mobilization would become, and he certainly would have altered his plan as events unfolded. His strategic thinking was fixed upon restoring the Union at the least cost in blood and treasure, and in that sphere he was preeminent.

Among Scott's other important contributions was his advice in naming key commanders at the war's outbreak, when they were vitally needed. General Scott recognized the command potential of Robert E. Lee, his "favorite" from the old army "whose genius he estimated far above that of any other officer." Lee was considered for command of the field army intended for an advance on Richmond. Although it has often been mentioned in Civil War writing that Lee was offered command of all Federal armies, he was actually considered only for the command that eventually went to Irvin McDowell. Albert S. Johnston, who defected to the Confederacy and became an army commander, was also offered high command by General Scott after Robert Lee showed no interest. Scott later had a role in the naming of his eventual successor.[21]

Meanwhile the fledgling Confederacy was in the process of losing its most important remaining strategic initiative, control of the Border States and the northwest portion of Virginia. Maryland with its proximity to Pennsylvania and large pro–Union population was always a dubious ally. The same is true of what soon became the State of West Virginia. However, Kentucky and Missouri each had pro-slavery governors and significant public sympathy for the rebel cause. The situation in Kentucky was particularly mishandled by the Confederate leadership with deleterious consequences for the Confederacy.

As we have seen, Kentucky Governor Beriah Magoffin was sympathetic to the Southern cause, as illustrated by his response to Lincoln's quota for Kentucky troops. In a reply to Alabama Commissioner Hale's missive quoted at the beginning of this chapter, Magoffin wrote: "You have not exaggerated the grievous wrongs, injuries and indignities to which the slave-holding States and their citizens have long submitted ... our honor, our self-preservation alike demand that our interests be placed beyond the reach of further assault." Magoffin, however, was hoping for a peaceful settlement rather than a war.[22]

The situation in Kentucky was in some ways unique in regards to the national crisis. Kentucky had much in common with other Midwestern States like Illinois, Indiana and Ohio. On the other hand it was a slave state with little Yankee influence. Governor Magoffin himself favored a State convention to consider secession, and for a while he sanctioned secret Confederate recruiting within Kentucky's borders. But the Bluegrass State's leaders wanted no part of Civil War. By mid–May Kentucky's leaders had rejected secession, and the Kentucky House had voted to assume neutrality. Even the pro–South governor by proclamation warned both the Confederate and Federal governments not to send troops into the state.

The Federal policy toward Kentucky under Lincoln's direction "displayed masterly comprehension and alertness." The Confederate policy didn't. Kentucky, with a population of 1.2 million and a strategic position on the Ohio and Mississippi Rivers, was of vital importance to both sides of the conflict. Kentucky's declaration of neutrality stood in contradiction to the president's authority, and Lincoln believed he had an "unquestioned right" to march troops through the state at any time. Yet the president reacted to the Kentucky situation with patience and restraint. His policy allowed time for events to determine the status of Kentucky rather than forcing the issue.[23] Eventually, as will be seen, actions by the Confederates pushed Kentucky into the Federal fold. In Kentucky, at least, the Federals chose the proper course and policy to gain sway.

Events in Missouri unfolded in a strikingly dissimilar manner. An entirely different political calculus was in play here. Senator Stephen A. Douglas had carried the state for the Democrats in the 1860 election. Slavery was legal but not particularly widespread or intensive; only one county in the southeast corner, some counties along the Missouri River and Clay County near Kansas City had slave populations of over 25 percent. Missouri was as culturally variegated as any state in the Union. The northern border of the state was not unlike Iowa, much of the Ozark region was populated with poor, small-scale farmers with little use for slavery, but the mid-section along the river was known as Little Dixie for its southern sentiment. St. Louis was a magnet for foreign immigrants. With a population of nearly 60,000 Germans and 39,000 Irish, St. Louis was proportionally the most immigrant intensive city anywhere in America. The German segment in St. Louis was strongly influenced by liberal, anti-slavery refugees from the 1848 German revolution, and these and other immigrants spread across the state counterbalanced the native pro-slavery population.[24]

Missouri Governor Claiborne F. Jackson set the tone for the state when he replied to President Lincoln's call for troops. On April 17 Jackson replied from Jefferson City, Missouri, "Your requisition, in my judgment, is illegal, unconstitutional, and cannot be complied with. Not one man will the State of Missouri furnish to carry on such an unholy crusade." Jackson's reply was about exactly the same as what came from North Carolina, Tennessee and Virginia, but the Missourian was in no position to control his state's response. When Jackson called for a state-wide convention hoping to push Missouri into the Confederacy, a majority favored staying in the Union with neutrality. Afterwards Jackson focused his efforts on serving the Confederacy in ways he could.[25]

Unlike Kentucky, in Missouri thousands volunteered for the Union immediately following the president's call on April 17. A majority of the first pro–Union volunteers were German immigrants who perhaps rallied to Lincoln's party because of a common dislike for slavery. Lincoln's pro-immigrant politics also helped make him popular with the Germans in particular. Missouri soon became a civil war within a civil war as the state militia through Governor Jackson's efforts sided with the Confederacy. Soon after Jackson ordered about 700 state militiamen to an encampment near St. Louis, pro–Union troops surrounded the place and took the militiamen captive. Most of the pro–Union troops were German immigrants, and when the captured militiamen were marched under guard into St. Louis on May 10, a crowd hostile to the Germans attacked with rocks. Somebody fired at the soldiers, wounding several, one mortally, and then the soldiers opened fire on the crowd. With ninety civilians shot—twenty-eight fatally—the riot was tantamount to a massacre in the eyes of pro-southern Missourians. The ultimate result of this tragedy was to intensify the hatred that fueled vicious guerrilla warfare in Missouri and Kansas during the course of the war. The situation in Missouri at this stage of the national crisis could have, obviously, been handled better by leaders on both sides of the conflict.[26]

It required a remarkably brief period of transition for military operations and fighting to commence following the attack on Fort Sumter. On January 1, 1861, the Federal Army numbered only 16,367 officers and men, counting 1,704 absentees and those who would defect to the Confederacy. By July 1, 1861, the total strength of the Army was already 186,651. The loyal states had quickly furnished 91,816 men under the president's call for three-month volunteers. On May 3, 1861, the president called for another 500,000 volunteers, and over 700,000 eventually answered the call, 657,868 for three years. The following day President Lincoln authorized nine additional regular infantry regiments to augment the Regular Army.[27]

In these opening months of the war the South was better prepared to fight than her Northern foe. The Southern armies held some important advantages, otherwise the Civil War would likely have been unremarkable and of short duration. First, as mentioned previously in this chapter, Southern troops initially enlisted for a minimum of one year rather than ninety days as was the case of the first Federal volunteers. President Lincoln erred in calling for three-month volunteers for restoring the Union. The Confederate troops went into training sooner and with more determination than the troops taken in Lincoln's first call. In many cases the Federal three-month volunteers did not perform well when needed.

In comparing the contending armies, one should bear in mind that personal bias has clouded this subject since the close of the war. Douglas Southall Freeman, author of *Lee's Lieutenants*, touched on this bias when he mentioned that the children of Southern soldiers were inculcated with the belief that Confederate generals were great, and that the South would have won the war except that the North had overwhelming resources. To Southerners, all their old soldiers were gallant and all their officers able. As Freeman observed, "Criticism was disloyalty."[28] Generations inculcated with this perspective have without doubt had their effect on how the war is remembered and documented.

Nevertheless, the facts point to an overall Southern edge in its officer corps, especially early in the war and particularly the eastern army which became the Army of Northern Virginia (ANV). A disproportionately large number of Southerners had at least some military experience, particularly young men with a military school education who became officers or able noncoms. Nearly a third of the prewar military's commissioned officers resigned, a total of 313, and a large portion of these tendered their services to the Confederacy.[29] Of this group many were particularly suited for the type of warfare the Confederacy would have to wage. What this means: the Confederacy gained from the

Old Army a cadre of officers that would mesh with the Southern need for campaigns of maneuver and mobility, rather than officers with military engineering skills as their primary interests.

One reason the South had a larger proportion of officer-ready volunteers is because military schools were more popular and numerous in the South than in the North. West Point, in New York, and Norwich Academy (or Captain Partridge's School), in Vermont, were the North's two best-known military schools. Only fifteen military schools are known to have existed in the free states in the three decades before the Civil War. West Point is a government school with Northern and Southern cadets, and many Southern cadets who did or did not graduate from West Point served the Confederacy. In contrast, the South's military schools included the Virginia Military Institute (VMI), The Citadel in South Carolina, The Kentucky Military Institute, Brandon State Military College in Mississippi, and several military schools in Alabama. At least 12,000 men who had attended the ninety-six Southern military schools and an additional 304 West Point graduates went into Confederate service. The men who formed the ANV had military training in school "in far greater numbers" than any other Civil War army. According to one historian, this fact made the ANV "a far better military organization" than the rest, North or South.[30]

The Federal Army's overall officer policy worked to its disadvantage, especially during the first year of the war. Junior Regular Army officers were then required to resign their commissions before accepting appointments within state volunteer units. Resigning meant losing seniority in the Regular Army organization during the first year of the war. Afterwards officers were allowed to accept positions in volunteer outfits without resigning, often at a much higher grade. During that first year of the war, efficient Regular Army officers were reluctant to resign to accept commands in volunteer units. As a result, Northern governors and politicians often appointed unqualified civilians to command regiments and to other high ranking positions. Since the Confederacy was just forming its army, qualified officers were free to accept appointments without seniority concerns. In effect, young, efficient and qualified officers were found and placed in key positions more frequently in the Confederate Army, especially during the formation of the armies in 1861. President Davis with the help of advisors was able to find and appoint a large number of capable regimental and brigade commanders, still in their thirties, who proved to be exceptional leaders and fighters.[31]

Civil War officers who attended West Point were without doubt the single most influential contingent impacting the war's planning and outcome. West Point was founded in 1802 at President Thomas Jefferson's urging as a national military academy under the direction of the Corps of Engineers. The school was launched by engineers and always placed an emphasis on military engineering. By 1844 West Point was one of the best, if not the finest, engineering school in the country. It was more an engineering school than a military academy. Over half its graduates were going into private industry rather than pursuing an army career.[32]

Northern cadets often excelled in the engineering-channeled curriculum of West Point, two examples being Henry Halleck, third in the class of 1839, and George McClellan, second in the class of 1846. These two graduates were each destined for a pivotal role in managing the Federal war effort, especially in the eastern region. McClellan embraced a plodding, methodical, low-risk approach to military strategy that endured within the Army of the Potomac's leadership throughout the war. In many ways McClellan's approach was correct for the circumstances presented by the Federal situation of numerical and material superiority, but his leadership lacked boldness and timing. McClellan and Halleck were perhaps archetypical examples of many Northern West Point graduates; they were well suited for the technical aspects of warfare and military engineering. Overall, the Northern armies appeared more efficient in logistics and military engineering when compared to those of the Confederacy.

West Point professor Dennis H. Mahan presided over every cadet from 1832 until the after the war in his engineering class that included lessons on the art of war. According to his gravestone he was professor of civil and military engineering for forty years. He rightly deserves his stature as the "primary molder" of prewar American military theory. Mahan was famous for his book on strategy and tactics, *An Elementary Treatise on Advanced-Guard, Out-Post, and Detachment Service of Troops and the Manner of Posting and Handling Them in Presence of an Enemy*, which was a summary of his lectures.

After graduating first in the West Point class of 1824, Mahan had traveled in Europe to study and observe European military methods. He was particularly affected by his observations in France, and he based his engineering course in many ways on the French model. Mahan believed in the advantage of offensive warfare and boldness as practiced by Napoleon; indeed, he founded the Napoleon Club. Professor Mahan's overall influence on the cadets was powerful.[33]

Mahan was a Virginian who remained loyal to his duties at West Point and to the Union. His impact on the conduct of the Civil War is obvious yet dichotomous. Civil War generals no doubt recalled his lessons and his influence from their cadet days. Yet West Point graduates such as Thomas J. Jackson and George B. McClellan exercised a completely different implementation of what Mahan sought to inculcate. The same can be said of Henry W. Halleck, one of Mahan's favored students, when Halleck is compared to William T. Sherman or Ulysses Grant. Mahan's class, however it was absorbed and implemented, was presented to many of the most

The grave of Dennis H. Mahan, the influential instructor at the academy for forty years, at the West Point Cemetery.

important leaders on both sides of the Civil War. Mahan and West Point helped create an equilibrium in leadership that ultimately made winning the war difficult. While the South may have entered the war with an advantage in its proportion of efficient officers, West Point schooling and Regular Army experience rendered that factor indecisive, though not irrelevant, by providing a cadre of capable leaders and commanders to each side.

The first land battle of the Civil War occurred on June 5, 1861, as part of Major General George B. McClellan's campaign to secure western Virginia for the Union at Philippi, Virginia. This campaign yielded proportionately great advantages for the Federals and is important as an example of the Confederacy's inability to hold or even control territory wherein a majority of citizens did not support the rebel cause.

No study of the Civil War can overlook the impact of George B. McClellan. A West Point graduate, noted Mexican war veteran, emissary to Europe during the Crimean War, successful engineer and business leader, McClellan was one of the most qualified, familiar and influential generals of the war. Appointed major general in April 1861, McClellan was organizing Ohio's forces when General Scott ordered him to move 20,000 troops into western Virginia. A force under McClellan's command, McClellan himself was still in Ohio, surprised Confederates at Philippi, Virginia, on June 5 and routed them. While the action is considered the first land action of the Civil war, with less than twelve total casualties it was less costly in casualties than many minor skirmishes.[34] The results, however, were far more significant than many major battles.

McClellan reached Grafton in western Virginia on June 23 to oversee the Federal forces the region. General Lee, commanding Virginia's forces from Richmond, did not leave to supervise operations in western Virginia until late July. The fact that these two eminent commanders personally supervised operations in the region reflects the significance of the western Virginia campaign in 1861.[35]

The situation in western Virginia favored the Union in spring of 1861 because the inhabitants there had little in common with the Confederacy in general and eastern Virginia in particular. The Virginia counties along the Ohio River and those bordering Pennsylvania had much stronger commercial and social ties to neighboring Free states than to the Richmond Government and Tidewater society. Indeed, a Morgantown newspaper declared that the hill folk of western Virginia had ten times the grievances against Richmond as the slaveholders had against the Yankees. Twelve typical counties from the northwestern part of Virginia voted almost ten to one against secession in 1861. Most mountain folk northwest of the Shenandoah Valley had no desire to follow Virginia into the Confederacy, and the presence of Confederate troops in the area probably drove many to volunteer for the Union. In fact, a ratio of ten to one or more in some counties of what became the State of West Virginia likely favored Union over Confederates volunteers during the war.

After Virginia voted to secede from the Union, the trans-Allegheny portion of the state began to seriously consider forming a new state to secede from Virginia itself. Politics and circumstances prevented immediate action, but by June 1863 the new State of West Virginia would be admitted as the 35th state in the Union. Virginia and the Confederacy proved incapable of preventing the permanent loss of a large section of that state and an important strategic location to the United States.[36]

The fighting in western Virginia in 1861 resulted in a significant success for the North. McClellan planned and supervised the second battle of the campaign at Rich

Mountain on July 11. Brigadier General William S. Rosecrans, who later in the war would have an important role as an army commander, led a flanking maneuver that rendered the Confederate positions on Rich Mountain untenable. The Confederates retreated, but nearly 600 of them commanded by Lt. Colonel John Pegram surrendered on July 13. Brigadier General Robert S. Garnett commanding the rebel forces at nearby Laurel Hill abandoned that defensive position and retreated northward to Carrick's Ford. A force consisting of the 7th and 9th Indiana and 14th Ohio led by Brigadier General Thomas Morris attacked Garnett's retreating force at the ford on July 13. Twenty Confederates were killed, including General Garnett whose body was returned to his family under a flag of truce. This being one of the first battles, Garnett was the first Civil War general to be killed in action. These three defeats in small battles helped doom Virginia's hold on the trans-Allegheny region of that state. Federal troops, mostly from Ohio, would soon have sufficient control of the region for Congress to pass a law creating a new State of West Virginia on July 14, 1862.[37]

General McClellan was sufficiently convinced of victory in the region to wire General Winfield Scott on July 17 offering to "move on Staunton if you desire." The next day General Scott replied, informing McClellan that his suggestion "would be admirable," and he relayed the news that General McDowell would attack at Manassas. Scott hoped to unite McClellan's force with troops commanded by Major General Robert Patterson in the Shenandoah Valley. Patterson was making a feckless attempt at holding a Confederate force under General Joseph Johnston at bay in the valley. Patterson was "doing nothing," and Scott hoped that with reinforcements McClellan would "bag Johnston" in the valley before Johnston could reinforce enemy forces at Manassas. The outcome of the battle at Bull Run, which will be considered next, altered this plan and impelled the government to call McClellan to Washington instead.[38]

Defeat in western Virginia was a serious setback for the inchoate Confederacy. The situation in northern Virginia, particularly at Manassas, had monopolized the focus of Confederate leadership. With the Confederate victory at Bull Run, more resources and attention could be spared for western Virginia. General Robert E. Lee was being sent to the trans-Allegheny region to salvage the situation. On July 23 Lee informed Brigadier General H.R. Jackson, commanding at Monterey, Virginia, "Four Virginia regiments, one Arkansas, three Tennessee, and two Georgia regiments, and two field batteries are ordered to join the Northwestern Army. This force, with what ought to be organized from the hardy mountaineers, will be sufficient to drive back the invaders. There is a necessity for repelling them, and it must be done. Every assistance will be afforded to this quarter."[39] General McClellan was leaving the region just as Lee arrived, and indeed, the Confederates had sufficient resources to respond to Lee's expectations. Nevertheless, by winter the region would be controlled by the Federals and would remain so for the duration of the war. The outcome would prove to be lesson number one to the overconfident Southerners on the difficulty of campaigning in a region without substantial civilian support.

Robert E. Lee is known to many as the foremost general of the American Civil War. On July 28, 1861, when Lee left Richmond to coordinate Confederate operations in western Virginia, he had yet to garner fame or much recognition as a Confederate general. His subsequent reputation makes his contribution in western Virginia seem incongruent or perhaps sub par. In studies of the war his activities in this vital region are usually given little scrutiny. His lack of success is attributed to circumstances and the performance of his subordinate generals, who did not coordinate well. Ultimately, despite fairly even strength of forces, Lee's participation did not tip the balance in favor of the Confederacy in this important campaign.

It was during the difficult campaign in western Virginia that Lee grew his gray beard so familiar in wartime and postwar photographs. In the cramped and inconvenient conditions of his mountain camp, Lee decided to stop shaving. He found that the gray beard gave him a patriarchal appearance, and the soldiers took to referring to him as "Marse Robert" in casual though sincere respect. The sobriquet and the beard remained with him for the rest of his life.[40]

The fighting at Cheat Mountain is the one battle most associated with General Lee's presence in western Virginia. Lee helped devise a battle plan with Brigadier General William W. Loring to attack a Federal stronghold on Cheat Mountain along the Staunton-Parkersburg Turnpike. Loring had been the youngest colonel in the prewar Regular Army, being promoted to colonel of mounted rifles in 1856 when Lee was the lieutenant colonel of the 2nd U.S. Cavalry.[41] The battle plan called for Loring to advance on the Federals at Elkwater while two separate Confederate forces attacked the stronghold on Cheat Mountain. After skirmishing from September 12 to 15, Lee called off the operation and withdrew Confederate forces. During the operation Loring commanded about 11,000 men against a Federal force of 9,000 to 11,000 led by Brigadier General Joseph J. Reynolds. Despite the near parity in troop strength, this episode, like the previous Confederate attempts to control western Virginia, ended in a failure.

Other battles and skirmishes in the region included General Rosecrans' attack on Floyd's Confederate brigade at Carnifex Ferry on September 10, 1861, and actions at Greenbrier River on October 3 and Camp Allegheny on December 15. While none of these combats proved singularly decisive, the end result was to hold western Virginia for the Union.

The Federal push into western Virginia yielded several advantages for the Union effort. The immediate result was securing the Baltimore and Ohio (B&O) Railroad. This line was an important supply route connecting Ohio with Harpers Ferry. Washington was fed coal for winter heat and industry by this artery along with troops and supplies from western states. Federal control in the trans-Allegheny region enabled the creation of West Virginia as a pro–Union state in 1863, a state that eventually supplied the Union with seven cavalry regiments, nineteen infantry regiments and several artillery batteries. Finally, Federal success in the region "made it strategically impossible" for Kentucky, bordering Virginia on the east, to be steered into the Confederacy.[42] Confederate failure in western Virginia in itself did not doom the rebellion, but combined with other mistakes and oversights the campaign set the Confederacy on the road to defeat.

General Lee's role in the western Virginia campaign of 1861 is ambiguous, but his performance, like the campaign's outcome, was unsatisfactory for the Confederacy. It is unfair, however, to place all the blame upon Lee for the defeat. That blame mainly rests upon the strategy and direction generated in Richmond. President Davis apparently did not appoint Lee to overall command in western Virginia. Davis himself admitted that he had sent Lee to coordinate plans and create harmony among the generals running the campaign. Lee's actual role was more that of a consultant than a commander.

Lee himself erred in initially failing to perceive the true sentiment of the region's population. He apparently initially did not appreciate that movement into western Virginia was tantamount to invading a Northern state. Lee's most serious fault during the campaign involved his planning for the attack on Cheat Mountain. One historian described Lee's battle plan for Cheat Mountain as "horrendously complex." While Lee had good troops at his disposal, he failed to take into account their inexperience and the limitations of their officers.[43] Ultimately Lee's failure in western Virginia proved to be a mirror of his other forays into pro–Union territory.

The western Virginia Campaign as it relates to a comparison of the military performance and capabilities of Civil War forces is most pertinent as an indicator of the Confederacy's inability to successfully operate in any region without the advantage of local popular support. The prewar Southern assertion of martial superiority over Northerners was fully disproved in western Virginia. The familiar explanation for Southern failure, unequal resources and manpower, did not apply at Cheat Mountain and to the western Virginia campaign overall. This campaign, the first test of the Confederacy's ability to win outside the confines of strong local support, established a pattern of failure and defeat outside the Confederacy. Throughout the course of the war Confederate armies could and did win on Southern soil. Operating on Northern soil, or even neutral areas, the Confederacy usually did not prevail. The western Virginia Campaign of 1861 did not serve the Confederacy as an indicator of the difficulty of fighting on enemy ground, as it should have, and Lee and Davis would suffer greater defeats later in the war for not taking into account the challenges of invading Northern Territory.

While the western Virginia Campaign was in progress, a far more familiar and documented fight occurred near an important northern Virginia railroad center called Manassas Junction. General Lee had quickly recognized the significance of the junction. In early May he had informed Virginia Colonel Phillip Cocke: "You are desired to post at Manassas Gap Junction a force sufficient to defend that point against an attack likely to be made against it by troops from Washington. It will be necessary to give this point your personal attention."

The first major battle of the war fought along a small stream called Bull Run and known as First Bull Run or First Manassas garnered much more attention and historical recognition than was warranted by its long-term strategic significance. The battle was the first large-scale test of the military prowess of the contending sections. Even so, this fact is misleading for several reasons; the real significance of the battle as it played out was to reinforce the dubious sense of martial superiority in the minds of many, then and now.

As was referenced earlier in this chapter, in the spring of 1861 General in Chief Winfield Scott preferred a time-consuming method for defeating the Confederacy known to history as the Anaconda Plan. As General Scott anticipated, politicians and public pressure combined to force him to resort to an alternate plan. Scott presided over the buildup of Federal forces for the protection of Washington, but he realized he could not lead an offensive campaign against secession forces gathering in northern Virginia because of his age and infirmity. The aged general had hoped to hand command of the gathering eastern army to Robert E. Lee. When that failed, Scott preferred to give that command to fifty-seven-year-old Joseph Mansfield, the senior regular officer in the Washington area. Instead, that command was given through apparent patronage by Ohioan and Treasury Secretary Salmon P. Chase to fellow Ohioan Irvin McDowell.[44]

McDowell along with General Scott hoped to postpone the movement against the Confederates in northern Virginia until time permitted proper training and preparation for their unseasoned recruits. Several conditions and considerations impelled President Lincoln to override his top general's advice and to order an advance into northern

Virginia. Intense pressure from the press played a major role in pushing Lincoln to order the advance. Probably the one correspondent most responsible for Lincoln's distress was one Fitz Henry Warren writing for the *New York Tribune*. Warren badgered the government to break camp for an advance to capture Richmond, and thanks to Warren and the *Tribune*, soon the phrase "Forward to Richmond!" was being reprinted in newspapers across the entire North. The president, facing an apparent tide of public opinion calling for action, decided to disregard General Scott's advice; he called for a plan of advance against the Confederates in northern Virginia without delay. Lincoln also felt compelled to use the ninety-day regiments gathering around the capital before their service expired, for these men would soon be discharged and sent home. A Federal defeat in the skirmish at Big Bethel, Virginia, on June 10, also embarrassed the government and added to Lincoln's impatience. Lincoln has been portrayed in historical accounts as pressuring McDowell to go on the offensive because neither side was well prepared for such an important campaign. He is said to have told McDowell that each side was "green alike," meaning neither side held an advantage in experience. This familiar remark credited to Lincoln may have in fact never been spoken by the president. Nevertheless, Lincoln obviously felt enough confidence in his unpracticed volunteers to override the judgment of his army commanders.[45]

The situation relating to the First Battle of Bull Run was not especially complicated, but for all the commanders, indeed everyone involved, it was something of a trial run. No American had ever handled armies this large or experienced a campaign of this magnitude, let alone with so little preparation. The Confederates here had the advantage of better commanders and overall leadership, and had the advantage of being on the defensive. Brigadier General Pierre Gustave Toutant Beauregard, second in the West Point class of 1838, led the Southern forces near Manassas. Brigadier General Joseph Eggleston Johnston, West Point class of 1829, commanded another Confederate force in the Shenandoah Valley with a view of coordinating his operations with Beauregard.

Beauregard and Johnston, as their subsequent Civil War records would validate, were more able generals than the army commanders on the Federal side, McDowell and Major General Robert Patterson. Even more significant, the commanders at the division, brigade and regimental level favored the Confederates at Bull Run. Among these were Thomas J. Jackson, Jubal A. Early, Richard S. Ewell, Wade Hampton, Joseph Kershaw, James Longstreet, and J.E.B. Stuart. Perhaps the most able commander at any level on the Federal side was William T. Sherman, but even he was inexperienced at the time and would require time and seasoning to mature into the accomplished commander he later became.

Under General Scott's direction, McDowell submitted a well-conceived plan to drive the Southerners from Manassas, with a view of relieving pressure on the nation's capital. In sum, McDowell's plan called for a westward advance in three columns, for the sake of mobility, to capture outposts at Fairfax Court House and Centerville. The plan then called for two columns to attack the Confederates along Bull Run while a third column would move along the enemy's right flank to strike from the rear.

General Beauregard's plan was simply to use Bull Run as a barrier and then guard the creek's fords, concentrating on the crossings that were practicable for a large attacking force. Beauregard placed about half of his troops in position to guard Mitchell's Ford, Blackburn's Ford and McLean's Ford along the creek south of the Warrenton Turnpike, the suspected route of the Federal advance. A small brigade was assigned to watch the turnpike's crossing at the Stone Bridge; Beauregard expected the Federals to attack at one of the fords below the turnpike.[46]

An important collateral factor in the Bull Run Campaign involved General Johnston's force in the Shenandoah Valley. Johnston commanded around 11,000 troops at Winchester. Generals Scott and McDowell realized that this force had to be kept isolated in the Valley. Otherwise Johnston could unite with Beauregard at Manassas and cancel McDowell's planned numerical advantage for the fight along Bull Run. General Scott assigned his longtime friend Major General Robert Patterson the task of confronting Johnston and forcing him to remain on the defensive in the Shenandoah Valley. Patterson led a force of nearly 18,000 men on his mission to occupy Johnston; nevertheless, Patterson was somewhat disadvantaged.

Johnston superseded Colonel Thomas J. Jackson in command of the Confederate troops in the Valley. Jackson had gathered a dependable nucleus of troops before Johnston arrived, and he now served under Johnston's command. The Valley force also included the 1st Virginia Cavalry commanded by Colonel J.E.B. Stuart. Patterson, on the other hand, led a force that included at least eighteen ninety-day Pennsylvania regiments manned by unhappy and dissatisfied short timers. Patterson had little faith that these troops would stay even one day past their enlistments, and discipline was declining daily. Apparently the sixty-nine-year-old Patterson had little confidence in his disgruntled Pennsylvanians or perhaps even in himself. He proved to be a disappointment to Scott, showing little initiative or determination. Patterson did, however, have the benefit of the services of some able subordinates including Colonel George H. Thomas who would later earn an outstanding reputation as an army commander. This and a numerical advantage suggest a probability that Patterson could have succeeded in his mission. Johnston should have been forced to remain in the Valley.[47]

Patterson finally did move against the enemy near Martinsburg, Virginia, (now West Virginia) skirmishing with Jackson's troops on July 2. Jackson fell back and the federals slowly followed, reaching Bunker Hill by the 15th. At this point, Patterson, worried about the condition of his three-month volunteers and their impending departure for home, decided to discontinue pressuring Johnston at Winchester. On the critical day of July 16, as McDowell's army moved out of Washington to attack Manassas, Patterson informed General Scott that on the morrow he would "move upon Charlestown" with the object of holding Harper's Ferry. On the 17th Scott informed Patterson, "I have nothing official from you since Sunday (14th), but am glad to learn, through Philadelphia papers, that you have advanced. Do not let the enemy amuse and delay you with a small force in front whilst he re-enforces the Junction with his main body." In effect, Patterson's move to Charlestown allowed Johnston to do exactly what General Scott had warned Patterson to prevent. General Scott explained Patterson's failure thusly in a report the following year:

> 5. But although General Patterson was never specifically ordered to attack the enemy, he was certainly told and expected, even if with inferior numbers, to hold the rebel army in his front on the alert, and to prevent it from re-enforcing Manassas Junction by means of threatening maneuvers and demonstrations—results often obtained in war with half numbers.
>
> 6. After a time General P. moved upon Bunker Hill, and then fell off upon Charlestown, whence he seems to have made no other demonstration that did not look like a retreat out of Virginia. From that movement Johnston was at liberty to join Beauregard with any part of the army of Winchester.[48]

Patterson's decision to fall back on Charlestown on the 16th enabled Johnston to reinforce Beauregard. However, McDowell, leaving Washington on that same day, certainly could have reached Manassas and attacked before Johnston's force could have intervened. A series of miscues, that might have been avoided, led to the Federal defeat at First Bull Run. First, McDowell allowed the advance on Manassas to move at a much too leisurely pace. Next, McDowell was forced to change his battle plan after learning, in route, that he could not expect to be able to turn the rebel right flank at Union Mills Ford on Bull Run east of Manassas. The terrain there was too cumbersome for a large-scale rapid movement. McDowell should have learned this during the planning stage, but somehow he failed to discover it. These factors were only part of McDowell's eventual troubles, but combined they threw his timing off schedule, forcing him to improvise.

The next blunder in the Federal advance occurred on July 18 when McDowell sent out a reconnaissance to probe the rebel line along Bull Run. Out from Centerville went troops commanded by Brigadier General Daniel Tyler, a sixty-two-year-old West Point graduate commanding the Federal 1st Division. Tyler had been an artillery and ordnance expert at one time, but long before the war he had repaired to civilian life as a successful investor and businessman. He returned to the service as colonel of the 1st Connecticut Infantry at the outbreak of war. Tyler and his force reached Bull Run in the vicinity of Blackburn's Ford without incident, but then he proceeded to provoke the concealed rebels by sending forward a brigade as "skirmishers to scour the thick woods with which the whole bottom of Bull Run was covered." The reconnaissance escalated into a hot skirmish before Tyler withdrew. The unnecessary and unauthorized action cost the Federals nineteen killed, thirty-eight wounded, and several missing, along with the humiliation of having to withdraw under fire from the enemy. The end result of Tyler's reconnaissance was to alter and delay McDowell's movement against Beauregard.[49]

Federal command missteps by now had begun to accumulate, eroding and eventually negating McDowell's advantage. Instead of immediately pressing an attack with superior forces, McDowell delayed for two days at Centerville to reconstruct his battle plan. Beauregard had concentrated his forces along the Bull Run fords south of the Warrenton Turnpike, leaving his left flank vulnerable to attack from the stream crossings north of the turnpike. Seeing this, McDowell decided to utilize the northern crossings as an avenue of attack and adjusted his battle plan accordingly. The plan was good and probably would have proved successful. Unfortunately for the Federals, further oversights and delays plagued their efforts and contributed significantly to their eventual defeat.

McDowell's most damaging mistake, other than his unnecessary delays, was his failure to adequately scout and carefully examine the Bull Run crossings and fords between the Turnpike and Sudley Springs for his new route of attack. McDowell was well aware that Patterson might fail to detain Johnston's force at Winchester. Nevertheless, he delayed two days at Centerville to prepare another battle plan. During that time some attempt was made at scouting Bull Run and its crossings. The task of locating the best crossing was assigned to McDowell's chief engineer, Major John Barnard. Barnard twice attempted to search for practicable fords on the 19th and again on the 20th.[50] However, the route Barnard recommended for the attack was a few miles farther north than another practicable track. With a better knowledge of stream crossings, the Federals could have saved the attacking columns time and fatigue. McDowell's flank attack thusly would have commenced at first light with the advantage of greater surprise.

Meanwhile, on July 19, as McDowell revised his tactics at Centerville, Johnston abandoned the Valley to the not-so-threatening Patterson and sped off to reinforce Beauregard. Marching his troops quickly from Winchester to Piedmont Station, Johnston sent them via a rickety railroad line to Manassas Junction. Jackson's Virginians reached that place by the afternoon of July 19. By the following day, most of Johnston's men had arrived to bolster the Confederates along Bull Run. Other reinforcements including a brigade led by Brigadier General Theophilus Holmes, arriving from Aquia Creek, and Colonel Wade Hampton with the infantry and artillery of his Hampton Legion showed up by the 20th.[51] Now the rebels along Bull Run, being on the defensive, actually held the advantage.

With the two Confederate armies consolidated along Bull Run, General Beauregard recommended an attack across the stream with a view of turning McDowell's left flank and cutting the obvious Federal retreat route to Washington. Instead, it was the Federals who initiated the action in the wee hours of July 21, 1861. McDowell set his army in motion around 2:30 a.m. on the 21st, before the Confederates were ready to attack.

Just as the Federal foray from Washington had been plagued with delays and missteps, the attack on the 21st was fumbled from the onset. McDowell's plan called for Brigadier General Daniel Tyler to march west with his 1st Division on the Warrenton Turnpike to the Stone Bridge. His assignment was to demonstrate there to draw attention away from the main attack coming from the northwest. Colonel David Hunter's 2nd Division and Colonel Samuel Heintzelman's 3rd Division, about 13,000 men, were the main attack force. These troops were to follow Major Barnard's recommended route, crossing Bull Run at Sudley and Poplar fords and to then sweep down the Sudley Road to outflank the Confederates south of the Turnpike. A series of mistakes in the marching order and delays, which will not be recounted here, put the Federal attack three hours behind schedule. As a result, Confederate Colonel Nathan Evans had time to shift most of his brigade from the pike to confront the attacking Federals.[52]

The tardy arrival of the Federal flanking columns at Sudley Springs and the perceptive adjustment by Colonel Evans proved decisive in the outcome of the First Battle of Bull Run. The pugnacious Evans, by confronting overwhelming odds, bought time for the brigades of Colonel Francis Bartow and Brigadier General Barnard Bee to shift into position to blunt the Federal attack. Hunter's force, by using a shorter route, should have arrived in position to outflank Evans before he could have reacted. Instead, fighting on Mathews Hill and along the Sudley Road bought time for Beauregard and Johnston to react and shift troops by interior lines to meet the unexpected threat.

The attacking Federals fought well enough, despite the long, fatiguing predawn march to the battlefield, to drive the Confederate brigades across the Warrenton Turnpike. The somewhat disordered Southerners fell back to a defensive position atop Henry House Hill. At this point in the battle, about noon, McDowell still stood a good chance of whipping the rebels. It was the crucial point in the battle, the point where adjustments would determine the outcome. Further mistakes could not be overcome. It was here that the Confederate leadership advantage proved decisive.

A concerted and coordinated attack by the units McDowell had at hand around noontime could have swept Henry House Hill and imperiled the entire rebel army. Instead, General McDowell chose more conservative and cautious tactics. It was a pattern, even method, of Federal leadership destined for repetition in the Virginia campaigns for much of the war. Somehow McDowell and his subordinates lacked the intuition necessary to grasp the opportunity at hand. McDowell delayed further attacks

This monument on the Bull Run Battlefield near the Henry House was one of the first Civil War monuments erected.

for two hours while he sent for reinforcements and gathered his troops. Meanwhile Johnston and Beauregard dropped their planned offensive and began sending troops to respond to the Federal success.

Continuing tactical errors by McDowell and his subordinates doomed the Federals that July afternoon. When McDowell finally did resume the attack at Henry House Hill, he made a serious mistake by sending Griffin's and Rickett's artillery batteries onto the hill near the Henry House. These batteries became the focus of the fighting atop the hill. The batteries were positioned too close to the enemy and without sufficient infantry support. According to Chief of Artillery Major William Barry: "…a regiment of the enemy's infantry … not more than sixty or seventy yards distance … delivered a volley full upon the batteries and their supports." The 11th and 14th New York regiments, protecting the guns, "instantly broke and fled in confusion to the rear." Advancing rebel infantry drove off the surviving artillerymen. For the rest of the battle the two armies fought for control of the hill and possession of the unmanned artillery. Ten guns, nine of them 10-pounder Parrott rifles, were eventually captured by the Confederates there.[53]

One further command mistake by McDowell worthy of mention here was his piecemeal commitment of units to the attack, especially during the critical phase of the battle in the afternoon. To be fair, Civil War commanders, on both sides, were guilty of this oversight to some degree in nearly every battle. Unfortunately for the Federals, McDowell's fault of sending regiments rather than brigades into the fight on Henry House Hill doomed his army to defeat. Many of his regiments were already fatigued to the point of

The grave of Judith Henry near the Henry House at Bull Run Battlefield. She was killed by an exploding shell in her house during the First Bull Run Battle.

ineffectiveness by the afternoon. He did not use his reserves effectively. Instead, he fed regiments into the fight on Henry House Hill a few at a time. A single concentrated attack with his reserves probably would have proved successful.

General Beauregard understood the necessity of massing troops for an attack. He once wrote that the "science of war" amounts to positioning a mass of troops in the right place at the right time in numbers too great for an enemy to oppose. An attack, Beauregard wrote, should never be made when "a short delay" will gather sufficient masses for success.[54] Notice he stipulated *short delay*, not time enough for an enemy to prepare. McDowell no doubt understood this principle also. However, in the crucible of battle he neglected to send his available forces forward in a concerted and effective attack. Beauregard and Johnston used the advantage of interior lines to bring reinforcements to Henry House Hill, thwarting McDowell's piecemeal attacks, fatiguing and demoralizing the unseasoned Federals. In the end, the battle faded from a Federal victory into an embarrassing rout, mainly as a result of the McDowell's feckless tactics on Henry House Hill.

Thus the First Battle of Bull Run transformed from a near Confederate defeat to an immense morale-boosting triumph for the South. The battle ended with McDowell's army fleeing the field in a humiliating and ignominious rout. The story of the Federal army's panicked escape from the battlefield has done more than probably any other Civil War event to perpetuate the aura of Southern martial superiority. The Federal defeat and rout was indeed an embarrassment to American arms. It was not, however, the last

View taken from Henry House Hill on the Bull Run Battlefield.

episode of its kind, and similar examples were repeated in later battles by the Southerners themselves.

In reality the battle's outcome was fortuitous for the Confederates, but the behavior of the defeated Federals provided ammunition for partisan Southern newsmen. A comment from a Louisville newspaper column after the battle succinctly portrayed the Southern outlook in familiar terms. According to the wag, the South had always ruled the North much as its Norman ancestors had lorded over the Saxon churls. A few more thrashings like Bull Run, he noted, "will bring most of them once more to the yoke," just as docile or perhaps circumspect as the most loyal "Ethiopian chattels." The familiar reference to Northerners as Saxons and Southerners as Normans was particularly apropos, to Southerners, in light of the humiliating Federal defeat.[55]

All things considered, the battle was not such an overwhelming triumph for Southern arms. A glance at the casualty reports reveals that the Confederates suffered more killed and wounded, those actually hit in combat, than did the Federals. Confederate killed and wounded totaled 1,969 while 1,492 Federals were killed and wounded.[56] The old Southern-held belief that their men were superior marksmen and thusly soldiers wasn't sustained in this battle. Remarkably, though they were driven from the field in a panicked rout, the Northern soldiers probably delivered more accurate fire than did the rebels. A statistician analyzing the battle's casualties years after the war determined that the Federals actually managed to hit about 100 rebels per 1,000 Federals in combat while the rebels hit about eighty Federals per 1,000 rebels in action.[57] This was a standup fight, neither side had the advantages of field works for protection and pre-selected fields of fire. Later in the war the Confederates would often inflict heavy casualties from behind the protection of earthworks. This battle was actually a better indicator of the ability of the soldiers from each army to face and return fire than were the battles later in the war when Federal casualties often greatly exceeded those of the well-protected Confederates.

In comparison the Confederates performed better overall than the Federals in this campaign. Johnston was able to elude Patterson's force in the Shenandoah Valley and reinforce Beauregard at Manassas. This was a complicated task, and Johnston overcame difficulties in getting his army moved in time to decisively impact the battle. Although somewhat unprepared for the Federal attack north of the Warrenton Turnpike, the Confederate leadership was able to adjust by sending reinforcements to the right place in a timely fashion. Southern morale appears to have been superior, demonstrating greater determination. The Southern units were defending while the Northerners were invading. A natural behavioral trait called "The Territorial Imperative" applies here. Even insects, fish, birds and animals, observation reveals, will fight harder when an invader approaches their niche.[58]

McDowell had been assigned a difficult, challenging mission, one he did not believe he was prepared for. He had agreed with General Scott that the army was not sufficiently trained and ready for this campaign. He was correct. Many of the Federal regiments were three-month units, almost due for a return home and muster out. These ninety-day troops were being sent into battle to risk their lives when they would be going home in a few days in any event. Naturally the men thought of surviving first, and it showed when panic swept the retreating Federals. In contrast, the Confederate soldiers were committed for at least one year and had many months of service ahead, win or lose.

McDowell's tactics during the battle did more to defeat the Federals than any other single factor. According to one source, the Confederates engaged nearly 32,000 men at First Bull Run while McDowell "managed to engage only some 18,500" of his available force of 35,000.[59] McDowell should have attacked with sufficient force to overwhelm Henry House Hill shortly after noontime. He obviously had reserves available to send into the fight that were not used effectively. Instead, regiments were onto Henry House Hill one or two at a time, wasting the slight advantage won during the morning.

The collapse of the Federals following the debacle on Henry House Hill reinforced an impression of ineptness, even recreance, which helped to substantiate the long-held perception of Southern martial superiority. Even greater overconfidence swept the South following this battle. The experience of First Bull Run should have had the opposite effect, despite the undisciplined Federal rout. The fact that the Confederates were unable to crush the defeated Federals should have pointed to the fact that the armies were in most respects equal in fighting ability and competence. According to a Naval Academy instructor, a "rough equilibrium" existed in the overall competence of the two armies. "Morale, unit cohesion, and the unpredictable vagaries of battlefield fortune" were the deciding factors in this battle, as was the case in most Civil War battles. This battle was decided by a "razor-thin margin."[60] Command decisions dictated the outcome to a much greater degree than the fighting ability of units or individual soldiers. As noted previously, McDowell's delays and missteps coupled with Patterson's inability to hold Johnston in the Valley were the decisive factors in the Federal defeat.

Because First Bull Run was the first major land battle of the war it has through the years garnered much greater importance and notoriety than is merited. The victorious rebels were unable to threaten Washington or even assume an offensive campaign soon after the battle. While the Confederates came away with an impressive victory and Confederate leadership from the brigade to army command level outperformed the Federals, no meaningful advantage was gained. The real lesson of the battle was to demonstrate that there would be no quick, easy ending to the war. Fortunately for the Federals, the administration took notice and reacted accordingly. Old General Scott's prediction that invading Virginia would precipitate a war costly in blood, time and treasure proved accurate, even understated. Under Lincoln's leadership the North began to shift to a long-term approach to the crisis.

The Confederate victory did very little to benefit the South. Even if the rebels had been defeated at Manassas, the Federals, with many regiments scheduled for discharge, probably would have been unable to continue the offensive meaningfully. The Confederates would later retreat southward from Manassas anyway. Perhaps the most significant and unfortunate impact of the battle was to encourage Southerners with resolve and confidence to continue the war effort, much to the sorrow of the country. Although the fighting disproved the fatuous adage that one Southerner could defeat five to ten Yankees, many, perhaps most, Southerners would forever cling to the notion that Northerners made for poor warriors. First Bull Run, happening as it did at the outset, established a pattern for the war in the East and how it would be remembered.

News of the battle buoyed the South with a sense of assurance that ultimately proved unfounded. In the months immediately afterwards the Confederate leadership accomplished very little to improve their odds for victory. Instead, operations and movements allowed by or directed from Confederate high command soon contributed to the loss of Kentucky, Missouri and western Virginia to Federal control. The later half of 1861 was the crucial period for the South to consolidate its resources and implement an effective defense strategy. President Davis and his military brain trust, it seems, lacked the capability to develop and implement a comprehensive defense strategy. Meanwhile, it was during this period that the Federal leadership demonstrated superior strategic planning and implementation. It was not simply Northern superiority in numbers and resources that led to victory in the Civil War. Northern superiority in allocating and managing resources, through more able supply administration and overall efficiency, coupled with superior strategic planning proved the key factors in the eventual Northern victory. First Bull Run removed all presumption of a short and easy end to the war. In the months immediately afterward, the North took huge strides toward victory by means of a comprehensive, multifaceted offensive war strategy.

4

1861

The North Initiates Comprehensive Warfare

The Federal debacle at First Bull Run casts a long shadow on American History despite its comparative insignificance. McDowell's demoralized army scurried back to Washington, making an uninspiring and unmilitary sort of impression upon its arrival. Washington and its residing politicians were justifiably unnerved by the sight of a defeated army milling about town in obvious need of discipline. Nevertheless, General in Chief Winfield Scott was not particularly worried about the safety of the nation's capital. Scott realized that more than enough forces were on hand to defend against Beauregard's and Johnston's battered troops, should they attempt an attack. On the day following the battle Major General George McClellan was summoned to the capital to assume command of McDowell's army. Propitiously for the Federals, a more able and suitable officer for the task of reorganizing, refitting and preparing that army could not likely have been found. Although the government failed to recruit sufficiently, Federal activities in the second half of 1861 to mobilize for war, train, equip and supply the army and navy, and implement an effective war strategy proved remarkably effective and impressive by any comparison. The road to Northern victory was laid out in the months immediately following First Bull Run.

Conversely, the Confederates, flush with victory and confidence, failed to develop even a comprehensive and effective defensive strategy. Instead, the Confederates established a series of defensive positions and forts at places deemed strategically significant. Forces were mostly scattered thinly at stations throughout the South leaving the western field army too weak to counter a Federal invasion. President Davis's plan for concentrating forces by means of interior lines to counter Federal incursions did not succeed in the West. Confederate command decisions and allocations implemented in late 1861 ultimately led to defeat.

In July 1861 the fate of Kentucky and Missouri had yet to be determined. Of the two states Kentucky had the stronger ties to the South. In both states, however, a majority preferred to remain in the Union. Kentucky secession advocates received a "crushing moral blow" in May when election results delivered a clearly pro–Union verdict, and a special Congressional election on June 30 gave nine of ten districts to "staunch Union men." Meanwhile the Kentucky House voted 69 to 26 to refrain from participation in the war, in effect a declaration of neutrality. Governor Magoffin, who had welcomed a Kentucky secession vote, felt compelled to inform President Davis of the situation in his state: "The people of this state desire to be free of the presence of soldiers of either belligerent, and to that end my efforts are now directed." Davis had been duly informed: Kentuckians did not want rebel troops even moving across their borders. Unable to overtly support the secessionists, Magoffin decided to ask the legislature to grant funds to arm Kentucky's State Guard through the efforts of State Adjutant General Simon Buckner, who later would become a Confederate general. The legislature took action to counter Magoffin's move to strengthen the apparently pro–Confederate Guard by creating a home guard and a pro–Union military board to oversee the state arsenal and all military supplies within the state. The destiny of Kentucky's role in the conflict still remained uncertain; political and strategic acumen would have a decisive impact on the state's eventual course.[1]

In Missouri Federal policy was far less patient and lenient. Pro-Union factors Frank Blair, Jr., and Brigadier General Nathaniel Lyon quickly acted to challenge the pro-secession state militia. Unlike Kentucky, Missouri would not be granted a period of neutrality. Missouri Governor Claiborne F. Jackson and former governor Sterling "Old Pap" Price took a decidedly pro–Southern stance, gathering the Missouri State Guard (MSG) in an effort to oppose Federal efforts to preserve the state within the Union sphere. As mentioned in the previous chapter, Jackson's militia was captured at its encampment in St. Louis in May. With Old Pap's assistance Jackson formed and recruited a new force, the MSG. Price was named as its commander. Price had previous military experience as a colonel and brigadier general of Missouri troops during the Mexican War, and he was popular with Missourians. The ranks of the MSG quickly swelled, partly due to Old Pap's popularity, with many joining who wanted only to serve Missouri's interests rather than supporting secession. As was the case in Kentucky, many Missourians had difficulty in deciding their loyalty. By June Lyon had identified Jackson and the MSG as the enemy, and he moved on Jefferson City, the state capital, to scatter the secessionist element there. On June 17 Lyon routed a MSG force at Boonville commanded by Colonel John Marmaduke, sending Jackson's boys scurrying to the southwest. Jackson and Price then split apart, intending to consolidate later. Price planned first to join forces with Confederates coming from Arkansas commanded by Brigadier General Ben McCulloch near the border in southwest Missouri. Lyon's aggressive moves had preserved Missouri's governmental infrastructure for the Union, but all hope of state unity was destroyed. Intense internecine warfare would plague Missouri for years to come.[2]

Following the skirmish at Boonville, Frank Blair, Jr., Lyon's political ally and the colonel of the 1st Missouri Infantry, decided to resign his commission. Blair believed he would be more useful in Washington, where his brother served as postmaster general in the Lincoln cabinet. Lyon continued his movement toward Springfield, Missouri, consolidating along the way with the First and Second Kansas Infantries and some regulars marching from Fort Leavenworth, Kansas. This column included future major generals Samuel D. Sturgis and Gordon Granger.

From Springfield troops were dispatched into southwest Missouri to chastise Governor Jackson and his guardsmen. This force, led by Colonel Franz Sigel, a politically connected, quintessential German immigrant from St. Louis, was composed of the 3rd and 5th Missouri Infantries and Backoff's artillery battalion. Sigel's infantry regiments were recruited from St. Louis German gymnastic societies. Sigel, though no gifted tactician, knew something about drilling soldiers, being a graduate of a German military academy and a former German military officer. Sigel's Germans had been well drilled in St. Louis "by the best rules of European warfare." They were much more efficient in tactical maneuvers and marching evolutions than Jackson's rag-tag Missouri Guardsmen.[3]

By the beginning of July Sigel had learned that Governor Jackson and several of his pro–Confederate political cohorts were marching in his direction with over 4,000 guardsmen, cavalry and recruits. Although outnumbered by at least three to one, Sigel turned his Germans northward hoping to check Jackson's force until Lyon and reinforcements could arrive to crush them.

On July 4, having closed on Jackson, Sigel's Germans camped just southeast of the pro–Southern town of Carthage, about a dozen miles east of the Kansas border. The appearance of the St. Louis Germans on the following morning at the town's edge rattled many of its citizens. No doubt they had heard of the "massacre" in St. Louis involving German troops, and many fled into the countryside to escape. Sigel kept his men moving quickly through the town and northward until he spotted Jackson's column about nine miles north of Carthage. The ensuing battle between raw Missouri militia and Sigel's carefully-drilled Germans soon regressed into a paragon of one of Sigel's few military talents—a careful and efficient retreat.[4]

Sigel soon realized that numbers would prove decisive in his little battle, and he set about withdrawing in an orderly and brisk fashion. By accounts he managed the retreat admirably, at least the German newspapers nationwide thought so. For his splendid defeat at Carthage, Sigel became a national hero to pro–Union and Republican German immigrants. He contributed more to the Federal war effort by bringing immigrant recruits, joining to fight mit Sigel, than with his battlefield endeavors, as we shall see. He proved as incompetent as any political general during the Civil War. His flawed leadership and mercenary behavior would darken the reputation of immigrant soldiers and officers in the Federal Army, probably contributing more to the adverse opinions of xenophobes, North and South, than any other participant in the war.

After the battle at Carthage the governor and his guardsmen gave up the chase and continued their march southward to link with General Sterling Price and Brigadier General Ben McCulloch, combining with their troops. Price then marched his Missourians to Cowskin Prairie in the far southwest corner of the state to drill and train his recruits. Some of the finest troops in the Confederate Army would come from Price's guardsmen. Meanwhile, the Germans retreated from the dusky woods east of Carthage, marching nearly all night and reaching Sarcoxie at 3 a.m. Sigel, finding that Jackson did not pursue, languidly made his way to Springfield, uniting with Lyon's small force there. Sigel's St. Louis troops, like Sigel himself, would make a poor showing in the next major battle of the Civil War.[5]

Even after uniting in Springfield the Federals were heavily outnumbered in southwest Missouri. Lyon, with a difficult supply situation and realizing that further reinforcement was unlikely, decided to move his army towards Cassville with a view of defeating Price before he could prepare an attack on Springfield. In the opinion of his adjutant general, "He saw clearly the inevitable necessity of either retiring to Rolla, and abandoning to the enemy all the southwest portion of Missouri and Southern Kansas, or of risking the utter destruction of his little army and the loss of all his material of war in a desperate engagement with a vastly superior force of the enemy." Unwilling to retreat, during the first week of August Lyon led a foray against the guardsmen southwest of Springfield. After skirmishing at Dug Springs and Curran's post office, Lyon realized that the enemy had joined forces; the objective of his advance had been rendered impracticable. By August 5 the Federals had returned to Springfield with Price and McCulloch following closely behind.[6]

Back in Springfield again, Lyon faced a perplexing dilemma. General Fremont, his department commander, was then concentrating on clearing the Mississippi River on Missouri's eastern border and had little interest in Lyon's operations. Lyon was heavily outnumbered by Price and McCulloch, and Fremont would not be sending more troops to southwest Missouri. Yet Lyon realized his obligation to the pro–Union residents of eastern Kansas and southwest Missouri. Calling his commanders to a council of war, Lyon explained his decision to attack:

> Gentlemen, there is no prospect of our being re-enforced at this point; our supply of provisions is running short; there is a superior force in front; and it is reported that Hardee is marching with 9,000 men to cut our lines of communication. It is evident we must retreat. The question arises, what is the best method of doing it. Shall we endeavor to retreat without giving the enemy battle beforehand, said run the risk of having to fight every inch along our line of retreat, or shall we attack him in his position, and endeavor to hurt him so that he cannot follow us. I am decidedly in favor of the latter plan.[7]

The original plan of attack was basically to strike the enemy's camps along Wilson Creek, a few miles southwest of Springfield, hoping that surprise and fury would stun the rebels. Unfortunately for the Federals, Colonel Franz Sigel somehow persuaded Lyon to give him an independent assignment for the impending battle. Although Lyon's other commanders opposed the plan, Sigel was given a brigade, about 1,200 strong, to attack the rebel encampment from the rear, in effect dividing Lyon's force in the face of a superior foe. The result has been termed "a pretentious little battle" in one familiar Civil War history.[8] While Lyon probably should have retreated to Rolla, the Battle of Wilson's Creek was envisioned as and manifested more than just a pretentious fight.

This battle, though of relatively minor significance and impact on the outcome of the war, meshes well with the theme of this study. It serves as an example of what can go wrong when an outnumbered army attacks with divided forces, particularly when a weak commander is assigned a crucial role. Many participants on both sides were strongly motivated and fought with uncommon intensity. The Federal troops here were a hodgepodge collection of immigrants, native-born pioneers, Jayhawkers, and abolitionists, many of them with a score to settle. Over half of the pro–Southern troops were Missourians; the rest were from Arkansas, Louisiana and Texas. The pro–Confederate Missourians were largely experienced fighting men: most of them had fought against Plains Indians or in bushwhacking expeditions against Kansas during the prewar "Bleeding Kansas" days, and many were Mexican War veterans.[9] As was usually the case, the rebel forces here were overwhelmingly comprised of non-immigrants.

A considerable amount of research has been done on the ethnic composition of the Federal infantry units that participated in the Battle of Wilson's Creek. Three regiments and a battalion of Missouri infantry fought in the battle. The 1st Missouri Infantry was 48 percent German, 44 percent American, and about 8 percent Irish. The 3rd and 5th Missouri Infantries, in Sigel's brigade, as we have seen, were almost exclusively comprised of German immigrants. Of the two Kansas regiments at Wilson's Creek, the 2nd Kansas, a ninety day unit, was manned largely by Kansas residents with common American surnames. The 1st Kansas was 18 percent German (mostly Companies I & K from the Atchison and Leavenworth areas) and 25 percent Irish with the balance being Americans born in Northern states including Ohio, New York, Massachusetts and Pennsylvania. As Kansas was a new state and being recently and sparsely settled, only two men serving in the regiment were born in the territory that became Kansas.[10]

At about 5 a.m. on August 10, 1861, Lyon's attacking column hit the northern edge of the rebel encampment with surprise. By this point in time the MSG had aligned with the Confederacy; thus, MSG units will be hereafter classified as Confederates. A skirmish line and a few shots from a Federal battery initially scattered the Confederates from their northern camps. Then Lyon deployed the 1st Kansas and 1st Missouri Infantries to press the attack. These troops pushed the Confederates off an elevation now known as Bloody Hill, thus gaining a slight tactical advantage despite the brushy and wooded nature of the hill.

Price's Missourians came swarming out from their camps, crossing the creek and ascending through the heavy vegetation on the south face of Bloody Hill. By about 6:30 a.m. enough of Price's men had reached the slope of Bloody Hill to check the Federal advance. Most of the Confederates were armed with shotguns or short-range arms, so the battle lines pressed forward to unusual proximity atop the hill. Soon the fighting on Bloody Hill, though utterly fierce, became a stalemate with each side attacking and retreating, swaying back and forth through the brush and timber.[11]

Sigel's brigade also had arrived well-timed and deployed undetected on the southern edge of the Confederate encampments. Sigel waited until around 5:30 a.m. when the roar of battle sounding from the north signaled that it was time to launch his coordinating attack. To this point the Federal attack plan had unfolded flawlessly. Unfortunately for the Federals, Sigel fumbled his role in the battle. With his small brigade, Sigel could have hoped for only a limited impact in any case. As it played out, Sigel's artillery succeeded in scattering some of the Confederates from their encampments on the southern edge of the battlefield; the Southerners were surprised while cooking breakfast. Little else was accomplished by Sigel's detachment. In all probability, Sigel's troops would have been of much greater use under Lyon's direction as part of the main attacking force.

When he launched his initial attack, General Lyon had ordered Captain Joseph Plummer to cross to the east side of Wilson Creek to protect his left flank. Plummer took his battalion of U.S. Regulars, about 300 strong, after a delay in finding a suitable ford, into the Ray Cornfield east of the creek as ordered. Many of the regulars in this fight were recent recruits, but they were mostly armed with the latest Springfield rifle muskets. By about 6:30 a.m. Plummer was well into the Ray Cornfield. He observed the Pulaski Arkansas Battery shelling Lyon's force from a position on his side of the creek. As Plummer moved to attack the Pulaski Battery, he was challenged by the 3rd Louisiana Infantry and the 2nd Arkansas Mounted Rifles, combined about 1,100 strong, near the southern edge of the cornfield.

A standup firefight ensued before Plummer's regulars could pass through the cornfield. Here the Confederates held an advantage in numbers and in cover afforded by brush and tall weeds along the edge of the cornfield. Plummer's regulars formed a firing line along a rail fence and in the corn, fully visible to the enemy when standing to fire. According to one account the Federal officers derisively heckled the Confederates before the shooting commenced. The shootout was at extremely close range, perhaps twenty paces; thus, the rifled muskets used by Plummer's men were actually less effective than the easier-loading smoothbore muskets in use by of some of the rebels. Smoothbore muskets could fire buck and ball cartridges that effectively increased firepower at close range, sending at least four balls downrange rather than the single bullet fired by rifle muskets.

Smoke soon shrouded the field, but remarkably the volleying continued for perhaps thirty minutes. No doubt several thousand rounds were fired at them while standing in full view and at short range, but less than a fourth of the Regulars were killed or wounded

The fence adjacent to the corn field on the Wilson's Creek Battlefield.

in the cornfield fight. Colonel James McIntosh of the 2nd Arkansas Mounted Rifles, Plummer's West Point classmate, seeing that the regulars were creating "havoc" with his troops, led most of the 3rd Louisiana and part of his regiment over the fence to attack the regulars. Heavily outnumbered, Plummer's battalion fell back hurriedly through the corn. A Federal battery on the west side of the creek efficiently covered Plummer's retreat, enfilading McIntosh's men with shell and canister. Plummer was wounded during the retreat, but he managed to lead his battalion back across the creek before relinquishing command to Captain Arch Houston.

The enfilading artillery fire shook the 3rd Louisiana severely, and the regiment basically skedaddled out of the cornfield in some disorder. McIntosh and the rest of his men also fell back from the artillery barrage, allowing the regulars to rejoin Lyon's force west of the creek without further menace. In effect Plummer accomplished his mission because the Confederates made no successful effort to assail Lyon's left flank from the Ray Farm area.[12]

In comparing the performance of the contending troops at Ray's Cornfield, it would be biased to contend that one side proved superior. The casualties here were probably about equal, perhaps the Confederates losing about a dozen more men than the regulars. Although heavily outgunned and outnumbered, the regulars stood their ground until McIntosh charged with an overwhelming force. Confederate regiments involved here were commanded by West Point trained colonels, and these troops proved their mettle in other battles including Pea Ridge, Stones River and Vicksburg.

While Lyon's column was fighting desperately and with remarkable tenacity atop Bloody Hill, Sigel's command delivered perhaps the poorest battlefield performance of any brigade during the war. The embarrassing Federal rout at Bull Run shrinks in comparison. Sigel had caught the Confederates by surprise and might have accomplished much more with better tactics. However, by about 8:30 a.m. Sigel apparently must have thought the battle was won. He spied approaching troops marching toward his position from the Confederate camps along the Wire Road. Apparently Sigel did not deploy both of his infantry units into a battle line as a responsible commander would have. According to Sigel, "it was reported to me by ... some of our skirmishers that Lyon's men were coming up the road." Sigel told his artillerymen not to fire and so did his regimental commanders to their infantrymen. Suddenly enemy artillery opened on Sigel's Germans, and the approaching Confederates, by then at point-blank range, fired. The incoming fire brought "frightful confusion" in Sigel's words, as his soldiers believed Lyon's infantry and artillery were mistakenly firing into them. In effect, the Germans simply scattered in complete panic while Sigel "recklessly" attempted to rally them. Four cannons were immediately abandoned to the enemy and another was also later given up. Almost instantly as the Confederates opened fire, Sigel's Brigade collapsed in a panicked run for safety, despite the fact that it outnumbered the attackers by about three to one.[13]

Sigel and his officers did not or could not rally enough men to make a stand or take any further part in the Battle of Wilson's Creek. The Confederates did not even send out a large force in pursuit of Sigel; therefore, Price was able to throw most of his army against Lyon's column still fighting on Bloody Hill. Sigel's men broke into groups of fugitives, thinking only of getting back to Springfield safely. Most of those killed and captured from Sigel's Brigade were lost while fleeing en route to Springfield.

Shortly after Sigel's defeat, Price launched an attack along the entire length of Lyon's front. By then the last Federal reserves had already been sent into the fight. Most of Lyon's infantry had been severely bloodied but continued to fight with fierce determination. Lyon himself was wounded in the leg and head and his horse was killed as he was rallying his troops on Bloody Hill. After a short rest to recover from the shock of his wounds, Lyon obtained a mount from Major Samuel Sturgis's orderly and rode farther to the Federal right where the situation required his attention. A gap had inadvertently opened in the Federal battle line. Though the Confederates did not exploit the situation, Lyon reacted by moving the 2nd Kansas to close the gap. Colonel Robert Mitchell brought his

Sigel's troops were routed on this field at Wilson's Creek on August 10, 1861.

Kansans as ordered into the gap and was joined by Lyon at the head of his regiment. A sudden volley from the brush dropped part of the lead rank of the column and wounded Colonel Mitchell. General Lyon, as he turned in the saddle to his right to encourage the Kansans, was struck in the left side of his chest. The bullet passed completely through Lyon's chest and out of his upper back, hitting both lungs and the aorta. Still conscious, Lyon slid from his horse and collapsed into the grasp of his aide. In probably less than a minute Lyon was dead, his shirt soaked with blood. Nathaniel Lyon was the first Union general officer killed in the Civil War.[14]

Just after Lyon was killed, the 2nd Kansas closed the gap in the Federal line, and Price's attack was thwarted. General McCulloch at this time ordered a cavalry attack aimed at the far right of the Federal battle line. Colonel Elkanah Greer, a Texas planter who had served in Jefferson Davis's regiment during the Mexican war, led a charge upon McCulloch's order with his South Kansas–Texas Cavalry. He and his horsemen spurred past a section of Federal artillery towards a battalion of the 2nd Missouri Infantry "with a shout for Texas."

Colonel Greer was a somewhat prominent Texan and erstwhile grand commander of the Knights of the Golden Circle, and his cavalry regiment, about 800 strong, was one of the first Texas cavalry regiments organized for Confederate service. Greer's recruits, it is safe to assume, were steeped in the rebel credo and highly motivated. Although Greer reported that his charge caused "considerable confusion" to the Federals and

This small monument was erected on Bloody Hill on the Wilson's Creek Battlefield to mark the spot where General Lyon was believed to have fallen. Researchers now believe that Lyon probably was killed at a different location on the hill.

"intimidated" them, his attack was a failure and was quickly repulsed. Captain James Totten, whose artillery battery shifted to fire on Greer's charge, reported that the attack was driven off "with ease." In Totten's opinion the rebel cavalry charge "was so *effete* and ineffectual in its force and character as to deserve only the appellation of child's play."[15]

Although Greer's cavalry charge accomplished little, it enabled Price to regroup his forces atop Bloody Hill. A lull quieted the battlefield as Price disengaged and prepared for yet another attack. Command of the Federals devolved upon Major Samuel D. Sturgis, the senior regular active on the field. The "great question" for Sturgis's and the other Federals on Bloody Hill was "Where is Sigel?" Sturgis noted that the ammunition "was well-neigh exhausted," and "should the enemy make this discovery," the Federals risked "total annihilation." He summoned his fellow officers for a consultation, but before Sturgis could determine the next move Price launched yet another fierce attack.[16]

As for Sigel, not only was his command flushed from the battlefield, he and a portion of his men were chased and hunted down by Confederate cavalry on their retreat to Springfield. Sigel's column had suffered few killed and wounded in the debacle on the southern edge of the Confederate encampment. However, during the retreat while attempting to ford the James River, Sigel and approximately 400 of his troops were ambushed and attacked by an equal force of Confederate cavalry. Among the cavalry were two companies from Greer's South Kansas–Texas regiment, the Deadshot Rangers and the Cypress Guards. Greer sent these two companies from his regiment along with a company, the Windsor Guards led by Lt. Colonel James Major, to "follow after and capture" Sigel and his routed band.

The cavalry sent by Greer charged upon finding Sigel's men at the ford and scattered them once again. The cavalry that Captain Totten had disparaged for its performance in the fight with Lyon's column completely dominated Sigel's demoralized band, rounding up prisoners for miles around the countryside. As Sigel termed it, his retreating group was "attacked incessantly" by the enemy cavalry. Lieutenant Colonel Anslem Albert of the 3rd Missouri Infantry and another 146 of Sigel's fugitives were captured. Sigel escaped by dodging into a cornfield and concealing his rank and thus his identity with a blanket. Mounted on a good horse, he was chased for several miles before making his escape to Springfield.

Sturgis reported a loss of 267, mostly missing and only fifteen killed, for Sigel's Brigade. The Confederates reported finding sixty-four dead Federals along Sigel's retreat route. However, the staff at Wilson's Creek National Battlefield compiled a list of casualties from the rolls of Sigel's units and found the total number of killed to be much lower. The Confederate units involved in the fight with Sigel probably suffered few casualties, excepting those captured before the battle actually began.[17]

While Sturgis consulted with the "principal officers" at approximately 11:00 a.m., Price attacked and commenced "the fiercest and most bloody engagement of the day." The outcome proved costly to the Confederates, as the Federal line "maintained its position with perfect firmness." According to Sturgis, the fighting closed with "a perfect rout ... throughout the rebel front" while the Federals maintained "a galling fire into their disorganized masses." The failed Confederate attack gave Sturgis an opportunity to disengage and fall back to a new defensive position.

As the Federals fell back Sturgis learned from one of Sigel's noncoms who happened by that Sigel's column had been routed. Sturgis now had no reason to continue the fight in order to assist or coordinate with the defeated Sigel. Sturgis noted that most of his troops "had fired away all their ammunition and all that could be obtained from the boxes of the killed and wounded." Although some of his officers still thought the battle was or could be won, Sturgis decided to make good on his opportunity to retreat unmolested to Springfield. In effect, although it cost him his life, Lyon had accomplished his objective for the battle. He had injured the enemy enough to ensure a safe retreat to Rolla or on to St. Louis. Now Price and McCulloch would not follow, and the Federals would not have to make the precarious retreat Lyon had fought to avoid.[18]

The Battle of Wilson's Creek stands as possibly the best individual battle of the war to compare the fighting qualities of Northerners to Southerners. The fight between Lyon's column and the Confederates on Bloody Hill was exceptionally intense. General Sturgis once opined that "for downright, hard, persistent fighting, Wilson's Creek beat them all." While the armies had comparatively few Yankees from New England or cavaliers from the Tidewater, the Northern army here serves as a sort of microcosm of the Union army overall. The Southern army at Wilson's Creek was comprised of troops from the slave-intensive states of Louisiana, Texas and Arkansas along with pro–Confederate Missourians and is thus a good representation of men inculcated with and motivated by the Southern creed. Most of these soldiers had not had sufficient time to master the arts of soldiering; hence, the men on each side brought to this fight their native aptitude for combat. Lyon's men differed in one respect from the average Federal soldier. Counting Sigel's Germans, probably over fifty percent of the soldiers in Lyon's army were foreign born. Nearly seventy-five percent of the veterans of the Federal army were American born, so the Federals at Wilson's Creek had a much higher complement of immigrants, even in the regiments of Lyon's two brigades of Regulars, Kansans, Missourians and Iowans.[19] The infantry led by Lyon into the fight had a strong cadre of able officers and a core of highly-motivated, American-born volunteers to galvanize and cohere them. Sigel's units did not.

Sigel's tactical mistakes and procedural lapses alone account for much of the onus for his poor showing at Wilson's Creek. Private Otto Lademann who participated in Sigel's morning attack believed that the colonel's tactical "skill" left the Germans with no option except to run.[20] This, however, does not explain the even worse debacle that befell the Germans during their retreat to Springfield. The complete collapse of unit cohesion by Sigel's men when attacked by enemy cavalry at the river ford indicates that other factors played a role in their panicked flight.

The remarkably poor performance of Sigel's troops at Wilson's Creek would be reflected by the defeats of other predominately German outfits later in the war. These unusually poor showings in battle gave German troops a perhaps unfair reputation for being unreliable. Nevertheless, the unfavorable image of German outfits did not transfer or necessarily apply to other predominately immigrant outfits such as the famous Irish Brigade. In any case, regiments recruited from German immigrants that were brigaded with non-immigrant regiments usually proved as reliable and efficient as any troops.

The qualitative differences in the performance of Sigel's troops as compared to the ethnically mixed regiments of Lyon's command cannot be explained by any single condition or circumstance. The same is true of debacles involving similar predominately German unit groupings that will be examined later. What is obvious concerning Sigel's command at Wilson's Creek is that poor leadership coupled with procedural and tactical mistakes induced demoralization and panic. Cultural and conditional factors, difficult to ascribe here, no doubt also played a role in Sigel's defeat. The unvarnished crux here is that Sigel's participation in the battle was of little if any benefit to the Federal effort.

Unfortunately for the Northerners, there would be other similar examples of this phenomenon later in the war.

Problems with Sigel's leadership continued during the Federal retreat from Springfield. Once the retreating Federals reached Springfield, Major Sturgis "resigned his command to Colonel Sigel." A council of officers agreed that the army should continue the retreat to Rolla "before the enemy could organize for a pursuit." Major John Schofield, who later would become a major general and an army commander, saw to the details of preparing the army to move by 2 a.m. At about 1:30 a.m. Schofield checked on Sigel's camp and discovered that his wagons had not been loaded and his men were preparing to cook breakfast. Schofield noted, "I could find no officer to execute my commands nor anyone to pay the slightest heed to what I said." He immediately rode to Sigel's quarters "and found him asleep in bed." The rear guard did not depart Springfield until about 6 a.m., about the time a Confederate attack would be anticipated.

The marching order for the retreat to Rolla was arranged by Sigel. Not too surprisingly he placed his brigade, or what was left of it, in the vanguard of the army. The same marching order was preserved during the first three days of the retreat. No only did the regiments behind the vanguard have to endure the clouds of dust, they also performed "the fatiguing duties of the rear guard" and remained on the road until "long after dark" while Sigel's men made camp and cooked their supper. Sigel's management of the retreat favored his brigade while many men from other brigades "were compelled to go twenty-four hours without a morsel of food and some much longer." Sigel's favoritism reflected a familiar yet troublesome trait of German soldiers relishing their ethnicity as a means of improving their status and quality of life at the expense of Americans. On the third day of the retreat the column was detained for three hours while Sigel's Germans killed and cooked beef for breakfast. Now the "clamor" for Sigel's relief from command "became such that almost total anarchy reigned." During this halt while Sigel's brigade cooked breakfast, "the officers, having become disgusted with the manner in which Sigel conducted the retreat, insisted that Major Sturgis should assume command. Sigel yielded, on the ground that he had no commission." Major Sturgis relieved Sigel and resumed command of the retreating army.[21]

While it is true that the Confederate armies had units and regiments that were predominately organized from immigrants, Germans and Irish for example, the vast majority of Confederate soldiers were Americans by birth and a great many Confederate soldiers had roots in America for generations. The problems described above, if they existed at all in the Confederate armies, are not well known and documented. Clearly the troubles resulting from commanders like Franz Sigel were much more common in the Federal armies than in the Confederate armies, and this factor disadvantaged the North by comparison.

The casualties for the Battle of Wilson's Creek demonstrate that this was an even struggle, excepting Sigel's participation, despite the fact that the Federals were on the attack and heavily outnumbered. Sturgis's report on August 20 listed the combined Federal losses as 223 killed, 721 wounded and 291 missing for a total of 1,235. The average loss for the Federal brigades was approximately 25 percent, one of the highest loss percentages of any battle during the war. General McCulloch reported from Springfield on August 13, "Our loss was 265 killed, 800 wounded and 30 missing." The losses in Sigel's Brigade reported by Sturgis amounted to 267, including thirty-five listed as killed and wounded. Sigel's troops likely were responsible for few Confederate casualties but accounted for a significant portion of the Federal losses. Another source, excepting the missing, listed Federal losses as 258 killed and 873 wounded compared to Confederate losses of 277 killed and 945 wounded. Yet another source lists Confederate losses as 281 killed and 1,055 wounded, somewhat higher than the Federals when the missing are not included.[22]

Price, now with about 10,000 men, planned his next move to reclaim his state. He chose the Missouri River town of Lexington, a wealthy pro-slavery community about sixty miles east of Kansas City, as his objective. Before turning north Price made an easterly march towards Fort Scott, Kansas. On September 2, 1861, along Dry Wood Creek near the Kansas border Price skirmished with Kansas troops from Senator James Lane's command. Lane, known as The Grim Chieftain, learned from some captured or perhaps deserting Missourians that Price's real target was Lexington. Lane forwarded this bit of intelligence and, being heavily outnumbered, cleared out of Price's way. Fremont was duly informed of Price's destination, so he ordered Lane to proceed to Ft. Leavenworth, Kansas, near Kansas City. Fremont then ordered Sturgis and Brigadier General John Pope to send troops to defend Lexington.

Colonel James Mulligan, an erstwhile Chicago politician, and his 23rd Illinois Infantry happened to be stationed at Jefferson City, Missouri, since July 21. Mulligan was an Irish immigrant, and so was most of his regiment, also known as the Irish Brigade. Scouts informed Mulligan that Price was heading northward, obviously targeting Kansas City or Lexington. The 23rd Illinois marched to Lexington, arriving before Price's column. Mulligan's Irishmen joined some home guards and an undersized Illinois cavalry regiment in fortifying the Masonic College on the outskirts of Lexington. Mulligan, being the senior officer, took command of the Federals at Lexington. Another German Missouri outfit commanded by Colonel Everett Peabody arrived from Kansas City, giving "a strong foreign flavor" to the town's defenders. Peabody himself was, however, from a prominent Massachusetts family and was a Harvard graduate. Yet the presence of so many immigrant troops with an Irishman in command gave the American-born troops "another reason to complain about Lincoln's rule by foreigners."

Soon Old Pap Price arrived and leisurely surrounded the Federal fortifications. Mulligan had a fairly strong position to defend but no source of water. Fremont failed to get relief to Lexington quickly, and within just a few days the Federals were in desperation. Many local farmers and county citizens came to town in wagons to watch the "furriners get licked."

Lexington was known for its hemp production for the manufacture of rope. Apparently a citizen suggested to the Confederates that hemp bales could be used as rolling cover for an attack on the Federal works at the Masonic College. On September 20 the Confederates used hemp bales rolled up slope to attack Mulligan's works. As the bales slowly rolled closer to the Federal works, the defenders grew apprehensive and some raised white cloths to signal surrender. Mulligan called his commanders together and found that most of them wanted to surrender. It seems that Mulligan's Irishmen wanted to continue to fight, but Mulligan acquiesced to his fellow officers and surrendered his command including about 2,800 men, five cannon and 3,000 muskets on September 20.[23]

The Anderson House, one of the finest homes constructed between St. Louis and Kansas City before the Civil War, was used as a hospital during and following the battle. It still stands on the battlefield site, the back porch pocked with bullet holes and battle damage. At the downtown courthouse a cannon ball can be seen lodged at the top of one of the building's white columns. These structures bear mute testimony of the battle's fury.

The Anderson House on the Lexington, Missouri, Battlefield. Multiple bullet holes still pock this face of the house which was used as a hospital during the battle.

Evidence of the 1861 battle at Lexington, Missouri, still exists at the town's courthouse.

Price had taken advantage of Fremont's inability to coordinate available forces to challenge him in western Missouri. Fremont had adequate troops in the region to check Price but failed to marshal them. Mulligan was a valiant and ambitious man, both he and Peabody would later die heroically in battle, but Mulligan's decision to defend at the Masonic College proved costly and gained nothing for the Federals. Poor leadership at the department level hampered the Federals and enabled Price to gain a relatively easy victory at Lexington. Nevertheless, within two weeks Price was marching southward again, and the Federals had yet managed to keep Missouri in the Union. The rebel victory at Lexington did little to change the balance of power in Missouri. Soon Price retreated to Neosho in Missouri's southwest corner, and gradually the Federals consolidated their control of the state.

While Missouri's fate was being decided by bloodshed, Kentucky had assumed a virtual state of neutrality. That is until the Confederates blundered. Kentucky was vitally important to both sides. Lincoln believed that losing Kentucky was tantamount to losing "the whole game." He believed that if that state joined the Confederacy then Missouri and Maryland could not be held. A sort of domino effect, he believed, would result that included the loss of the capital itself, being adjacent to Maryland. Lincoln watched Kentucky closely and considered his military options there with great care.[24]

Major General Leonidas Polk commanded the Confederate forces adjacent to Kentucky in 1861. Polk was a West Point class of 1827 graduate, one year before Jefferson Davis was graduated there. Polk had left the Army shortly after graduation to study for the ministry. Before the war Polk had been an Episcopal bishop with a career in the clergy and since his West Point days a close friend of Jefferson Davis. His friendship with Davis no doubt accounts for his appointment to high command, as he had not pursued a military career and had no obvious qualifications for his position.

General Polk had been concerned about the Federal troop movements near western Kentucky. He recognized the strategic value of the bluffs above the Mississippi River at Columbus, Kentucky, where cannon could attack shipping and thereby block river traffic, and he knew the Federals would want to secure that place. As mentioned previously, Kentucky Governor Beriah Magoffin had cautioned President Davis about the risk of sending Confederate troops onto Kentucky soil. Magoffin anticipated that a Confederate movement into Kentucky would push the state into the Union camp. Nevertheless, Polk, who had been anxious to occupy and fortify Columbus for some time, finally sent troops into Kentucky for that purpose on September 3, 1861.

Brigadier General Ulysses S. Grant was then commanding Federal troops at Cairo, Illinois, and Grant quickly moved to counter Polk by occupying Paducah, Kentucky. Grant's movement gave the Federals control of access to the Cumberland and Tennessee rivers from the Ohio River and threatened the new Confederate post at Columbus. At about this time General Albert S. Johnston assumed command of all Confederate troops west of the Alleghenies. Johnston was highly regarded by both the U.S. and Confederate governments at the outbreak of war. Like President Davis he had attended Transylvania University and then was graduated from West Point. Johnston's resume included extensive military experience. He had served in the Black Hawk War, in the Texas War for Independence and as the Texas secretary of war, in the Mexican War and as colonel of the 2nd U.S. Cavalry before resigning his commission in May of 1861. President Davis "had implicit confidence in him," which, of course, bestowed tremendous influence with it. Before long Johnston would send more troops into Kentucky in reaction to Grant's occupation of Paducah.[25]

Kentucky's legislature reacted to Polk's occupation of Columbus much as Governor Magoffin had expected. As historian Shelby Foot explained it, the Kentuckians were determined to have peace in their state, and they were "willing to fight for it." On September 11, 1861, the Kentucky Legislature demanded that the Confederates leave the state. One week later, when the injunction wasn't obeyed, the legislature passed an act creating a military force to expel the Confederates. President Davis had allowed Polk to retain troops at Columbus, and, in effect, his decision to allow his commanders to send troops into Kentucky had pushed Kentucky into the Union fold. Kentucky was lost to the Confederacy, and with it went the "best chance" for the Confederacy to win the war.[26]

Even as Kentucky Legislature acted in response to the Confederate invasion, General Albert S. Johnston decided to move more troops into the state in a line stretching from Columbus on the western border through Bowling Green and on to Cumberland Gap near the southeast border. In a letter to President Davis dated September 16, 1861, Johnston mentioned that the governor and legislature of Kentucky had required the "prompt removal of all Confederate forces." Johnston declared that his troops would not be withdrawn because the forces in Kentucky were "essential to our present line of defense as well as to any future operations." Instead of "yielding" to Kentucky's demand to remove his troops, he would "occupy Bowling Green at once." Although Johnston explained his tactics as a reaction to anticipated Federal movements, his invasion of Kentucky was a serious blunder. Polk and Johnston had cast the Confederacy in the role of aggressor and thus justified Federal movements into Kentucky. The Confederate invasion of Kentucky was a "cataclysmic strategic mistake" comparable to the folly of attacking Fort Sumter.[27]

By October 14 a force of about 5,000 men commanded by Brigadier General Simon Bolivar Buckner was in place at Bowling Green. As mentioned previously, Buckner had been Kentucky's adjutant general and commander of the pro–Confederate state guard. General Buckner was a graduate of the West Point class of 1844 and a Mexican War veteran.[28] My grandmother Clara's father was a farmer in Butler County, Kentucky, about twenty miles north of Bowling Green, at that time. According to his obituary he was a lifelong Democrat and his family had migrated from the South, but apparently he too did not approve of the Southern violation of Kentucky's sovereignty. He and his four brothers-in-law enlisted in the 11th Kentucky Volunteer Infantry, Union. My great grandfather, like two-thirds of Kentuckians who served in the Civil War, chose to follow the legislature's call to expel the Confederate invaders and went with the Union. Kentucky eventually furnished seventeen cavalry regiments and forty-four infantry regiments for the Union.[29]

Kentucky probably would have rejected secession in any case, but the Confederate invasion of the state gave the Federals opportunity to take offensive operations within its borders sooner. When General Johnston chose to ignore the legislature's injunction to remove his troops from Kentucky, the pro–Union political element found their justification for alliance with the North. President Lincoln had managed the political situation in Kentucky with wisdom that yielded success. The strategic benefit as well as ensuring the contribution of Kentucky to the Federal war effort was well worth Lincoln's patience and restraint. Here Lincoln's political and strategic acumen was demonstrably superior to that of Davis, Johnston and Polk.

Further indication of Northern superiority in strategic planning is found in the Federal effort to blockade the South and in the proposals generated by the Blockade Strategy Board, a temporary advisory committee convened during the summer of 1861. The board was an amalgamation of Navy and Army officers and the superintendent of the U.S. Coast Survey. The U.S. Navy required coaling stations and bases to service the blockading fleet. Advice from the board helped initiate military operations to secure ports and stations along the Confederate coastline. Major General Benjamin Butler's successful capture of Confederate Forts Hatteras and Clark in late August of 1861 was the first military operation generated on the board's advice.[30] Butler's operation was the first of many to follow during the war in the effort to strangle Southern imports and access to foreign markets. Northern planning in this field of strategy completely outclassed that of the South and contributed significantly to winning the war. The blockade and coastal operations conducted by the North presented a challenge that proved beyond the capability of the Confederate military to answer.

By the later part of 1861 the Federals were finding success in multiple military operations. Due in part to Lincoln's shrewd political strategy, Kentucky was well on its way to rejecting the Confederacy. Missouri was soon to be permanently under Federal sway despite setbacks in the western portion of the state. On November 7 a Federal joint operation captured Confederate Forts Beauregard and Walker at Port Royal Sound near Savannah, Georgia. Seizure of these forts provided a valuable refueling site and a station for blockading ships operating against Savannah and Charleston. On the strategic level the Federals were identifying objectives and invasion routes that provided the genesis for campaigns delivering significant territorial gains. A comprehensive strategy combining Naval and land forces, including amphibious landings, in joint operations was being planned and would soon be implemented. Facing an enormous task in securing and occupying a vast region of the continent, the Federals required a practical and systematic method for defeating the Confederacy. Effective and comprehensive planning in the second half of 1861 paved the way to Federal victory.

While the Federal war effort was progressing favorably overall, stinging tactical defeats in minor battles continued to discourage the North. In addition to the September defeat at Lexington, Missouri, the Federals were soundly defeated near Leesburg, Virginia, at Ball's Bluff on October 21, 1861. The fighting at Ball's Bluff was a Federal fiasco only made possible by an unlikely succession of command errors and failures of communication. The fighting was the result of a misplayed demonstration intended to cause the Confederates to abandon Leesburg, Virginia. Colonel Edward Baker, an Oregon senator and longtime friend of President Lincoln, led a Federal brigade into the fight with marked insouciance. Baker ignored advice from a more seasoned colonel on the field and deployed his troops in a vulnerable position atop a bluff overlooking the Potomac River. The Confederates benefited from an advantage in command tactics. Hard-drinking and hard-fighting Colonel Nathan Evans, a West Point graduate, led the Confederates. Evans had faced the initial Federal attack at First Bull Run with tactics that delayed the Federal advance, and here his direction proved decisive. Evans deployed his troops on higher ground on the Federal left and within the cover of a wood fronting the Federals. Colonel Baker, yards out in front of his battle line, was killed by a rebel firing a revolver. Baker had unwisely stepped out to proximity of enemy pistol range when he was killed. Soon after Baker fell the Federals attempted to retreat. The terrain at Ball's Bluff, with a steep slope leading to a deep river crossing, made for a perilous escape path. As the sun was setting, the Confederates charged and drove the Federals down the slope to the riverbank. There the rebels completely ignored their professed chivalry, firing into the Yankees as they discarded their arms and attempted to swim across the rain-swollen Potomac. The rebels continued to shoot at the helpless Yankees until darkness ended it. What had stared as an even contest ended with disaster for the Federals at the riverbank. When it was over the Federals counted forty-nine killed, 158 wounded and 714 missing, 529 were reported as prisoners by Evans. Many of the missing drowned while trying to cross the Potomac. Confederate losses were thirty-six killed, 117 wounded and only two missing. The debacle so astonished Northern politicians that a congressional committee was established to investigate the conduct of the war.[31]

Having long since cultivated the image of the swashbuckling cavalier destined for an easy victory over the mudsill Yankees, early in the war the Southerners reveled in their indecisive victories, battles usually poorly managed by opposing Federal commanders. Although the Confederates won several battles in 1861, the tide of the war was against them. By the year's end Kentucky was siding with the Union, as were the other Border States so vital to Southern hopes for victory. The Federals were planning and executing a strategy to secure bases along the Southern coastline to support the blockade and provide launching points for invasive operations. The Confederacy didn't attempt offensive operations into Northern States in 1861 and never succeeded in later attempts. The Federals simply *had* to undertake offensive operations to reclaim lost territory and put down the rebellion. Obviously the United States faced the more arduous path to winning the Civil War. Despite having the simpler road to victory and the favorable trend of winning battles early in the war, the Confederacy failed to take advantage of momentum or to even devise and implement a successful war strategy.

Southerners had overestimated their odds for victory before the war escalated, and once it had escalated, they seemed unable or unwilling to grasp the true state of affairs. Two examples of this delusional appraisal of the war's progression are found in the admission of Missouri to the Confederacy on November 28, 1861, and the secession ordinance adopted by Confederate soldiers at Russellville, Kentucky, which led, without foundation, to Kentucky's admission as the Confederacy's thirteenth state on December 10, 1861. As mentioned previously, Kentucky's voters had rejected secession, and the state legislature had demanded Confederate troops leave the state. Missouri was also predominately pro–Union and was controlled by Federal forces. Yet Southerners shrugged off the obvious, clinging to faint hopes of a thaumaturgic change of fate. This trend would persist, as we will see, even after all reason for conflict had been eliminated.

On November 1, 1861, Lieutenant General Winfield Scott retired from active duty and was replaced by Major General George B. McClellan. General Scott had performed his duties as general in chief remarkably well for a man of his age and infirmities. Frustrations from interaction with the Lincoln administration and McClellan surely must have discouraged the old soldier enough to compel him to relinquish his post. McClellan's opinion of the aged general was revealed in letters to his wife referring to Scott as either a "dotard or a traitor," "a perfect imbecile," "the great obstacle," and "an incompetent." McClellan believed that Scott was an impediment to his plans, being unable to understand or appreciate McClellan's objectives. McClellan groused that the "confounded old Genl … is ever in my way." It is strange that McClellan could even suggest in frustration that General Scott could be a traitor, or refer to a man of Scott's brilliance as an imbecile. Yet these unmasked sentiments reveal a facet of McClellan's complex personality, which doubtless played a role in his downfall. After his resignation General Scott left the country briefly and then retired to West Point. The old general highly esteemed the school and its graduates and must have felt at home there.[32]

The grave of General in Chief Winfield Scott at the West Point Cemetery.

George McClellan was a key figure in the Civil War. His influence, for better and worse, was pervasive in the Federal Army of the Potomac and the Federal war machine for much of the war. So it is necessary here to briefly consider his personality and outlook to better understand his command strengths and weaknesses.

George McClellan was a prodigy. He attended the University of Pennsylvania and then was accepted by and admitted to West Point at the age of fifteen, by special permission. He was somewhat disappointed at graduating second in his West Point Class of 1846, a class of fifty-nine that eventually produced twenty generals, but he did not disappoint his reputation as a prodigy during his pre-war military service and career as a railroad executive. His personality was a dichotomous mixture of traits not to be expected from a man of his abilities. Spoiled by success, he could be petulant and arrogant, yet affable and kind to supporters and loyal subordinates. He appeared self-confident, but he often overstated the difficulty of his tasks and the strength of his opposition. His behavior as a general betrayed the weaknesses of self-doubt and timidity.

The key aspect of McClellan's psyche relating to his command methods was described by one historian as a "Messiah complex," and complex describes his psyche well. McClellan believed his was a Divine calling to the great task of saving the country. He demonstrated religious fervor, once mentioning his belief that he alone was chosen for this great work and that his previous life had been unwittingly crafted to prepare him for his calling. These beliefs and sensibilities brought great energy and diligence in the performance of his duties. McClellan thus viewed himself as indispensable to his country's salvation. His country could not afford to lose him, whether from death on the battlefield or by interference from politicians. This belief was manifested in his disregard for the suggestions and directions of President Lincoln, and in his obvious reluctance to expose himself to the dangers of the battlefield. He was a perfectionist who only took action in his "own time": that is, when all was in perfect readiness and he was certain of success. Perhaps because of his "Messiah complex" McClellan did not seem to apprehend the fact that his success depended on his cooperation with and the approval of the president.

While there should be no doubts as to his gifts as a military organizer, planner and strategist, McClellan was hobbled by unfortunate character flaws. If McClellan was dissatisfied with the level of support he was receiving, fairly or unfairly, he felt betrayed and assumed the mentality of a martyr. He was seemly unable to accept fault for any setback and was quick to find scapegoats when things went wrong. As he demonstrated by his comments about General in Chief Scott, McClellan was wont to doubt the competence of his superiors and to unjustifiably disparage and even disrespect them. Because of his belief in his calling and his obvious gifts, he seemed to disregard his obligations to the government. He took good care of his soldiers, but being a patrician he failed to recognize the importance of public support for his methods. He chose to ignore or appreciate the impatience of the common people and the political consequences of his overcautious manner.[33]

Days after McClellan ascended to the top command spot, on November 9, 1861, Major General Henry Wager Halleck was given command of the new Department of Missouri, effectively replacing the marginally capable Major General John C. Fremont. Henry Halleck, like McClellan, was a very influential figure in the Civil War. Halleck's paternal ancestors were Yankees of Puritan stock, the first having arrived in New England in 1640. His mother's Wager family was of German ancestry. Halleck's paternal ancestor had migrated to Westernville, New York, where Halleck was born in 1814. After schooling at the Hudson Academy and Union College, Halleck was appointed to West Point, graduating third in the class of 1839. While at West Point Halleck was influenced by Professor Dennis Hart Mahan's emphasis on military history. His subsequent military career was far more noteworthy for his writings on military science than for participation in actual combat. In fact Halleck's reputation for comprehensive military expertise perhaps led the sobriquet "Old Brains" by which he was known in the Army. Halleck was so highly regarded for his intellect that General Scott recommended him to President Lincoln for high command. Appointed to major general in August 1861, Halleck was fourth in rank seniority behind Scott, McClellan and Fremont. Although obviously gifted, Halleck suffered from various medical ailments and temperamental defects that perhaps contributed to his overcautious and halting command reputation. His contribution to the Federal cause would be clouded by his unwillingness to assume responsibility for the inevitable risks associated with military command.[34]

On November 15, 1861, Brigadier General Don Carlos Buell was assigned to command of the Department of the Ohio. Buell was a friend of General McClellan and may have owed his promotion to that relationship. President Lincoln's plan and expectation for Buell's command was for a move into eastern Tennessee to liberate the pro–Union population there. Once Buell controlled the region he was to sever the railroad connections linking Virginia to the Southwest Confederacy. Buell's command consisted of the states of Indiana, Ohio, Michigan, Tennessee, and the portion of Kentucky east of the Cumberland River.

Buell was a graduate of the West Point class of 1841 with a middling standing that resulted in an assignment to the infantry, as was the custom in those days when cadets of higher standing could and often did choose the engineers or artillery. After service in Florida and in the Mexican War, where he was severely wounded at Churubusco, he was assigned to the adjutant general's department until outbreak of the Civil War. For a few months prior to his assignment to the Department of the Ohio, Buell had worked with McClellan in Washington to organize and train the new outfits assigned to the Army of the Potomac.[35] Don Carlos Buell's tenure as an army commander would prove as insipid and unproductive as Halleck's.

President Lincoln had defined his plan for Buell's troops in October. Unfortunately for Lincoln, Buell shared McClellan's aversion to risk; also like McClellan he would never move unless all was in order with success assured. Of course Buell would have faced some difficulties had he complied with the president's expectations. A large Confederate force occupied Bowling Green, Kentucky, on Buell's right, had he moved towards Knoxville. And the route to eastern Tennessee was fraught with supply and logistics complications. Buell soon concluded that the president's plans for eastern Tennessee would have to wait. He preferred an advance using the Cumberland River as a waterborne route to capture Nashville rather than attempting the much more difficult overland route to Knoxville. While Buell aptly recognized the advantages of using the Cumberland and Tennessee rivers for transport and supply, he failed to develop a solution to meet the president's directive for his command. Buell's intransigence here and later would deprive the Federals of opportunities to shorten the war.[36]

In the last months of 1861 the pace of the war slowed with the onset of cold weather. Still, much had been accomplished to restore the Union during the first six months of Lincoln's presidency. The Border States were largely secured for the Union. Kentucky, probably the most essential and vulnerable of the Border States, was supplying troops in large numbers for the Federals and was now allied with the North. The Federal Navy was growing rapidly and starting the work of blockading Southern ports. The Federal Army had captured outposts on the Southern coast, and more such operations were planned. Northern military might was increasing daily, far outpacing the Confederacy. Few had anticipated the extreme difficulty of restoring the Union, yet the government had responded with alacrity as the situation unfolded. By the last days of 1861 the plans and means for winning the war were largely conceptualized and were being implemented.

Meanwhile the Confederacy had already passed it zenith; henceforth it would continually forfeit territory and strength. Confederate strategic miscalculations in the immediate months ahead would doom the Confederacy. Yet in the late months of 1861 the Confederacy still should have stood a good chance of winning the war. No single cause or failure doomed the Confederacy, but poor planning and faulty strategy in the western theater at this stage of the war proved costly.

Historian James McPherson in seeking an explanation for the Confederacy's ultimate defeat pondered why the Southerners were initially so confident of victory, seeing that the North had superior resources. He asked, were they "Inexcusably arrogant?" The answer, as we have seen from their antebellum perceptions of Northerners, is yes.[37] By December 1861 the Confederates knew that Northerners would fight for the Union and fight well. Confederate defeats in the coming year, perhaps partially resulting from lingering over confidence, were certainly not inevitable. In comparison, Northern strategic operations, especially early in 1862, were simply superior. The Confederacy failed to answer with an effective defensive response. In retrospect, the Federals probably should have won the war by the end of 1862, but as it was, failures by the Federal high command and administration ultimately prolonged the war by an additional two years.

5

1862

A Disastrous Year for the Confederacy

The focus of the war in terms of immediate and significant activity in the first months of 1862 was in the western theater of operations. It was here that the Confederacy faced its greatest difficulty in defending national territory. Unlike the East, where the geography strongly favored the defender, here the geography strongly favored the invader. Three rivers accessible from the Ohio River provided invasion routes into the western Confederacy. The Cumberland River was navigable as far as Nashville, which represented an invasion route to capture that important city and middle Tennessee. Both the Cumberland and Tennessee rivers were accessible from the Ohio River, the Tennessee at Paducah, Kentucky, and the Cumberland just a few miles upriver. The Tennessee River provided a route deep into Confederate territory and thereby an opportunity to outflank Nashville and Memphis. The river flowed through northern Alabama and past Chattanooga, Tennessee, an important railroad junction. At several locations along the Tennessee a vital rail line linking the eastern and western Confederacy could easily be severed by gunboats or small contingents of troops landed by Navy vessels.[1] Also accessible from the Ohio, the Mississippi River, as was recognized by General Scott in his initial blueprint for the war, would serve as a transportation route for an invasion of the entire western Confederacy. Federal control of the Mississippi would divide the Confederacy and seal off communications and supplies from Arkansas and Texas. Texas was of some importance as a place to smuggle imports past the blockade. Imports passing through Mexican ports could be transported into Texas without Federal interference. Control of these rivers and the associated defense of the cities of Memphis, Nashville, and New Orleans were the key objectives of Confederate military strategy for 1862 in the West.

In the East, Major General George B. McClellan, having replaced the retired General Scott, was already proving a disappointment to many. McClellan resisted urging to push the Confederates back from northern Virginia. His priority in the East was to assemble and train his new Army of the Potomac before undertaking a serious offensive operation. In no way would he risk another Bull Run fiasco. By January 6, 1862, members of Congress, hoping for a more aggressive replacement, approached the president asking to have McClellan relieved. Lincoln refused to name another commander, although he was as anxious as anyone for an advance, especially for Buell's troops to occupy eastern Tennessee. The lone aggressive movement worthy of note during this period was an expedition led by Brigadier General Ambrose Burnside sent to establish a beachhead on the North Carolina coast.[2]

Offensive operations in the West commenced in January after Brigadier General

Buell dispatched two forces from his Department of the Ohio to deal with the Confederates in eastern and south central Kentucky. On December 17, 1861, Buell ordered Colonel James A. Garfield, the future 20th president, to take his 18th Brigade on a mission into the valley of the Big Sandy River to drive back a Confederate force from Virginia commanded by Brigadier General Humphrey Marshall, West Point class of 1832. On January 7, 1862, Garfield drove the Confederates from Paintsville, Kentucky, and then on January 10 he attacked Marshall's force at Middle Creek near Prestonsburg, Kentucky. Garfield claimed his force "drove the enemy from all their positions." However, Marshall claimed that the Federals "did not move me from a single position I chose to occupy." Each side claimed victory, but Marshall retreated into Virginia. Garfield had accomplished "precisely what General Buell" had expected of him.[3]

Another Confederate force led by Brigadier General Felix Zollicoffer had advanced early in December from Cumberland Gap to a camp called Beech Grove. Zollicoffer's camp was located just north of the Cumberland River. It was a poor position for a defense with the river impeding Zollicoffer's logical retreat route. Major General George B. Crittenden, Zollicoffer's superior, ordered him to move his troops and camp south of the river near Mill Springs, Kentucky, a much safer position. Zollicoffer convinced Crittenden that moving across the river was too risky, so the Confederates remained at Beech Grove. On December 29, 1861, Buell sent orders to Brigadier General George H. Thomas, then at Lebanon, Kentucky, with three brigades of Federals, to move by way of Columbia, Kentucky, to link with another brigade led by Brigadier General Albin Schoeph near Zollicoffer's camp. Thomas and Schoeph rendezvoused at a place called Logan's Crossroads near the rebel camp. Buell had correctly surmised that if Thomas and Schoeph attacked, the "result ought to be at least a severe blow to him (Zollicoffer) or a hasty flight across the river."[4]

Thomas departed from Lebanon, Kentucky, some sixty-five miles northwest of Mill Springs, on New Year's Eve. George Thomas is not remembered for his alacrity. It took him until January 17 to negotiate the nearly sixty miles to Logan's Crossroads. Despite having the Confederates trapped with the Cumberland at their back, Thomas was reluctant to attack. Crittenden, feeling vulnerable, instead made the attack, hoping that his essentially equal force would drive the Federals off and obviate the possibility of a risky retreat across the rising Cumberland River. Thomas' one salient quality was his ability to steadfastly defend a position, as he would again prove later in the war. Crittenden attacked on January 19 in a frigid rainstorm that disadvantaged his army to a greater degree than the Federals. Many Confederates, troops from Tennessee, Mississippi and Alabama, were armed with outdated flintlock muskets, which often failed to fire in the rainy conditions. General Zollicoffer, wearing a white raincoat, rode forward and mistook the Federal 4th Kentucky for his own men. While shouting orders to the wrong side, he was cut down by a Federal volley. Both sides sent more men into the fight after Zollicoffer fell, but the Federals gradually gained control and Crittenden's troops gave way.

The Confederate retreat began in an orderly fashion, but, like the Federal debacle at First Bull Run, it became a disorderly flight from the battlefield. Thomas, pausing to replenish ammunition, was slow to press the beaten rebels. Crittenden managed to gather his men behind fortifications at the Beech Grove camp. By the time Thomas deployed at Beech Grove, it was evening. Crittenden managed to hold until dark, and then had his army ferried across the Cumberland aboard a steamer and a few barges. In the darkness

Thomas failed to crush Crittenden's demoralized army, and he did not attempt to follow the enemy the following day. His explanation was:

> The steam and ferry boats having been burned by the enemy in their retreat, it was found impossible to cross the river and pursue them; besides, their command was completely demoralized, and retreated with great haste and in all directions, making their capture in any numbers quite doubtful if pursued. There is no doubt but what the moral effect produced by their complete dispersion will have a more decided effect in re-establishing Union sentiments than though they had been captured.

Confederate casualties were more than double the Federal's. Crittenden reported 125 killed, 309 wounded and ninety-nine missing, also twelve cannons with caissons, 150 wagons and 1,000 draft animals were lost to the Federals. Thomas reported thirty-nine killed and 207 wounded. Crittenden withdrew, leaving Johnston's defensive line broken in eastern Kentucky and opening the way for a Federal invasion of eastern Tennessee. Unfortunately for President Lincoln, Buell did not and would not attempt to press on into the region east of Knoxville. Although the Confederates were vulnerable in eastern Tennessee, the much more feasible invasion route was down the Tennessee River. Buell focused his attention on clearing Bowling Green, Kentucky, and capturing Nashville. Lincoln's plans for eastern Tennessee would remain unfulfilled for many months ahead.[5]

The battle, called Logan's Crossroads or Mill Springs, again demonstrates the difficulty for the Southerners in winning battles outside the Confederacy. Here Southern troops were routed as completely as any Federal troops were during the war. The Confederates here were in some ways disadvantaged by their commanders and their outdated firearms. Crittenden also mentioned "a want of proper drill and discipline" in his troops.[6] Ultimately the outcome helped buoy spirits in the North, and demonstrated that in an overall equal contest the rebels were not superior man for man in fighting as was presumed by many Southerners before the war.

General Albert S. Johnston by now realized his position in Kentucky was in peril. For some time Johnston had been requesting reinforcements. In January he had sent a personal envoy to President Davis to explain his need for more men and arms. Confederate strategy at the time entailed defending as much territory as possible; Davis told the envoy that he could do nothing further to assist Johnston, and he would have to rely on his present resources. Perhaps Davis felt constrained for political reasons, but in fact over 29,000 troops were idle on the Southern coasts and in Florida. Most of these troops could have been sent to reinforce Johnston.[7] With the defeat at Mill Springs, and without reinforcements, Johnston faced a dilemma. He would have to concentrate his forces to defend one crucial place, or he would have to withdraw and cede vital defensive positions to the Federals.

While Johnston pondered his dilemma, Brigadier General Ulysses S. Grant sought permission to attack one of Johnston's defensive positions on the Tennessee River, Fort Henry. Grant recognized that with the capture of Fort Henry the Federals "had a navigable stream open to us up to Muscle Shoals," Alabama, and the Memphis and Charleston Railroad, "of vast importance to the enemy, would cease to be of use to them" after Fort Henry fell. Grant met with General Halleck in St. Louis to explain his plan to attack Fort Henry. Grant was received by Halleck with "little cordiality," and Halleck showed almost no interest in what Grant had to say. He returned to his station at Cairo "very much crestfallen." Nevertheless, Grant, this time with support from Navy Flag Officer Andrew H.

Foote, again suggested a move against Fort Henry. Halleck finally agreed, possibly fearing that Confederate reinforcements were on the way. Grant commenced his expedition against Fort Henry on February 2, 1862.[8]

The capture of Fort Henry on February 6 was accomplished almost entirely by the efforts of Foote's Navy gunboats. Grant's infantry did not reach the scene until after Fort Henry had surrendered. Most of the garrison had left for Fort Donelson, about twelve miles east on the Cumberland River, before the attack commenced. Almost immediately after Fort Henry fell, Grant began preparations to capture nearby Fort Donelson.

News of Fort Henry's capture reached General Johnston at Bowling Green, Kentucky. General Pierre Gustave Toutant Beauregard, of Fort Sumter and Manassas fame, had arrived from Virginia to assume duties as deputy commander to Johnston in the West. On February 8 General Johnston informed Secretary of War Judah P. Benjamin of the loss of Fort Henry. In this message Johnston expressed doubt that Fort Donelson would hold, and he informed Benjamin that a withdrawal to Nashville was in the works. Bowling Green was to be evacuated; but Johnston had not decided to vacate Fort Donelson, in fact he mentioned forces were available to reinforce it. Johnston expressed his assessment of Fort Donelson with the following:

> ... Operations against Fort Donelson, on the Cumberland, are about to be commenced, and that work will soon be attacked. The slight resistance at Fort Henry indicates that the best open earthworks are not reliable to meet successfully a vigorous attack of iron-clad gunboats, and, although now supported by a considerable force, I think the gunboat of the enemy will probably take Fort Donelson without the necessity of employing their land force in co-operation, as seems to have been done at Fort Henry.

Johnston also noted, "Generals Beauregard and Hardee are, equally with myself, impressed with the necessity of withdrawing our force from this line at once."[9] The decision to abandon the Kentucky defensive line was a crucial turning point in the war. Soon Nashville would fall and the stronghold at Columbus, Kentucky, would also have to be abandoned. President Davis's refusal to send available troops to reinforce Johnston was now haunting him. An interrelated series of Confederate defeats was now unfolding because of Davis's troop allocation policies.

A more aggressive commander might have immediately attacked Grant with troops available to reinforce Fort Donelson. The defeats at Middle Creek and Logan's Crossroads did not represent an immediate threat to Bowling Green, so Johnston could have sent an overpowering force to defeat Grant and save Fort Donelson. But since Johnston had decided to retreat into middle Tennessee, he logically could have abandoned Fort Donelson to save the garrison from capture. Instead, Johnston gradually sent more men to defend the fort, eventually 21,000 Confederates were committed to its defense. Apparently Johnston somehow ultimately thought this partial reinforcement of Fort Donelson would suffice. Major General Braxton Bragg in Mobile, Alabama, wrote on February 12, "General A.S. Johnston, from whom I heard yesterday, feels confident of holding Fort Donelson and driving the enemy from Tennessee soon."[10] Johnston's gamble to hold Fort Donelson seems inscrutable from hindsight; the futility of simply attempting to hold Fort Donelson should have been obvious even then.

Grant with a force of 15,000 marched from Fort Henry on February 12, 1862, to capture Fort Donelson. By then 21,000 Confederates manned the Fort Donelson defenses. Even though Grant was initially outnumbered significantly, the Confederates did not attack until after Grant was reinforced. A Navy gunboat attack on the 14th similar to the one at Fort Henry failed at Fort Donelson. Discouraged, Grant sent a message from the field near the fort: "Appearances indicate now that we will have a protracted siege here. The ground is very broken, and … I fear the result of an attempt to carry the place by storm with raw troops." The next day a strong Confederate attack, while Grant was away for a meeting with Flag Officer Foote, punched a hole in the Federal cordon, opening an escape route to Nashville for the rebels. Despite this success the Confederates returned to the fort and surrendered the following day. The total Federal losses were over 500 killed and 2,100 wounded. Confederate casualties were lighter, about 450 killed and 1,500 wounded, but over 15,000 Confederates surrendered along with 20,000 stand of arms, forty-eight cannons and seventeen heavy guns.[11]

The loss of Fort Donelson and its garrison was a catastrophe for the Confederacy. The defeat would have a domino effect leading to the loss of an enormous amount of territory and several key cities. President Davis was late recognizing the cost of spreading his forces too thinly in order to defend the entire Confederacy. After the Fort Donelson debacle this strategy would be shelved for a concentration of forces to deal with the Federal incursion into the western Confederacy. A paragraph from a letter from Major General Braxton Bragg to Secretary Benjamin serves as an explanation of the changing perception of strategy early in 1862:

> Our means and resources are too much scattered. The protection of persons and property, as such, should be abandoned, and all our means applied to the Government and the cause. Important strategic points only should be held. All means not necessary to secure these should be concentrated for a heavy blow upon the enemy where we can best assail him. Kentucky in now that point. On the Gulf we should only hold New Orleans, Mobile, and Pensacola; all other points, the whole of Texas and Florida, should be abandoned, and our means there made available for other service. A small loss of property would result from their occupation by the enemy; but our military strength would not be lessened thereby, whilst the enemy would be weakened by dispersion. We could then beat him in detail, instead of the reverse. The same remark applies to our Atlantic seaboard. In Missouri the same rule can be employed to a great extent.[12]

Almost immediately after the loss of Fort Donelson, troops were being forwarded from several locations to Johnston in an effort to combine sufficient strength to confront the Federal advance into the western Confederacy. On February 20 the bastion at Columbus, Kentucky, was abandoned with all but 5,000 of General Polk's garrison going to join Johnston. The remaining 5,000 men of Polk's command were sent to defend Island No. 10 near New Madrid, Missouri, a fortification built to support Columbus and to block the Mississippi River. Another 10,000 troops commanded by Major General Braxton Bragg were sent from Pensacola and Mobile. Brigadier General Daniel Ruggles brought 5,000 troops north from New Orleans to augment Johnston's army. When combined with his troops retreating from the Kentucky line, Johnston would have an army of about 40,000.[13]

While the Confederates were losing ground in Kentucky and Tennessee, a rebel force from Texas was making an invasion into New Mexico Territory. Although President Davis had clearly stated in April 1861 that the Confederacy did not seek additional territory through conquest, a Confederate force did attempt to conquer the New Mexico and Arizona Territories. Federal Colonel Edward R.S. Canby attempted to halt the rebel incursion led by Brigadier General Henry H. Sibley along the Rio Grande River in south central New Mexico Territory. On February 21, 1862, near Fort Craig, the first major battle in the Southwest was fought at Valverde Ford. Canby's force totaled about 3,800 against over 2,500 Confederate effectives. Only about 900 of Canby's troops were Regulars from the 5th, 7th, and 10th Infantries with troopers from the 1st and 3rd U.S. Cavalry regiments. Most of Canby's troops were New Mexico Volunteers, for whom Canby had little respect or confidence. Among the New Mexican troops was Colonel Christopher (Kit) Carson's 1st New Mexico Infantry. Carson, of course, was the famous scout and mountain man familiar in Western lore. He and his troops gave a creditable account of themselves at Valverde. Unfortunately for Canby, some of the other New Mexican troops fled from their assignment as support for a Federal battery, and the guns were captured by charging Texans. Canby reported, "The battle was fought almost entirely by the regular troops (trebled in number by the Confederates), with no assistance from the militia and but little from the volunteers, who would not obey orders or obeyed them too late to be of any service." Unable to retake the guns, Canby decided to return to the protection of Fort Craig. After two days Sibley continued his march northward to Albuquerque. Canby reported losses of sixty-eight killed, 160 wounded and thirty-five missing. Only twenty of the killed and wounded were from the six New Mexican outfits on the field, giving credence to Canby's report. Thirty-six Texans were reported killed and 150 wounded.[14]

Valverde is an intriguing example of the variable impact of troop quality and weapons upon the outcome of battle. Here, as Canby documented, the outnumbered Regulars did most of the fighting for the Unionists. The territorial troops appear to have been more of a liability than an asset in the battle. Confederate Colonel Thomas Green, in command of the Confederate force during most of the battle, confirmed this in his report. Green stated that the locals "were not made of as good stuff as the regulars.... They fled from the field ... in the utmost disorder." The gritty Texans prevailed over greater overall numbers. In this battle, as was the case at Wilson's Creek, the superior small arms of the Regulars had an indecisive affect on the outcome. The close-range nature of the combat seems to have advantaged the Confederates armed with shotguns and pistols over the usually favored rifle muskets carried by the Regular infantry.[15]

There is little reason to doubt that Colonel Canby was overall the best officer and commander on the field at Valverde, despite his defeat. General Sibley was taken ill during the battle, and Colonel Green earned the credit for the victory. Sibley was known during the war for "his alleged predilection for the bottle." He is best known as the inventor of the Sibley tent, which was widely used by both sides early in the war. Colonel Green, however, was an able leader and performed admirably during the war.[16] But Canby had a limited potential for victory at Valverde, as he was severely handicapped by the performance of his undisciplined and disrupted volunteer regiments during the decisive phase of the battle. Here a quality Federal commander did not win, essentially because of his doubts as to the quality of the bulk of his soldiers. Valverde demonstrated that having a quality commander with superior numbers does not guarantee victory in battle. Many unaccountable variables and the vagaries of chance affected the outcomes of Civil War battles. To Sibley's credit, he continued with his mission into New Mexico, leaving Canby in his wake at Fort Craig rather than fearing to push on with an enemy force at his rear. Whatever his faults, Sibley in effect demonstrated resoluteness and initiative following the battle, qualities uncertain in other more famous Civil War commanders.

Sibley's column of Texans marched into Albuquerque and then farther north to capture the capital city of Santa Fe. Canby remained at Fort Craig awaiting reinforcements he hoped would arrive from California, Colorado or Kansas. To complete the conquest of New Mexico, Sibley sent his Texans eastward through the mountains intending to capture Fort Union in the north central region of the Territory. Manned by about 800 troops commanded by Colonel Gabriel Paul, a class of 1834 West Point graduate and experienced combat veteran, the fort was about the only obstacle preventing complete Confederate control of New Mexico Territory. Capture of Fort Union would also give the Confederates a base for invading Colorado Territory.

On March 11 the 1st Colorado Infantry arrived at Fort Union, at about 900 strong, having marched over 400 miles from Colorado camps. Colonel John P. Slough, commanding that regiment, superseded Colonel Paul in command at the fort, much to Paul's dismay. Slough was a prominent Denver attorney with only months of military service. Colonel Paul was understandably ruffled by Slough's determination to assume command. Colonel Paul had experience against the Seminoles in Florida and earned a brevet promotion for gallantry at the Battle of Chapultepec during the Mexican War. He was a major in the Regular Army and had recently accepted the colonelcy of the 4th New Mexico Infantry, technically making him junior to the inexperienced Colonel Slough. In a report to the adjutant general in Washington Paul vented his frustration:

> On the arrival of Colonel Slough, with his regiment of Colorado Volunteers, I had the mortification to discover that his commission was senior to mine, and thus I am deprived of a command which I had taken so much pains to organize and with which I expected to reap laurels. Thus, also, an officer of only six months' service, and without experience, takes precedence of one or many years' service, and who has frequently been tried in battle.[17]

The Confederate Government had hopes of annexing the New Mexico and Arizona Territories, as evidenced by an act to organize the new Confederate Territory of Arizona. The act, which stated that the Confederate Constitution and "all laws of the Confederate states" would have "the same force and effect" within the new Arizona Territory "as elsewhere within the Confederate States," was approved on January 18, 1862.[18] Sibley's column had nearly succeeded in conquering most of the eastern portion of the proposed new Territory when Colonel Slough sallied forth from Fort Union, against orders, to challenge the Texans on March 22, 1862.

Slough's force included his 1st Colorado, Companies A and G of the 5th U.S. Infantry, some Regular cavalry, some New Mexican volunteers, four mountain howitzers and a battery of two six pounders and two twelve pounders, a total of 1,342 men. On the 26th Slough sent his regiment's major (John M. Chivington, infamous for the Sand Creek Indian massacre) with about 380 troops towards Santa Fe through the pine-covered Sangre de Cristo Mountains. Chivington attacked the Confederate vanguard at Apache Canyon at the western entrance of Glorieta Pass. The aggressive Chivington succeeded in driving back the rebels, inflicting much heavier casualties and capturing about seventy Texans. Chivington then fell back to rejoin the main Federal force.

On the 28th Slough moved into the mountain pass "with a view of reconnoitering" the Confederate position at Johnson's Ranch at Apache Canyon. Major Chivington "with about 430 officers and picked men" was sent via an obscured route to attack the Texans from the rear. At about 10 a.m. Slough's column encountered the main Confederate force commanded by Lieutenant Colonel William R. Scurry in the pass near an oddly-named site known as Pigeon's Ranch. Slough, not expecting to encounter the enemy in the pass, fought defensively and stubbornly withdrew during a six-hour fight. Chivington meanwhile reached Johnson's Ranch undetected and found the Confederate supply train of around seventy wagons lightly guarded. Chivington's men captured the entire train then burned the wagons and killed the draft animals before Scurry could intervene. Chivington crippled the rebels by destroying all their reserve ammunition, baggage, and provisions required for the campaign. At around dusk Scurry called for a truce, having heard of the destruction of his supply train. Scurry fell back to Santa Fe by the 30th, reporting that the loss of supplies had compelled his men to go two days without food and blankets in the cold mountains. Scurry wrote, "I was compelled to come here (Santa Fe) for something to eat."[19]

Sibley's Texans were able to commandeer some supplies and wagons by ransacking Santa Fe, but their progress in New Mexico was over. By May Canby had managed to push the Confederates back into Texas, and the Confederate plan to expand westward to California had evaporated. The Federals would control the Southwest for the remainder of the war. Here again the Confederates were unable to successfully mount an operation outside the Confederacy. The outcome of the New Mexico invasion underscores the difficulty faced by the Federals in constantly operating on enemy ground throughout the war, something the Confederacy was never able to accomplish. The Federals had to and did invade and conquer every Confederate state, an immensely difficult task. Conversely, the Confederates, though thoroughly convinced of their martial superiority, were unable to even successfully invade and occupy neighboring Border States, much less loyal Northern States.

Other operations in the Trans-Mississippi region in March were related to Major General Henry Halleck's plan to secure the Mississippi River. A force commanded by Brigadier General Samuel Curtis was sent to secure southwest Missouri while another Federal force commanded by Brigadier General John Pope concentrated on eliminating the Confederate stronghold at Island No. 10 near New Madrid, Missouri. Halleck intended these operations to secure Missouri for the Union and thusly enable further operations to control the Mississippi River. Curtis's advance was aimed at finally ridding the threat posed by Pap Price's Missourians and McCulloch's small army in northwest Arkansas that had combined to defeat Lyon the previous August at Wilson's Creek.

In January 1862 President Davis appointed Major General Earl Van Dorn to command of the troops of McCulloch and Price, which Van Dorn combined and named the Army of the West. Van Dorn was graduated near the bottom of the West Point class of 1842. He remained in the Army serving in the Indian campaigns and with some distinction in the Mexican War. Just before the Civil War he had attained the rank of major in the 2nd U.S. Cavalry, assigned to the same regiment as Albert S. Johnston and Robert E. Lee. After resigning his Army commission in January 1861, at the onset of war he was commander of the Confederate Department of Texas and was later transferred to Virginia with the rank of brigadier general. After General Braxton Bragg and another officer refused appointment to command of the Trans-Mississippi District, Van Dorn accepted command there.[20]

Van Dorn's opponent was Brigadier General Samuel R. Curtis, a fifty-seven-year-old West Point graduate with a diverse occupational career. After only about one year following his graduation from West Point, Curtis resigned his commission to become a civil engineer, lawyer, politician and occasional military officer. He served as colonel of the 2nd Ohio under General Zachary Taylor during the Mexican War and later as a three term congressman from Iowa. In 1861 he was named colonel of the 2nd Iowa and then was appointed brigadier general to rank from May 1861. He resigned his seat in Congress to accept his promotion to brigadier general.[21]

On February 10, 1862, Curtis set out from Lebanon, Missouri, with about 12,000 men and fifty cannon. The object of Curtis's advance was to push Pap Price and his MSG out of Missouri so that St. Louis and the Missouri River transport route would not be threatened while General Halleck concentrated on an advance down the Mississippi River. Outnumbered, Price evacuated Springfield and retreated down the Wire Road with Curtis on his heels. After some skirmishing in far southern Missouri, Curtis had managed to fulfill his objective by mid–February. Price fell back to Cross Hollow, about a dozen miles south of the Missouri border in northwest Arkansas.

In northwest Arkansas Price again combined forces with Brigadier General Benjamin McCulloch's small army. After a clash with the Federal vanguard east of Bentonville, Arkansas, along Little Sugar Creek, the Confederates withdrew to camps in the Boston Mountains near Strickler's Station. General Curtis wisely decided not to follow. The Federal supply route from Rolla, Missouri, was a logistical nightmare. Curtis instead decided to build a defensive line along Little Sugar Creek blocking the Wire Road, which was the obvious return route for a Confederate invasion of Missouri.

By March 3 General Van Dorn had arrived at Strickler's Station to personally assume command of his Army of the West. The command situation in both his and Curtis's armies was far from ideal. Price and McCulloch had disagreed about the retreat into the Boston Mountains, with Price wanting to remain closer to Missouri to invite an attack by the Federals and McCulloch insisting on the withdrawal further south. McCulloch had correctly pointed out that the Federals would overtax their supply line should they press on into Arkansas. Price had become quite indignant over McCulloch's decision, and he did what he could to circumvent McCulloch's authority and status. Cooperation between the two generals had not been satisfactory for Price since the Battle of Wilson's Creek the previous August.[22]

Van Dorn had initially seized upon the idea of invading Missouri with hopes of capturing St. Louis when spring weather arrived. When Curtis sallied forth from Lebanon, Missouri, in February, the focus of Van Dorn's ambition shifted to driving Curtis from Arkansas and then liberating Missouri from the southwest corner of the state. Once he reached the Confederate camps in the Boston Mountains, he wasted no time in making preparations; he immediately sent out the combined forces of Price and McCulloch on the following day, March 4, to drive the Federals out of Arkansas.

With difficulty Curtis managed to concentrate his army behind trenches situated on a bluff along Little Sugar Creek, thus blocking the Wire Road. It was a strong position, and Curtis probably hoped the Confederates would attack him there. He now had a reduced force of about 10,250 men with forty-nine guns. Several hundred troops of his original force had been scattered behind to protect his supply line from Rolla. Unfortunately for Curtis and the Federals, Van Dorn declined to attack the fortified position along Little Sugar Creek.

Van Dorn's army outnumbered the 10,250 Federals with approximately 14,000 men reaching the field out of about 16,500 that set out from the Boston Mountains on March 4. General McCulloch was familiar with the area adjacent to the Federal position, and he suggested a flanking maneuver on the Federal right rather than a direct assault on the trenches along Little Sugar Creek. Curtis wasn't blind to this possibility; he took measures to react in case Van Dorn attempted to turn his right flank. But Van Dorn decided on a more aggressive battle plan. He discovered that a road, the Bentonville Detour, circled behind the Federal position to Elk Horn Tavern a little farther north on the Wire Road. If the Confederates could reach Elk Horn Tavern undetected, Curtis would be isolated with his retreat route blocked. Van Dorn thus decided to attempt to envelop the Federals with a view of destroying Curtis's army rather than simply driving it back into Missouri.[23]

Against McCulloch's advice Van Dorn sent his army out on the night of March 6 attempting to reach Elk Horn Tavern on the Wire Road by daylight. McCulloch advised his commander to rest his weary troops and march to Elk Horn Tavern at dawn. The Confederates had been on the march for two days in cold and snowy weather; the ordeal of an all-night march would obviously deplete their remaining stamina before the anticipated battle commenced. Van Dorn, apparently not expecting much of a fight from the Federals and valuing surprise over preparation, ignored McCulloch. The night march proved arduous, more a detriment than an advantage for the rebels.

Well before Van Dorn's column reached the Wire Road the vanguard was snagged by a blockade of cut trees and branches emplaced earlier that night by the direction of Iowa Colonel Grenville M. Dodge. Dodge was a Norwich Academy graduate and a capable engineer who would garner a distinguished reputation during the Civil War. The colonel and his crew managed to build yet another blockade near the Wire Road north of Elk Horn Tavern before returning to camp. The already creeping Confederate movement, hindered by a creek crossing and darkness, was further delayed while exhausted soldiers worked to clear the timber blockades cannily emplaced by Dodge.

Van Dorn's troops were still making their way to Elk Horn Tavern when General Curtis grasped the tactical situation and reacted. By about 10:30 a.m. Curtis had dispatched troops to meet the Confederate threat. Colonel Peter Osterhaus was sent with a force of artillery, cavalry and infantry to intercept the Confederates at Twelve Corner Church on the western end of Big Mountain where the Bentonville Detour and Ford Road forked on separate paths to the Wire Road. Then Curtis directed Colonel Eugene A. Carr to take Dodge's Brigade, the 4th Iowa and 35th Illinois infantries, 3rd Illinois Cavalry and 1st Iowa Battery, up the Wire Road to Elk Horn Tavern with orders to hold that place.[24] Van Dorn's advantage had evaporated; now he was forced to react.

By 11:30 a.m. Osterhaus had passed through a hamlet called Leetown and encountered McCulloch's troops marching near the intersection of the Ford and Leetown roads. Several cavalry companies and three twelve-pounder James rifles ordered out by Osterhaus commenced firing at McCulloch's column around noon. Brigadier General James McIntosh responded by sending the 6th, 9th, and 11th Texas cavalry regiments, the 1st Texas Cavalry Battalion and the 1st Arkansas Cavalry Battalion charging at the Federal guns and cavalrymen. Outnumbered six to one, the Federals were soon swept from the field. The three James rifles were abandoned in the melee. Companies A and B of the 3rd Iowa Cavalry had been sent northward from the artillery position before McIntosh ordered the charge. Having moved about three hundred yards beyond the deployed artillery, the two cavalry companies were attacked by Brigadier General Albert Pike's brigade of Cherokee, Chickasaw, Choctaw and Creek troops from the Indian Territory. Pike's 2nd Cherokee Mounted Rifles and a Texas cavalry squadron hit the Iowans hard and sent them reeling to the rear. The rest of Pike's brigade followed afterwards and murdered several of the wounded Iowans. The adjutant of the 3rd Iowa Cavalry reported: "I discovered that eight men of that regiment had been scalped. I also saw bodies of the same men which had been wounded in parts not vital by bullets, and also pierced through the heart and neck with knives, fully satisfying me that the men had first fallen from gunshot wounds received and afterwards brutally murdered."[25]

By around 11:30 a.m. Colonel Carr had deployed Dodge's Brigade just north of Elk Horn Tavern and along the Huntsville Road which branched off eastward from the Wire Road at Elk Horn Tavern. Carr realized he couldn't repulse Price's entire command with only Dodge's Brigade. He sent a message to General Curtis requesting reinforcement from Colonel William Vandever's 2nd Brigade, which belonged to Carr's 4th Division. Curtis, though concerned with the threat near Leetown from McCulloch, agreed with Carr and pulled Vandever's Brigade from the works along Little Sugar Creek to reinforce Carr. By now Curtis was realizing that the battle probably would not develop along Little Sugar Creek, but he was reluctant to strip all of his forces from his strong defensive line until he could determine where they were most needed.[26]

Shortly after noon General McCulloch was informed that thousands of Federals, obscured from McCulloch's view by a patch of trees, were forming in a nearby field to the south. Rather than continuing the march to join Van Dorn and Price, McCulloch gathered his command and turned it southward to confront the unexpected enemy threat. Before informing Van Dorn of his situation, McCulloch rode into the patch of trees adjacent to the open field where the Federals had been observed. The 36th Illinois Infantry, a comparatively large regiment about 830 strong, was deployed with two companies thrown out as skirmishers on the north edge of the field. Two companies of the 16th Arkansas Infantry went forward with McCulloch on his personal reconnaissance, but McCulloch, mounted and dressed in a black suit rather than a uniform, appeared first to the waiting Federal skirmishers. The captain of the company nearest to McCulloch ordered his men to fire when the general was spotted about seventy yards distant riding through the trees. McCulloch was hit but once, through the heart, and killed instantly. His mount was struck four times and still managed to run off. The accompanying Arkansas companies fell back without noticing that the general had fallen. Private Peter Pelican of Company B, 36th Illinois, was the first to reach McCulloch. He claimed the general's gold watch and credit for killing McCulloch.[27]

Brigadier General James McIntosh soon learned of General McCulloch's death, which meant he, being the senior officer, assumed command of the division. He immediately called for an attack and went forward with his old regiment, the 2nd Arkansas Mounted Rifles. As division commander his duty was to oversee and coordinate the movements of the units under his command. McIntosh was the goat of his West Point class; his actions at Pea Ridge seemed to justify his class standing. As he rode through the same patch of trees where McCulloch had just died, he too was struck down in much the same manner, shot through the heart. The attack on the west side of the Leetown Road stalled, and the Confederates there withdrew to a field near the Ford Road beneath Big Mountain, a relatively safe place but well out of the fight.

Colonel Louis Herbert, unaware of the deaths of McCulloch and McIntosh, heard the firing west of the Leetown Road and pressed southward with his 3rd Louisiana and three Arkansas regiments belonging to his brigade. The area where Herbert advanced was thickly forested, limiting the range of vision to less than 100 yards. Hebert pushed through the tangle, struggling to maintain unit cohesion, until his regiments collided with two Illinois infantry regiments from Colonel Julius White's 2nd Brigade sent in as reinforcements by General Curtis. Herbert was making progress in a confused firefight

The landscape of Pea Ridge Battlefield from the heights of Big Mountain.

within the smoke shrouded forest until he was hit from the left flank by troops sent in by a Federal Colonel with the unlikely name of Jefferson Davis. Hebert's fatigued brigade disintegrated as his men retreated through, around and behind the Federal line. The scattered rebels then retraced their path through the dense forest to rejoin the rest of McCulloch's Division. Hebert also passed through a gap in the Federal battle line with several men, but he then wandered in the wrong direction and was eventually captured well with the Federal lines.

Confederate command on the western portion of the battlefield was essentially paralyzed by the loss of McCulloch, McIntosh and Herbert. Brigadier General Pike was occupied with simply attempting to reorganize his brigade, and the remaining colonels seemed unable to take charge or agree on any offensive action. The fighting fizzled out on the Leetown Battlefield, and most of the Confederates moved on to join Van Dorn near Elk Horn Tavern. Some Confederate units, about 1,200 men in total, turned back to join the army's trains far to the rear.[28]

While the Confederate effort at the Leetown Battlefield was ending in disarray, Federal Colonel Eugene Carr was making an impressive stand against Van Dorn and Price near Elk Horn Tavern. In fact Carr's gallantry there earned him a Medal of Honor. Reinforcements were gradually sent to assist Carr, but not enough arrived to check Van Dorn's attack down the Wire Road. By sunset the Federals had been pushed back from Elk Horn Tavern but not defeated.

After dark Curtis gathered his army in support of Colonel Carr just a few hundred yards south of Elk Horn Tavern. By morning the Federals were arrayed stretching east

A reconstructed Elk Horn Tavern stands on the site of the original tavern at Pea Ridge Battlefield.

to west in a long line intersecting the Wire Road. Brigadier General Alexander Ashboth of Sigel's command was justifiably worried that the he, Sigel and their troops would be trapped because the Confederates blocked the Wire Road north of the Federal position. The Wire Road was the best avenue of escape for the Federals. Ashboth, a Hungarian émigré and Fremont minion, met with Sigel well before dawn and convinced him that the only recourse for them was to cut through the enemy line and retreat into Missouri via Cross Timber Hollow and the Wire Road. Sigel apparently absorbed Ashboth's take on the battle thoroughly. As we have seen by his record at Carthage and Wilson's Creek, Sigel was at his best on the retreat. His performance on March 8 at Pea Ridge would demonstrate that he intended to make for the Missouri border, what happened to the rest of Curtis's army was not his worry.[29]

On the morning of March 8 the Federals massed twenty-one cannons and commenced pounding the Confederate positions from higher ground. Sigel helped direct the bombardment, contributing to the dominance of the Federal artillery. The Federal artillery proved superior to its rebel counterpart, softening the Confederate positions as the Federal infantry prepared to attack. At some point during the artillery barrage, Van Dorn learned that his ammunition train had not followed during the night and remained hours away in the Federal rear. It is unclear why Van Dorn and Price were surprised to learn that the ordnance trains were far to the rear and unavailable. Not surprisingly the Confederate artillery was running low on ammunition on the second day of battle. With his artillery unable to respond effectively to the Federal bombardment or to help repel an infantry attack, Van Dorn ordered a withdrawal. When Curtis sent his infantry forward, most of the Confederates retreated to the southeast via the Huntsville Road. Others made their escape as best they could westward around Big Mountain.

Federal casualties at Pea Ridge totaled 1,384, of which 203 were killed and 980 were wounded. Confederate casualties were underreported and are consequently more difficult to determine. A conservative estimate put the Confederate casualties at 2,000. The Confederate defeat at Pea Ridge ended Van Dorn's dream of capturing St. Louis, as well as Price's hopes of returning to Missouri.[30]

As the Confederates retreated, Sigel led his divisions northward through Cross Timber Hollow on the Wire Road. Ashboth and two of Sigel's colonels disobeyed instructions from Curtis to remain south of the hollow. Instead they followed Sigel with their troops northward beyond the battlefield. Curtis expressed his displeasure thusly: "I regret exceedingly that so much force separated from this position; and Colonels Schaefer and Greusel and General Ashboth must account to me for neglecting my instructions not to go down the hill.... I certainly need all the force I have to maintain my position." In effect, Sigel had led half of Curtis's army on a retreat towards Missouri while Van Dorn's defeated army scattered in an attempt to escape southward. It seems that once again Sigel behaved selfishly and acted in accordance with his own interests or, in this particular case, his fears.[31]

Confederate defeat at Pea Ridge resulted from overall poor leadership at the command level. General Van Dorn appears to have been promoted beyond his capabilities. He made several dubious command decisions and overall asked more from his men than could be reasonably expected. One prominent example was his decision to send his army on a night march behind the Federal position despite its fatigued condition. As a result his army failed to consolidate and deploy according to plan. Instead, the Confederate divisions were met separately as Curtis used interior lines to confront them. If Curtis would have had more troops, he could have crushed McCulloch first and then concentrated to defeat Price at Elk Horn Tavern. Van Dorn failed to control and supervises his entire force during the battle, having almost no influence on the fighting near Leetown. His inexplicable failure to account for the army's ordnance train by the second day of battle was the crucial factor in his defeat.

The Confederates succeeded in getting beyond the Federal right flank undetected; thus, Van Dorn effectively avoided attacking the strong Federal position along Little Sugar Creek. In effect, the Confederates were initially in exactly the proper position to defeat Curtis. But Van Dorn, against advice, insisted on blocking the Wire Road near Elk Horn Tavern in an effort to envelop and possibly destroy Curtis's army. Instead of trapping the Federals, McCulloch's tired division was unable to reach Elk Horn Tavern before being engaged near Leetown. McCulloch and McIntosh were soon killed before an attack could be organized, creating a leadership vacuum at the Leetown Battlefield. When Van Dorn learned of the situation at Leetown, he failed to devise an alternative plan to adjust to the unanticipated setback.

Van Dorn attempted to deny blame for the defeat at Pea Ridge in a report dated March 18: "I attempted first to beat the enemy at Elk Horn, but a series of accidents entirely unforeseen and not under my control and a badly-disciplined army defeated my intentions. The death of McCulloch and McIntosh and the capture of Herbert left me without an officer to command the right wing, which was thrown into utter confusion, and the strong position of the enemy on the second day left me with no alternative but to retire from the contest." Van Dorn claimed to have learned during the night of the 7th that "the ammunition was almost exhausted," and "the officer in charge of the ordnance supplies could not find his wagons." He also estimated enemy strength at 17,000 to 24,000. The reader here can judge the validity of Van Dorn's excuses.[32]

By comparison, General Curtis demonstrated poise and tactical savvy at Pea Ridge. This battle was also Franz Sigel's best performance of the war. Unfortunately, his motivation was not really about defeating the rebels. He was obviously anxious to secure a retreat route back to Missouri. Fortunately for Curtis, the Confederates were already defeated when Sigel made his move to escape from the battlefield. Curtis, nevertheless, benefited from capable subordinates in Colonels Carr, Davis, Dodge and others. Although the Federals also benefited from Confederate mistakes and fortuitous circumstances, Curtis accomplished his objective and won a significant victory with commendable skill and boldness at a time when few Federal commanders were doing so.

The beginning of 1862 brought an impressive succession of victories for the Federal war effort. Indeed, it would have been reasonable to anticipate the Confederacy's defeat and capitulation by year's end—had the trend continued. In the West, Kentucky and Missouri had been secured, Nashville captured, and the invasion of New Mexico turned back. On the eastern coast, Fort Pulaski had been reduced, closing the vital harbor of Savannah, Georgia, to the Confederacy. On March 14, General Burnside's expeditionary force on the North Carolina coast captured New Bern, North Carolina, establishing a base for further incursions into Confederate territory. A Federal effort was underway that would lead to the capture of New Orleans, Louisiana, by far the most populous city in the South. Almost everywhere except in Virginia the Confederacy was reeling in March 1862.

The narrative of Federal military operations in Virginia during the spring and summer of 1862 is complex and requires at least one volume if not a series of volumes to adequately address. It is beyond the scope of this book to explain fully the details of the Peninsula Campaign and operations in the Shenandoah Valley. However, these operations, which resulted in perhaps the foremost Confederate successes of the war, should be examined and contrasted.

Major General George McClellan, under pressure from President Lincoln, had by March 1862 developed an offensive plan to satisfy the Northern public's demand for an advance against Richmond, Virginia, the Confederate capital. McClellan's plan sagely bypassed the Confederate defenses around Centerville, Virginia, and would enable McClellan to reach Richmond without a series of costly battles required by an overland campaign. The plan called for transporting the Federal army by sea to Urbanna, a small tobacco port on the Rappahannock River. After landing the Federals could use the port as a base of operations for a quick move westward to invest Richmond. It was a good plan, but it was rendered impracticable when Confederate General Joseph Johnston withdrew from Centerville by March 9. McClellan sent the Army of the Potomac out from Washington toward Centerville, but the Confederates fell back to the south bank of the Rappahannock. McClellan realized that Johnston could oppose his landing at Urbanna; the plan to outflank Johnston required the Federals to shift their landing site farther south to the York River. McClellan devised an alternate plan calling for a movement up the York River and the Peninsula between the James and York rivers to approach Richmond.

Meanwhile the Confederates at last began concentrating at Corinth, Mississippi, as part of a strategy to combine forces in order to overwhelm a Federal army considered vulnerable in the West. General Braxton Bragg had recommended this strategy to Secretary

Benjamin. In March his advice was being implemented. By March 27 troops from scattered commands throughout the South had arrived at Corinth to create an army of over 40,000 to be led by General A.S. Johnston. Van Dorn's army, defeated at Pea Ridge, was ordered to Memphis, Tennessee, on March 24. But Van Dorn's troops would not be available to augment Johnston's army at Corinth in time to participate in the next battle.[33]

The target for Johnston's consolidated army would be the Federal Army of the Tennessee. These troops had moved from Fort Donelson up the Tennessee River to camps around Savannah and Pittsburg Landing, Tennessee. The move from Fort Donelson had been conceived by Major General Henry Halleck, Grant's superior officer, with a view of ultimately capturing Corinth, Mississippi. At first Halleck limited his objective to raiding the Memphis & Charleston and the Mobile & Ohio railroads. But when Halleck won command of the Department of the Mississippi on March 11, 1862, he took charge of General Buell's Army of the Ohio as well. Lincoln's War Order No. 3 stated: "Ordered further, that the two departments now under the respective commands of Generals Halleck and Hunter, together with so much of that under General Buell ... be consolidated and designated the Department of the Mississippi, and that until otherwise ordered Major General Halleck have command of said department." Halleck had hoped Buell would cooperate with his plan to take Corinth, but Buell had not complied. After assuming command of the department with authority over Buell, Halleck ordered the intractable general to reinforce the Federals at Savannah. Halleck was concerned that the Confederates were consolidating, as they actually were, and would move to attack at Savannah. On March 17 he informed Buell that seemingly reliable information indicated that a Confederate force of 26,000 was moving to operate against Savannah. He told Buell: "I fully understand these movements. Move on, as ordered, to-day to re-enforce Smith. Don't fail to carry out my instructions. I know that I am right." When Buell moved to comply with Halleck's orders, General Johnston was compelled to make his attack (the object of the Confederate consolidation) on the Federals gathered along the Tennessee River at Pittsburg Landing before Buell's army could reinforce them.[34]

By late March the stage was set for a showdown along the Tennessee River just north of the Mississippi state line. General Bragg's concept of concentration "for a heavy blow upon the enemy" would be put to the test. President Davis and his brain trust were risking the loss of more territory in order to gather sufficient strength to defeat the Federals "in detail, instead of the reverse."[35] The Confederates had already lost the garrison at Fort Donelson and would soon lose another at Island No. 10 on the Mississippi. Their continuing strategy of holding defensive strongholds in key locations was failing. The capture of most of the Fort Donelson garrison and the failure of Van Dorn to participate in the upcoming battle significantly weakened Johnston's chances for success, but Johnston knew he had to strike before Buell could arrive at Pittsburg Landing. Once Buell's Army of the Ohio combined with Grant's Army of the Tennessee, the Confederates would be heavily outnumbered. The Confederates had already stripped troops from areas throughout the South in hopes of checking the Federal incursion into Tennessee and Mississippi. The Confederate leadership knew that victory in the looming battle could change the course the war in the Confederacy's favor. Johnston made the call to attack the Federals at Pittsburg Landing without further delay, thus committing the Confederacy to the first of a series of battles it could not afford to lose.

Johnston's army got underway, behind schedule, on April 3. With Buell's army closing on Savannah, Johnston could not afford any delay. Nevertheless the Confederates used two days to march the short distance, about twenty miles, from Corinth to the Federal encampments around Pittsburg Landing. On the afternoon of the 4th, pickets from Colonel Buckland's Federal brigade clashed with Confederate cavalry near Brigadier General William T. Sherman's divisional encampment. General Grant was, of course, informed of this. He informed General Halleck of the incident, telling Halleck he had gone out from his headquarters to investigate, "but found all quiet." Somehow Grant discounted the possibility of a Confederate attack, despite the fact that he guessed that the number of enemy troops within striking distance could exceed 80,000. On the 5th Sherman told Grant, "I do not apprehend anything like an attack on our position." Grant apparently fully concurred, telling General Halleck that same day, "I have scarcely the faintest idea of an attack (general one) being made upon us, but will be prepared should such a thing take place."[36] There is little to indicate that Grant actually did anything meaningful in preparation for an attack, despite assuring Halleck otherwise. Apparently Grant expected Johnston to repeat the mistakes he made at Fort Donelson, and he believed that Corinth would be easier to capture than Fort Donelson had been. Grant in his memoirs never explained why he did not adequately fortify his encampments or even take reasonable precautions for an attack by Johnston.

Johnston finally did attack on Sunday, April 6, 1862, at about dawn, completely surprising the Federals. Before the Confederate attack could get underway, an unscheduled Federal patrol stumbled into the lead elements of the attacking army. Shots were exchanged at about 5 a.m.; the first casualties of the Battle of Shiloh fell in the pre-dawn dark at Fraley Field. Despite the roar of musketry on the southern edge of their encampments, the Federals did not believe a major battle was commencing. Most of their camps went about with business as usual as the Confederates approached.

With the advantage of surprise, the Confederate attack swept through the unfortified camps and pushed back the Federals on all fronts. A great many Federal soldiers, in their first battle, panicked and made their way to Pittsburg Landing, there to skulk along the riverbank hoping to escape the enemy onslaught. In some places the resistance stiffened and slowed the attackers. In the Federal center, Brigadier General Benjamin Prentiss formed his battered division with other units to form a salient along a worn former stage road known to history as the Sunken Road. Elements of three Federal divisions combined to defend the salient, which proved such a wicked place to fight that the Confederates dubbed it "the Hornet's Nest." According to Prentiss, "After having once driven the enemy back from this position Maj. General U.S. Grant appeared upon the field ... and I received my final orders, which were to maintain that position at all hazards."[37] Prentiss's determined stand at the Hornet's Nest attracted Confederate units that assaulted the salient time and again, allowing the rest of the Federal army to withdraw to a strong defensive line and await reinforcements.

Brigadier General Daniel Ruggles, a Massachusetts-born West Point graduate serving as commander of Bragg's 1st Division, collected sixty-two cannons to bombard the Hornet's Nest. Attacks on both sides of the salient, combined with the shelling, eventually caused the Federal position to crumble. Determined to follow Grant's order, Prentiss and several units along the Sunken Road that did not retreat were cut off and surrounded. Prentiss and his resolute band fought on to "retard" the Confederate onslaught, sacrificing themselves to, in Prentiss's words, "save the army from destruction." Prentiss described the end at the Hornet's Nest: at about 5:30 "finding that further resistance must result in the slaughter of every man in the command, I had to yield the

The field adjacent to the Federal line at the Hornet's Nest, Shiloh Battlefield.

fight. The enemy succeeded in capturing myself and 2,200 rank and file, many of them being wounded."[38]

During the fight at the Hornet's Nest, General Albert S. Johnston participated in a charge against the Federal front in an adjacent peach orchard. The peach blossoms were in full bloom that day, contrasting to the violence and mayhem in that otherwise soothing pastoral setting. Johnston, who was responsible for command of the entire Confederate West, had no business assuming the role of a line officer; nevertheless, he went forward with the attackers. During the charge Johnston was nicked on his uniform in a few places and his boot heel was cut away by bullets. He apparently told Tennessee Governor Isham Harris, who was with the general, that he was unhurt. Actually he had been wounded in the right leg behind the knee at some point during the charge. It was later found that Johnston had been struck in three places, but only the leg wound was serious. An artery had been sliced behind his right knee, and he was bleeding profusely. Incredibly none of his assisting staff officers managed to find the wound and stop the flow of blood; the general bled out in minutes from a wound that an ordinary hospital steward probably could have treated. General Beauregard had virtual command of most of the Confederate army before Johnston was shot anyway, as Johnston at the start of the battle had assigned Beauregard the role of supervising army movements. About thirty minutes after Johnston's death, around 3 p.m., Beauregard was informed and assumed overall command in Johnston's place.[39]

The Confederates had focused so much time and attention on reducing the Hornet's Nest that most of Grant's battered army managed to regroup and form a strong defensive line along a road leading eastward to Pittsburg Landing. General Prentiss had held until 5:30 p.m., and the Confederates were then further delayed in gathering Federal

5. 1862: A Disastrous Year for the Confederacy

These cannons mark Grant's final line on the Shiloh Battlefield. A James shell sits atop the James rifle in the foreground.

prisoners before continuing their attack. Grant correctly anticipated that Confederate attacks would next focus on his extreme left near Pittsburg Landing. Federal artillery was concentrated there, and the U.S. Navy gunboats *Lexington* and *Tyler* steamed along the riverbank throwing large shells at presumed Confederate positions for hours after dark. General Beauregard suspended the Confederate offensive around sunset, a little over a half hour following the surrender of Prentiss. Nearly the entire Confederate army had been sent into the fight, so Beauregard had no fresh reserve to send against Grant's strengthening defensive line anyway.

Most of Major General Lew Wallace's Third Division tardily arrived from Crump's Landing and Stoney Lonesome, north of the battlefield, to reinforce Grant's line. Historians still study the controversy surrounding his delayed arrival and its implications. Brigades from General Buell's Army of the Ohio crossed the Tennessee River after dark and throughout the night, and other troops from Buell's army debarked from transports at Pittsburg Landing to further strengthen Grant's position. Grant planned to renew the battle in the morning with an attack. With the arrival of Buell's Army of the Ohio, Grant would send forward 45,000 men against the approximately 20,000 fatigued troops Beauregard could depend upon to resist the attack.[40]

The Confederates, for good reason, thought they had won the battle, and they expected a mopping-up operation for the next day. Yet they were badly disorganized, and a large portion of their troops were out ransacking the overrun Federal camps for food, clothing, equipment and other plunder throughout the night. The Confederates had concentrated their forces from throughout the South for this battle. Their hopes for victory in the western theater depended upon winning decisively here. But, although Beauregard did not realize it, the opportunity for Confederate success in the West was over by the wee hours of April 7, 1862.

The Federals steadily regained all lost ground on the 7th, although the Confederates gamely resisted. The regiment to which my Grandmother Clara's father belonged advanced as part of Brigadier General Thomas Crittenden's Federal division against rebel regiments from his native Kentucky. One of my great grandfather's brothers-in-law, serving in the same regiment, was mortally wounded that day. By late afternoon the rebels had been forced to yield the entire field. By dusk they began retreating to Corinth, Mississippi.

On following morning around 10 a.m., General Sherman was sending out a superficial probe to determine if the rebels intended to make a stand south of the battlefield. The 77th Ohio Infantry, to which three of my paternal grandfather's uncles and some of their cousins belonged, went forward as skirmishers when rebel cavalry was spotted south of Shiloh Church near a field known historically as Fallen Timbers. The rebel cavalry was led by Colonel Nathan Bedford Forrest, later a lieutenant general and arguably the foremost cavalry commander of the Civil War. Forrest and his riders charged the Ohioans across the field and blasted them with shotguns and revolvers at close range. The 77th scattered. According to the regiment's commander, "The rebel cavalry literally rode down" his infantrymen. "We sustained a loss in killed, wounded, and missing of 57 men. Nineteen were killed on the spot," he reported. General Sherman was forced to flee for his life to escape the rampaging Forrest, but one of his infantrymen pushed his musket into Forrest's side as he rode by and fired. The bullet lodged next to Forrest's spine. Somehow he remained in the saddle and pulled a Federal up behind his saddle to shield himself from being shot again, finally throwing the soldier to the ground as he made his escape. Forrest recovered from the serious wound and returned to duty a couple of months later. The affair at Fallen Timbers had been a close call for two of the Civil War's best-known commanders, but of little overall significance.[41] A few years ago a relic hunter visited this same field and found a Federal coat button. The button was dented at the top edge from being struck by buckshot—a vintage buckshot ball fitted perfectly into the indentation. The long-lost button, its eagle motif still sharply visible, had resurfaced after 150 years in the battlefield sod, giving evidence of the shotgun blasts that peppered the Ohioans that day.

The Battle of Shiloh was a pivotal event with important consequences not to be overlooked. It demonstrated that, in the West, even with concentration of forces and the advantage of surprise the Confederates could not be assured a decisive victory, as had been and would be the case in Virginia. The Federal victory enabled the North to continue its sweeping conquest of territory and strategic Southern cities. Island No. 10, one of a dwindling series of Confederate strongholds on the Mississippi River, fell to General John Pope's Federal force by April 8, continuing the string of Confederate defeats in the West. Federal forces in the West were enabled by the victory at Shiloh to concentrate in overwhelming force. Only logistical limitations and overcautious command decisions prevented the Federals from ending the war in the West by the spring of 1863.

A comparison of the command leadership of both sides relating to Shiloh reveals more significant flaws on the Federal side, yet the Confederate mistakes ultimately proved more costly. Concisely, General Grant was egregiously over confident, seemingly insouciant, in the days leading up to the battle. He inexplicably neglected to take reasonable precautions to prevent being surprised by the enemy at Pittsburg Landing.

General Sherman also contributed to Grant's faulty situational assessment by assuring his commander that a Confederate attack was very unlikely and by failing to order sufficient reconnaissance in the days prior to the battle. In light of procedure later during the war, Grant's failure to fortify his camps seems particularly puzzling. General Lew Wallace's late appearance on the battlefield also must be counted as a contributing negative affecting how the battle played out. The Confederate commanders also made critical mistakes. General Johnston, regardless of the circumstances, was late in making his attack on Grant's encampments. His objective was to ultimately defeat each of the Federal armies before they could unite. Buell's army was the smaller and would have been easier to overwhelm. Still, Johnston targeted Grant for the first strike, and despite delays that obviously reduced his chances for success, he committed his army to attack on April 6. Once battle was joined, the Confederate attacks were not well coordinated. Concentration on the Hornet's Nest front wasted daylight. The position could have been bypassed and isolated. Instead, by the time the Hornet's Nest was reduced, it was nearly dusk, and Grant had consolidated his forces and established a strong defensive line. Grant's final defensive line, with support from Navy gunboats, was probably too strong for the Confederates to overcome. The effect of Johnston's death on how the battle progressed cannot be determined, but General Beauregard was a capable substitute. Ultimately Beauregard, Bragg and the other Confederate commanders failed to exploit an excellent opportunity for a significant victory at Shiloh.

A few days after the battle Major General Henry Halleck arrived at Pittsburg Landing to assume command of the burgeoning Federal forces there. On April 21 Major General Pope brought his army of 30,000 into camp a few miles north of the battlefield. His troops brought the combined strength of Halleck's command to over 100,000 men. By that time General Grant was finding his reputation imperiled because of the severe losses suffered at Shiloh and the fact that his army had been attacked by surprise. The casualties at Shiloh were actually fairly evenly divided except for the capture of Prentiss and his men at the Hornet's Nest. Federal losses totaled about 13,000 compared to Southern losses of nearly 11,000. Grant believed the report of Confederate casualties, especially those killed, was too low.[42]

Halleck led a Federal advance on Corinth, Mississippi, the object of his attention since the capture of Fort Donelson because of its importance as a rail hub. Halleck, in his first field command, proved unnecessarily over cautious and plodding in his approach. It required over a month for Halleck to capture the town with an overpowering force. His advance wasted time and personnel that could have been directed against Chattanooga or other strategically-important objectives. General Grant, with the benefit of hindsight, observed that Corinth might have been taken in two days had the Federals advanced aggressively with the reinforced army following the Battle of Shiloh.[43] With General Halleck replacing Grant in the West, the progress of Federal success slowed at mid-year.

Activity in the East had been going at a languid pace in early 1862, but things began to stir in the spring. Major General McClellan, having been relieved of his duties as general in chief and under heavy political pressure to do something, finally got his campaign to capture Richmond underway on March 17, 1862. McClellan had altered his Urbanna plan to adopt a similar scheme calling for a move up the peninsula between the York and James rivers as his approach to besiege Richmond. Essentially it was one of the best operational plans of the Civil War. It was practical, practicable, and well conceived. It should have succeeded.

From the Confederate perspective, McClellan's movement to the Peninsula couldn't have been more unwelcome. The region between Washington and Richmond was replete with obstacles to thwart a Federal advance. Several eastward-flowing rivers blocked the overland route to Richmond without providing advantageous supply and transport avenues. Plentiful strong natural defensive positions throughout the region also favored the Confederates. McClellan had recognized that an advance through northern Virginia would require many costly battles and would be plagued with supply challenges. His move to the Peninsula bypassed these Confederate advantages and presented a serious threat to the Confederate capital. General Joseph E. Johnston, facing McClellan on the Peninsula, had no plan or option to repel McClellan's sound campaign scheme. The Federal initiative became apparent as McClellan slowly advanced on the Peninsula; the Confederate capital seemed imperiled indeed.

A collateral operation to the Peninsular Campaign was playing out in the Shenandoah Valley while McClellan slowly crept up the Peninsula and into the Richmond environs. Operations in the Shenandoah known as Jackson's Valley Campaign had a decisive affect upon the outcome of McClellan's efforts to capture Richmond. Major General Thomas J. Jackson, already noted for his accomplishment at First Bull Run, became truly famous because of his overwhelming domination of larger Federal forces in the Shenandoah Valley in the spring of 1862.

Jackson's Valley Campaign was crucial to the Confederacy's ability to change the progress of the war in 1862. Jackson won a series of victories over inept Federal commanders in a genuinely impressive fashion. His army performed well in battle and was so rapid on the march that his infantry troops afterwards were called "foot cavalry." Nevertheless, history has portrayed the campaign in the Shenandoah as something impeccable and brilliantly nonpareil while overlooking the fact that the opposing Federal commanders were some of most incompetent of the entire war. The effect has been to enhance Jackson's reputation as an independent commander beyond his merit. The Federal commanders in the Shenandoah in 1862 would have been overmatched by any competent general. While Jackson clearly showed considerable strategic skill and initiative while operating in the Valley, his campaign there does not compare in difficulty or even scope with many Civil War campaigns. Jackson's Shenandoah Valley Campaign obviously has contributed to the perception of Southern martial superiority because of the apparent ease of Confederate mastery over the opposing poorly led and poorly supplied Federal troops. It is true that few, if any, Civil War campaigns compare with the domination Jackson demonstrated in the Valley against inferior competition, but probably in no other circumstance was such a feckless collection of generals arrayed in opposition to any army commander.

McClellan's campaign against Richmond has received an antithetical assessment by most historians in comparison to Jackson's Valley Campaign. Few historians have appreciated the difficulty of McClellan's task, and perhaps fewer still have fully understood the strategic and operational methodology adopted by that general. McClellan designed his campaign with sound military principles. His planning was devised to absolutely ensure that he would not be soundly defeated. In effect McClellan chose the correct place to attack and the best approach to get there, but because he exercised excessive caution during a period of great impatience, his campaign ultimately failed.

McClellan began his advance from Fort Monroe on the tip of the Peninsula on April 4. There were obstacles barring the way to Richmond, the old Revolutionary War battleground at Yorktown being the most significant. McClellan's conservative approach wasted time and opportunity by unnecessarily laying siege to Yorktown. Confederate army commander Joseph E. Johnston reinforced the place to no avail, later deciding to retreat with the loss of scores of naval cannon left behind. The next major action occurred on May 5 near the old Virginia colonial city of Williamsburg. Here again the Confederates had decided to withdraw, and the battle was actually unnecessary and brought neither side any significant advantage.

As McClellan closed on his objective along the Chickahominy River east of Richmond, he would be deprived of the powerful I Corp that had initially been selected to take part in the Peninsular Campaign. President Lincoln refused to send that corps, which had already advanced to Fredericksburg on the overland route to Richmond. Worried about the security of Washington, Lincoln decided to utilize these troops to neutralize the threat posed by Confederate General Thomas Jackson's presence in the Shenandoah Valley. As a result of Lincoln's change of plan, McClellan would be deprived of nearly 40,000 troops he had expected to have available when he devised his campaign. The effect on McClellan's psyche was as detrimental as it was damaging to the prospects of the campaign itself.

Meanwhile, Confederate Major General Thomas Jackson stepped up his efforts in the Shenandoah Valley. Jackson had by May been reinforced by Major General Richard Ewell's nearby division and Brigadier General Edward Johnson's force sent in from the Alleghenies, swelling Jackson's available force to about 17,000 men. The opposing Federal forces commanded by Major General John Fremont and Major General Nathaniel Banks, both politically connected generals with minimal command experience and talent, heavily outnumbered the Confederates. But the Federal forces were separated and never operated with effective coordination during Jackson's campaign in the Valley.

It is superfluous here to narrate in detail Jackson's moves in the Valley, as they are quite familiar to most students of the Civil War. Ever since, Jackson has received unstinted praise for his bold campaign. One historian, for example, called it "a classic feat of modern warfare."[44] Following a defeat at Kernstown, near Winchester, Virginia, on March 23, Jackson won a series of small battles that ultimately distracted President Lincoln and affected the outcome of McClellan's campaign against Richmond. Under Jackson's direction the Confederates won against Fremont's 15,000 troops positioned near the Valley and Banks' 19,000 operating within the Valley.[45] His success ultimately neutralized McDowell's additional 40,000 troops that had been slated to reinforce McClellan.

Jackson's first successful Valley foray was against Fremont's vanguard at McDowell on May 8, 1862. Here, on the northern edge of the Valley, Jackson attempted to crush an advanced element of Fremont's force as it moved from the Alleghenies to confront the Confederates in the Valley. Before Jackson could do much, Federal Brigadier General Robert Milroy, a Norwich Academy graduate later known as the "Gray Eagle," attacked despite being outnumbered by about 3 to 2. Four Ohio infantry regiments and the 3rd West Virginia Infantry did the fighting for Milroy with considerable success, inflicting nearly twice their casualties on Jackson's Confederates. Milroy's aggression served it purpose as the Federals were enabled to retreat unmolested to Monterey and escape. Nevertheless, Jackson had successfully held Fremont at bay, and he then devoted his attention to dealing with Banks' Federals at Front Royal and Winchester.

Banks had scattered his command at three separate towns in the Valley, and Jackson took advantage by attacking and overpowering a 1,500 man force at Front Royal, Virginia, on May 23, 1862. Banks fell back from his main position at Strasburg to Winchester and attempted to hold that place to thwart Jackson's advance toward the Potomac. Two days later on the 25th, Jackson struck Banks' outnumbered force at Winchester. Banks engaged only a portion of his troops and was easily overpowered and driven through the town.

The Federals reported 2,019 total casualties for the period of May 23 through May 25 in the Shenandoah Valley, which included the fighting at Front Royal and Winchester. Only sixty-two Federals were killed during that period, but 1,714 were reported as missing or captured. Jackson reported losses of sixty-eight killed, 329 wounded and three missing for the same period. The Federals, being on the retreat in both actions, were captured in masses as a result of poor battlefield management. Jackson also reported taking 9,354 small arms and two pieces of artillery in total.[46]

After Banks' debacle at Winchester, President Lincoln grew even more apprehensive about the safety of Washington. Rather than forwarding the I Corps from Fredericksburg to join McClelland, he focused his attention on crushing Jackson in the Valley. His plan called for coordinating the separate commands of Fremont, Banks and McDowell to trap and then annihilate Jackson's troublesome Valley Army. Any strategy directed at annihilation of an enemy army proved supremely difficult during the course of the Civil War, and Lincoln's efforts here against Jackson were no exception. His generals in the Valley fumbled the operation from the onset.

President Lincoln's obsession with Jackson's operations in the Valley proved to be one of the greatest mistakes of the war. In chasing Jackson he was reliant on two feckless political generals to defeat an obviously able enemy commander. Lincoln at this point in the war had yet to learn how to anticipate the probabilities of success in his military delegations. Fremont, whom Lincoln already knew as an incompetent, immediately disappointed him by failing to follow the president's directions. On the 24th Lincoln ordered Fremont to "move against Jackson at Harrisonburg ... immediately." Instead, Lincoln learned that Fremont had marched to Moorefield, many miles off his assigned route. "I see you are at Moorefield," Lincoln observed to Fremont on the 27th. "You were expressly ordered to march to Harrisburg. What does this mean?" Fremont replied with excuses, including the veritable fact that his army was poorly supplied and could obtain rations on the way to Moorefield. Lincoln accepted Fremont's explanation and ordered him to proceed to Strasburg. On the 30th Lincoln again inquired of Fremont, "Where is your force? It ought at this minute to be near Strasburg. Answer at once." Fremont replied that his army was "pushing forward" and he intended to "carry out operations proposed." It didn't play out as Fremont proposed. Jackson beat him to Strasburg, and, due to Fremont's lassitude, escaped Lincoln's trap.[47]

In truth, Jackson's troops had marched and covered distances better than Fremont's. But Jackson was outnumbered by Fremont and another Federal force under Brigadier General James Shields who was moving up the Luray Valley from Front Royal. Shields hoped to crush Jackson if Fremont could block the Confederate's retreat route.

Days passed before Fremont finally attacked on June 8 at a hamlet called Cross Keys. There Jackson had posted Ewell with about half as many troops as Fremont. In 1862 the Federal forces in the Shenandoah Valley had the highest percentage of foreign-born troops of any army on either side.[48] Fremont's army was rife with foreign officers of dubious military capability. Fremont attacked with a division commanded by Brigadier General Louis Blenker, a German revolutionary immigrant who, like Franz Sigel, had sought refuge in America. Blenker accomplished little except for suffering nearly 500 casualties.

Such was the essence of Fremont's efforts at Cross Keys. Although Fremont claimed Ewell was in retreat and that his men camped on the battlefield, Ewell had actually pushed Fremont back. The next day the Confederates burned a bridge behind them and thereby isolated Fremont's force from any further threat. Federal losses totaled 684 including 114 killed. Ewell reported 288 casualties with forty-one killed.[49]

On the following day Jackson withdrew Ewell's Division from the Cross Keys battlefield and across a fork of the Shenandoah River. Being essentially safe from attack by Fremont, Jackson went after the vanguard of Shields's force arriving from Front Royal. Outnumbering the Federals on this side of the River by about four to one, Jackson attacked without bothering to reconnoiter. Two Federal brigades, commanded by Brigadier General Erastus Tyler and Colonel Samuel Carroll, posted in a strong defensive position near the hamlet of Port Republic stoutly resisted several Confederate attacks. Fremont did not find a means of assisting the outnumbered Federals across the river, although his army was nearby. After repulsing several Confederate attacks and inflicting heavier casualties on the enemy, Shield's Federals abandoned six of their cannons and withdrew. Jackson's troops followed for a few miles and captured hundreds of retreating Federals. The Federals reported sixty-seven killed, 393 wounded and 558 missing. Confederate casualties, as is often the case, are more difficult to determine. Several Confederate regiments did not report their casualties, but Jackson certainly suffered nearly twice as many killed and wounded as the Federals did.[50] Jackson was fortunate in this battle that Carroll and Tyler were not reinforced. Their Ohio, Indiana, Pennsylvania and West Virginia troops had given Jackson all he could handle as it was.

So Jackson's celebrated Valley Campaign came to an end as Shields, Banks and Fremont never managed to corner the wily Jackson. Although General Jackson earned lasting admiration for his impressive and significant accomplishments in the Valley, his campaign has been overrated by historians. Against more able commanders or a single capable coordinating commander Jackson's Valley Campaign quite possibly would have had a much different outcome. Jackson's chief subordinate Major General Richard Ewell expressed his contempt for Fremont's troops, providing an example of the confidence the Confederates enjoyed during the Valley Campaign. "Their troops are very much scattered and demoralized," he opined to Jackson. Ewell described Blenker's troops in particular as "stupid, ignorant Dutch ... as cowardly as villainous. I doubt even if they intend, when united, to attack you."[51] The true fault for the Federal debacle in the Valley, despite Ewell's observation, was not with the common soldiers. The onus for the Federal defeat belonged to the two principal commanders, Nathaniel Banks and John Fremont. Radical Republican politicians had looked to these men as potential champions to vanquish the rebels. They, like other politically-connected Northern generals, were instead an asset to the Confederacy.

Jackson's success in the Valley was of immense value to the efforts of Davis, Johnston and Lee to repel McClellan's movement on Richmond. His Valley Campaign was the first significant good news for the Confederacy in a year that had to that point brought nothing but bad tidings. On June 11 General Lee informed Jackson that his victories had "been the cause of the liveliest joy in this army as well as in the country." But Lee wanted Jackson to bring his army south to cooperate in the effort against McClellan. Lee explained: "Unless McClellan can be driven out of his intrenchments he will move by positions under cover of his heavy guns within shelling distance of Richmond." Lee comprehended that McClellan's campaign was a grave threat to the Confederacy. He concluded, "The present, therefore, seems to be favorable for a junction of your army and this."[52]

As Jackson was making his move against Banks at Winchester, McClellan was shifting his corps to approach Richmond's defenses. So far General Johnston had not attempted to check his slow approach to the Confederate capital, so McClellan took a risk in sending his III and IV Corps across the Chickahominy River south of his main force. McClellan had other options which he preferred, one being use of the James River as his approach rather than this northern approach across the Chickahominy. The Chickahominy River was prone to widespread flooding in the bottoms and lowlands adjacent to the streambed. As it happened heavy rains turned the Chickahominy into significant barrier, making it difficult for McClellan to shift troops to reinforce or withdraw across the river. McClellan felt obliged to hold part on his force north of the river, as he explained: "The entire army could probably been thrown across the Chickahominy immediately after our arrival, but this would have left no force on the left bank to guard our communications or to protect our right and rear." He also needed to position his troops to allow for the possible arrival of McDowell's Corps. "It will be remembered," he later wrote, "that the order for the co-operation of General McDowell was simply suspended, not revoked, and therefore I was not at liberty to abandon the northern approach (to Richmond)."[53] McClellan's decision here to maintain his conservative manner enabled the Confederates to finally go on the offensive. Once the rebels concentrated to attack rather than man the trenches at Richmond McClellan's campaign began to unravel, and soon he would abandon his plan to lay siege to Richmond by this northern approach.

At this point in 1862 the Confederacy was in serious peril. The Federal war effort was succeeding simultaneously in nearly every quarter. The important Southern city of New Orleans had formally surrendered on April 29. The Federals had won at Fort Donelson, Pea Ridge and Shiloh. Now, having moved up the Peninsula, McClellan threatened to lay siege to the Confederacy's capital. June of 1862 was a crucial juncture in the Civil War. A victory at Richmond, capturing the rebel capital, could have ended the war in favor of the Union within less than a year. Instead, the tide of the war's progress shifted dramatically during the summer of 1862. Historians have nearly unanimously laid the blame for this reversal on George McClellan. That assessment, though partially correct, is an oversimplification. President Lincoln and his cabinet made critical mistakes in their management of military operations in the East in 1862. McClellan, for one, correctly discerned the purpose and limits of Jackson's movements in the Shenandoah. When Lincoln overreacted to Banks' defeat at Winchester, telling McClellan he might have to recall his army to defend Washington, it was McClellan who interpreted the situation correctly. He informed the president, "The object of this movement (Jackson's in the Valley) is probably to prevent re-enforcements being sent to me."[54] Despite his many flaws as an army commander, McClellan had positioned his forces in the best position to defeat the Confederacy that could have been had at any time during the war. The administration, rather than McClellan, should be faulted for failing to allocate all possible resources to the effort against Richmond.

With McClellan paralyzed by awaiting reinforcement and protecting his communications, General Joseph Johnston saw an opportunity to finally attack. McClellan had pushed his III and IV Corps across the Chickahominy. Since the river was swollen these two corps were somewhat exposed. They were not quite isolated, but sending reinforcements would prove difficult. Johnston attacked on May 31 following a night of very heavy downpours. McClellan had not fully anticipated the onslaught, and, although the Federals had prepared some fieldworks, the attack drove the IV Corps' Second Division commanded by Brigadier General Silas Casey out of its works. Casey's Division was considered the Army of the Potomac's "worst division," inexperienced, somewhat indifferent and lacking efficient officers. McClellan criticized the outfit after the battle for retreating "discreditably."[55] Nevertheless, Union II Corps troops managed a frightful crossing of the flooding river over rickety, makeshift bridges and then blunted the Confederate attacks. The battle ended the following day in a stalemate. General Joseph Johnston was severely wounded on May 31, and his successor Major General Gustavus Smith temporarily replaced him with undistinguished results. Despite the presence of able commanders, including Wing Commander James Longstreet and Major General D.H. Hill, the Confederate attacks lacked coordination. The Confederate effort also suffered as a result of miscommunication at the command level.

The Confederates named this battle Seven Pines after the crossroads where they had success; the Federals called it the Battle of Fair Oaks after the area where they had bested the rebels. Brigadier General Silas Casey saw his reputation tarnished as his division was unable to hold on the defensive notwithstanding the benefit of a redoubt and fieldworks. Casey was the editor of a widely-used textbook on infantry tactics. His troops turned in a less than impressive performance, despite his apparent military expertise. The Confederates initiated the fighting with a considerable advantage; thus, the stalemated outcome reflects more credit on the Federals. Casualties were also heavier in Johnston's army. Casualties totaled 6,134 for the Confederates including 980 killed and 4,749 wounded. McClellan's army lost 790 killed, 3,594 wounded and 640 missing.[56]

The weeks following the fight at Fair Oaks/Seven Pines were largely wasted by General McClellan, but for the Confederacy June 1862 marked two of the most significant events of the entire year in the East. First, General Robert E. Lee assumed command of the Army of Northern Virginia at Richmond. Second, Brigadier General James E.B. "Jeb" Stuart led a cavalry reconnaissance that made a circuit around McClellan's army. General Lee immediately concentrated his attention upon going on the offensive and seizing the initiative. He instructed cavalry commander Stuart to scout McClellan's right flank in anticipation of the arrival of Jackson's army from the Shenandoah. By the time Stuart was finished he had led his troopers completely around McClellan's army during the period of June 12–15. The impact of Stuart's ability to threaten McClellan's supply and communications line upon McClellan's decision to shift his supply base to the James River is debatable. At the least Stuart's accomplishment was rightly perceived as a daring deed by Southerners and provided a morale boost for the Confederacy. In addition, Stuart's reconnaissance revealed that the Federal right was vulnerable to attack; thus, Lee decided to assume the offensive soon against McClellan.

In any case, McClellan began to focus his attention on the James River as a new base of operations after Stuart's reconnaissance. According to McClellan:

> In anticipation of a speedy advance on Richmond, to provide for the contingency of our communications with the depot at White House being severed by the enemy, and at the same time to be prepared for the change of base of our operations to the James River if circumstances should render it advisable, I had made arrangements ... to have transports with supplies ... sent up James River. Events soon proved this change of base to be, though most hazardous and difficult, the only prudent course.[57]

The superiority of Confederate cavalry at this stage of the war was examined and defined in an article by Ethan Rafuse of the U.S. Army Command and General Staff College. Besides the often-cited cultural factors supposing that Southerners were bred to be better horsemen, Rafuse noted that the Federal Government was quite slow to augment its cavalry forces while the Confederacy accepted cavalry regiments immediately after the war commenced. The Federals, hoping to spare the expense of purchasing horses and equipping cavalry regiments, initially did not accept volunteer cavalry regiments. The few Regular U.S. Cavalry were scattered mostly in the West and were too few in numbers to adequately serve the Federal needs. There is little in the way of accomplishments for arguing that the Federal cavalry early in the war was any match for Stuart's cavalry.

Another factor negatively affecting the Federal cavalry was the preference of the pre-war Army's elite officers to accept assignments in the more technical branches—engineers and artillery. Northern West Point cadets regularly outperformed their Southern counterparts and selected the more prestigious technical branches over cavalry and infantry. As a result, more Southern West Point graduates were relegated to the cavalry. Before the Civil War, Northerners held over 72 percent of the Corps of Engineer commissions and about 68 percent of artillery officers were from the North. This preference for technical occupations has been recognized as a Yankee stereotypical trait. It apparently has some demonstrable validity. Over 59 percent of the cavalry officers in the pre-war Army and four of the five colonels of mounted regiments were Southerners.[58]

After a delay of over three weeks in awaiting dry weather, and recovering from sickness, McClellan finally set aside his seemingly endless preparations and ordered an offensive move to initiate his plan to capture Richmond. He had devised a feasible plan within the constraints imposed by the president, and, despite his anxieties about his communications and his overestimation of enemy strength, he sent the III Corps and units from the II and IV Corps forward to push back the Confederate lines in preparation for his final offensive against Richmond. On June 25 McClellan launched an attack from a redoubt near Seven Pines against the southern portion of the Confederate line commanded by Major General Benjamin Huger. The combat known as The Battle of Oak Grove began around 8 a.m. and lasted until near sunset. McClellan was satisfied with the result, pushing back the enemy pickets, "with but little loss" and accomplishing "all that could be desired." This "affair of Heintzelman's corps," as McClellan termed it, resulted in higher casualties than McClellan apparently realized. The Federals losses were sixty-eight killed, 503 wounded and fifty-five missing. Confederates, being on the defensive with fieldworks, lost sixty-six killed, 362 wounded and thirteen missing. The fighting at Oak Grove was the first of a series of battles near Richmond known to history as The Seven Days Battles. Sadly, as often occurred during this tragic war, the battle was of no real significance. McClellan abandoned his objective and the purpose for this "affair" immediately after the fighting ended on that day.[59]

As the fighting at Oak Grove was ending under his supervision at Casey's Redoubt, McClellan was assessing disquieting reports from several sources convincing the anxious general that he was soon to be outnumbered by massive Confederate reinforcements. There on the evening of June 25, McClellan's plan to invest Richmond collapsed; the course of the war was altered dramatically. Reports that General Jackson was just north of his right flank, marching in from the Shenandoah, and rumors that reinforcements from General Beauregard had arrived from the West, convinced McClellan that his northern approach to Richmond would fail. Shaken by the rumors and convinced that he was now heavily outnumbered, McClellan returned to headquarters and sent the following message to Secretary Stanton at 6:15 p.m.:

> I have just arrived from the field, and find your dispatch in regard to Jackson. Several contrabands just in give information confirming the supposition that Jackson's advance is at or near Hanover Court-House, and that Beauregard arrived, with strong re-enforcements, in Richmond yesterday.
>
> I incline to think that Jackson will attack my right and rear. The rebel force is stated at 200,000, including Jackson and Beauregard. I shall have to contend with vastly superior odds if these reports be true....[60]

It was true that the Confederates intended to attack the Federal right and soon. Indeed, Jackson was assigned to attack the Federal V Corps commanded by a McClellan friend and supporter, Brigadier General Fitz John Porter. Porter's corps was separated from the rest of McClellan's army on the north side of the Chickahominy River near Mechanicsville, Virginia. General Lee had confirmed through Stuart's cavalry reconnaissance that Porter's corps could be overwhelmed and possibly destroyed with Jackson's arriving army before McClellan could intervene. Lee assembled an attacking force of nearly 56,000 by combining Jackson's army with the divisions of A.P. Hill, Longstreet, and D.H. Hill against Porter's corps numbering about 28,000.[61]

Porter occupied a strong position on bluffs along Beaver Dam Creek near Mechanicsville. He deployed about half of his men in a line of fieldworks and rifle pits above the creek and kept the rest of his corps in reserve. Lee hoped that a turning movement by Jackson from the north would force Porter to evacuate his strong position, but he committed a large portion of his army to overwhelm Porter if necessary.

Lee's decision to concentrate against Porter required him to strip most of the troops available to man the defenses around Richmond. His move presented McClellan with an opportunity to smash through the undermanned defenses before Lee could check him. It was a risk Lee was willing to take because he doubted McClellan would seize the opportunity with its associated risks. McClellan, succinctly, was committed to a methodology prioritizing risk avoidance. As one historian observed, McClellan's fears "had mastered him" as a commander even before the Peninsular Campaign began. McClellan had confided to his wife that he could not allow himself to "run the slightest risk of disaster," which he supremely feared at this point in his campaign.[62]

General Lee's attack on Porter's position at Mechanicsville on June 26 was his first large-scale battle. It was poorly executed, but Lee had limited control of the outcome. His plan was heavily dependent on Jackson's assigned role, and Jackson failed to reach the field in time to even participate in the fighting. As the day waned, General Lee realized that some effort was required to retain the initiative. Lee apparently allowed attacks by A.P. Hill's Light Division and Brigadier General Roswell Ripley's Brigade from Major General Daniel H. Hill's Division in an effort to occupy McClellan's attention. Lee felt obliged to attack so that McClellan would not move against the depleted Richmond defenses or shift his focus towards Jackson's incoming army. The result was a costly repulse and a thorough pounding for the Confederates. Lee ultimately engaged about 11,000 men against the 14,000 posted in Porter's defenses. The heaviest loss for Porter was the seventy-five men captured from the 13th Pennsylvania Reserves "Bucktails." While Lee's losses totaled 1,475, the Federal losses were 361 of which forty-nine were killed and 207 were wounded.[63] Lee had assumed a substantial risk in concentrating his forces against Porter but had seemingly accomplished nothing at Mechanicsville. However, for Lee the battle had the desired affect upon McClellan. He abandoned his northern approach to besiege the rebel capital and instead initiated a withdrawal to Harrison's Landing on the James River.

General McClellan's decision to shift his base of operation to the James River came with a bundle of negative ramifications. The move was exactly what General Lee and President Davis desired. It handed the initiative to Lee and relieved the imminent threat to the rebel capital. Moving to the James required McClellan to retreat in an insecure manner from a powerful enemy force superior in maneuverability and numbers. With reinforcements sent to Richmond by June 25, 1862, Lee had 112,220 men present for duty against McClellan's 101,434.[64] Lee's army was also favored by a lighter marching order and secure supply communications. The political considerations relating to a Federal retreat also were weighty. McClellan, being a Democrat, was at odds with the Lincoln Administration and Radical Republicans in Congress.

The move to the James offered a number of advantages for McClellan besides the preeminent one—security. McClellan believed that the advantages of moving his base to the James were obvious. He had lost hope of obtaining McDowell's cooperation, and he feared Jackson's movements as a threat to his long supply line from White House Landing. McClellan was correct in seeing the James River route as superior to his other options. From the James he could threaten the railroad supply routes from the Deep South, he would have, with naval superiority, a secure supply line, and he could assail Richmond or the also vital city of Petersburg as Grant did two years later. Nevertheless, history has sided with the viewpoint that the shift to the James was an indication of McClellan's enervation. McClellan's behavior during the Seven Day's Battles did little to convince observers otherwise. Yet in actuality, McClellan's behavior can be explained by his overarching fear of the possibility of a massive defeat. The general, concisely, simply was convinced that he and his army were indispensable. If he were killed or captured or if his army were destroyed, he believed, the result would be the irreconcilable collapse of the United States. To McClellan, his survival was paramount for the country's future. He could not allow himself to be exposed to death or capture; the country, he was convinced, counted on him too much.

A word here is necessary to assess the Confederate tactical response as directed by General Lee. Some historians have criticized Lee's aggressive offensive tactics against McClellan during the Seven Days Battles. The valid implication is that the Confederacy could not afford risking heavy casualties usually associated with offensive operations. While this is true, Lee had no alternative other than submitting to a siege and ultimately the surrender of Richmond. The loss of Richmond at this stage of the war, coupled with defeats in the Confederate West, could have resulted in a swift collapse for the Confederacy. Lee hoped to destroy McClellan's army and deal a crushing blow to the Lincoln Administration, something that could not be accomplished in resisting a siege. Lee's success vindicated his strategy. In fact the acclaim for Lee's generalship in these battles has often been amplified in Civil War histories. One historian remarked that Lee's response transformed an "almost certain defeat" into "the greatest victory" of the South's "fight for independence."[65] In truth, Lee's success in turning McClellan away from besieging Richmond resulted more from the risk aversion modus operandi of the Federal high command and administration than anything Lee and his army carried out.

Immediately following the Confederate attacks on the 26th, McClellan began withdrawing his army towards Harrison's Landing. His first step in shifting to the James involved preparing a defensive position for Porter's corps which was still on the north side of the Chickahominy River and thus apart from the bulk of his army. McClellan assigned General John G. Barnard, the Army of the Potomac's chief engineer, the task of locating a provisional defensive position to secure the bridges across the Chickahominy accessing the withdrawal route to the James. While the fighting was still ongoing at Mechanicsville on the 26th, Barnard selected a strong defensive line near a tiny hamlet with the odd name of New Cold Harbor. Barnard was doubtless a quite capable civil and military engineer, albeit his performance during the First Bull Run Campaign was less than satisfactory. On the morning of June 27, Porter spread his V Corps along the line selected by Barnard. Unfortunately for Porter, he had only hours to prepare his defensive position. Lee was immediately following on his heels from Mechanicsville. Porter's men threw up improvised fieldworks in mere hours consisting of felled trees, fence rails and whatever could be piled upon that to stop a bullet.

South Carolina troops from A.P. Hill's Light Division opened the Battle of Gaines's Mill around 2 p.m. on June 27. The battle took its name from a nearby mill owned by a prominent and outspoken Southern loyalist, one Dr. William Gaines. Here again Lee had a significant manpower advantage over Porter. The 1st Division from the VI Corps reinforced Porter from across the Chickahominy; nevertheless, Lee outnumbered the Federals by about 17,000 men. General McClellan was not numbered among the Federals present at the battle. The general remained at his headquarters south of the Chickahominy, nervously monitoring the situation on both sides of the river while attempting to direct the fighting by telegraph.

By late in the afternoon the Federals had held against repeated attacks across their lines. Jackson was again late arriving, but he did manage to engage his command effectively against the Federal center and right. Finally near dusk an especially determined attack by Brigadier General W.H.C. Whiting's Division with the brigades of Brigadier General John B. Hood and Colonel Evander M. Law cracked the Federal left sufficiently to alter the outcome of the battle. General Lee had personally explained to Hood that the enemy line here had to be carried. The front line of defenders gave way and ran for the rear, blocking the second line's field of fire. Retreating Federals completely disrupted the secondary defenders, and, with the frenzied attackers closing with bayonets, the Federal line collapsed. Hood's Brigade, which was composed of the only Texas infantry regiments in Lee's army and the 18th Georgia, garnered most of the credit for breaking through the Federal line. The attack did much to enhance Hood's reputation as a determined fighter as well.

Casualties at the Battle of Gaines's Mill were the heaviest of the Seven Days Battles, and the total casualties amounted to one of the costliest single-day battles of the entire war. Lee's army counted nearly twice as many killed and wounded as the Federals with 1,483 killed, 6,402 wounded while 104 went missing. Federal casualties totaled 894 killed, 3,107 wounded and over 2,800 missing or captured.[66] The large loss in captured men plagued McClellan's army throughout the campaign, as many were unable to stay with the retreating army and were caught while straggling. Well over a third of the total casualties incurred by the Federals during the Seven Days were captured or missing.

The outcome of the battle was a Confederate victory, despite the fact that McClellan's intention to retreat would have left Lee in possession of the field in any case. Lee accomplished his objective of driving the Federals away from a siege of Richmond, and, seeking to destroy McClellan's army, Lee followed the Federal retreat towards the James. The Army of the Potomac here was in a critically dangerous position and fought admirably, considering the circumstances, in one of the fiercest battles of the war. The Confederate army's ability to overcome the advantage of Porter's strong defensive position through grit and determination deserves perhaps greater yet admiration, if not great praise for the tactical acumen of Lee and his commanders. Confederate tactics consisted of straight-ahead attacks with little or no finesse. Jackson was late in reaching the battlefield; had his force arrived in a timely manner the Confederate attacks would doubtless have been more effective earlier in the battle.

Coming off his victory at Gaines's Mill, Lee could not immediately pursue the retreating Federals across the barrier presented by the Chickahominy River. General Lee delayed for a day in attempting to determine McClellan's next move. Lee was unsure whether McClellan would attempt to retain his supply line from the York River and resume his plan to lay siege from this northern approach or retreat. McClellan had three reasonable options available. He could have remained in his defenses south of the Chickahominy to threaten Richmond, or he could retreat back out via the Peninsula, or he could retreat to the protection of Navy gunboats on the James River.

While Lee gathered and assessed intelligence, fighting continued near the recent battlefield of Oak Grove. Here on the 27th and 28th at Garnett's and Golding's Farms, Confederate political-general Robert Toombs's brigade clashed with Federals from the VI Corps. The Confederate probes were easily repulsed with more than twice as many rebel casualties, 458 for the Confederates compared to 189 Federals.[67]

By the following morning, the 29th, Lee had discerned McClellan's intent to retreat to the James River. He ordered his somewhat scattered forces to pursue the retreating Federals immediately. Delays in repairing bridges over the Chickahominy prevented an effective concentration of Lee's army in time to press the retreating Federals making a difficult passage through White Oak Swamp en route to the James. However, Major General John B. Magruder, though heavily outnumbered, managed to inflict punishing attacks against the Federal II Corps at a railroad depot called Savage's Station on the 29th. The Federal II Corps, functioning as the army's rear guard, outnumbered Magruder's command by nearly two to one. Yet where the Confederates attacked they brought superior numbers to the point of combat. The fighting at the train station ended with the II Corps in possession of the field, but Federal losses were more than double those of Magruder's command. Brigadier General Edwin V. Sumner commanding the Federal II Corps believed that the battle at Savage's Station could have resulted in a "crushing blow" to Magruder's outnumbered command on the 29th if the Federals had cooperated properly.[68]

Lee pressed his effort to inflict a decisive defeat on the retreating Federals yet again on the 30th without delaying for concentrating his forces or making time-consuming preparations. McClellan focused his attention on getting his artillery, supply train and troops to a strong position on the north bank of the James River. In fact, McClellan's fixation on the new base at Harrison's Landing dominated his activities on the 30th. According to General McClellan:

> I extended my examination of the country as far as Haxall's, looking at all the approaches to Malvern, which position I perceived to be the key to our operations in this quarter, and was thus enabled to expedite very considerably the passage of the trains and to rectify the positions of the troops. ...it would be necessary for the army to fall back to a position below City Point,

as the channel there was so near the southern shore that it would not be possible to bring up the transports should the enemy occupy it. Harrison's Landing was ... the nearest suitable point.[69]

While McClellan was occupied in the rear with assessing his options for a new and secure supply base, Lee was striving to destroy his army at another crossroads called Glendale. Here again the Confederates outnumbered the retreating Federals. The Federal IV Corps and two divisions from the V Corps had reached Malvern Hill near the James and thus were not involved in the fighting at Glendale. The Confederates had success at Glendale in attacking the battle-fatigued Pennsylvania Reserves Division holding the Federal center. The Reserves were driven back, and for a time it appeared that the Confederates would push through the Federals retreat route along the Quaker Road. Reinforcements from the Federal right stemmed the Confederate breakthrough as sunset brought an end to the fighting. Once again McClellan had dodged a disaster without taking part in the battle. The situation at Glendale had presented Lee with his best opportunity yet to deal a crippling blow to the Army of the Potomac. He had failed at Glendale to exploit his advantage resulting as much from poor coordination among his subordinates as from the determined fighting of the Federals. Lee revealed his disappointment in a single sentence in his battle report: "Could the other commands have co-operated in the action the result would have proved most disastrous to the enemy."[70]

Casualties were overall about equal at Glendale with over 3,660 each. Yet again the attacking Confederates lost twice as many men killed and substantially more wounded, but the retreating Federals lost many more men captured than did the Confederates. The fighting had been desperate and at times vicious at close quarters. Had the Southerners been truly superior man for man as they had been wont to believe, the outcome at Glendale would certainly have differed.

After dark on the 30th the battle-fatigued Federals followed the Quaker Road the short distance to Malvern Hill and joined the rest of McClellan's army in a very strong defensive position. Basically all of McClellan's army was packed into a compact plateau about a square mile in area. On the Federal left the Malvern Cliffs provided strength for the position. To the right two small streams converged in marshy bottomland creating an obstacle to attack. The Federal center covered the gentle down slope of Malvern Hill with a wide and clear field of fire. It was here in the center that the Confederates saw their only opportunity to make an effective attack.

Lee and his army had dogged the retreating Federals over the preceding week and the trend would continue on July 1. Lee should have held back and allowed the Federals to fall back to the James, but he sought a decisive victory rather than the limited objective of relieving the threat to Richmond. Lee recognized the great strength of Malvern Hill as a defensive position and delayed to devise a practicable method of attack. At first Lee hoped to pound the Federals with a concentrated artillery barrage and then follow up with an infantry assault on the north slope of Malvern Hill. However, Federal artillery overpowered the Confederate batteries, rendering the planned supporting barrage ineffective. Hours passed while Lee assessed the situation and looked for an opportunity to attack.

During the afternoon, while the artillery dueled, some Confederates advanced toward the Federal center to drive back some skirmishers. Believing this limited foray was part of a planned attack, Confederate brigades began charging up the open slope of Malvern Hill into a field of fire swept by Federal artillery and infantry. Several brigades were fed into the attack with the result being heavy Confederate casualties and repeated repulse. Fortunately for the Confederates, the Federals had not dug in with earthworks, as would be the case in battles later in the war. Even so, the battle was a one-sided defeat for Lee. Overall, the battle reflected a dismal performance by the Confederate command.

Malvern Hill was the final battle of the Seven Days series. The feckless attacks here cost the Confederates 869 killed, 4,241 wounded and 540 missing. Most of these missing men probably should have been counted as killed in action. Federal losses, which doubtless would have been even fewer had earthworks been prepared, were 314 killed and 1,875 wounded. While 818 Federals went missing, nearly all of these men were captured as stragglers on the retreat to Harrison's Landing following the actual fighting.[71]

With Lee's army battered at Malvern Hill and unable to mount an effective attack, McClellan nevertheless ordered his corps to withdraw very soon after the shooting ceased. His orders met with considerable resistance. Brigadier Generals Joseph Hooker and Phillip Kearny strongly criticized McClellan's decision to evacuate the Malvern Hill position. Even Brigadier General Fitz John Porter, McClellan's friend and supporter, urged his commander to assume a counteroffensive and move against Richmond. Such a move against Richmond without a secure supply line was completely beyond the range of McClellan's risk tolerance. Perhaps McClellan was beaten psychologically, as many historians have suggested, having seen his campaign plan disintegrate. In any case, his decision to evacuate his advantageous position at Malvern Hill was his worst misstep of the Peninsular Campaign.

In assessment of the Peninsular Campaign historians almost unanimously censure George B. McClellan for his generalship and laude Robert E. Lee for saving Richmond from siege. This traditional evaluation of this significant campaign is an over simplification, a cliché. While McClellan indeed was flawed as an army commander (and as a personality for that matter) his decisions and adjustments during June 1862 compare favorably to most Civil War commanders. The outcome of Lee's offensive that month probably would have been much worse for Lincoln and the Union had a different general been in command of the Army of the Potomac during this campaign.

McClellan's faults in directing the Peninsular Campaign have been well cataloged in narratives ever since the guns at Malvern Hill fell silent. Chief among his veritable flaws was his constant penchant for overestimating his enemy's strength in numbers and capability. His low risk tolerance and over cautiousness seriously limited his tactical options and decreased his effectiveness. As one Civil War military history observed, "McClellan campaigned without the confidence of Lincoln or Stanton."[72] His relations with the president and cabinet bordered on insubordination and overt disrespect. In alienating the president and his cabinet McClellan forfeited influence; he was unable to persuade his superiors to fully support his plan and to send needed reinforcements.

Despite the missteps of its commanding general, the Army of the Potomac had performed well during the Peninsular Campaign under trying and precarious circumstances. The Federal army had reached a secure base on the James River where it could threaten Richmond or Petersburg, Richmond's vital railroad hub. General Lee had the advantages of greater overall numbers and in fighting on home soil; nevertheless, his army suffered much heavier losses in killed and wounded, and he never won a substantial victory in any of the Seven Days Battles. Lee's losses totaled 20,614 with 3,494 killed and 15,758 wounded. Federal casualties were slightly over half as many in killed and wounded: 1,734 killed and 8,062 wounded. The Federals abandoned their wounded more than once during the Seven Days and lost perhaps thousands of stragglers during the retreat to the James River. With the extraordinary total of 6,053 men captured, Federal losses totaled 15,894 against 20,614 for the Confederates for the Seven Days.[73] At this stage of the war the Federals could regain their captured in exchanges for Confederates captured in the West at Fort Donelson and Island No. 10.

General Lee had accomplished his objective of delivering Richmond from immediate siege, but he had completely failed to win a battle of annihilation, as he had hoped, against the retreating Federals. Throughout the Seven Days Lee had to contend with indifferent performances from some of his key subordinates. Lee admitted his disappointment in his official report: "Under ordinary circumstances the Federal Army should have been destroyed."[74] No doubt some historians would agree. However, the Confederates were badly battered in three of the Seven Days Battles, and following the Battle of Malvern Hill it could be said that the Federals held the upper hand. Lee is criticized by some historians for the heavy losses incurred during the Seven Days. In fairness to Lee, there was no apparent alternative to the aggressive tactics he employed during the Seven Days Battles. While there was little in the way of finesse in his tactical approach, Lee demonstrated confidence and competence that proved sufficient in a critical setting. He fairly deserves the admiration and acclaim he has ever since received in most Civil War histories for his conduct of this campaign.

The outcome of the Peninsular Campaign has historically been portrayed as a Confederate victory resulting from General Lee's superiority as an army commander as compared to General McClellan. Yet in truth it was subsequent decisions by President Lincoln and his shift in military strategy in the East that facilitated Richmond's relief and a return to stalemate in Virginia until 1864. The superiority of McClellan's approach to attack Richmond was demonstrated by the failures of subsequent commanders who moved against Richmond via the overland route. The reality is that McClellan faced a much more difficult task in attacking Richmond in 1862 than General Grant did two years later. McClellan got to the James River in position to do exactly what Grant did in 1864, and he got there with far fewer casualties. McClellan's campaign was superior to Grant's. The difference is that Grant was allowed to fail repeatedly. McClellan, lacking the president's confidence, was not. We will never know whether McClellan would have been able to mount an offensive from Harrison's Landing that would have duplicated Grant's success later in the war. Given the resources and support that Grant received in 1864, McClellan probably would have accomplished the task in less time with less cost in blood and treasure. McClellan's conservative methods, devised to remove the possibility of defeat, were suited for the conditions he faced in 1862. The reality is that the Confederacy benefited from Lincoln's decision not to allow McClellan to continue his campaign from the Harrison's Landing base during the summer of 1862.

President Lincoln visited the Federal encampment at Harrison's Landing, arriving on July 8, 1862. The president had traveled by steamer up the James River, obviously confident that the rebels would be unable to prevent him from reaching his destination or to even threaten him during the passage. On the following day the president met with McClellan's corps commanders without McClellan in attendance. He asked these general their opinions about continuing the campaign or if the army should be withdrawn back to northern Virginia. Fitz John Porter commanding the V Corps, Edwin Sumner of the II Corps and Samuel Heintzelman commanding the III Corps opined that the army was secure at Harrison's Landing and should remain there. Erasmus Keyes of the IV Corps and William Franklin commanding the VI Corps advised the president to withdraw the army and evacuate Harrison's Landing. Erasmus Keyes was adamant about withdrawing the army. On July 10 Keyes sent a letter to President Lincoln giving his views on what should be done. Keyes suggested that the "sickliness of this camp would nearly destroy the army in two months." He anticipated that the Confederates would soon build fortifications manned with "abundant artillery" so as to cut off the Army of the Potomac from supplies. Addressing the president's obsession with the safety of Washington, Keyes informed Lincoln that if the army remained on the James River the enemy would have ample time "to capture Washington before we could possibly go to its rescue." He insisted that the army could not attack Richmond "with any hope of success" unless at least 100,000 "good troops" were sent to reinforce McClellan. New troops being recruited in the North, he observed, would be of no use because they would not be conditioned to the demands of campaigning on the James. "The raw troops," he wrote, "would melt away and be ruined forever."[75] McClellan had accomplished little to convince the president that he would successfully attack Richmond. He had continually called for substantial reinforcements, and Lincoln could not provide them. Ultimately, the views of men like Erasmus Keyes carried more weight than McClellan's supporters.

The summer of 1862 became a turning point in the war in favor of the Confederacy. This temporary but significant shift in the course of the war resulted almost entirely from poor operational performances and faulty strategic decision making by key ranking Federal generals. Much of the onus for enabling the Confederate resurgence during the second half of 1862 belonged to Major General Henry W. Halleck. The historical image of Halleck has often accentuated his unwillingness or inability to accept responsibility and his reputation for risk aversion. Halleck's record as an army commander certainly demonstrated these traits. He was, however, absolutely marked by a high intellectual capacity, and he was perhaps, with the exception of General Scott, the nation's foremost authority on military matters. Because of his reputation as a military savant, President Lincoln selected Halleck to assume the duties of general in chief on July 11, 1862. McClellan's performance and manner during the Peninsular Campaign had obviously discredited him with the Lincoln Administration. Lincoln sought and wanted sound military advice, and, with the recommendation of General Scott, he appointed Halleck to overall command of the Federal Army to fulfill this desideratum.

General Halleck's command record in the West prior to his appointment to general in chief was appropriately characterized by success. He had demonstrated, to an acceptable extent, sound judgment and competence in his area of operations. However, he benefited from able subordinates and occasionally took credit for victories and successes earned by others. Concisely, General Halleck was no bungler, yet he should have accomplished much more with the resources and opportunities dealt to him through mid-1862. Halleck's performance as a field commander following the Battle of Shiloh demonstrated, for all time, his limitations and liabilities.

General Halleck's command style, as briefly mentioned previously in this chapter, was displayed after he assumed command of Grant's and Buell's armies at Pittsburg Landing on April 11, 1862. Halleck set about the task of capturing the important rail junction at Corinth, Mississippi, on April 30, having wasted valuable time in preparation. The advance was carried out as a siege from its inception, and the Federal troops "were always behind intrenchments" as Halleck required his men to dig in practically each day. By late May Halleck's troops were in position to besiege Corinth, and the Confederates evacuated the town during the night of May 29. The operation squandered much valuable time and resources that could have been employed to greater effect with proper management. General Grant, acting as Halleck's XO, was "satisfied that Corinth could have been captured in a two days' campaign commenced promptly on the arrival of reinforcements after the battle of Shiloh." Corinth was certainly close enough to the encampments at Shiloh to be reached within two days, and obviously General Grant did not believe the Confederates could have successfully contested its capture.

Immediately after Corinth fell, Halleck should have sent sufficient troops to capture Chattanooga or to secure the Mississippi by taking Vicksburg and Port Hudson, the remaining Confederate strongholds on the river. General Buell was sent towards Chattanooga with the Army of the Ohio. A much smaller force led by Major General Ormsby M. Mitchel had already practically paved the way for Buell. But Buell was a poor choice for any assignment requiring expeditious effort. General Grant, however, believed that even Buell could have captured Chattanooga "with but little fighting, and would have saved much of the loss of life which was afterwards incurred" had Buell marched there as rapidly as possible.[76] It is quite probable that the war would have been shortened significantly had General Halleck taken measures to ensure a rapid advance against Chattanooga and Vicksburg during the summer of 1862.

General McClellan wanted Chattanooga captured to sever the Confederacy's single east-west railroad connection. He considered its capture an integral factor in his strategy to take Richmond. Unfortunately for the Federals, Halleck split his armies and assigned them to various posts in Tennessee and Mississippi. It is probable that both Vicksburg and Chattanooga could have been captured and held with the forces available to Halleck in June 1862. Certainly he could have spared sufficient troops to capture Vicksburg. Ultimately Halleck's decisions after the capture of Corinth accomplished little and extended the war's duration and cost. He squandered the opportunity to extend the pattern of Federal success in the West by dispersing his armies with inconsequential assignments rather than concentrating on meaningful objectives.

Halleck's actions in the West followed a pattern of miscalculations by the Federal high command during the spring and summer of 1862. In April, for unclear reasons, Secretary of War Edwin Stanton closed the Federal recruiting offices. It was part of an overall mismanagement of the recruiting process in the North. When recruiting did resume, new regiments were raised at the expense of recruiting replacements for the veteran regiments. Veteran regiments were far more effective than newly recruited ones. New recruits sent into veteran regiments benefited from instruction by seasoned soldiers and experienced leaders. The recruitment of new regiments was a politically-driven policy that hampered the Federal war effort greatly. Apprehending the error of closing the recruiting offices in the various Northern states, President Lincoln issued a call for 300,000 men for three years service on July 2, 1862. These men were desperately needed during the Peninsular Campaign, but instead the 421,465 men furnished by the states under this call were not available until months after that campaign ended.[77]

Equally significant in its negative impact on the Federal war effort was the decision to recall the Army of the Potomac from Harrison's Landing. By July President Lincoln had concluded that General McClellan would never advance from the James against Richmond without resources Lincoln believed were unavailable. McClellan had continually requested more troops before resuming the offensive, and he had habitually overstated the troop strength of Confederate forces operating against him. Perhaps Lincoln had concluded that McClellan would never manage to reach Richmond without overwhelming superiority in numbers, something Lincoln could not immediately provide. With the concurrence of General Halleck, Lincoln decided to abandon the effort to capture Richmond from the James River base and instead to return the Army of the Potomac to Washington's environs.

Lincoln's decision here on the surface seemed fitting; however, from hindsight it was obviously one of the worst strategic moves of the war. At the time McClellan was being criticized for his retreat to the James because the move allowed Lee the option of moving towards Washington. But a move by Lee against Washington was never a serious concern as long as McClellan posed a viable threat to Richmond from his base on the James. With the strong fortifications surrounding Washington it is unlikely that Lee could have captured the capital defended by available troops even with the Army of the Potomac remaining at Harrison's Landing. This, or course, is a simplification of the conditions in the East in July 1862; but, concisely, McClellan made the correct call in pleading to sustain his campaign from the James. We will never know what sort of success McClellan would have achieved from his base on the James, but we know that the decision to recall McClellan's army resulted in a Confederate resurgence in the East and the West during the summer of 1862.

Conversely the Confederates assumed a successful strategic policy in reaction to the overly cautious Federal operations that summer. To some historians the Confederate reaction and subsequent resurgence demonstrated something like strategic brilliance. Actually, the Confederates reacted as required given the circumstances. The willingness of Lee and the Confederates to assume a risky posture in the summer campaigns certainly deserves some of the acclamation bestowed traditionally by Civil War historians. As events played out that summer General Lee engineered a significant, if temporary, reversal of fortunes. However, Lee's success was due as much to poor operational performances on the part of his opponents as to the boldness and rectitude of his tactics. Lee's subsequent accomplishments following the withdrawal of McClellan's army from the James were in any case impressive. It is unlikely that but few, if any, commanders could have accomplished more with the resources Lee was dealt that summer. In that respect the Confederate success was impressive and demonstrated obvious superiority to the Federal operational performance following the Peninsular Campaign.

The Confederate resurgence in the East began with a telegraph from General Halleck to McClellan on August 3, 1862: "It is determined to withdraw your army from the Peninsula to Aquia Creek. You will take immediate measures to effect this, covering your movements the best you can." McClellan answered the following day with a lengthy explanation as to why the move was a grave mistake: "...I am convinced that the order to withdraw this army to Aquia Creek will prove disastrous to our cause. I fear it will be a fatal blow." McClellan went on to point out that he was in position to advance "in any direction" with a secure supply line protected by gunboats. He observed that his army could move to within ten miles of Richmond without meeting an enemy force "sufficient to fight a battle." The withdrawal, McClellan argued, would demoralize the army and depress the Northern people. As to the threat to Washington, he observed that General Burnside's troops could be sent to the capital as well as "portions of the Army of the West not required for a strict defense there." Perhaps the most prescient observation McClellan offered that day was: "It is here, on the banks of the James, that the fate of the Union should be decided."[78]

McClellan was correct in asserting that a continuance of the campaign against Richmond from his base on the James was the proper course and strategy to defeat the Confederacy. However, Federal successes in the West had perhaps shifted the focus and priority to that area of operations. And from the West, President Lincoln in June had selected Major General John Pope to command the reorganized Federal armies that Stonewall Jackson had whipped in the Shenandoah Valley earlier that month. On June 26 the corps of Generals McDowell, Banks and Fremont were reorganized as corps of the newly organized Army of Virginia and placed under Pope's command. The I Corps of the newly organized army went to Major General Franz Sigel who replaced the feckless Major General John Fremont. As we have seen, Sigel was a poor selection for any command assignment and was not an improvement. Major General Nathaniel Banks, who had been thoroughly outgeneraled in the Shenandoah, led the II Corps. The hapless Major General Irvin McDowell commanded the III Corps of Pope's Army of Virginia.

Major General John Pope was a politically-connected graduate of the West Point Class of 1842. His credentials were impressive enough, being from a family with a distinguished history of governmental service and having served with distinction prior to his assignment in Virginia. Under his leadership New Madrid and the fortress at Island No. 10 on the Mississippi River were captured. But instead of inspiring confidence at his new command, he instead got off to a controversial start. His reputation in the East proceeded to decline from its disenchanting inception.

Learning of Pope's newly organized army gathering to the north of Richmond and of Pope's rigorous policy towards Virginia's civilian population, General Lee sent Stonewall Jackson and A.P. Hill northward to confront Pope. By August 1 Jackson had over 24,000 troops in position at Gordonsville, Virginia, to thwart Pope's route to Richmond. On August 3, the same day that Halleck ordered McClellan to withdraw from the James, Lee received information indicating that Burnside's command, moving north from the Carolinas, would not be sent to reinforce McClellan on the James. Burnside instead was heading farther north to reinforce Pope's army in northern Virginia. Another action by McClellan contributed to Lee's correct assessment of Federal intentions. McClellan believed he needed to have possession of Malvern Hill to comply with the order to withdraw or to move against Richmond or Petersburg, so on August 5 a force led by Brigadier General Hooker drove the Confederates off Malvern Hill. McClellan claimed that 100 Confederates were captured by Hooker's column. On the 5th he messaged Halleck from Malvern Hill: "This is a very advantageous position to cover an advance on Richmond ... and I feel confident that with re-enforcements I could march this army there in five days." Halleck replied the next morning, "I have no re-enforcements to send you."[79] McClellan then abandoned Malvern Hill yet again. By August 7 General Lee, seeing the retreat from Malvern Hill as further evidence that McClellan was likely to withdraw from Harrison's Landing, began focusing on operations in northern Virginia.

Lee was not content to react to the next Federal initiative. His immediate intent was to defeat Pope decisively. Pope's Army of Virginia was still scattered with the largest corps, McDowell's with 30,000 men, at Fredericksburg and Sigel's I Corps still marching in from the Shenandoah Valley. Only Banks' II Corps was in position to confront Stonewall Jackson's force. By August 8 Lee had decided to move in strength against Pope before McClellan could interfere.

Meanwhile General Pope ordered General Banks to prevent Jackson from advancing from Gordonsville towards Culpeper, Virginia. Pope needed to secure Culpeper with its strategic road junctions as an assembly point for his army. Pope's orders to General Banks were "clear and unequivocal" for Banks to assume a defensive posture to block Jackson's route to Culpeper. Jackson had over 20,000 troops in his column moving from Gordonsville by August 7. Banks had about 8,000 troops facing Jackson on the Orange and Culpeper Road near Cedar Mountain when Jackson's column appeared on August 9, 1862. On the afternoon of August 9 Banks, though heavily outnumbered, attacked Jackson at Cedar Mountain.[80]

Nathaniel Banks' decision to attack was and remains as inscrutable as it was unsound. Banks later denied responsibility for ordering the attack, but the Federal division and brigade commanders involved in the heaviest fighting at Cedar Mountain reported that they advanced on orders, apparently from Banks. Division Commander Alpheus Williams in his report mentioned that "by direction of the major-general commanding the corps" he sent a brigade into a position that eventually led to an attack on the Confederates. The resulting Battle of Cedar Mountain proved to be one of the more pointless engagements of the war. The battle had no meaningful impact on the outcome of the campaign that summer. Nevertheless, in the words of Federal Brigade Commander Samuel Crawford describing his experience in the fighting, "The slaughter was fearful."[81]

At Cedar Mountain the unexceptional Banks nearly defeated the renowned Stonewall Jackson before overwhelming numbers forced his troops to retreat. In the early stages of the fighting the Federals routed Jackson's vaunted Stonewall Brigade and forced the Confederates to fight desperately to avoid defeat. In the end both sides claimed a tactical victory at a cost of 2,377 Federal and 1,355 Confederate casualties. The Federals reported 622 men as missing, so the overall losses in killed and wounded were similar on each side.[82]

The battle overall was as poorly managed as it was inconsequential. Banks should have remained on the defensive awaiting reinforcements rather than attacking Jackson's much larger force. Jackson himself was resting on the porch of a farmhouse rather than observing the field when the Federals attacked and nearly swept his front line away. He was fortunate to have reinforcements arrive at the proper time to swing the battle in his favor. Pope arrived around sunset to supervise the deployment of reinforcements in a strong defensive position, and Jackson halted his counterattack at nightfall. Ultimately Jackson fell back to Gordonsville within a few days of the battle, having accomplished nothing meaningful to compensate for the 1,355 casualties his army incurred at Cedar Mountain.

The campaign in Virginia that followed the Battle of Cedar Mountain in August 1862 played out in manner that completely favored the operational advantages of the Confederate Army of Northern Virginia and General Lee's style of command. To further benefit the Confederates, the Federal high command of Generals Halleck, McClellan and Pope each contributed in their own way to the dismal fortunes of the Federals in Virginia that summer.

Throughout the war the Army of Northern Virginia demonstrated marked superiority over its counterparts in two key elements: maneuverability and flexibility. The Confederate army was free of the impediment of lengthy supply lines and could react faster to changing circumstances than the Federals. In a fluid situation requiring quick reaction, the Confederates held a significant advantage.[83] By comparison the Federal army in the East was more powerful but far more ponderous. These two important advantages were never more apparent or better demonstrated by Lee and his army than during the summer campaign of 1862.

Following the Battle of Cedar Mountain Pope was constrained by General in Chief Halleck to remain north of the Rapidan River. Halleck sent the following message to Pope on August 16: "I think it would be very unsafe for your army to cross the Rapidan. It would be far better if you were in the rear of the Rappahannock. We must run no risks just now, but must concentrate, so as to secure full co-operation."[84]

General Lee had reasoned correctly that McClellan's army would remain inert or would withdraw from Harrison's Landing; therefore, on August 13 he dispatched Longstreet's command by train to deal with Pope in northern Virginia. By shifting Longstreet northward Lee kept only 25,000 troops behind to defend Richmond. It was as if Lee had a copy of McClellan's orders to evacuate his position on the James, and Lee couldn't have made a better move in response to McClellan's shift. It was a risky, somewhat desperate, response by the Confederates. Had Lincoln and his generals reacted with equal audacity the Confederacy might well have fallen during the summer of 1862. Instead, Lee launched a brilliant and successful campaign that prolonged the war.

By August 24 Lee had devised a plan to defeat Pope and shift the fighting away from Richmond. He assumed a high risk course of action by dividing his army in the presence of a larger enemy force. Jackson with 25,000 troops was sent on a circuitous route to outflank Pope and threaten his supply line. Longstreet with 30,000 men remained in place demonstrating along the Rappahannock to distract Pope. The movement left Jackson quite vulnerable to a concentrated and crushing attack from Pope, but mistakes by Pope enabled Jackson's risky foray to succeed incredibly well.

Jackson was the right choice to lead Lee's risky flanking maneuver. He could drive his men hard and cover prodigious distances remarkably fast. On the other hand, Pope, thinking offensively and looking to his front, neglected to guard his supply base and watch his rear. By August 26 Jackson had passed through unguarded Thoroughfare Gap to menace Pope's supply line and place his force between Pope's army and Washington. On the morning of August 27 Jackson's troops pillaged the Federal supply depot at Manassas while Pope's scattered army was out of position to respond.

Despite being surprised when Jackson's troops burned his supplies at Manassas, Pope at least then knew where to look for Jackson's vulnerable force. But Jackson did not remain at Manassas or attempt to escape. Instead he chose a strong defensive line along an unfinished railroad embankment on the First Bull Run battlefield and awaited reinforcements from Lee and Longstreet. While Pope's troops marched about seeking to corner and crush Jackson, Lee followed Jackson's flanking route through Thoroughfare Gap. Lee's passage through the gap was feebly countered by Brigadier General James E. Ricketts 2nd Division from McDowell's III Corps. Rickett's troops, heavily outnumbered, could not turn back Longstreet's command. Here at Thoroughfare Gap Pope blundered once again: he failed to keep track of Longstreet's force and prevent its passage to reinforce Jackson. Pope's mistakes were compounding, and each error and oversight contributed to Lee's odds of achieving a decisive victory.

Unfortunately for the Federals, Pope was unable to locate exactly where Jackson went after sacking Manassas Junction. Pope focused his attention almost exclusively on finding and crushing Jackson, and in the process he lost track of Longstreet's command. With more and better cavalry Pope might have prevented Jackson from moving behind his army undetected. As it was, Pope never managed to assess Lee's plan. He proved incapable of even finding and defeating Jackson, something he certainly should have done. Worse yet, Pope failed to prevent Longstreet from passing Thoroughfare Gap to unite with Jackson. Thus, Pope's strategy to crush Lee's divided army separately came to naught. Lee's risky plan worked to perfection simply because Pope failed to account for it and implement fundamental precautions to prevent it.

On August 28 Pope was gathering his army to deal with Jackson, confident he would bag that famous general and his command. That afternoon Brigadier General Rufus King's 2nd Division of McDowell's III Corps, while marching in compliance to Pope's orders, brushed into some of Jackson's concealed troops near Groveton. The 2nd U.S. Sharpshooters, one of the best Federal light infantry outfits for scouting, skirmishing and sniping, discovered some of Jackson's troops near the Brawner farmstead as King's division marched along the Warrenton Turnpike. Colonel Henry Post of the sharpshooters sent a messenger to warn 1st Brigade Commander John Hatch "that the rebels were in line of battle" as the brigade marched by. General Hatch "refused to believe it ... saying there were no rebels anywhere near there, and took no heed" of Post's report. Hatch kept his brigade moving toward Centerville as Stonewall Jackson watched its passage. Jackson decided to attack the next Federal brigade marching by, Brigadier General John Gibbon's 4th Brigade, later known to history as the famous Iron Brigade.[85]

Jackson ordered out six brigades led by Brigadier General William Taliaferro and Major General Richard Ewell, about 6,400 men, to attack Gibbon's lone brigade, about 2,100 strong. Gibbon responded by deploying his brigade of three Wisconsin infantry regiments and the 19th Indiana Infantry along with some artillery to engage the enemy. It was late afternoon when the two sides formed battle lines and began blazing away at about seventy-five yards apart. The fighting at the Brawner Farm was simply a stand up shootout beginning after 6 p.m. and lasting through the twilight of dusk. By 9 p.m. darkness had snuffed out the fighting except for snipping by Confederates targeting Yankees aiding the wounded. Casualties are difficult to determine with exactness; some sources estimate the losses at about 1,300 each. The Federals likely suffered at least 912 casualties and the Confederates perhaps as many as 2,200. At any rate, the Federal losses amounted to about a third of those engaged in the battle, a staggering percentage for a fight lasting about two hours. Both Taliaferro and Ewell were wounded. A bullet from a Federal volley struck down Ewell with a leg wound that required amputation.

The battle on the 28th had little impact on the outcome of the campaign, but it could have had a significant role. After the fighting subsided, General King decided to move on rather than awaiting reinforcements. The action had revealed Jackson's location, and King's division was "the one Federal force interposing between" Jackson and Longstreet. Some historians have criticized King's decision to withdraw after engaging Jackson. Certainly if Pope could have concentrated his forces and attacked at Groveton early the following day, Jackson might have been defeated, and then Pope could have concentrated against Lee with overwhelming numbers. An expert on this campaign, however, concluded that King made the correct decision. Jackson might have succeeded in destroying King's division before Pope could send reinforcements. The ongoing lack of coordination and alacrity in Pope's army casts doubt on the likelihood of Federal success even if King had remained at Groveton.[86]

Pope now knew where Jackson had posted his half of Lee's army, and he was anxious to take advantage of his superior numbers. The opportunity to crush Jackson and then go after Lee and Longstreet had finally presented itself. On the verge of an immense opportunity for victory and personal glory, Pope, simply said, failed miserably. On August 29, as Pope's forces converged to attack Jackson, Longstreet's command was arriving undetected to bolster Jackson and even the odds of another Confederate victory. Pope's unwieldy command structure, with its triumvirate of mediocre to incompetent corps commanders, proved too great a handicap to overcome against the capable Lee, Jackson and Longstreet.

Still unaware of Longstreet presence within supporting distance, Pope ordered attacks along Jackson's defensive line posted along the unfinished railroad embankment. On the morning of August 29 Major General Franz Sigel commenced piecemeal attacks on Jackson as ordered by Pope. As always, Sigel proved ineffective. At least this time he was not driven ignominiously from the field, as he had been at Wilson's Creek the previous August. After a few hours Sigel's troops were pulled back to allow them to recuperate. Pope continued the somewhat disjointed attacks with several divisions, including Hooker's and Kearny's from the III Corps, Army of the Potomac and Reno's and Stevens' from the IX Corps. By evening Jackson's line had been severely pressed on the left, but it had held. Lee and Longstreet awaited their opportunity to counterattack.

On the 30th Pope, thinking that Jackson was retreating, ordered another advance. Remarkably, Pope still did not know that Longstreet's 30,000 troops had reached the battlefield the previous day. As the Federal divisions renewed the attack along the railroad embankment at places known to Civil War relic hunters as the "Deep Cut" and "The Dump," Longstreet prepared to attack from south of the Warrenton Turnpike. Hatch's division had clashed with some of Longstreet's troops on the evening of the 29th near Groveton; nevertheless, Pope had no idea of Longstreet's whereabouts. Pope's attention

The "Deep Cut" on the Second Bull Run Battlefield, where Jackson repulsed Federal attacks.

was fixed on Jackson to the exclusion of all else. His failure to account for Longstreet's command enabled General Lee to gain the upper hand in this Second Battle of Bull Run.

Pope hurled heavy attacks against Jackson on the afternoon of the 30th, but massed Confederate artillery and infantry firing from the cover of the railroad embankment checked them effectively. Pope's uncoordinated attacks failed to hit a soft spot in Jackson's line, and the Federal commander never concentrated sufficient strength to punch through the enemy line with a single well-executed assault. Later in the afternoon, with Pope's army bloodied and weary following its costly and ineffective attacks north of the turnpike, Lee launched Longstreet's command on a sweeping attack south of the main battlefield. Throughout the battle Pope had practically ignored the possibility of attack from that quarter, just as he had failed to keep track of Longstreet's command. As a result, few Federal units were covering Pope's left flank south of the Warrenton Turnpike. Longstreet's attack struck the Federals in a vulnerable spot, completely altering the course of the battle and the campaign.

The 5th and 10th New York infantry regiments of Colonel Gouverneur K. Warren's 3rd Brigade, 2nd Division, V Corps stood alone facing Longstreet's onslaught. The 5th New York, a Zouave outfit with colorful red and blue uniforms, had distinguished itself at the Battle of Gaines's Mill a little over a month prior to this battle. Five regiments from the rebel Texas Brigade swarmed out from the cover of the woods along Young's Branch and charged the New Yorkers. Unable to fire for fear of hitting skirmishers from the 10th New York, the 5th held until the friendly troops had cleared the field of fire. By the time the 5th had fired its first volley, the Texans had them in a deadly enfilading fire and nearly surrounded. With the Texans closing with bayonets, the 5th turned and raced for cover rather than surrendering. The Texans shot them down by the scores; and when the final tally was counted, 297 of the 490 men present with the 5th New York were casualties. Perhaps as many as 124 men from the 5th New York were killed outright or died of their wounds at Second Bull Run, making this the highest number of men killed in a single battle from any Federal infantry regiment during the entire Civil War.[87]

The situation for the rest of Pope's army was not quite as dire as it was for the 5th New York that afternoon; but after Longstreet's unexpected strike, Pope struggled to prevent a complete Federal disaster. There is no consensus as to how serious Pope's defeat at Second Bull Run truly was. Historian Jeffry Wert suggested that Lee got closer to "shattering a Union army into pieces" here than in any other battle during the war.[88] But as it had been at the Battle of First Bull Run the previous summer, the Confederates were bloodied and fairly spent by nightfall on the 30th. It was a humiliating defeat for the North, for sure. However, Lee and his army had accomplished more than could be expected, mostly as a result of very poor generalship on the Federal side. As it played out, the Federals managed to make a stand on Henry House Hill, disengage and retreat. Lee certainly would have destroyed Pope's army if he could have that evening. In brief summary, the Second Bull Run Campaign was a monumental example of how poor Federal generalship altered the course of the war in favor of the Confederates during the second half of 1862. Pope failed to discern Lee's plan and did not adapt tactics to take advantage of the opportunity to attack the divided Confederate army.

Pope regrouped at Centerville, a few miles east of the battlefield on the road to Washington. Lee dispatched Jackson yet again in an attempt to cut off the Federal retreat route to Washington. Pope suspected this potential turning movement, for once, and sent Major General Jesse Reno with IX Corps troops and Major General Phillip Kearny and his III Corps troops to ensure Jackson would not further molest his retreat to Washington. On September 1, Reno launched a late afternoon attack on Jackson's command near the Chantilly Plantation during an intense thunderstorm. Brigadier General Isaac Stevens, a promising, capable commander who had graduated first in the West Point Class of 1839 ahead of General in Chief Halleck, was shot through the head and killed while leading his brigade in a charge at Chantilly. The widely-admired Major General Phillip Kearny rode into a cornfield alone and was shot and killed by a soldier from the 49th Georgia as he spurred his horse to escape. The loss of these two able Federal leaders deprived the Federal Army of potential future corps or army commanders of considerable talent and ability. The fighting at Chantilly ended on the evening of September 1 with no clear victor. Pope, thoroughly demoralized, continued his retreat to Washington rather than making another attempt to crush Jackson's detached command.

The Campaign of Second Bull Run was so poorly managed by the Federal high command that perhaps only the Federal performance in the 1862 Shenandoah Campaign compares for ineptitude by either side during the entire war. Pope could have anticipated Lee's plan and reacted swiftly to crush his separated commands in succession. Had the situation been reversed and had Lee faced a divided Federal army that summer, there is little reason to doubt that he would have crippled at least one of the divided enemy commands. While it is obvious that Lee benefited from a more versatile, flexible and maneuverable army and operational situation, he also demonstrated savvy, intuition and audacity at a level far superior to his foe that August. His tactical plan was supremely precarious, making the outcome seem all the more remarkable.

When the casualties for the Second Bull Run Campaign including Chantilly and Brawner's Farm were tallied, the sum for Federal losses came to 14,462 of which 4,263 were listed as captured or missing. Some of these missing would later return to their commands, but most of them were taken prisoner. Confederate losses totaled 9,474 with at least 8,353 men killed and wounded at the Bull Run battlefield alone.[89] The retreating Federals again lost far more captured men than did the Confederates, but the losses in men actually shot in combat were comparatively even considering that Pope launched several attacks on well-protected Confederate positions on August 29 and 30.

Having succeeded incredibly well in accomplishing his objectives that summer, General Lee proceeded to attempt the first meaningful Confederate offensive into Federal territory. On September 3, 1862, Lee wrote to President Davis opining that the Federal armies in Virginia were "much weakened and demoralized," and the newly recruited troops remained unorganized, requiring "time to prepare for the field." He suggested that it was the "most propitious time since the commencement of the war for the Confederate army to enter Maryland," and "afford her an opportunity of throwing off the oppression to which she is now subject." Lee believed that moving into Maryland would at least draw the Federals north of the Potomac; and if even if the move were to be "prevented," the outcome would "not result in much evil." On September 4, Lee wrote to advise his president that he was "fully persuaded of the benefit that will result from an expedition into Maryland, and I shall proceed to make the movement at once.... Should the results of the expedition justify it, I propose to enter Pennsylvania, unless you should deem it unadvisable upon political or other grounds."[90]

The Confederate intent to invade Pennsylvania and accomplish much more than a brief raid would have been difficult enough, but a happenstance on September 13, 1862, shifted all the advantage to the Federals. Two soldiers from the 27th Indiana Infantry found a copy of General Lee's Special Orders No. 191 in a meadow near Frederick, Maryland, a document of ten parts giving directions to different commanders in Lee's army for the forthcoming week. The paper, signed by R.H. Chilton, Lee's adjutant, was quickly forwarded to General McClellan. In effect Lee's orders divided his army into four separate forces scattered over twenty-five miles. Lee intended to capture the Federal post at Harpers Ferry, the former national armory. A Federal garrison of about 14,000 occupied the place, and Lee did not wish to leave it intact behind his invasion route. Lee ordered the divisions of Generals McLaws and R.H. Anderson to "take the route to Harper's Ferry, and by Friday morning … endeavor to capture Harper's Ferry and vicinity." General Walker with his division was to "take possession of Loudoun Heights" commanding the Federal post from across the Shenandoah River. General Longstreet was directed to march his command to Boonsboro, Maryland, and, after the capture of Harpers Ferry, "the commands of Generals Jackson, McLaws, and Walker" were ordered to "join the main body of the army" and Longstreet at Boonsboro.[91]

Major General George B. McClellan had been restored to command of all troops assigned to the defense of Washington, D.C., on September 2. Most of the troops from Pope's army were transferred to the Army of the Potomac, giving McClellan an even larger command to confront Lee. With the reorganization of the Army of the Potomac completed, on September 5 McClellan led his army from Washington's environs to the northwest into Maryland to turn back the invading rebels. With him went the I, II, V, VI and XII Corps from the Army of the Potomac accompanied by Major General Ambrose Burnside's IX Corp, about 95,000 men counting infantry, artillery and cavalry. The III and XI Corps remained behind, posted to defend the capital's forts.[92]

Several new and green regiments had been assigned to McClellan's army just before it left Washington. Many of these new regiments had only recently organized, having been mustered into the service in August. Two months previously in July, President Lincoln had issued a call for 300,000 men to serve for three years. In August 1862 two of my ancestors answered Lincoln's call. James Earley enlisted in the 116th Ohio Infantry, and Joseph Craven enrolled in a cavalry company assigned to the Ringgold Cavalry Battalion from western Pennsylvania, these men were my father's two grandfathers. All across the Union new army units were organized to replace the losses incurred from the first year of fighting. Over 420,000 men were furnished by the loyal states in answer to Lincoln's July call for recruits, and McClellan's army had its share of new regiments manned by those inexperienced soldiers.[93]

General McClellan, nevertheless, was highly confident that he would whip Lee's seasoned veterans, despite the influx of green outfits sown into his army corps. On September 13, the day he was handed Lee's Special Orders No. 191, Lee's battle plans, McClellan informed the president: "I think Lee has made a gross mistake, and he will be severely punished for it. The army is in motion as rapidly as possible. I hope for a great success.... I have all the plans of the rebels, and will catch them in their own trap if my men are equal to the emergency." In a letter to General in Chief Halleck sent the same day, McClellan advised Halleck that he would "do everything in my power" to rescue the Federal garrison at Harpers Ferry. McClellan still believed he would be outnumbered if Lee could reunite his commands, and he believed "the fate of the nation" depended upon his success in Maryland. McClellan also advised Halleck that he was confident that no enemy force was "immediately threatening Washington or Baltimore"; thus, his looming battle with Lee should take precedence. Yet again McClellan overestimated the strength of Lee's army; he informed Halleck that he believed that "120,000 men or more ... commanded by Lee in person, intended to attempt penetrating Pennsylvania."[94] McClellan's penchant for grossly overestimating enemy strength would again have a grave impact on the outcome of the campaign.

By September 13, the day McClellan obtained Lee's plans, the Confederates were already getting into position to besiege Harpers Ferry. When Lee's army began moving northward in early September, General McClellan had urged General in Chief Halleck to withdraw Federal garrisons from Martinsburg and Harpers Ferry. Halleck, however, believed that Harpers Ferry could be defended despite the fact that the place was obviously vulnerable to attack from surrounding mountainous terrain. One Confederate general once said that he would rather capture the place forty times than defend it once. Halleck's decision to leave 14,000 troops in such a vulnerable position, inviting capture, remains a mystery. The folly of defending Harpers Ferry parallels the Confederate situation at Fort Donelson earlier that year.[95]

With General Lee's plans revealed, McClellan felt sufficiently confident to finally take the offensive. He planned to send the bulk of his army through the northern gaps of South Mountain to attack the divided rebel army at Boonsboro. To relieve the garrison at Harpers Ferry he ordered Major General William Franklin to take three divisions through Crampton's Gap, the southern approach to Harpers Ferry through South Mountain. McClellan obviously hoped that Franklin's three divisions combined with the 14,000 defenders at Harpers Ferry would be sufficient to save Harpers Ferry while his main force crushed the outnumbered rebels at Boonsboro. General Lee had accompanied General Longstreet with his command to Hagerstown, leaving only Major General D.H. Hill's Division and a small cavalry force to defend Fox's Gap and Turner's Gap along the National Road at South Mountain. McClellan's route to Harpers Ferry or Boonsboro passed through these gaps at South Mountain; the task of delaying McClellan until the Confederate commands could reunite was assigned to D.H. Hill with his division and Brigadier General Howell Cobb's Brigade from McLaws' Division.

McClellan thought he could push through the South Mountain gaps with little opposition. The I, VI and IX Corps were sent into the road passages through South Mountain on September 14, but a determined stand by D.H. Hill's Confederates necessitated a daylong battle at South Mountain. Fighting in heavily forested mountain terrain, cut with ravines and overgrown with tangles of thick vegetation, the Federals made slow progress against fierce opposition. By evening of the 14th, the Federals had pushed through the South Mountain gaps and cleared the way for an attack on Lee's scattered forces. The battles at Turner's Gap and Crampton's Gap were impressive Federal victories. Outnumbering the Confederates by less than two to one, the attacking Federals had overcome difficult terrain to throw Hill's troops off the mountain passes. Confederate losses were not fully reported but were probably around 2,300 in total. The Federals suffered about 1,800 casualties, including Major General Jesse L. Reno who was killed while leading the IX Corps at Fox's Gap.[96] D.H. Hill failed to prevent McClellan's army from making the passage through South Mountain, but his efforts succeeded in delaying McClellan's plans to assail the divided Confederate command at Boonsboro.

General McClellan, having brushed aside Hill's defensive stand at South Mountain with comparative ease, was in position and on time to fulfill his plans to relieve Harpers Ferry and crush Lee's divided forces. He was in an enviable position, holding the keys to victory. On September 15, 1862, George B. McClellan possessed perhaps the greatest opportunity for annihilating an enemy army granted by fortuity to any commander in American history. His performance during the following three days squandered this incredible boon, rendering the bloodshed and horror at South Mountain meaningless and inconsequential. McClellan's mistakes, here again, were essentially sins of omission spawned by a consuming fear of failure. The events of these three September days were representative of the flaws that plagued the Army of the Potomac, America's star-crossed army, for most of its existence.

After the fighting on South Mountain, General Franklin had access to Pleasant Valley, just a few miles north of Harpers Ferry. The bulk of McClellan's army passed through Turner's Gap and was free to move against Longstreet's vulnerable command or to move down Pleasant Valley to relieve Harpers Ferry and perhaps crush Jackson's command. There was no time to spare in order to save the garrison at Harpers Ferry. Nevertheless, General McClellan did practically nothing on September 15. He explained in his report dated October 15, 1862, that he had ordered his corps to attack at once if the rebels were encountered in marching columns, but if they were found deployed for battle his corps were to prepare to attack and await his arrival at the front. When McClellan finally reached the front on the afternoon of the 15th, he found that the Confederates were in line of battle. Despite his purported order for his corps "to be placed in position to attack," only two divisions, Richardson's and Sykes', were "in position" when he arrived at the front. At that point McClellan "found that it was too late to attack that day." Somehow the original priority to rescue the garrison at Harpers Ferry, with the promise of "forced marches" for that purpose, was set aside when Franklin encountered active rebel forces at Pleasant Valley. Yet again McClellan had concentrated his efforts to ensure that he could not be beaten decisively; thus, the garrison at Harpers Ferry was left to its fate. As shrouding mists cleared on the 15th, Confederate batteries at Maryland Heights and Loudoun Heights coupled with Jackson's artillery began a destructive cannonade hitting the Federals from all angles at Harpers Ferry. At around 8 a.m. white flags went up as the garrison signaled its surrender. Garrison commander Colonel Dixon Miles was mortally wounded by one of the final Confederate salvos fired after the white flag went up. Over 11,000 Federals were surrendered along with seventy-three cannons and 13,000 small arms. It was the largest surrender of Federal troops in any battle of the Civil War.[97]

A dense fog again shrouded the region on the following morning, Tuesday, September 16. The curtain of fog could have benefited a Federal attack to some extent, and McClellan then had 60,000 troops near Sharpsburg in position to attack Lee. With a large part of Lee's army still separated for the Harpers Ferry operation, McClellan enjoyed odds of nearly four to one in his favor against Longstreet and Lee that morning. Still he delayed. At 7:45 a.m. he informed General Franklin, "If the enemy is in force here, I shall attack him this morning." He also sent a message to General Halleck saying he did not know the strength of the enemy "position just in front of Sharpsburg," but he would "attack as soon as situation of enemy is developed." McClellan should have known that much of Lee's army could not have consolidated, even though Harpers Ferry had surrendered the previous day. In his report McClellan offered the following explanation: "The morning of the 16th (during which there was considerable artillery firing) was spent in obtaining information as to the ground, rectifying the position of the troops, and perfecting the arrangements for the attack."[98]

With the benefit of the delay on the 16th McClellan devised his attack plan. He somewhat cryptically described his tactical plan in his report about a month later: "The design was to make the main attack upon the enemy's left—at least to create a diversion in favor of the main attack, with the hope of something more by assailing the enemy's right—and, as soon as one or both of the flank movements were fully successful, to attack their center with any reserve I might then have on hand." His report also mentioned that on the afternoon of the 16th Major General Joseph Hooker and his I Corps were sent across Antietam Creek "with orders to attack, and, if possible, turn the enemy's left." The wording was ambiguous as to whether the attack was intended for the 16th. The shifting of the I Corps was, in any case, too late in the day to accomplish much.[99]

Early on the morning of Wednesday, September 17, 1862, having wasted two indispensable days in preparation, General McClellan attacked Lee's Army of Northern Virginia on the outskirts of Sharpsburg, Maryland. The fighting, known to history as the Battle of Antietam after the stream flowing across the battlefield, inflicted more American casualties than any single day of combat in any war. This single bloodiest day in American history, as students of the Civil War are aware, marked a pivotal point, a transition affecting the past, present and future of the United States. But students of the war now can only contemplate what might have been altered, what blood and treasure might have been saved, if General McClellan had managed the Maryland Campaign and the Battle of Antietam another way.

General McClellan did not, in fact, manage the Battle of Antietam particularly well even after he finally authorized the I Corp to attack around 5:30 a.m. on the 17th. The Federal attacks succeeded in driving back Lee's Confederates across most of the

The Miller House on the Antietam Battlefield in the area where the Federal I Corps attacked, as it appears today.

A view of the Miller House taken around the time of the War. Library of Congress Civil War Collection.

The sunken road known as Bloody Lane on the Antietam Battlefield. The lane was nearly filled with dead Confederates during the battle.

battlefield, but the attacks were not well coordinated and were delivered piecemeal in some instances. Major General Ambrose Burnside directed the assault on Lee's right quite poorly. He chose to cross Antietam Creek via Rohrbach Bridge, funneling his regiments across this narrow passage under fire from higher ground. There were other locations not far distant from the bridge to ford the creek. His attack was needlessly delayed as a result of his time-consuming crossing at the bridge. The slow progress of Burnside's attack allowed time for Confederate reinforcements to reach the field from Harpers Ferry, changing the reckoning of the battle and ultimately its outcome. The Federal soldiers fought well at Antietam, well enough to earn a victory. They were certainly the equals of their rebel counterparts. And despite a pedestrian performance in this key battle, McClellan succeeded in positioning his forces for a decisive victory by the evening of September 17.

General Lee fought his army skillfully at Antietam. He anticipated the main Federal effort on his left along the Hagerstown Turnpike and made preparations to meet it. Lee adeptly shifted his troops to parry and blunt threatening Federal attacks throughout the day. Conversely, McClellan failed to reinforce success where Lee was threatened. Lee was a splendid commander when fighting on the defensive; and the Antietam battlefield was good defensive ground, playing to Lee's advantage. Lee also benefited at Antietam from opportune adjustments by his able subordinate commanders. At a critical stage of the battle, Brigadier General Jubal Early checked an attack by the Federal II Corps in the West Woods that threatened disaster for the rebels. Early later explained: "Had we retired

Burnside Bridge over Antietam Creek viewed from the Confederate position. Here the Federal attack on Lee's right was stalled for hours by a small number of Georgia troops.

from the fear of being flanked or cut off, the enemy must have obtained possession of the woods ... which would have resulted in a decisive defeat to us, and a probable destruction of our army."[100] Yet the most important element benefiting Lee at Antietam was luck. He was very fortunate that Burnside's plodding attack, which by afternoon threatened to collapse his right flank, was checked by A.P. Hill's Light Division arriving just in time from Harpers Ferry.

At the end of the day the Army of Northern Virginia remained on the field outside Sharpsburg. Both armies were severely battered, but McClellan had an additional 32,300 fresh troops available to continue the battle while Lee had already committed almost every available man to the fight. The casualties, while staggering, were remarkably even considering the terrain of the battlefield and that the Federals were on the attack. On the 17th the Federals had engaged 53,632 men against 30,646 Confederates. Federal losses were 2,157 killed, 9,716 wounded, and 1009 missing compared to 1,754 killed, 8,649 wounded and 1,127 missing for the Army of Northern Virginia. The casualties amounted to 24 percent of the Federals and 38 percent of the Confederates engaged at Antietam. McClellan and his Army of the Potomac were disadvantaged somewhat in the Maryland Campaign because of the large number of green regiments that had been recently added as reinforcements. Overall these newly organized Federal regiments suffered casualties at about twice the percentage rate of the veteran units.[101]

On the morning of September 18, McClellan did not feel confident of success without receiving substantial reinforcements. It was a curious assessment of the situation considering the large number of fresh troops he still had available. Rather than being thankful that Lee remained on the field awaiting renewal of the conflict, McClellan feared the loss of what little had been gained on the previous day. His reasoning, from hindsight, seems somewhat inscrutable. Had the Confederates been driven from Sharpsburg, their retreat would have required a crossing of the nearby Potomac River while being pursued. In sum, McClellan, by hesitating to attack on the 18th, passed on a very rare opportunity to achieve a victory of annihilation over the Confederacy's best field army.

A comparative assessment of the Maryland Campaign reveals much to criticize regarding both sides of the conflict. As it played out, the campaign served as a Federal victory; it presented President Lincoln with an opportunity to issue the Emancipation Proclamation, made public a few days after the battle. The Confederates had little hope of accomplishing more than a raid into the North when the campaign began, so a withdrawal back into Virginia was, barring the unexpected, inevitable. But McClellan's victory at South Mountain and Lee's retreat from Sharpsburg rendered the impression of an overall Confederate defeat.

President Davis's approval of the Maryland Campaign in September 1862 suggests a lack of reasoned strategic perspective. Confederate successes during the summer of 1862 doubtless played a significant role in building over confidence in the capabilities of Lee and the Army of Northern Virginia. Pope's defeat at Second Bull Run coupled with McClellan's timid generalship during the Peninsula Campaign was sufficient to convince the Confederate high command that an invasion of Northern territory could succeed. General Lee had succeeded time and again by taking calculated risks that ignored accepted tactical doctrine. He continued his high risk modus operandi during the Maryland Campaign, dividing his army and making tactical adjustments that should have brought catastrophic defeat to his command. It is not the purpose of this study to suggest alternative strategies that might have applied; instead, the purpose here is to assess and compare the merits of the decisions of the principals and the outcomes of their strategies as events unfolded. Concisely, the Maryland Campaign as planned by the Confederate high command was an ill-advised concept that should never have been attempted. Worse yet, Davis and Lee failed to learn from this failure and were doomed to repeat it. Unlike General Lee, many of the common soldiers who participated in the Maryland Campaign realized that the Confederacy could not successfully invade the North. Confederate Brigadier General Dorsey Pender tersely summarized the reality of the Confederacy's limitations after the Battle of Antietam: "Our Army has shown itself incapable of invasion and we had best stick to the defensive."[102] It was unfortunate for the Confederates that Lee and Davis simply couldn't see it.

The Federal approach during the Maryland Campaign was equally flawed. While the Confederates undertook the campaign with methods bordering on rashness, McClellan and Halleck managed the campaign with the limited goal of turning back Lee's invasion attempt. Much more could and should have been accomplished by the Federals. Halleck himself was fixated on the security of the capital. Halleck cautioned McClellan about the priority of Washington's defense on September 13, the day Lee's lost order was found: "I am of the opinion that the enemy will send a small column toward Pennsylvania, so as to draw your forces in that direction; then suddenly move on Washington … you attach too little importance to the capital. I assure you that you are wrong." Two complete army corps were withheld to defend Washington during the Battle of Antietam, as it turned out, unnecessarily.[103] McClellan's decision not to concentrate on Jackson's separated command at Harpers Ferry, knowing as he did that Lee and Longstreet were north of the Potomac in limited force, was the foremost error of the campaign. When McClellan opted to concentrate on Longstreet's command rather than Harpers Ferry, he inexplicably failed to press the attack immediately after his army had forced passage of South Mountain. Ultimately, McClellan accomplished his primary goal of repelling the rebel incursion into Maryland. Unfortunately for his historical reputation, McClellan failed to severely punish Lee for the mistake of dividing his army in the presence of the concentrated Federal army, something he had asserted that he would do. The old adage that fools rush in did not apply in McClellan's situation on September 13. His chance to take advantage of Lee's vulnerability came with a brief window of opportunity. McClellan's slavish obsession with safety was fully displayed during the Maryland Campaign. While McClellan was unquestionably an able strategist and quite capable of winning the war if given an unbridled command free of time restraints, he again proved incapable of adjusting rapidly to fluid situations. At Antietam, as he had done during the Peninsular Campaign, he failed to take charge of the battle, relying instead on his corps commanders to fight the battle incrementally. McClellan's inability to adjust and react with alacrity enabled the Confederates to escape a potentially catastrophic defeat during the Maryland Campaign.

After the Battle of Antietam Lee and the Army of Northern Virginia fell back into Virginia without much interference. The series of far-reaching mistakes on the part of the Federal high command inaugurated in the summer of 1862 continued in the West while the situation in the East stalemated. General Halleck had, in effect, botched the Federal war effort after the Battle of Shiloh with his sluggish, safety-first methods. In a short period following the capture of Corinth, Mississippi, the Confederacy was able to change the nature of the war, reversing a trend that had been leading to defeat and collapse in the West.

Most of the onus for enabling the Confederate resurgence in the West in the second half of 1862 should be ascribed to General in Chief Halleck and Major General Don C. Buell. As early as June 11, 1862, Halleck had informed Buell that Chattanooga would be his operational objective. He told Buell, "...I am satisfied that your line of operations should be on Chattanooga.... By moving on Chattanooga you prevent a junction between Smith and Beauregard and are on the direct line to Atlanta."[104] Chattanooga could and should have been captured immediately after the Confederates withdrew from Corinth, Mississippi. Chattanooga, in fact, was a more important objective than Corinth, as was demonstrated later in the war when it was captured and used as a springboard for the Atlanta Campaign. The Confederates recognized its importance and, by reinforcing it, altered the course of the war.

Buell probably had sufficient strength to capture Chattanooga, which was a priority for President Lincoln. But he was a poor choice for the assignment. Halleck should have known that Buell shared some of the negative traits of General McClellan. Like McClellan, Buell was a good organizer and disciplinarian, and also like McClellan he was methodical and apparently incapable of adjusting speedily to fluid situations. Buell's attitude towards Confederate civilians was much like McClellan's in that both tried to spare Southerners from the ravages of war. His policy towards civilians greatly increased his logistical difficulties by restricting foraging. Halleck had observed Buell's limitations and drawbacks prior to the Battle of Shiloh, so he should have expected more of the same from Buell when he assigned him to operate against Chattanooga. General Grant would have been a better choice for that assignment or even Brigadier General Ormsby Mitchel for that matter.

By July 24, 1862, the vanguard of General Braxton Bragg's Army of the Mississippi, traveling via a long and circuitous route, reached Chattanooga. After the capture of Corinth, Bragg had assumed command of the Confederate Western Department in place of General Beauregard. Reacting to Halleck's dissipation of his forces after Corinth was captured, the Confederates assumed an offensive stance in the West while General Lee was winning battles in the East. The Confederates took steps to protect Vicksburg and Chattanooga and to recover lost territory in Tennessee and Kentucky.

The Confederate operational plan for the fall of 1862 envisioned an invasion of Kentucky to seize that state for the Confederacy and an effort to threaten Louisville and Cincinnati. Confederate forces that had been concentrated prior to the Battle of Shiloh were divided and assigned separate tasks. Confederate troops in Mississippi under Generals Van Dorn and Price were to occupy General Grant's force around Corinth while forces commanded by Generals Bragg and Smith invaded Kentucky. Major General Edmund Kirby Smith launched the Confederate western offensive from Knoxville, Tennessee, on August 14. Smith made Lexington, Kentucky, his initial objective. Smith's movement into Kentucky outflanked Federal Brigadier General G.W. Morgan at Cumberland Gap in eastern Kentucky; Morgan was eventually forced to abandon that strategic position. Bragg began his advance from Chattanooga on August 28. Bragg's advance initiated a flurry of activity in the West and precipitated several battles and engagements in September and October.

When Bragg headed northward from Chattanooga in late August, he presented the Federals with an opportunity to shorten the war and accomplish one of the requirements for defeating the Confederacy. The Confederate operational plan was flawed from the onset. Smith and Bragg each held separate commands and were thus doomed to act according to their own advantage. In effect, the Confederate Western offensive in the fall of 1862 lacked essential coordination; ultimately, Bragg's offensive amounted to an attempt to do too much with too little. Unfortunately, General Buell failed to take advantage of the situation.

General Buell should have seized Chattanooga immediately after Bragg departed. Capturing Chattanooga would have left Bragg without a base for operations, leaving his army cut off from supply and stranded. One historian suggested that Buell could have set the stage for the destruction of Bragg's army by taking Chattanooga in September. Instead, Buell decided to withdraw toward Nashville, in effect abandoning Federal gains in northern Alabama and allowing Bragg to take the initiative.[105] Buell's command style mirrored that of the majority of Federal commanders during the Civil War. Far too often Federal generals overestimated enemy numerical strength and fighting prowess. Interestingly, General Halleck addressed this phenomenon in a message to Buell himself in the fall of 1862. Halleck mentioned that President Lincoln could not understand "why we cannot march as the enemy marches, live as he lives, fight as he fights, unless we admit the inferiority of our troops and our generals." Buell replied by basically suggesting that the rebels were, in some important ways, actually superior to the Federals. Buell replied, "We can give good reasons why we cannot do all that the enemy has attempted to do … without ascribing the difference to the inferiority of our generals, though that may be true. The spirit of rebellion enforces a subordination and patient submission to privation and want which public sentiment renders absolutely impossible among our troops…. It is absolutely certain that … the discipline of the rebel army is superior to ours."[106] Buell's attitude to some extent was justified by his awareness of the rebel's basic morale advantage. Nevertheless, his fearful approach to operations was unjustified. Concisely, Buell failed miserably at a crucial point. A confident and aggressive commander in his situation would have inflicted a serious defeat upon the Confederacy.

Events in the weeks following Bragg's departure from Chattanooga unfolded quite favorably for the Confederates. Bragg's column marched northward without much interference, as Buell chose to shadow rather than confront the enemy. Buell followed northward to Murfreesboro and then to Nashville. He pushed his army across the state line to Bowling Green, Kentucky, eventually falling back to Louisville on the Ohio River while Bragg roamed in Kentucky.

After days of maneuvering in the drought-plagued Kentucky hills, units from both armies stumbled into a skirmish while looking for a source of water at Doctor's Creek near Perryville, Kentucky. The fighting commencing in the early hours of October 8, 1862, intensified and expanded into a full-scale battle without either army commander realizing it. General Buell could not hear the roar of the battle although his headquarters was only a few miles away, and Bragg did not realize until the next day that his troops were confronted by the entire Army of the Ohio. The battle was not well managed by either side, but the Federals blundered enough to allow Bragg to escape from a potentially perilous situation. Aggressive leadership by subordinate commanders on both sides, including Confederate Major General Benjamin F. Cheatham and Federal Brigadier General Phillip Sheridan, resulted in a hard-fought and bloody battle at Perryville. Federal III Corps Commander Charles Gilbert put in a mixed performance that contributed to what success the Confederates achieved. He was later condemned for not supporting McCook's corps on the Federal left, which ultimately exposed this own left flank. Gilbert was replaced and never again held a field command during the war.

Bragg realized during the night that he was outnumbered, so he arranged for an immediate withdrawal to cover his retreat route back to Tennessee. The Confederate invasion in Kentucky was checked at Perryville, despite the fact that the battle was essentially a draw. Bragg fell back to Harrodsburg intending to "form a junction" with Kirby Smith. Once there he "offered the enemy battle," but Buell was having none of that. Federal casualties at Perryville totaled 4,241. Confederate casualty reports were more difficult to determine, but a total of 3,396 is estimated. The casualty rate as a percentage of troops engaged was one of the highest of the war, demonstrating the severity of the fighting there.[107]

While Bragg was invading Kentucky, two Confederate forces in Mississippi led by Major Generals Sterling Price and Earl Van Dorn battled Federals commanded by Major General Ulysses Grant. On September 14, Price seized the Federal supply depot at Iuka, Mississippi. The move against Iuka placed Price's army dangerously close to a superior Federal force around Corinth. Van Dorn and his army remained several miles to the west, beyond supporting range. General Grant, acting on General in Chief Halleck's suggestion, reacted quickly by sending two separate forces commanded by Major Generals William Rosecrans and Edward O.C. Ord to trap Price at Iuka. Grant's battle plan called for Ord to move on Iuka from the north and await the sound of Rosecrans attacking from the south. On the afternoon of September 19, as Rosecrans' force neared Iuka, Price sent two brigades south of town to attack the Federals. Rosecrans wasn't ready; his column was stretched out and was slow to shift into line of battle in wooded terrain. Price's two brigades drove the Federals back and captured some artillery before Rosecrans was able to deploy his force and check the rebel attack. Grant had accompanied Ord on the march to Iuka, and Ord's column arrived there before Rosecrans. Grant's plan called for a coordinated attack to commence when Rosecrans approached Iuka from the south. However, Grant and Ord did not hear the roar of battle and thunder of artillery as expected from the fighting south of town. Grant and Ord remained inactive, waiting for the battle to begin until darkness rendered the battle plan obsolete.

After nightfall General Price managed to slip away with his army on a southbound road that Rosecrans unaccountably left unguarded. Price joined forces with General Van Dorn on September 28, 1862, at Ripley, Mississippi, southwest of Corinth. Price's aggressive reaction at Iuka worked in his favor, and he wisely retreated before Grant could take advantage of his superior numbers. The Federals reported 790 casualties, including 141 killed and 613 wounded. Reports and estimates of Confederate casualties vary from a total of 693 to 1,516.[108] Confederate Brigadier General Henry Little also was a casualty of the fighting at Iuka; he was shot in the forehead and killed while conferring with General Price shortly after the battle began.

Defeated Major General Sterling Price replied to a letter from Tennessee Governor Isham G. Harris from Ripley, Mississippi, on the day he arrived there. Governor Harris in his letter asked Price when he would arrive in the Nashville vicinity. The governor assured Price that he would arrange forage for Price's army, and that he was ready to aid Price in any way possible to facilitate his movement into Tennessee. Price explained that his reason for being at Iuka was in "obedience to instructions from General Bragg" to march to Nashville. "Your Excellency may rest assured," wrote Price, "that I most earnestly desire the liberation of your State, and shall leave nothing undone to secure it." Price informed the governor that he had joined forces with Van Dorn; and that together they intended to "at once proceed northward, endeavoring" to defeat the Federals in their front. Price also explained that the Federal force at Corinth proved much larger that he anticipated, and that alone kept him "from carrying out General Bragg's orders."[109] Van Dorn was given command of the combined armies at Ripley. After considering his options, Van Dorn chose to attack Corinth before proceeding to Tennessee.

Immediately after the fighting at Iuka, General Grant was unsure of what to expect from Van Dorn. Grant believed that other stations under his command were threatened sufficiently to prevent his going after Van Dorn with a concentrated force. Grant decided to await developments and react accordingly. By October 1, it was clear to Grant that Van Dorn intended to attack Corinth with Price and what forces he could concentrate. General Rosecrans with about 23,000 troops manned the defenses at Corinth awaiting Van Dorn's attack on October 2, 1862. Grant ordered in reinforcements from Bolivar, Tennessee, for Rosecrans, but as Van Dorn was advancing from the northwest, these outnumbered troops could not reach the Corinth defenses before the Confederate attack.

Van Dorn launched his attack around 10 a.m. on October 3, hitting the outlying defenses northwest of Corinth. The Federals were driven in and retreated to another line of earthworks near and around the town. Federal Brigadier General Pleasant A. Hackleman was mortally wounded and two other Federal brigade commanders were also wounded while attempting to rally their men during the first day of battle. Van Dorn renewed his attacks the following morning around 10 a.m. The temperature had already reached ninety degrees on a day destined to become fiercer than the heat itself. The battle is best remembered for the combat around a Federal earthwork known as Battery Robinett. There five Confederate regiments were severely mauled in a desperate effort to overrun that earthwork. Colonel William Rogers of the 2nd Texas Infantry, who had served with Jefferson Davis during the Mexican War, was riddled with bullets and killed while carrying his regimental flag in front of Battery Robinett. The 11th Missouri and 27th Ohio infantry regiments fired a devastating volley into the rebels from a position thirty yards away just as Confederates swept over the battery's earthen walls. A counterattack by fresh Federal units pushed the Confederates back at bayonet point in brief hand-to-hand fighting. Van Dorn's rebels scrambled for the rear across a field thickly strewn with their dead and dying comrades. The Confederates at least had limited success in capturing a redoubt and overrunning a battery on the Federal right flank, but here again the attackers were soon cut off and driven back. Before noon the fighting was over; Van Dorn, realizing the day was lost, quickly withdrew and retreated to the northwest.

General Grant had given Rosecrans specific orders to pursue the Confederates immediately should they retreat. Van Dorn began his withdrawal before noon, so lack of daylight was not a factor that could inhibit a Federal effort to pursue the enemy. Grant was concerned that the reinforcements he had ordered in from Bolivar would be imperiled if Rosecrans did not immediately go after Van Dorn's defeated army. He repeated the order for Rosecrans to follow the enemy after the fighting ceased. Nevertheless, Rosecrans waited until the morning of October 5 to start his pursuit of Van Dorn's army and then started out on the wrong road. Grant, of course, was critical of the delay. Rosecrans followed from Corinth with a wagon train for supply; therefore, his march was naturally slower Van Dorn's. Grant observed that the mistake of waiting, and worse yet, taking the wrong road, deprived the Federals of an opportunity to possibly annihilate Van Dorn's army. Grant wrote, "…if Rosecrans had followed the route taken by the enemy, he would have come upon Van Dorn in a swamp with a stream in front and Ord holding the only bridge"; in other words, he would have put Van Dorn in serious jeopardy.[110]

Casualties for the Federals at Corinth totaled 2,520 including 355 killed and 1,841 wounded. Van Dorn reported his casualties as follows: "our loss in the several conflicts with the enemy and on the march to and from Corinth, viz: Killed, 594 wounded, 2,162; prisoners and missing, 2,102." Van Dorn's total of 4,858 was nearly twice the Federal losses. Higher Confederate casualties were the result of making attacks against earthworks and fortifications. Van Dorn's selection of Corinth as an operational objective seems dubious because he knew in advance that, under usual circumstances, an attacking force going against earthworks requires a numerical advantage of at least two-to-one. Nevertheless, Van Dorn explained his decision with the following: "...after mature deliberation I determined to attempt Corinth. I had a reasonable hope of success." He hoped to surprise Rosecrans "and carry the place" before reinforcements could arrive. In the end he must have realized his error in judgment, as he admitted, "In my zeal for my country I may have ventured too far with inadequate means."[111] While this may be true, the outcome would have been much worse for Van Dorn had Grant's orders been carried out with alacrity and competence.

Of all the Civil War army commanders one can bring to mind, Ulysses Grant suffered the most from subordinates who failed to execute his orders in a timely, competent and efficient manner. Only President Lincoln, as commander in chief, experienced more disappointment in the performances of his generals. Grant's disappointment in the outcome of the Battle of Corinth resulting from Rosecrans' failure to follow instructions was only one of many such episodes he would undergo during the course of the war. Grant usually devised a feasible and promising tactical or operational plan during his campaigns only to have poor or tardy execution by subordinate generals spoil the outcome. The Battle of Corinth demonstrated one of the faults General Grant was never able to alter or overcome during the course of the war. He too often depended upon his subordinates to carry out their assignments and orders without ensuring that they could and would complete them. Unlike General Lee, Grant was never able to generate the kind of loyalty and confidence in his ability to deliver victory that Lee instilled in his lieutenants.

By the middle of October 1862 the only concentrated Confederate effort at a two-theater offensive during entire war had ended in failure. Lee's invasion of Maryland and Bragg's sojourn in Kentucky each netted significant captures of men and material, but neither invasion attempt seriously threatened the Northern states. The outcome proved two salient facts beyond reasonable doubt: Southerners were not as militarily superior to their Northern neighbors as they had previously believed, and the South stood no realistic chance of successfully invading and holding Northern territory. President Lincoln's proclamation freeing slaves in rebellious states sent notice to Southern slaveholders, the people who instigated the war in 1860, that soon the very motivation for Southern independence would be irrelevant. Northern forces were operating throughout much of the South, freeing slaves and capturing important Southern cities almost at will. The Confederacy's leadership had proved incapable of defending Southern soil, and invasion of Northern states had proved completely beyond Southern military capability. As the winter of 1862 approached, the South's hope for independence depended on two factors that yet seemed beyond the Confederacy's grasp. The South desperately needed recognition and assistance from France and England. In addition the South needed to erode the North's will to maintain the war. The later of these two factors was both the most important and obtainable in order for the Confederacy to survive.

Following the Battle of Perryville, General D.C. Buell, much like his friend and colleague General McClellan, refused to engage the enemy. Despite his advantage, he failed to even follow Bragg out of Kentucky. He let yet another opportunity to shorten the war slip away. General Halleck suggested and then insisted that Buell drive Bragg's army out of Kentucky and eastern Tennessee. Buell replied with excuses: the roads and logistics and other circumstances rendered the task too difficult. On October 19, Halleck told Buell, "I am directed by the President to say to you that your army must enter East Tennessee this fall, and that it ought to move there while the roads are passable." Buell quickly replied, "I have no doubt that you realize that the occupation of East Tennessee with a suitable force is an undertaking of very considerable magnitude, and that if undertaken unadvisedly it will fail." Next he informed Halleck that "To continue the pursuit (of Bragg) would exhaust and throw the troops out of position without any fruits. I am therefore putting them on other lines toward Tennessee."

Pressure on Buell was building from sources outside of Washington. On October 21, Indiana Governor O.P. Morton complained to President Lincoln: "The butchery of our troops at Perryville was terrible, and resulted from a large portion of the enemy being precipitated upon a small portion of ours. Sufficient time was thus gained by the enemy to enable them to escape. Nothing but success, speedy and decided, will save our cause from destruction. In the Northwest distrust and despair are seizing upon the hearts of the people."

President Lincoln, having no political reason to retain Buell, or military justification for doing so, finally chose to fire the general. Buell's military career was effectively finished. On October 23, General Halleck sent this terse message to Major General W.S. Rosecrans at Corinth, "You will immediately repair to Cincinnati, where you will receive orders. Telegraph your arrival. Go with the least possible delay." The following day Halleck informed Buell that President Lincoln directed him to turn over his command to General Rosecrans and then "repair to Indianapolis." Governors Yates of Illinois and Morton of Indiana expressed their approval to the president on the 25th with the following: "The removal of General Buell and appointment of Rosecrans came not a moment too soon."[112]

In the East President Lincoln's patience with the performance of General George McClellan was rapidly running out. Both McClellan and Buell were viewed as unfriendly to the Lincoln Administration, McClellan was a Democrat, and both had been retained in command only because of perceived military necessity. The state of Lincoln's temper is revealed in the messages he sent to General McClellan in late October. McClellan had correctly reported to General Halleck on October 13 that "the service suffers from our deficiency in the cavalry arm." He again reported to Halleck on the 25th problems with cavalry horses, including fatigue, sore backs and sore tongues. Lincoln somewhat sarcastically replied "I have just read your dispatch about sore-tongued and fatigued horses. Will you pardon me for asking what the horses of your army have done since the Battle of Antietam that fatigues anything?" McClellan attempted to explain why the horses were tired, to which Lincoln replied, "To be told, after more than five weeks' total inaction of the army ... that the horses were too fatigued to move, presents a very cheerless, almost hopeless, prospect for the future, and it may have forced something of impatience in my dispatch."

Lincoln's impatience was justified and didn't end there. McClellan next suggested, quite judiciously, that drafted men should be sent to bring existing regiments up to strength. Throughout the war the Federal government continued to recruit new regiments rather than sending recruits to fill veteran units. It was a malignant practice that

General William T. Sherman also reproved. But McClellan's message was sent at a time when Lincoln had been urging both Buell and McClellan to move against the enemy. Lincoln answered on the 27th, "…I ask a distinct answer to the question, Is it your purpose to not go into action again until the men now being drafted in the States are incorporated into the old regiments?"[113] Yet the president's frustration was a direct result of his own failings as commander in chief. Lincoln always seemed to suggest rather than give orders for his plans and expectations to his generals. The political genius and tremendous scope of his intuitive capabilities were wasted because Lincoln was unable or reluctant to impose his will upon his army commanders. It was this flaw in his disposition as president that enabled his commanders to circumvent his directions and intentions. Lincoln shares responsibility for the failures of his army commanders because he did not fully assert his authority during the war. Lincoln often perceived what needed to be done strategically and operationally better than the generals themselves, but too often he failed to demand compliance when nothing less would suffice.

McClellan continued to frustrate the president's aims until Lincoln decided that the general was dispensable. Lincoln waited until shortly after the November elections and then fired McClellan. Lincoln ordered the dismissal on November 5. The orders arrived by the hand of Brigadier General Catharinus P. Buckingham in an unseasonable driving snowstorm on November 7, 1862. Just as it would be with Buell, McClellan's military career was finished. Unlike Buell, McClellan possessed military talents that were too useful to waste. Nevertheless, McClellan would never be reassigned to another command in the army. Other generals would come and go as commander of the Army of the Potomac and then accept another command assignment. McClellan never did.

Lincoln selected Major General Ambrose Everett Burnside to succeed McClellan in command of the Army of the Potomac. The change of command was not an improvement. In Burnside the president found someone who would attempt to obey his orders, and not much else. There is nothing in the record of Burnside's military career to suggest that he was qualified for or capable of replacing General McClellan.

General in Chief Halleck immediately ordered Burnside to report upon assuming command the position of his troops and exactly what he was going to do with them. This message went out the same day, the 5th, that the president dismissed McClellan. To his credit, and as an indication of his willingness to comply with directives, Burnside completed a document detailing his proposal for immediate operations of the Army of the Potomac on November 7. Burnside's apparent willingness to commence operations immediately upon approval was a sharp contrast to McClellan's record of constant delays.

Burnside's plan of operations called for a concentration of troops near Warrenton, Virginia, to "impress upon the enemy a belief" that he would attack Gordonsville or Culpeper. Instead of moving against those towns, his plan called for "a rapid move of the whole force to Fredericksburg, with a view to a movement upon Richmond from that point." Burnside believed that the route to Richmond via Fredericksburg would be quicker, shorter and easier to supply than the Gordonsville approach. He also stressed that the Fredericksburg "line would render it almost impossible for the enemy to make a successful move upon Washington by any road on this side of the Potomac." He expected to beat Lee to Fredericksburg and upon reaching that place to attack at once. Another reason why Burnside believed the Fredericksburg route was superior was that if the army were "detained by the elements," it would be better "to be on that route." Also mentioned in his November 7 document were details about his supply wagon train to be "preceded by pontoon trains enough to span the Rappahannock with two tracks."

Burnside asked Halleck for an answer to his plan of operations on November 13. Halleck himself seemed to favor the Gordonsville line of advance over the Fredericksburg route. President Lincoln appeared skeptical of Burnside's plan, but he made his decision in reply to Burnside's request. On the 14th, Halleck sent this message from Washington: "The President has just assented to your plan. He thinks it will succeed, if you move very rapidly; otherwise not."[114]

While Burnside was preparing for his move against Fredericksburg, both sides were planning operations and adapting to the circumstances wrought by the vagaries of war. President Davis had retained the hapless General Braxton Bragg in command despite the failure of his Kentucky invasion. Bragg moved to occupy Murfreesboro in middle Tennessee with a view of recapturing Nashville. However, the Confederate priority in the West in late 1862 was retaining possession of Vicksburg, Mississippi, and other points south on the Mississippi River, including Port Hudson, Louisiana. The importance of Vicksburg was explained by General Grant. Vicksburg, Grant noted, occupied the first high ground on the river bank below Memphis. An important railroad at Vicksburg functioned as the only channel connecting parts of the Confederacy divided by the river. Perhaps most important, as long as the Confederates held Vicksburg they could prevent free passage on the river from the Midwest to the Gulf of Mexico.[115] Control of the Mississippi River was of crucial political importance to Northern politicians in the Midwest and also to President Lincoln. The Confederacy had other operational priorities in the West including defending Chattanooga and retaining and regaining territory, but ultimately holding Vicksburg would have had the most impact on winning the war for the South. Unfortunately for the Confederacy, General Joseph Johnston who had overall command of Confederate forces in the West considered middle Tennessee the most important area to defend. Johnston would ultimately fail to find a means of holding Vicksburg.

Grant commenced a campaign to capture Vicksburg on November 2, 1862. In addition to Vicksburg, the Federals had other operational objectives in the fall of 1862. Major General Rosecrans, having replaced Buell, was tasked with pushing the rebels out of Tennessee and occupying east Tennessee in particular, as President Lincoln had so intently desired for some time. The Federals also hoped to occupy the rest of Arkansas and even invade Texas soon. Eventually the Federals made the correct choice in prioritizing Grant's campaign sufficiently to produce success.

General Bragg soon abandoned the idea of attacking and capturing Nashville, realizing that he would be required to attack a more numerous, entrenched enemy there. Instead, Bragg sent out cavalry raids led by Colonel John Morgan and Brigadier General Nathan B. Forrest. By late November Bragg had managed to reach Murfreesboro, south of Nashville about twenty-five miles, and occupied the place with his army. Apparently Bragg decided his best option was to fight a defensive battle around Murfreesboro and attempt to hold onto middle Tennessee. The choice of Murfreesboro as a defensive position was dubious at best. There were better areas for a defensive stand nearby to the south along the Duck River and at the base of the Cumberland Mountains.[116] Bragg naturally wanted to retain as much territory and foraging area as possible; he made his stand around Murfreesboro and awaited Rosecrans' likely advance.

Rosecrans, after assuming command of the Department of the Cumberland from Buell in late October, continued the familiar practice of delaying operations to satisfy preparations he deemed necessary for an advance. General in Chief Halleck attempted to spur Rosecrans forward. On November 27 and again on December 4 Halleck sent dispatches to caution Rosecrans that he must not remain inert at Nashville. "The President is very impatient at your long stay at Nashville," he wrote. "If you remain one more week at Nashville, I cannot prevent your removal … the Government demands action, and if you cannot respond to that demand someone else will be tried." Rosecrans immediately replied to Halleck that "I have lost no time.... To threats of removal or the like I must be permitted to say that I am insensible."[117] The delay at Nashville allowed Bragg to occupy Murfreesboro, which ultimately resulted in a battle that might not have been necessary if Rosecrans had immediately moved in the direction of Chattanooga after replacing Buell.

West of the Mississippi River, Brigadier General John M. Schofield was clearing troublesome southwest Missouri of rebel detachments and outposts. Brigadier General James G. Blunt advanced his division, which included eight Kansas units and two infantry regiments of Native Americans, into northwest Arkansas. Two Federal divisions commanded by Brigadier General Francis Herron remained in camp near Springfield, Missouri. In northwest Arkansas, Confederate Major General Thomas Hindman led a force of about 11,000 troops, many of them recent conscripts of dubious loyalty. In late November Blunt defeated a rebel cavalry force at Cane Hill, Arkansas, and, being isolated and outnumbered, he sent for Herron to bring his two divisions from southwest Missouri to help secure his position. Herron received Blunt's message on December 3 and marched his divisions out of camp on the following morning. His movement in relief of Blunt was perhaps the most impressive forced march of the war, covering 125 miles in three days without tents or camp equipment. As Herron approached from Fayetteville on December 7, General Hindman deployed his army for a defensive stand on a hill near Prairie Grove Church. Herron did not realize that he was vastly outnumbered, so he deployed his exhausted troops to push on towards Cane Hill where he expected to rendezvous with General Blunt. Herron's tired infantry regiments soon went forward to occupy a hill near the Borden House. Two Confederate divisions held the brow of the hill, vastly outnumbering Herron's infantry regiments. Although some of Herron's men were armed with Colt revolving rifles, increasing their firepower, his infantry was driven off the hill with heavy losses. Meanwhile, General Blunt had heard the sounds of the battle and hurried his division to Prairie Grove. Although Hindman's force heavily outnumbered Herron's, he reacted with excessive caution and thereby missed an opportunity to defeat the divided Federals in detail. When Blunt arrived the advantage swung to the Federals, and the fighting ended in a stalemate. After dark, Hindman, his army now low on ammunition and his artillery battered, withdrew.

Casualties at the Battle of Prairie Grove were about even in numbers of killed and wounded, although many of Hindman's conscripts deserted. By the time Hindman halted his retreat, his force was considerably reduced. The outcome of the fighting in northwest Arkansas in the fall of 1862 was a Federal tactical victory. The Confederates were unable to reclaim northwest Arkansas and southwest Missouri. The Battle of Prairie Grove is an example of an outnumbered Federal force achieving a significant tactical victory in a Confederate state, something no Confederate force achieved on Northern soil.

In Virginia, Burnside's planned advance via Fredericksburg, so dependent upon rapid movement, was doomed to failure because the Army of the Potomac was simply too ponderous and inflexible to accomplish such a mission. Burnside's vanguard reached the Fredericksburg vicinity around November 17, but the pontoons needed to bridge the

Prairie Grove Battlefield.

The reconstructed Borden House, the scene of heavy fighting on the Prairie Grove Battlefield.

Rappahannock had not yet arrived. Halleck, it seems, was at least partially responsible for the delayed pontoons; he had "failed to oversee a prompt execution of his orders." The pontoons did not arrive at Falmouth, near Fredericksburg, until the November 25. The delay had allowed time for General Lee to send General Longstreet's divisions to Fredericksburg. By the 25th the Confederates were digging fieldworks in the hills above the town and posting artillery batteries to oppose a crossing of the river.

Burnside was delayed further by a meeting with the president on the 26th. Lincoln proposed an alternative plan involving a crossing of the river at Port Royal, Virginia, southeast of Fredericksburg. Halleck suggested an immediate attack, saying the president's plan was infeasible. Lincoln left the decision to Burnside, and the general returned to Fredericksburg to try to salvage his plan.[118] At this point it was Burnside's plan that had become infeasible; it should have been shelved.

Burnside delayed yet another week before holding a council of war with his senior commanders. Most of Burnside's generals believed that his plan would fail and that it would be rash to proceed with it at that point. Yet Burnside remained convinced that his plan would be unexpected and could still succeed. Simply stated, Burnside lacked the versatility and flexibility to alter his plan or abandon it. He was certainly under pressure to do something and do it soon. So he ordered the engineers to bridge the river commencing in the predawn hours of December 11, 1862, and sent his army on a forlorn mission at Fredericksburg.

The Battle of Fredericksburg involved the greatest total number of troops engaged in a single battle during the entire war. It was General Burnside's legacy to command two of the worst mishandled Federal operations of the entire war, and the Battle of Fredericksburg was one of them. Burnside superintended one of the truly tragic military blunders in American history here. It may be possible that the Army of the Potomac could have accomplished Burnside's objectives at Fredericksburg if he had attacked Lee's right south of town at his first opportunity. Instead, Burnside, seemingly disorientated, went about preparations as if time were not a factor in the outcome. When he did order an attack, his instructions to his generals were vague and simply inadequate. He did not sufficiently reconnoiter or probe the Confederate positions across the river before deciding when and where to attack. Overall, Burnside's conduct of the battle was so inept that it is difficult to determine just what his tactical plan entailed.

The fighting at Fredericksburg from December 11 to 15 basically amounted to a two-pronged attack. One force crossed bridges south of town and attacked upslope along a railroad embankment. This attack achieved limited success but was of insufficient strength to create a breakthrough. The other attack was made upslope just west and outside of the town at Marye's Heights. The objective of this attack was to occupy Lee and prevent him from reinforcing his right, south of town. Unfortunately for the Northern soldiers, Burnside pressed this obviously forlorn effort into a debacle by reacting as if it could change the outcome of the battle, in effect making it the main attack. The Federal attacks on Marye's Heights above Fredericksburg have long been remembered for their courage and carnage but also for their folly. There is very little about the battle to regard on the Federal side, except for the bravery and determination of the American soldiers who attacked despite impossible odds against them. The Irish Brigade, the 2nd Brigade, 1st Division, II Corps, five infantry regiments composed mostly of Irish immigrants, lost 545 men by attacking the impregnable wall on Marye's Heights. These Irishmen manned probably the best-known brigade in the Federal service, "having made an unusual reputation for dash and gallantry."[119] They earned a large measure of their fame at Fredericksburg and proved that some immigrant outfits performed as well as any soldiers on either side.

General Lee, as usual, made the correct adjustments during the Fredericksburg Campaign. He was a superb defensive commander, and it showed here. Lee had actually wanted to establish a defensive line closer to Richmond along the North Anna River. Instead, his defense at Fredericksburg proved quite sufficient. He correctly chose not to try to defend the town itself, instead selecting defensive positions along the ridges beyond. Fredericksburg must be considered as perhaps the easiest Confederate victory of the war.

Casualties at the Battle of Fredericksburg for Burnside's army were more than twice those of Lee's. The Federal report listed a total of 12,653 including 1,284 killed and 9,500 wounded. Confederate losses might have been as high as 5,300, but the Confederate medical director's report listed only 448 killed and 3,743 wounded.[120] The disparity in casualties reflected heavy losses incurred by attacks against Marye's Heights, where the Federals charged across open space against walls and field works manned by the Confederates. The Confederates held an even greater advantage here than McClellan's army enjoyed at Malvern Hill in July; the outcome was similar but reversed.

During the night of December 15, 1862, Burnside withdrew the Army of the Potomac back across the Rappahannock. The Battle of Fredericksburg was over. Like many other Civil War battles, Fredericksburg had very little impact on outcome of the war, except to extend its duration. It was a hollow Confederate victory that, when viewed by its dominance, gives an impression of Southern fighting supremacy. However, had the two armies exchanged places and tactics, the outcome would have favored the Federals to the same extent.

It was shortly after the Battle of Fredericksburg when General in Chief Halleck's advice to Burnside demonstrated the strategy evolved by Lincoln and the Federal high command in 1862. This "headquarters doctrine," as termed by historians Herman Hattaway and Archer Jones, focused the Federal war effort in Virginia on Lee's army rather than on the capture of Richmond. Obviously a siege would be required in order to capture Richmond, and Lincoln believed that a siege would amount to a political liability and would lower morale in the North. In a message to Burnside, Halleck reminded him, "In all our interviews I have urged that our first object was, not Richmond, but the defeat or scattering of Lee's army, which threatened Washington and the line of the Upper Potomac.... The great object is to occupy the enemy ... and to injure him all you can with the least injury to yourself."[121] The strategy of concentrating on Lee's army rather than Richmond has been largely accepted by historians as the proper replacement to the "on to Richmond" policy dominant early in the war. However, the emphasis on Lee's army rather than Richmond predicated an overly-cautious approach in Virginia that prioritized the security of Washington at the expense of shortening the duration of the war.

It had been a mistake for President Lincoln to order McClellan to withdraw from Harrison's Landing in the summer of 1862. Some of the generals in the Army of the Potomac held out hope for a return to the James River as the launch point for a new campaign against Richmond. Shortly after the Federal defeat at Fredericksburg, two corps commanders from the Army of the Potomac wrote to President Lincoln on this subject. The two generals informed Lincoln that they believed Burnside's operations, or an overland campaign, would fail. A move to the James River, they observed, would place the army "within twenty miles of Richmond without the risk of an engagement." The overland approach would allow the enemy to "post himself strongly" along the route to Richmond and inflict "enormous" losses on the Federals while sustaining "comparatively slight" losses themselves. President Lincoln, as noted in the paragraph above, disagreed. Lincoln believed that a return to the James River would leave Washington uncovered. Brigadier General John Barnard, a prominent officer of the engineers, also observed in a missive dated November 28, 1862, that "the James River is probably better than any other single line of approach" to Richmond. Barnard suggested a limited campaign with about 50,000 men landing on the south bank of the James to cut Richmond's communications with the South while Burnside pressed "with utmost vigor" his attack on the Rappahannock.[122] The significance of these observations, devised in late 1862, is that they anticipated the future keys to the capture Richmond and the defeat of Lee's army. Indeed, the overland route to Richmond in 1864 proved almost too costly to sustain, but operations once Grant reached the James brought ultimate victory. Much of the cost of the war in blood and treasure might have been saved if McClellan had been allowed to continue his campaign from Harrison's Landing in 1862.

While Burnside's campaign was being fumbled in Virginia, General Rosecrans remained in Nashville gathering supplies and making preparations to confront Bragg in middle Tennessee. Although General in Chief Halleck had suggested to Rosecrans that he must advance by the middle of December or possibly face removal, Rosecrans waited until Christmas Eve to inform Halleck he would finally make his move. Rosecrans told the general in chief on December 24, "…having now the essentials of ammunition and … rations in Nashville, shall move on them to-morrow morning at daylight…. If we beat them, I shall try to drive them to the wall." Rosecrans left almost half of his army in Nashville and on duty guarding the railroad line to Louisville. He set out from Nashville on the 26th with about 44,000 troops to battle Bragg's army of around 34,000 in the Murfreesboro vicinity.[123]

The march to Murfreesboro was delayed by Confederate cavalry stands along the way, allowing Bragg time to consolidate his army around Stones River near Murfreesboro. Rosecrans had expected to fight within a day or two after leaving Nashville, but after some skirmishes no battle had materialized by the 30th. Coincidentally both armies were arrayed around Stones River, and both Rosecrans and Bragg decided to attack on the 31st. Also coincidentally both generals decided to attack the enemy's right. As often happened during the war, the Confederates were quicker to make their move.

Rosecrans planned to open his attack across Stones River at McFadden's Ford with two divisions from Major General Thomas L. Crittenden's left wing. Sometime after 7 a.m. two Federal brigades crossed at McFadden's Ford and deployed. My Grandmother Clara's father splashed across Stones River there with his regiment that morning, participating in Rosecrans' anticipated attack. However, Bragg struck first, hitting the Federal right with overpowering force at about 6 a.m.

Bragg had initially thought to attack along the Nashville Turnpike, intending to concentrate on the Federal left. Instead, he chose a turning movement aimed at the Federal right flank. The attacking rebel divisions appeared out of the gray dawn mist immediately in front of the Federal bivouacs. Many of the Federal regiments were caught preparing breakfast with their weapons stacked and unloaded. In quick order the units on the Federal right flank were crushed; seven Confederate brigades hit two Federal brigades, overlapping the far right of Rosecrans' line.

Bragg's unexpected flank attack gave the Confederates momentum along much of the Federal front. Rosecrans recalled most of Crittenden's brigades from his left, including my great grandfather's regiment, to shore up threatened positions along his front in response to the morning chaos. By afternoon the situation had stabilized for the Federals as Crittenden's troops filled gaps, allowing routed Federal units to collect and reorganize in the rear. Crittenden's troops, having moved in after the initial shock of the Confederate attack, held their positions at every point they had reinforced, and the jaded Confederates could make no further headway. The fighting sputtered out at nightfall with Bragg confident that the Federals would fall back to Nashville, defeated.

Bragg was surprised to find on New Year's Day that Rosecrans's army remained essentially in the same positions held at dusk on the 31st. Neither army commander attempted to renew the battle on January 1. Bragg expected Rosecrans to quit the field and waited for a Federal withdrawal. Instead, the Federals dug in and realigned units to restore their jumbled battle line. Parts of Crittenden's divisions, including my great grandfather's regiment, were returned to the McFadden's Ford area, just north of the main battlefield. New Year's Day passed in relative quiet as Bragg weighed his options, seemingly incapable of deciding what to do next.

January 2, 1863, dawned with rain turning to sleet and neither army commander yet ready to quit the field. Although Rosecrans outnumbered Bragg, he refused to take the initiative and continued adjusting and strengthening his lines. Colonel Samuel Beatty of the 19th Ohio Infantry had assumed command of Crittenden's 3rd division, replacing the wounded Brigadier General Horatio Van Cleve. On the 2nd, Beatty's Division, and my great grandfather, were posted across McFadden's Ford on the east bank of Stones River

This broken Wiard cannon rests among the rocky shelves in a wood on the Stones River Battlefield where General Sheridan's troops made a determined stand.

to protect a hill commanding the Federal positions on the west side of the river. General Bragg realized during the morning that if he could seize this high ground, Confederate artillery could enfilade the Federals. Just as important, Bragg realized that Federal artillery posted atop this hill could enfilade his battle line. Bragg decided that he must have Beatty's division driven off the hill and back across McFadden's Ford. He ordered Major General John C. Breckinridge, a former vice president of the United States, to attack with his division at 4 p.m. Bragg chose the late hour for the attack so that dusk would prevent Rosecrans from counterattacking.

Breckinridge's division was selected for the attack because his was the only Confederate division available and in position near McFadden's Ford. But Breckinridge wanted no part of the assignment and so informed Bragg. The reluctant general pointed out that he had already examined Beatty's position and found that the hills occupied by the Federals would dominate the approach of his attacking force. Breckinridge argued that his attack would be devastated by Federal artillery fire and would fail. Bragg disagreed and informed Breckinridge that his order would stand. Bragg obviously believed that he could still achieve a victory by capturing this high ground along the river. Unfortunately for the Confederates, Bragg did not sufficiently support Breckinridge's attack, despite the fact that he considered it a key to victory.

The attack commenced at 4 p.m. as planned. Breckinridge's attacking line was over a half-mile wide. His front was six ranks deep "succeeded by a second of the same depth, and a third of apparently greater." Federal artillery on both sides of the river opened fire

The Federals held this position on the banks of Stones River near McFadden's Ford. General Bragg's attack was repulsed here on January 2, 1863.

with a barrage of at least fifty-eight guns, sustained until the Confederates closed with the Federal infantry. Beatty reported that his front line sheltered behind the crest of a hill until the rebels approached to within 100 yards and then fired its first volley into Breckinridge's attacking column, "which checked it for a moment." When the Confederates closed to within a few yards of the defenders, Beatty's front line began to give way and carried the second line away with them. Beatty's reserve from his 1st brigade, which included my great grandfather's regiment, "advanced most gallantly toward the crest of the hill and poured a destructive fire" into the Confederates. The Confederate ranks were broken "more than once, their colors shot down several times, but their ranks were speedily filled with fresh troops." At this time 1st Brigade Commander Colonel Benjamin Grider rode back to Beatty and shouted, "Colonel, we have them checked; give us artillery and we will whip them."

But Grider's three regiments could not hold. The 19th Ohio, Beatty's own regiment, was assailed from the riverbank by a rebel regiment out of alignment with the rest of Breckinridge's attack. Grider saw the 19th begin to retreat and called upon Major Charles Manderson, commanding the 19th in place of Colonel Beatty, to rally his regiment. Major Manderson replied, "We are flanked on our right; we had better fall back and rally at the foot of the hill, if we can." With the 19th Ohio in retreat, Grider followed with his two Kentucky infantry regiments; "both of these regiments, almost in line with some of the enemy's troops, were the last regiments to quit the field."[124]

Breckinridge's troops pursued the Federals to the banks of Stones River, but the Federal artillery posted on the heights above McFadden's Ford was firing over 100 rounds per minute into the attackers. Although the Confederates were exhilarated by their apparent success, their ranks were now disordered and the attack stalled. Soon the Confederates, subjected to heavy incoming fire from Federal infantry and artillery, began milling around on both sides of the riverbank, and then the Confederates started retreating back up the hillside above the ford. Almost spontaneously, a Federal brigade and then others charged across the river, chasing the rebels back up the hill. The tide of the battle had been reversed; now the Confederate officers were frantically trying to rally their men and hold the hill they had just captured.

Winter twilight was darkening the landscape as the Federal brigades, including troops that had been pushed across the river, regained the lost ground. By 4:45 p.m. the Confederates had been completely routed and driven back to their original lines. In the gloaming of one of the shortest days on the calendar, the Federal officers decided not to press on beyond the point where Breckinridge's attack had sallied forth less than an hour earlier. Once again darkness extinguished the fighting at Stones River.

The official total of Federal casualties for the Stones River Campaign was 13,249 of which 1,730 were killed and 7,802 wounded, but this total was for the period of December 26 through January 5, which would have included other skirmishes. The official casualty list for Bragg's army was somewhat lower, but another estimate for Confederate losses totaled 11,739.[125] The Federals incurred heavy losses on December 31 when the Confederate attacks caught many Federal outfits unprepared or cooking breakfast. The terrain at the battlefield of December 31, just north of Murfreesboro, was heavily wooded with dense stands of red cedars and areas with limestone outcroppings. These geographical features allowed the Confederates to close on the Federals without being exposed to excessive musket and artillery fire. The wooded and rocky landscape created difficulties for artillery movement and limited fields of fire. Confederate attacks also sometimes heavily outnumbered Federal defenders at the point of combat despite the fact that overall the Federal army was larger. These factors partially account for the higher total for Federal casualties.

Rosecrans did not renew the battle on January 3, although he probably should have. The Confederates were in a precarious position with parts of Bragg's army on both sides of Stones River. Winter rain kept falling, and the usually shallow Stones River was rising. If the river were to flood with the continual rains, about half of Bragg's army could have been practically isolated. Bragg decided by the afternoon of January 3 that the risk or remaining at Murfreesboro was too great. After 10 p.m. Bragg's troops abandoned their positions along Stones River and began retreating southward. The week of marching and fighting in the chilling winter rain after leaving Nashville had been an ordeal for Rosecrans' army. Thus, Rosecrans did not seriously consider pressing his advantage. A commander of a different ilk might have continued the battle on January 3 or at least called for reinforcements to pursue Bragg as he retreated. Rosecrans, however, was apparently satisfied with his limited success at Murfreesboro, and there he remained.

General Bragg was criticized in the Southern press for retreating from Murfreesboro after his army had fought the Federals to a standstill. Some of his of his corps and division commanders also hoped for his removal from command. But it was Rosecrans who deserved criticism for not accomplishing more. After the debacle at Fredericksburg, President Lincoln was desperate for any good war news. Bragg's retreat provided a favorable outcome to at least partially offset the gloom cast over the North that December. So Rosecrans was allowed to operate in the West essentially in the same manner as McClellan did in Virginia before his removal. However, in fairness to Rosecrans, few Federal generals would have handled his situation after the Battle of Stones River differently or better. Federal generals seldom looked past the battle just fought; they usually devoted their efforts to avoiding a catastrophic defeat rather than achieving a comprehensive victory. Rosecrans was no exception.

Farther west, General Grant was enduring frustration and failure in his campaign to capture Vicksburg, Mississippi. Grant feared that a political general and former Illinois congressman, Major General John A. McClernand, would be placed in command of a portion of his army intended to strike Vicksburg from the river. Grant did not believe that McClernand was competent for the task. Grant later explained, "...I was very much disturbed ... that General McClernand was to have a separate and independent command within mine.... I feared for the safety of the troops intrusted to him."[126] Before the ambitious McClernand could assume command of his corps, General Grant ordered his friend Major General William T. Sherman to cooperate with the Navy for an expedition launching an attack from river transports at Chickasaw Bluffs just north of Vicksburg. Grant planned to move the rest of his army towards Vicksburg overland simultaneously to prevent the Confederates from concentrating against Sherman's attack.

Unfortunately for Grant and Sherman, Lieutenant General John C. Pemberton in charge of Vicksburg's defense ordered a raid on Grant's supply depot at Holly Springs in northern Mississippi before Grant was fairly away. Major General Earl Van Dorn, the Confederate general defeated at the battles of Pea Ridge and Corinth, led a cavalry raid on Holly Springs successfully. It seems that Van Dorn, who was a cavalry officer in the Old Army, was better at leading cavalry raids than at leading armies. Van Dorn captured the base and its garrison of 1,500 men and destroyed munitions, food and forage intended for Grant's advance on Vicksburg. Grant later suggested that the base commandant, one

Colonel Murphy of the 8th Wisconsin, surrendered disgracefully. Grant observed that along the railroad "Van Dorn did not succeed in capturing a single garrison except the one at Holly Springs, which was larger than all the others attacked by him put together."[127] While Van Dorn was destroying Grant's supply base, the cavalry raid dispatched by General Bragg from Tennessee (before the Battle of Stones River and led by Brigadier General Nathan Bedford Forrest) successfully damaged Grant's railroad supply line between Jackson, Tennessee, and Columbus, Kentucky. Grant was compelled to abandon his advance on Vicksburg, and he was unable to communicate with Sherman. Damaged railroads and downed telegraph lines prevented Grant from informing Sherman that he was canceling his advance toward Vicksburg. Sherman went ahead with his planned attack at Chickasaw Bluffs without knowledge that Grant had called off his campaign temporarily.

General Sherman hoped to approach Vicksburg by surprise with his force of 30,075 men. It didn't play out that way. As Sherman's force reached its landing point about four miles northwest of Chickasaw Bluffs on December 26, the Confederates were aware and reinforcements were arriving to meet the attack. Sherman reported that during "the night of the 27th the ground was reconnoitered as well as possible," and he learned that it would be a daunting task indeed to attack the defenses along the Chickasaw Bluffs. Although Sherman admitted that not "a word could" he hear from General Grant about his supporting operation, he decided to attack anyway because timing was essential to the success of his Grant's plan. On the 28th the Federals probed the Confederate defenses during the day and night. Confederate Brigadier General Stephen D. Lee, West Point Class of 1854, had deployed his defenders well by the time Sherman launched his main attack on December 29. The outcome of the fight at Chickasaw Bluffs was, by comparison, a worst defeat for Sherman than Burnside's defeat that earlier month at Fredericksburg.

Sherman described the terrain of the battleground in detail in his report after the battle. He did not exaggerate when he wrote that the ground "was found to be as difficult as it could possibly be" for an attacking force to approach and assault. Grant later called Sherman's attack "unfortunate" and suggested that the rebel defenses were "impregnable against any force that could be brought against its front." From hindsight it appears that Sherman should have realized that the odds of success were too low, but he ordered the attack on the 29th nonetheless. The casualties totaled 1,776 for the Federals, of which 208 were killed in action and 1,005 were wounded, against only 187 for the Confederates. Sherman had charge of probably the most uneven defeat of the entire war.

After finally realizing that he could not dent the Confederate line at Chickasaw Bluffs, Sherman planned another landing and attack at another point on the ridge above the Yazoo River. He hoped to continue his effort to take Vicksburg and compensate for his defeat at Chickasaw Bluffs. In the end he thought the better of it and withdrew to Milliken's Bend on the Louisiana bank of the river.[128] As the year closed, Grant's initial attempt to take Vicksburg had failed miserably. It was a gloomy conclusion to the outgoing year for the Union.

Overall 1862 was a disastrous year for the Confederacy. The war's second year certainly could have and would have been indeed ruinous for the secessionists if not for mistakes by the Federal high command and several poor performances by Federal army commanders. Impractical strategy by the Confederate high command had resulted in the loss of several key fortresses and their garrisons including Forts Henry, Donelson, Pulaski and others and in the captures of New Orleans, Nashville, and Memphis. Kentucky and Missouri had gone over to Federal control, partly as a result of inept political decisions. Arizona, New Mexico, and western Virginia were also under Federal control, and parts of nearly all Confederate states had been penetrated or lost by the end of the year. President Davis had failed to develop a comprehensive strategy to identify and implement the requirements for winning the war. Instead, Davis and the Confederate high command had fixated on defending as much Southern territory as possible, and they had failed in this impossible and unreasonable objective. The Confederate command structure, especially in the West, was inefficient and often poorly coordinated. The ultimate blow to the future of the Confederacy was delivered after the Battle of Antietam when President Lincoln issued the Emancipation Proclamation. Southerners then realized that even if the Confederacy were somehow sustained by force of arms, possession of slaves in the South would become increasingly difficult and perhaps impossible to maintain. The slaves in rebellious states had been declared legally free and thousands had left the plantations forever. Now there would be no fugitive slave laws or other means of regaining slaves fleeing to the Northern States as practiced before the war. By December of 1862 it was becoming clear that the Southern states had chosen the hard road and had mistaken its destination.

The one area where the Confederacy had best frustrated Federal military operations was in Virginia. General Robert E. Lee has historically received most of the credit for keeping the Federals in check there, as well he should. But even General Lee warrants some criticism for his direction of the Maryland Campaign in September 1862. As Lee moved into Maryland, he divided his army into four separate forces miles apart. In the end he managed to escape from General McClellan's delayed attempt to crush his army at the Battle of Antietam. Lee's judgment in attempting to invade Pennsylvania is uncertain and suggests that the general was perhaps prone to excessive risk taking. His tactics in Maryland had presented the Federals with an opportunity to destroy his army. More puzzling yet was his intention to return Maryland just days after Antietam, where he had been lucky to escape with his army intact. Lee was slow to recognize that the Confederacy was incapable of operating on Northern soil with any realistic expectation of success. It was a miscalculation he was destined to repeat.

For the Union the year 1862 was marked by its own miscalculations and by several lost opportunities; 1862 closed with a pervasive feeling of despondency in the North. The greatest single error by the Federal high command in 1862 was its decision to withdraw McClellan and the Army of the Potomac from Harrison's Landing in July. Many historians would disagree and assert that General McClellan would have failed to capture Richmond anyway because he was a weak commander. This simplistic traditional assessment is flawed. McClellan's management of the Peninsular Campaign was imperfect indeed, but he had placed his army on the James and in position to accomplish exactly what was done two years later by a different general. McClellan is condemned by most historians for constantly demanding reinforcements and for overestimating enemy troop strength. True perhaps, but McClellan needed the numbers he demanded in order to reasonably expect to invest Richmond successfully in 1862. It required massive troop and material superiority and a long siege to eventually capture Petersburg and Richmond at the war's close. Why should McClellan be expected to accomplish that task with numbers roughly equal to Lee's in 1862? It was the Lincoln Administration that called off recruitment in the spring of 1862. As a result the government lacked troops to send to McClellan at Richmond when they were most needed. In addition, President Lincoln's obsession with protecting Washington severely limited options for offensive operations in Virginia. By the close of 1862, Federal operations in the East allowed for stalemate, provided that Washington remained safe. Instead of besieging Richmond, the Federal high command pursued an unlikely if not impossible goal: annihilation of Lee's army.

Buell's failure to capture Chattanooga immediately after the Battle of Shiloh was another strategic blunder allowed by the Federal high command. The course of the war was altered significantly as a result. General Halleck scattered his forces after Shiloh. Had he concentrated his attention upon Corinth and then Chattanooga, the path to a Federal victory would have been shortened considerably and there would have been no Confederate incursion into Kentucky that fall.

Despite the melancholy mood pervading the North as the New Year arrived, the Southern resurgence in Virginia would wither. Success in Virginia would delude the South in the months ahead with belief that the war could be carried into the North. But without foreign intervention and support the Confederacy could only win by causing the North to quit. The failure of the Maryland and Kentucky Campaigns in 1862 had demonstrated that the Confederacy could not operate in Northern territory, yet Lee would attempt another invasion and fail again. Southern hopes would blossom in the months ahead, but in the coming year the North would find its way and begin to demonstrate its dominance.

6

1863

The Year of Northern Ascendency

President Abraham Lincoln had little to cheer him during the frosty January days of 1863. Rosecrans' narrow victory at Stones River just after New Years Day prevented a clean sweep of despairing war news. On January 5 Lincoln sent his thanks to the general with the following message: "Your dispatch announcing retreat of enemy has just reached here. God bless you and all with you! Please tender to all, and accept for yourself, the nation's gratitude for your and their skill, endurance, and dauntless courage." Later Lincoln reflected on the dismal days at the beginning of 1863 and confessed that if Rosecrans had been defeated that January, "the nation could scarcely have lived over" it.[1] Lincoln was destined for a litany of continuing discouraging news that winter, but the Union's war effort was ascending, waxing stronger each day while the Confederacy was on the wane.

Jefferson Davis, and for that matter President Lincoln, had concentrated their attention on the contest for control of the Mississippi River. Two Confederate strongholds on the river were all that prevented the North from navigating from St. Louis to the Gulf of Mexico. Davis, like President Lincoln, recognized "the exigent demand of the Northwestern States for the restoration to them of the unrestricted use of that river." In a letter to General T.H. Holmes on December 21, 1862, Davis identified what he believed were the two primary Federal military objectives for 1863. "It seems to me," he wrote, "now clearly developed that the enemy has two principal objects in view, one to get possession of the Mississippi River and the other to the capital of the Confederate States." He further explained his views on his strategy for the war: "We cannot hope at all points to meet the enemy with a force equal to his own, and must find our security in the concentration and rapid movement of troops. Nothing will so certainly conduce to peace as the conclusive exhibition of our power to hold the Mississippi River, and nothing so diminish our capacity to defend the Trans. Mississippi States as the loss of communications between the States on the eastern and western sides of the river."[2] Davis was confident, after the Confederate victory at Fredericksburg, that the stalemate in Virginia would continue, and thus Richmond would remain secure for the foreseeable future. The challenge for Davis and the Confederate high command was determining how to shuffle troops to defend as much territory as possible.

Although President Davis had identified Vicksburg as a crucial point to defend in December of 1862, his senior army commanders did not share his viewpoint. General Joseph Johnston commanding in the West considered middle Tennessee more important than Vicksburg. General Robert E. Lee commanding in the East opposed sending troops west and argued for another invasion of Pennsylvania instead. By the summer of 1863 the Confederates would be frustrated at all three of these operational fronts.

Intrigue by generals under Burnside's command attempting to have him removed from command finally convinced President Lincoln that a change was incumbent for the Army of the Potomac. On January 26, 1863, Major General Joseph Hooker replaced Burnside as commander of the Army of the Potomac. Burnside had suggested that General Hooker be dismissed from the service; instead, Burnside was relieved and later sent to command the Department of the Ohio. The fractious behavior of officers in the camps around Fredericksburg reflected the deteriorated morale of the Federal Army during the winter of 1862–1863. General Hooker, despite his many character flaws, proved quite able in rebuilding morale and confidence within the Army of the Potomac after assuming command.

Hooker was graduated from West Point with a middling class standing in 1837. During the Mexican War he served as a staff officer and demonstrated considerable administrative and leadership talents. He came through that war with brevets for all grades to lieutenant colonel for gallantry and merit. His record was second to none for any first lieutenant during the Mexican War. During the first years of the Civil War he had earned a justified reputation as a fighting general. He was, in fact, known nationally as "Fighting Joe Hooker." He was confident and looked the part of a warrior general.[3] These attributes overcame the more odious aspects of his character, and he was granted a shot at the daunting task of facing General Lee and his Army of Northern Virginia.

In January Grant realized he would have to lead the effort to capture Vicksburg rather than to delegate the duty to a subordinate. The task was of ever increasing importance to both sides of the conflict, but Grant at first considered alternative methods to bypass Vicksburg without a direct attack on the place. During the winter Grant conceived various plans to skirt the Vicksburg defenses, all of them failed. One of his better-known plans involved digging a canal across a bend of the river near Vicksburg to provide a channel to bypass the fortress and guns commanding the river. Other schemes involved attempts to utilize nearby watercourses to get around Vicksburg. By April Grant had decided that he would have to undertake a campaign from below Vicksburg with his army and invest the town to capture it.

In February General Lee concluded that it was necessary to send troops south to counter Federal activity in North Carolina and as insurance against a possible return of Federal troops to the James River region south of Richmond. On February 18 he dispatched General James Longstreet and his corps of 16,000 men from Fredericksburg to North Carolina. The movement weakened Lee's ability to counter a Federal offensive in Virginia. Longstreet's move south helped provide forage and food supplies for the Confederates operating in Virginia, and little else.

During the winter in Virginia only a few minor skirmishes at various locations were recorded. The most significant combat of the period occurred at Kelly's Ford on the Rappahannock River west of Fredericksburg. Brigadier General William Averell, one of Hooker's cavalry division commanders, asked for and obtained permission to go after rebel cavalry along the Rappahannock commanded by his old West Point classmate Confederate Brigadier General Fitzhugh Lee, General Robert E. Lee's nephew. On March 17 Averell's troopers splashed across the Rappahannock at Kelly's Ford and captured about two dozen enemy pickets. Fitzhugh Lee deployed his five Virginia Cavalry regiments soon after the Federals crossed the river. A cavalry battle erupted near Kelly's

Ford featuring charge and counter charge with the saber frequently put to use. Major John Pelham, one of the South's most popular young officers, was mortally wounded by a shell explosion soon after he joined in the fighting. Pelham didn't belong in the fight and was actually on leave when he took part. Averell's troopers seemed to be gaining the advantage when he decided to withdraw back across the Rappahannock. The fight bolstered morale in the eastern cavalry corps, as this fight marked a turning point in the performance of Federal cavalry in Virginia. The Confederates also suffered heavier losses, 133 compared to seventy-eight Federals; and the loss of young Major Pelham, who was a gifted artillery commander, was a blow to the Confederate cavalry corps.[4] But the fighting itself was pointless and served practically no military purpose or advantage.

It was General Ulysses S. Grant's lot to command the most significant, challenging and complex military operations of the war for the Federals. The Vicksburg Campaign might well have been the most difficult and impressive operation of the entire war, for it required tactical savvy, innovation, daring, and versatility to a greater degree than perhaps any other campaign. Most of Grant's schemes and undertakings during the winter and early part of spring were intended to keep his troops and officers occupied while active campaigning was impossible due to heavy rains and flooding. In April Grant commenced the serious work for his task of capturing Vicksburg.

While Grant was commencing the real work of his campaign against Vicksburg, General Robert E. Lee was reacting to Major General Joseph Hooker's maneuvers in what one Civil War writer selected as "the most complex campaign of the Civil War." In the spring of 1863, Hooker's offensive in Virginia was checked at the Battle of Chancellorsville. The Chancellorsville Campaign is usually recognized as Lee's greatest and most remarkable victory. It absolutely ranks as one of the most disappointing outcomes of the war for the Federals. Confederate brigadier general, author and historian Edward Porter Alexander believed that Hooker's campaign was "decidedly" the best strategy "conceived" and utilized against Lee's army during the war.[5]

Hooker's campaign plan wasn't especially resourceful, but it was astute and well executed at the onset. In essence Hooker's final plan was a turning movement utilizing crossings on the Rappahannock to outflank Lee on his left and threaten Lee's supply line. The object of Hooker's plan was to force Lee to withdraw from Fredericksburg and then to fight him on ground and terms selected by Hooker himself. Most of Hooker's cavalry was to make a raid in the direction of Richmond for the main purpose of ensuring the destruction of Lee's supply line. Major General George Stoneman, a West Point graduate serving as Hooker's chief of cavalry, was assigned to lead the raid with most of the Army of the Potomac's cavalry forces. Civil War author Stephen Sears opined that Hooker's plan was more innovative than anything devised by his predecessors.[6] Perhaps the most impressive aspect of Hooker's plan was his success in moving a large portion of the Army of the Potomac onto Lee's left flank before Lee was aware and able to react to it. By almost any calculation the Chancellorsville Campaign should have resulted in a significant Federal victory. Somehow happenstance and feckless leadership at the Federal corps level combined to defeat Hooker's otherwise excellent battle plan.

On the morning of April 27, 1863, Hooker launched his campaign by sending the V, XI and XII Corps up the Rappahannock to cross the river at Kelly's Ford. The VI Corps, the largest corps in the Army of the Potomac, staged a diversion two miles below Fredericksburg at Franklin's Crossing. About two miles downstream the I Corps also staged a crossing to confuse the Confederates about Hooker's intentions. The III Corps remained temporarily in camps across from Fredericksburg in view of the Confederates while most of the II Corps slipped away en route to U.S. Ford and Bank's Ford upstream on the Rappahannock. Stoneman's cavalry raid would commence the following day.

By April 29 General Lee suspected that something was afoot, but he didn't know exactly what it was. Hooker had managed to obscure his exact intentions, and the diversions mounted by the I Corps and VI Corps demanded Lee's attention. Lee was then aware of the Federal crossings at Kelly's Ford and at Germanna Ford. His messages to President Davis on the 29th reveal his uncertainty: "Their intention, I presume, is to turn our left, and probably get into our rear.... Taken with the reports received from our left, it looks like a general advance; but where his main effort will be made, cannot say. Troops not wanted south of James River had better be moved in this direction, and all other necessary preparations made." Concerned about the possibility of a turning movement on his left, Lee dispatched Major General Richard Anderson with his division of the Confederate I Corps westward to cover his left flank. Anderson and his division marched toward Chancellorsville on the night of the 29th in compliance to Lee's order "to cover the road leading from Chancellorsville down to the river, taking the strongest line you can, and holding it to the best advantage."[7] Anderson reached Chancellorsville by midnight; but, learning that a large Federal infantry force was bearing down on Chancellorsville, he withdrew to a ridge near Tabernacle Church to cover the roads leading to Fredericksburg.

While General Lee was pondering how to react to the puzzling Federal movements, Hooker was in a celebratory mood. From his headquarters near Falmouth on April 30, Hooker announced to his army "that the operations of the last three days have determined that the enemy must either ingloriously fly, or come out from behind his defenses and give us battle on our own ground, where certain destruction awaits him."[8] With most of four army corps already there and more troops on the way, Hooker arrived at Chancellorsville on the evening of the 30th to assume command in the field. Unfortunately for Hooker and the Federals, his prediction of victory was not only premature but also overly confident.

As the afternoon waned on the 30th, General Lee reached a decision about how to counter Hooker's maneuvers. In fact Lee was in serious trouble. Hooker's announcement was correct in that the Confederates would have to retreat or give up their advantage at the Fredericksburg defenses and fight on less favorable ground. Lee decided to march nearly all of his available forces to Chancellorsville and leave Major General Jubal Early's division behind to confront the Federal VI Corps at Fredericksburg. The Confederates would be heavily outnumbered on both fronts and in danger of the fate predicted by Hooker. Lee was doing exactly what Hooker had hoped he would do. It was a very audacious move by Lee, one that few commanders would have risked.

Stonewall Jackson reinforced Anderson near Tabernacle Church on the morning of May 1. Both Hooker and Jackson ordered an advance, Hooker from Chancellorsville and Jackson from Tabernacle Church on the roads leading to Chancellorsville. The Battle of Chancellorsville beginning on that day was fought in the region of tangled, second-growth forest known to locals as the Wilderness. The fighting took place in an area somewhat like a jungle with scattered clearings as the only open space with much visibility. The terrain hampered Hooker's ability to maneuver and to deploy and utilize his artillery. If Hooker chose this place for a fight, the outcome of the first day's fighting suggested that it was his mistake. By the end of the day Hooker had recalled his corps back to the Chancellorsville crossroads. He had surrendered the initiative to Lee and assumed a defensive stance.

On the evening of May 1 General Lee and Stonewall Jackson met and conferred near an ironworks known as Catherine Furnace south of Chancellorsville. Lee had considered attacking the Federal left flank, but after doing some checking he decided that plan was impracticable. History has often credited Stonewall Jackson for devising the flank attack at the Battle of Chancellorsville. Lee, however, on the evening of the 1st "stated to Gen. Jackson, we must attack" the Federal right as soon as possible. The two generals instead discussed how to facilitate the attack and which troops to use for it. Jackson proposed sending his entire corps via roads connecting to the Orange Turnpike a little west of the Federal XI Corps positioned on Hooker's right flank. Lee accepted the plan despite knowing that only two divisions from the Confederate I Corps, about 14,000 men, would remain in place to face the 75,000 men available to Hooker near Chancellorsville. Jackson with about 26,000, perhaps as many as 33,000, men would attempt on the following morning to march undetected through the woods and then spring a surprise attack on Hooker's right flank along the Orange Turnpike.[9] Jackson's column would be strung out for miles for most of the day, and Lee with only his two divisions facing the Federals stood no chance against a vigorous Federal attack. Lee seemingly had no problem accepting the extreme risk of this dicey tactical plan. Thus, a path was opened for Hooker to totally crush the Confederacy's eastern army on May 2.

General Jackson was later than usual getting his troops on the road for his flanking march. It was around 7 a.m. on the morning of May 2 by the time Jackson got his column moving. The road was filled for several miles by marching rebel infantry, and Jackson's column was soon spotted by Federals on a ridge known as Hazel Grove about a mile to the north. Hooker informed XI Corps commander Major General Oliver O. Howard to look well to his right because he suspected that the enemy was moving in that direction. In the afternoon a division from the Federal III Corps pushed out from Hazel Grove to engage Jackson's column. The elite 1st and 2nd U.S. Sharpshooters were in the vanguard of this movement, and these crack regiments managed to capture most of the 23rd Georgia Infantry, which had been assigned the duty of guarding the rear of Jackson's column. Other than this interference, the Confederate II Corps managed to reach its objective on Howard's right flank and deploy in line of battle during the afternoon hours.

Unprepared is the best term to describe the condition of the XI Corps on the afternoon of May 2. Howard and his senior officers had been receiving several reports of enemy activity on the right, just as General Hooker had suggested. Yet General Howard did little in response. Apparently General Howard gave little credence to reports of heavy enemy movement from his picket lines. Howard believed that the dense undergrowth and tangled forest would prove impenetrable, at least for the deployment of an attacking battle line. Also, by that afternoon Federal officers had started to believe that the Confederates were retreating; therefore, the sightings near the XI Corps could be explained as rear guard activity of the retreating Confederate columns.

It was Jackson's good fortune to be attacking the XI Corps that afternoon. His target was the smallest corps in the Army of the Potomac and the least effective. About two thirds of its soldiers were German immigrants or children of recent German immigrants, although nearly half of its soldiers were citizens by birth. With many German officers speaking English as a second language, and perhaps not very well, confusion was inevitable. Eleven of its twenty-seven regiments had never seen combat, and those units that had seen fighting usually had been whipped. General Lee himself euphemistically referred to the outfit as one of the "smallest and most indifferent corps" in the Federal Army. The Germans clung to their ethnic identity, proudly proclaiming "I fights *mit* Sigel." Many of its soldiers harbored resentment after the feckless Franz Sigel was replaced as corps commander by General Howard that spring, and a good many wanted Major General Carl Schurz, the 3rd Division commander, as their corps commander.[10] The Germans naturally wanted a German to command them; morale suffered when Howard assumed command.

At around 5:30 p.m., General Jackson, having reached his objective and having deployed his forces for an attack, sent his corps forward through the thick underbrush and woods towards the unsuspecting XI Corps. The Confederate II Corps was more than twice the size of the Federal XI Corps, and the attacking battle line overlapped the Federal right flank by more than a mile perpendicularly. Jackson's attack couldn't have succeeded much better if he had sent it marching through an unarmed mob.

Over the years the XI Corps has been much maligned for what happened at Chancellorsville. Much of the blame for its poor showing has been rightly ascribed to General Howard and other ranking officers within the corps who ignored warnings of the impending Confederate attack. Nevertheless the facts are that some of the XI Corps regiments fled without firing a shot, and perhaps most of its men panicked and ran rather showing much resistance when the rebels charged out from the woods. More recently writers have observed that the XI Corps was unpopular, even before Chancellorsville, within the Army of the Potomac and was assessed with an unfair reputation after the battle. For sure, many Union veterans blamed the XI Corps for their defeat at Chancellorsville with the implication being that its many Germans or "Dutchmen" were cowards who failed the rest of the army.

The simple explanation for what happened to the XI Corps at Chancellorsville is to point to the poor showing of its senior officers. That explanation ignores the performance of the units within the corps itself in other battles. It also ignores the record of other similar immigrant units in other battles, particularly those associated with Major General Franz Sigel. It is now impossible, other than by researching their letters and writings for that matter, to get into the minds of the soldiers of the XI Corps who were there on May 2. Perhaps motivation, outlook, morale and fealty should also be considered in the appraisal of the XI Corps as a fighting force. For the most part immigrant regiments performed satisfactorily when they were brigaded with non-immigrant units rather than being functionally segregated and led by immigrant officers. The Irish Brigade could be considered as one prominent exception to this trend. That particular immigrant brigade compiled an admirable record for valor and dependability during the war on its own. For whatever reason or cause, the performance of the XI Corps at Chancellorsville must be considered as one of the worst showings of the entire war. The poor reputation of the XI Corps never recovered among Civil War veterans. An example is found in the observations of a Union veteran appearing in a veteran's publication in 1889:

> If it will not be out of order I will say that while on our way to establish the skirmish line that day we passed through the breastworks of the Eleventh Corps and the remark was often made by some of the boys that we would have considered ourselves very fortunate to be attacked by the rebels in such works as those. Indeed they looked impregnable. And I have heard the remark made since by many of my old regiment, that Griffin's old Division of the Fifth Corps, or Birney's old Division of the Third Corps could, in their opinion, repulse Jackson's 20,000 men.[11]

Strangely, General Hooker did little on May 2 except to concentrate on saving his army. He reacted with even more caution than McClellan did during the Antietam Campaign. Jackson's attack crushed the overmatched XI Corps and continued eastward almost to Chancellorsville. Hooker shifted his troops and artillery to face the onslaught from the west as evening set in. Jackson's attack was losing momentum when dusk snuffed it out.

Considering a night attack, Jackson rode out with his staff around 9 p.m. to reconnoiter near the Federal lines along the Orange Plank Road. Somehow Jackson and his staffers were mistaken for Federal cavalry and were fired upon, probably by pickets from the 18th North Carolina Infantry. The general was hit three times, twice in his left arm and in his right hand. The wound in his left arm was severe, breaking the bone near his shoulder. The wound would prove mortal. Major General A.P. Hill assumed command of the Confederate II Corps, but he was soon injured by an exploding shell. Hill selected Major General J.E.B. Stuart, the famed cavalry commander, to succeed him in command of the corps.

General Hooker continued with his dubious command decisions. He ordered Major General John Sedgwick to march his VI Corps from Fredericksburg at once to Chancellorsville. At daybreak on the 3rd, Hooker withdrew the III Corps from Hazel Grove, the low ridge commanding the Chancellorsville crossroads. The movement itself was difficult and risky under enemy pressure, but also it surrendered a key position to the Confederates. Hazel Grove separated Lee's two army wings; the ridge there provided the Federals with a launch point to attack the weaker portion of Lee's army. Lee would have had a difficult task in reinforcing his troops on the east side of the battlefield. The Confederates quickly occupied Hazel Grove as the III Corps withdrew and thus gained an excellent artillery position from which to shell Hooker's lines at Chancellorsville. Hooker then shifted his artillery to Fairview Heights near the Chancellorsville crossroads, a location vulnerable to shelling from Hazel Grove.

A view of the Confederate artillery position on Hazel Grove. Here the rebel guns had an open field of fire upon the Federal artillery at Fairview Heights near the Chancellor House at Chancellorsville.

The author at Stonewall Jackson's grave in Lexington, Virginia (photograph by Myrna Earley).

General Stuart continued the Confederate attacks from the west with the II Corps early on May 3. By 7:30 the Confederate battle line had achieved a breakthrough on the Federal line along the Orange Plank Road. Throughout the day the Federals would fall back northward from Chancellorsville while General Sedgwick struggled to push his corps through Fredericksburg against strong enemy positions there. Sometime around 9 a.m., General Hooker was knocked senseless while standing on the Chancellor House front porch. A Confederate solid shot, or bolt, struck one of the porch pillars very close to the general, and a large section of the column was hurled into Hooker's side from his head to his foot. Hooker wasn't seriously injured, but he was apparently addled, perhaps sustaining a concussion. He soon called for Major General Darius Couch, the II Corps commander, to assume command of the Army of the Potomac in his stead. Hooker ordered General Couch to fall back to a defensive line north of Chancellorsville that had been selected the previous night by Federal engineers. Hooker decided against counterattacking the Confederates and ordered a withdrawal.

Hooker had in effect been bullied and pushed around by a smaller adversary out of fear of failure. Hooker later explained to the president that his withdrawal was the result of "a cause which could not be foreseen," and after this happened, "the chances of success were so much lessened that I felt another plan might be adopted in place of that we were engaged in, which would be more certain in its results." He also mentioned that it was no fault of his troops that they were "not crowned with glorious victory…" except for "one corps" which, of course, referred to the XI Corps.

General Sedgwick and his VI Corps managed to do what Burnside had failed to do against Lee in December: his troops successfully assaulted Marye's Heights. The VI Corps pushed on from Fredericksburg on the Orange Plank Road, heading for Chancellorsville as ordered. But Sedgwick and his VI Corps were checked at Salem Church, a short distance west of Fredericksburg. Lee kept shifting forces from Chancellorsville to meet Sedgwick until only around 25,000 men were remaining to face Hooker at Chancellorsville by the morning of May 4. Somehow all of these movements failed to spur Hooker to go on the offensive, or, for that matter, to go to Sedgwick's aid. General Sedgwick informed Hooker that he might be "obliged to withdraw" as he was "hemmed in" near Banks Ford on the Rappahannock.[12] By 2 a.m. on the 5th, Sedgwick received authorization, finally, to withdraw across the Rappahannock. By 5 a.m. the VI Corps was across the river at Scott's Mill Ford and the pontoon bridges used for the crossing were being taken up. The Chancellorsville Campaign was finished; Hooker withdrew back to his camps around Falmouth.

General "Fighting Joe" Hooker put up a very uneven performance as an army commander during the Chancellorsville Campaign. His plan for the campaign was excellent, and initially it was well executed. However, once the fighting started his decisions and tactics became increasingly inscrutable, even illogical. Unlike McClellan, who usually claimed to be outnumbered, Hooker knew from the onset that his army greatly outnumbered Lee's army. He knew that Longstreet's troops were away and unavailable to Lee; nevertheless, he fought the battle with excessive caution. He had managed to bypass Lee's strong position at Fredericksburg, yet he opted to halt his advance in a terrible place to fight a battle with superior numbers. He decided to fight a defensive battle and then failed to select proper ground for a defensive stand. The XI Corps was unprepared for Jackson's attack because Hooker didn't ensure that it was ready—he mistakenly assumed that Lee was retreating. The vital position at Hazel Grove was unwisely abandoned at a crucial point, giving the Confederates a great advantage. His decision to send most of his cavalry on a raid deprived him of the ability to screen his movements and to keep track of Lee's movements. These were some of Hooker's glaring mistakes, but his most detrimental command fault was his inability to act aggressively when nothing less would suffice.

To be sure, there were mitigating circumstances that relate to Hooker's failure at Chancellorsville. Stoneman's cavalry raid proved disappointing, Jackson's flanking march should have been detected and then engaged by the III Corps, General Howard allowed the XI Corps to be surprised by ignoring reports of enemy activity and General Sedgwick could have made a better effort at threatening Lee from Fredericksburg. The Army of the Potomac as it existed in the spring of 1863 was a legitimate concern for Hooker. Several regiments, thousands of men, were at the end of their enlistments and would soon be discharged. Also several regiments had never seen combat; it was an unknown as to how these outfits would perform in battle. Hooker's doubts concerning the abilities of some of his troops perhaps played a role in his timid command performance at Chancellorsville.

At Chancellorsville it seemed that every move and decision by General Lee succeeded beyond reasonable expectation. Fortune smiled on Lee throughout the campaign. Hooker allowed Lee free reign to take desperate chances repeatedly. Lee was fortunate that Jackson's attacking column passed unchallenged to the Federal right flank and then met with feeble resistance and then panic. This single development proved decisive in Lee's victory. General Lee's ability to quickly and decisively adjust to battle situations without regard to the extreme risk of his tactical decisions was extraordinary. That rare quality was on display repeatedly at Chancellorsville, and a Confederate victory would have been very unlikely if not impossible without it.

A look at the casualties at Chancellorsville indicates that the battle was mostly even, except for the XI Corps' involvement. The XI Corps suffered 2,400 casualties of which forty-one percent were missing compared to about 800 casualties in Jackson's attacking column on May 2. The fighting on May 3 around the Chancellorsville clearing cost the Federals around 8,623 casualties. The estimate for the Confederates is 8,962 men in that part of the battle. The Confederates were attacking, which usually results in higher casualties, but the Federals were hard hit by artillery fire and were in retreat, also a situation prone to increase casualties. Total casualties for the Federals were 1,694 killed, 9,672 wounded and 5,938 reported missing, 17,304 all together. The Confederates lost 1,724 killed, 9,233 wounded and 2,503 missing for a total of 13,460. Slightly more Confederates were killed in the fighting than Federals; but, being in enemy territory and having some positions overrun, the Federals lost many more men captured.[13]

General Lee's victory at Chancellorsville delivers the impression of military genius on his part. He defeated a numerically superior army and inflicted heavier casualties than his army sustained. However, a number of unlikely and fortuitous circumstances combined to favor him during the Chancellorsville Campaign. First, Hooker took too long in getting his corps combined and moving once he had established a bridgehead over the Rappahannock. Hooker waited for developments that he hoped would absolutely guarantee his success. He expected Stoneman's cavalry raid to cut Lee's communications: that didn't happen. Second, the Federal battle alignment allowed Lee to attack nearly always with equal or superior forces at the point of combat. Jackson was thereby able to overwhelm the XI Corps, and on May 3 the Confederate attacks benefited from a superior artillery position and equal to superior numbers where the fighting was done. After Hooker was injured, his sole concern was building a strong defensive position to resist further attacks. When the Federals pulled back north of Chancellorsville, a very strong defensive line was established. Lee is fortunate that he did not attack that line on May 4. Lee was also fortunate that Hooker failed to shuffle his corps effectively to reinforce the threatened sections of his battle lines. Hooker had two army corps on the battlefield that had little involvement in the fighting. Lee's tactics at Chancellorsville succeeded so incredibly well because General Hooker repeatedly failed to respond aggressively. The Federals did not need to retreat from the field at Chancellorsville; but they did, and as a result Lee's victory seemed all the more impressive.

While General Hooker's promising operational plan in Virginia was deteriorating and then collapsing into defeat, General Grant was executing one of the most brilliant campaigns of the war. As mentioned previously, the Chancellorsville Campaign is sometimes considered the most complex campaign of the war. The Vicksburg Campaign, however, involved much more planning, resourcefulness, cooperation, and ingenuity than probably any other campaign. Grant's Vicksburg Campaign required assistance from the Navy, innovation, deception, a series of land battles and a siege. Grant's dominance after he arrived on the scene, despite a few errors in judgment, makes his success seem all the more remarkable.

Grant chose Grand Gulf, a river village south of Vicksburg, as the base of operations for his campaign. He needed transports and gunboats to land his army on the east bank of the Mississippi. The required vessels were on the river north of Vicksburg; the vessels would have to steam past Vicksburg to be of use in Grant's operations. On the night of April 16, 1863, Admiral David Porter ran a fleet of twelve vessels past the batteries at Vicksburg with the loss of only one transport and some barges. With the naval gunboats and transports then available to assist an amphibious operation, General Grant decided to concentrate on capturing Vicksburg. He had originally considered first assisting in the effort to capture the other Confederate stronghold at Port Hudson, Louisiana, but he chose to focus on Vicksburg instead.

To deceive the enemy about his intentions, Grant ordered Sherman to distract the Confederates by making a feint northwest of the city. To further deceive General Pemberton, Grant ordered a major cavalry raid through Mississippi on April 17. That operation, known to history as Grierson's Raid, proved highly beneficial to Grant's operations. Colonel Benjamin H. Grierson was selected to lead the perilous cavalry foray into enemy territory. Grierson was an unlikely selection for such a demanding task. At age 36 during the raid, he had been a music teacher and storekeeper before the war. Grierson entered the service as an aide to a volunteer officer and had served in the army for only about a year and a half. Like most volunteer officers, he had limited command experience. Nevertheless, Grierson led his raid with commendable daring, marching his troopers across Mississippi north to south and creating consternation and commotion in rebel territory for over two weeks.

Grant opted to ask Admiral Porter to capture Grand Gulf rather than attempting to land his troops there and attack from across the river. A Navy gunboat attack on April 29 failed to silence artillery posted on a bluff above the town, so Grant decided to land his troops a few miles downstream at Bruinsburg and then attack Grand Gulf from the rear. Once his troops debarked at Bruinsburg, Grant felt a great sense of relief, despite the fact that he was "now in the enemy's country, with a vast river and the stronghold of Vicksburg between" him and his base of supplies.[14] Grant was proving here in the West that he was as audacious as Lee was in the East.

As Grant's expedition marched eastward from Bruinsburg, a Confederate force of 8,000 commanded by Brigadier General John S. Bowen blocked Grant's route in difficult terrain featuring ridges and ravines that favored the defenders. On May 1, Grant's force overwhelmed the Confederates after a hard-fought battle near Port Gibson. Two days later Grant reached Grand Gulf; the place was prepared as a staging and supply base for Grant's operations against Vicksburg.

Rather than moving immediately against Vicksburg from the south, Grant discerned that the more practicable approach was from the east. While marching to the northeast, Grant's troops clashed with Confederate Brigadier General John Gregg's brigade near Raymond, Mississippi, on May 12. Although Gregg fought aggressively, his brigade was heavily outnumbered. The Confederate left flank collapsed after several hours of fighting, and Gregg's troops retreated through Raymond. The following day Gregg withdrew to Jackson, Mississippi.

After the fighting at Raymond, General Grant "decided at once to turn the whole column towards Jackson and capture that place without delay." General Pemberton's Vicksburg garrison was on Grant's left and a force was assembling at Jackson on his right. General Joseph E. Johnston had arrived from Tennessee in hopes of saving Vicksburg. Grant assumed that Johnston would be receiving reinforcements at Jackson, so he could not allow a threat from the rear. On May 14 Grant attacked the Confederate fortifications at Jackson. Johnston, having decided against trying to defend Mississippi's capital city, established a rear guard to cover his retreat. The hard-fighting General John Gregg commanded the Confederate covering force at Jackson, so the Confederates again put up enough of a fight to cause significant casualties. Federal casualties at Jackson totaled about 286. The Confederates losses were 845 killed wounded and missing and seventeen pieces of artillery.

While at Jackson, Grant obtained a copy of General Johnston's dispatch to General Pemberton from a spy acting as a Confederate courier. From the captured document Grant anticipated that Pemberton would march his army, about 23,000 men, eastward from Vicksburg to join forces with Johnston. Grant decided to move to meet Pemberton's approaching army and found Pemberton's force posted in a defensive line on a ridge at a place called Champion Hill. On May 16 the Federals attacked and again overwhelmed the rebels after "about four hours" of intense combat. At the Battle of Champion's Hill, Pemberton lost twenty-seven cannons and nearly 4,000 men. Federal casualties totaled 2,441. Pemberton retreated to Vicksburg, but he posted a division and a brigade on the east bank of the Big Black River to hold a bridge near Bovina, Mississippi. The Confederates were posted in strong fieldworks with an open field and a shallow bayou in their front as a field of fire. The Federals arrived at the crossing shortly after dawn, May 17, and began pounding the enemy works with artillery. Brigadier General Michael Lawler then led an audacious bayonet charge "that lasted only three minutes" before overwhelming the Confederate defenders. Another 1,751 rebels surrendered and about 200 more fell in the brief battle. Federal casualties were thirty-nine killed, 237 wounded and two missing.

Grant's high-risk campaign in Mississippi was as dominant as any comparable operation conducted by either side during the war. While Grant always brought superior numbers to bear in each battle, his army was always on the attack and yet still inflicted much heavier casualties on the enemy. In most of the battles during the campaign Grant's army probably lost slightly more men killed and wounded. However, the Confederates lost heavily in troops captured or missing. In the final tally the Confederates lost about twice as many men as Grant did in the series of battles leading to the siege of Vicksburg and also eighty-eight cannons.[15] Grant succeeded in separating the forces of Pemberton and Johnston, which were superior in total numbers to his army, and in isolating Pemberton at Vicksburg. He surprised Pemberton by operating without a supply line in enemy territory and proved that an invading army could function in that fashion. This campaign demonstrated that, when properly led, Federal troops were capable of achieving dominating results on par with anything Lee's army accomplished in Virginia.

After his defeat at the Battle of Champion's Hill, Pemberton retreated to Vicksburg, worrying that his defeated, demoralized army would not be capable of defending the city. On May 17 he sent a message to General Johnston, whom he disliked, informing him of the Confederate defeat at the Battle of Big Black River Bridge. His army had suffered heavy losses in the two battles fought after he marched out from Vicksburg to cooperate with Johnston. His remarks to Johnston reveal his state of mind: "I greatly regret that I felt compelled to make the advance beyond the Big Black, which proved so disastrous in its results." The inference here is that he thought that he should have remained in the Vicksburg defenses rather than following Johnston's plan.

Johnston replied to Pemberton's message on the 17th, acknowledging Pemberton's message and informing Pemberton that he should be prepared to withdraw from Vicksburg. "If, therefore, you are invested at Vicksburg," Johnston wrote, "you must ultimately surrender. Under such circumstances, instead of losing both troops and place, we must, if possible, save the troops. If it is not too late, evacuate Vicksburg and its dependencies, and march to the northeast." Pemberton had been ordered by President Davis to defend Vicksburg, and he held out hope that a relief force would be sent from somewhere in the Confederacy to save the place. Pemberton "summoned his generals" and informed them about Johnston's orders. He asked them if they should comply with Johnston's directive. His subordinates unanimously advised Pemberton to remain at Vicksburg because they believed that their army would be rendered "ineffective as a fighting unit" even if it managed to fight its way out of the city.

On the following day, May 18, Pemberton informed Johnston of the verdict of his "council of war," which had decided "that it was impossible to withdraw the army from this position." Pemberton continued, "I have decided to hold Vicksburg as long as possible, with the firm hope that the Government may yet be able to assist me in keeping this obstruction to the enemy's free navigation of the Mississippi River. I still conceive it to be the most important point in the Confederacy."[16] And with that Vicksburg's fate was sealed.

Grant's army sealed the city with a crescent of its own fortifications; Grant also took measures to prevent Johnston from assisting Pemberton. After his string of victories in May, Grant believed Vicksburg was vulnerable to assault. Perhaps his easy victory at the Battle of Big Black Bridge served to convince Grant that Pemberton's troops were demoralized and ready to quit. On May 19 Grant ordered an assault on the Confederate lines northeast of the city. The attack was a complete failure. Grant ordered another greater and more widespread assault on May 22. During the attack General McClernand, commanding the XIII Corps, disingenuously claimed a near breakthrough and called on Grant to renew attacks that had been repulsed along the enemy lines. Grant reluctantly ordered renewed attacks to support McClernand. The end result was a Federal bloodbath. The fighting on May 22 cost the Federals 3,199 total casualties of which 502 were killed in action. Confederate casualties totaled about 500.[17] The Federal attacks never seriously threatened a breakthrough, and Grant resolved to implement siege operations commencing on May 25.

The ill-advised assault on May 22 at Vicksburg claimed one noteworthy distinction: it resulted in the largest number of Medals of Honor ever awarded to a single group of soldiers for a single action during the entire war. On the evening before the attack, volunteers were requested for a hazardous mission later known as the "forlorn hope." Only unmarried men were accepted for the mission. These volunteers were tasked with making a bridge over a ditch in front of a Confederate fort, under fire. The men had to cross nearly a quarter-mile of open ground, vulnerable to musket and cannon fire, to reach the fort. Of course, not enough men reached the fort with materials to complete the mission, and the survivors, probably less than half of the original group, were forced to remain beneath the fort's wall until darkness allowed them to fall back to the Federal lines. Fifty-three men, survivors of the "forlorn hope," were later presented with the Medal of Honor for this action.[18]

As the weeks passed in May of 1863, General Johnston was under increasing pressure to do something about the situation at Vicksburg. On May 9 Secretary of War Seddon had asked General Lee to send two divisions (Hood's and Pickett's that had been absent at Chancellorsville) to reinforce Johnston in the West. Lee replied on the 10th, "The adoption of your proposition is hazardous, and it becomes a question between Virginia and the Mississippi. The distance and the uncertainty of the employment of the troops are unfavorable." President Davis added his endorsement of Lee's response with

A Federal artillery emplacement on the siege line at Vicksburg.

the following: "The answer of General Lee was such as I should have anticipated, and in which I concur." These two messages reveal the position of the Confederate high command regarding Vicksburg. Although President Davis had considered Vicksburg as vital to defend, he was siding with General Lee and prioritizing Virginia operations.[19]

The wisdom of Davis's decision to prioritize the Eastern Theater over Vicksburg is dubious, although it is understandable given Lee's victory at Chancellorsville. Lee wanted to try another invasion of Maryland and Pennsylvania. His plan was basically a repeat of the Maryland Campaign of 1862 that ended with his defeat at the Battle of Antietam. Lee again believed he could influence Northern public opinion with a victory on Northern soil. He also thought that his Army of Northern Virginia was virtually invincible after his unlikely victory at Chancellorsville. Lee told General John Hood, for example, that at Chancellorsville "had I the whole army with me, General Hooker would have been demolished."[20] Lee's remarks reveal his faulty appraisal of the balance of power in the East. The Federals were not in danger of being "demolished" at Chancellorsville as Lee believed, and having Longstreet's Corps present would not have enabled Lee to destroy Hooker's army as Lee suggested. His plan to invade Maryland demonstrated that Lee's military judgment wasn't infallible. He was yet to realize that successfully invading Northern territory was beyond the capability of any Confederate army.

The siege of Vicksburg lasted through May and June. General Grant was more prone to attempt unorthodox schemes than most generals. He attempted an experiment with mine warfare (not the naval mine warfare) in hopes of opening a passageway for an assault through the Confederate defenses. Concluding that an enemy fortification known as the 3rd Louisiana Redan was impregnable, Grant gathered coal miners from Federal regiments to dig a tunnel under the rebel fortification. The miners dug three branches from the main tunnel and packed them with gunpowder. On June 25 the powder-filled branches were detonated. The explosion left a large crater in the fort, and, as planned, a Federal brigade charged into the breach. The assault failed to create a breakthrough, so the mining and explosion scheme was attempted again at the same redan on July 1. Following this second explosion, the Federal commanders, not wanting to risk another costly repulse, decided not to go ahead with another assault. The mining and blasting experiments had little impact on outcome of the campaign.

While Grant was making headway in the effort to secure the Mississippi River for the Union, General Lee was dominating events in the East. General Hooker had no promising plan to defeat Lee in Virginia after Chancellorsville, but Lee had secured approval for another incursion into Pennsylvania. By June Lee was moving his army northward.

Lee's initial objective was to clear the Shenandoah Valley of Federal troops. His invasion route ran northward through the valley to Winchester and on to western Maryland. Federal Major General Robert Milroy with a garrison of nearly 7,000 troops blocked Lee's way at Winchester. My paternal great grandfather was a soldier in the 1st Brigade of Milroy's Division at Winchester.

Robert Huston Milroy, known to his men as the "Gray Eagle" for his eagle-like white mane, sharp nose and darker beard, was an ostensibly competent commander for the post at Winchester. He had earned a Master of Military Science degree from Captain Partridge's Academy, later known as Norwich Academy. He had more command experience than many generals in the Civil War, including General Irvin McDowell before First Bull Run. But at Winchester he placed excessive confidence in the security of a few fortresses about the town. General Halleck advised Milroy to withdraw his division to Harpers Ferry as the entire Confederate II Corps approached from the south. Milroy declined, believing he could defend the town against whatever force the rebels were likely to hazard against it.

Lee sent General Ewell and the Confederate II Corps northward on June 10, and by the 13th Ewell was positioned to attack the Federals at Winchester. Ewell sent Major General Jubal Early to attack south of Winchester at Bower's Hill on the 13th. After some skirmishing and shelling, Milroy withdrew to his forts in Winchester. President Lincoln and General Halleck concluded that Winchester should be abandoned, as evidenced by Lincoln's dispatch to Milroy's department commander on June 14: "Get General Milroy from Winchester to Harper's Ferry, if possible. He will be 'gobbled up' if he remains, if he is not already past salvation." Ewell continued his attacks against the West Fort and Star Fort at Winchester on the 14th. The Federals were hopelessly outnumbered but still held the town. After dark Milroy decided to evacuate, and he managed to successfully withdraw most of his troops to Stephenson's Depot northeast of town that night. Ewell had sent a division to block the road at Stephenson's Depot, and fighting raged there in the pre-dawn hours of June 15. In the darkness Milroy proved unable to coordinate his forces for a breakthrough, and at dawn, with Confederate reinforcements arriving, Milroy's troops surrendered or escaped as best they could. When it was over Milroy had lost twenty-three guns, 300 wagons, 443 men killed and wounded and 3,358 missing. Ewell's casualties totaled only 269 men.[21] My paternal great grandfather was one of those captured on June 15.

As Ewell was mopping up at Winchester on the 15th, the remaining two corps in

Lee's army began moving northward. General Hill's newly created III Corps followed Ewell's route towards Winchester from Fredericksburg while General Longstreet's I Corps moved from Culpeper through gaps in the Blue Ridge Mountains and into the valley. General Stuart's Confederate cavalry managed to screen Lee's movements by fighting a series of skirmishes at Aldie, Middleburg and Upperville. These small actions wore down the Federal cavalry and prevented detection of Lee's infantry as it moved into Maryland. Following these cavalry skirmishes, Stuart embarked on another sweeping ride through enemy territory, an excursion that ultimately deprived Lee of knowledge of the movements and location of the Federal army. By June 24 parts of Lee's army were roaming in southern Pennsylvania. Ewell's troops moved through Chambersburg with Hill's and Longstreet's corps not far behind. Some II Corps troops marched through Gettysburg to York while others made for the state capital at Harrisburg.

Meanwhile General Joseph Hooker was relieved of command of the Army of the Potomac on June 27. The details of Hooker's demise need not be covered here. His performance at Chancellorsville had demonstrated that a change of command was incumbent. Hooker provided the opportunity when he tendered his resignation on the 27th.

Major General George Gordon Meade was chosen to replace General Hooker in command of the Army of the Potomac on June 28. Born on the last day of 1815 in Cadiz, Spain, Meade was a son of an American merchant. He was graduated from West Point in 1835 with a respectable academic standing. Meade served in the Topographical Engineers Corps during the Mexican War, and most of his service involved engineering and surveying work. During his Civil War service up to the time of his selection for command of the Army of the Potomac, he had demonstrated competence in his various assignments. He had been promoted from brigade commander to command of the V Corps by the end of 1862. Meade fit the mold of Federal officers groomed under the leadership of General McClellan. In other words he was not one to resort to risky tactics, nor was he a general likely to be wasteful of his soldiers' lives.[22]

Before noon on June 30, 1863, Brigadier General John Buford's cavalry division rode into the heretofore peaceful village of Gettysburg, Pennsylvania. General Buford reported a sizeable Confederate infantry force had been in town and had then moved a few miles to the west. Meade ordered Major General John Reynolds, commanding the I Corps, to occupy Gettysburg. Meanwhile Buford deployed his cavalry division west of town and awaited reinforcements from Reynolds.

Early on the next morning, July 1, Brigadier General Henry Heth's Confederate division returned to the outskirts of Gettysburg, intent on confiscating shoes from a local shoe factory. Buford's cavalry division was there to meet them. Buford's cavalrymen were heavily outnumbered, but with the advantage of breech-loading carbines and artillery support they kept the rebels out of Gettysburg for hours. General Reynolds arrived to fulfill his assignment at Gettysburg during the cavalry fight and met with Buford. After a quick assessment of the situation, Reynolds rode back to rush his I Corps into the fight west of town.

The Battle of Gettysburg is probably the best-known battle in American history. The fighting didn't have to happen there; it wasn't preplanned. Historical tradition suggests that General Reynolds, and perhaps Buford, had examined the lay of the land south of Gettysburg and had recognized it as a good place for a defensive stand. Reynolds could have deployed his corps on that strong defensive ground south of town; instead, he hurried back to his troops and deployed them west of town. He also sent aides to order the

XI and III Corps to march to Gettysburg on the quick. He had been ordered to occupy Gettysburg, so he acted accordingly. Reynolds's decision to fight for the town probably shifted the advantage to Lee initially. The first day of the battle certainly played out that way.

General Reynolds returned with his I Corps troops and immediately deployed his corps on ridges running north to south a short distance to the west of Gettysburg. Major General Howard soon came up with his XI Corps via roads from south of town. The troops deploying that morning to defend Gettysburg were a dichotomous group. The soldiers in Reynolds's I Corps were doubtless some of the best in the Army of the Potomac. General Howard was at best an indifferent commander, and his XI Corps was the weakest corps in the Army of the Potomac. The manner in which the fighting played out on July 1 followed exactly, as one might expect, according to this assessment.

General Reynolds was shot from his horse and killed at McPherson's Woods west of town just as he arrived to supervise his infantry deploying for battle. Thus, at the onset of serious fighting for the town, the Federals were deprived of a dependable leader to manage the battle. Brigadier General Abner Doubleday, of baseball notoriety, assumed temporary command of the I Corps until General Howard, the senior general on the field, sorted things out and assumed overall command.

As Howard's XI Corps arrived, he sent two divisions north of town to align with the I Corps on his left. Howard later explained that he realized that he might "be obliged to fall back" during the fight, so he left "Steinwehr's Division with some batteries" at Cemetery Hill, on the southern edge of town, while the other two divisions deployed ahead.[23] Two Confederate divisions from Ewell's II Corps (Early's and Rodes') arrived to battle Howard's two divisions north of town while two divisions of General A.P. Hill's III Corps attacked from the west.

The Federal I Corps troops were more than holding their own, though outnumbered in the fight, when the XI Corps collapsed as it had done at Chancellorsville. The commander of one of Howard's divisions later wrote that his men began to run almost immediately after the Confederate skirmishers attacked. Conversely, one historian suggested that the XI Corps soldiers "fought tenaciously and bravely until Jubal Early's Rebels" outflanked them. Another expert on Gettysburg wrote that Howard's men "fought extremely well" under the circumstances; they were "let down once more by the decisions of their commanders."[24]

However anyone wishes to interpret the conduct of the Federal XI Corps at Gettysburg, General Lee observed the panicked retreat of its soldiers and decided to choose Gettysburg as the place to fight the Army of the Potomac on Northern soil. It must have seemed to Lee that he had a fortuitous opportunity to repeat his victories at Second Bull Run and Chancellorsville. His immediate objective was to drive the enemy off Cemetery Hill to secure command of the good defensive ground General Reynolds had recognized and had attempted to control. The real outcome of the day's fighting was decided on the evening of July 1.

Having decided to make Gettysburg his battleground, Lee recognized the importance of seizing the high ground south of town. A.P. Hill's two divisions, which had fought all day west of town and were low on ammunition, were not immediately available for the task. General Longstreet's I Corps was not yet on the scene, so General Lee sent his aide to suggest to General Ewell that he should attack Cemetery Hill, if Ewell thought he could. Generals Early and Gordon urged Ewell to attack the hills south of town. Early thought a division "could take the hill to which the enemy had retreated," and he "communicated" his views to Ewell. However, General Ewell informed Early that the remaining fresh division of his corps, Johnson's Division, "was coming up," and Ewell intended to use it to attack the hill adjacent to Cemetery Hill.[25] Ewell delayed until it was too late to make a successful attack that evening. Reinforcements from the Federal XII arrived and began to occupy Culp's Hill adjacent to Cemetery Hill on the Federal right. Had Ewell attacked immediately after the XI Corps was routed the outcome is uncertain, but because he didn't Lee had lost his best opportunity to benefit from the fighting around Gettysburg by nightfall of July 1.

General Hancock rode back to Taneytown, Maryland, to report to General Meade. Major General Henry W. Slocum, commanding the XII Corps, assumed temporary command at Gettysburg. General Hancock reached Taneytown around 9 p.m. He reported that the position at Gettysburg was a good place to fight it out with Lee. Meade by this time had already sent a message to General in Chief Halleck informing him that he hoped to concentrate his army at Gettysburg to defeat Ewell's and Hill's Confederate corps before the rest of Lee's army could intervene. Meade retained in his mind the option to fall back to a defensive line on Pipe Creek if the situation were to change. On the evening of July 1 Meade was unsure of what he would do next. He believed the field at Gettysburg provided a strong defensive position to hold against Lee, but he also was considering the option of attacking Lee if the situation warranted it.

Confederate Lieutenant General James "Old Pete" Longstreet, who commanded Lee's I Corps, played a highly controversial role at Gettysburg. Longstreet was graduated from West Point in 1842, and, like many Civil War generals, he had been brevetted for gallantry during the Mexican War. Longstreet has been traditionally viewed as an excellent battlefield tactician; however, his record as an independent commander proved unimpressive. At Gettysburg Longstreet disagreed with Lee's battle plan, and he was late in carrying out his assignments throughout the battle.

When Longstreet conferred with General Lee on the afternoon of July 1 and on the morning of July 2, he urged Lee to abandon the battlefield at Gettysburg. Longstreet offered an alternative campaign plan which he believed made better sense. Concisely, Longstreet suggested that the Confederate army should be fighting a defensive battle rather than attacking at Gettysburg. A change of tactics, Longstreet held, would not only be safer but also more likely to succeed. Longstreet wanted to slip Lee's army around the Federal left towards Maryland and deploy in a defensive position to await a Federal attack. The plan would place Lee's army between the Army of the Potomac and Washington or Baltimore. The plan, of course, assumed that Meade would remain at Gettysburg while Lee marched southward and that Meade would attack after the Confederates established a strong defensive line. The shift of position, Longstreet probably thought, might play out like the Battle of Fredericksburg.

General Lee disagreed with Longstreet's suggestion to quit the battle at Gettysburg. He had not yet heard from his cavalry commander, General Stuart. His army had already fought a costly battle at Gettysburg on July 1, a battle that had nearly used up his III Corps. Lee did not want another Antietam; he did not want another defensive stand being fought this time in Pennsylvania. The fighting on July 1, particularly the rout of the XI Corps, seemed very similar to the way Chancellorsville unfolded. An offensive victory similar to Chancellorsville this time on Northern soil would have been much more beneficial than a defensive stalemate similar to the Battle of Fredericksburg. Meade now knew the exact whereabouts of Lee's army, so breaking off contact and moving unchallenged in enemy territory was a dubious proposition. Lee had decided to fight it out at Gettysburg, confident he could best Meade much as he had bested Hooker in May.

General Meade reached the battlefield from Taneytown sometime around midnight and spent the predawn hours examining his army's positions. Most of the Army of the Potomac reached Gettysburg by 9 a.m. on July 2 except for the VI Corps, the largest corps in Meade's army. Meade concentrated his strength on the north end of his hook-shaped line with the XII Corps atop Culp's Hill on the right, the "indifferent" XI Corps on Cemetery Hill with two I Corps divisions posted behind, and the II Corps spread out southward on Cemetery Ridge. The V Corps was placed in reserve behind Cemetery Hill. On the far left edge of Meade's line stood two small eminences, Little Round Top and Big Round Top, dominating most of the Federal positions. Meade had assigned Major General Daniel Sickles and his III Corps to hold the ground south of the II Corps including the Round Tops. Unfortunately for Meade, Sickles did not deploy his corps according to Meade's expectations.

On the morning of July 2, General Lee concluded that his best chance of winning at Gettysburg required hitting the Federal left flank south of town. He selected General Longstreet's fresh I Corps arriving that day to make the attack, despite the fact that Longstreet opposed the plan. Lee could observe the concentration of Federal corps defending the hills south of town, and he correctly reasoned that Meade's left would be the weakest point of his line. Lee ordered Longstreet to attack the Federal left flank that morning.

A view from Little Round Top looking toward Cemetery Ridge.

To assist Longstreet, he wanted General Ewell to make a demonstration with his II Corps against the northern sector of Meade's defensive line at Culp's Hill and Cemetery Hill.

Up until July 2 Lee had been winning a nearly unbroken series of battles beginning during the Seven Days around Richmond in the summer of 1862. What had happened the previous day, July 1, fit the pattern of Federal failures. It was reasonable for Lee to expect another one-sided victory after the Federal XI Corps crumbled much as it did at Chancellorsville. Unfortunately for Lee, he did not have in General Longstreet the type of aggressive commander that he had with General Jackson at Chancellorsville. Longstreet did not act with alacrity in response to Lee's order to attack on July 2. In a difficult situation anyway, Lee's chances for victory at Gettysburg were lessened further by the unusually slow movement of General Longstreet's command.

Lee and Longstreet were granted an unearned and unexpected advantage when Federal Major General Daniel Sickles neglected to cover the two hills, Little Round Top and Big Round Top, at the southern edge of the battlefield with his III Corps. Sickles instead sent his corps out east of Cemetery Ridge along the Emmitsburg Road. The position looked good to Sickles, but by moving off Cemetery Ridge Sickles had exposed his heavily outnumbered corps to attack. The movement also isolated his corps by failing to link with the II Corps holding Cemetery Ridge in conjunction with the rest of Meade's army. Sickle's outnumbered III Corps was soon overmatched by Longstreet's corps, which consisted of a third of Lee's army.

It was after 3:30 p.m. before Longstreet got his divisions in position to make his assigned attack. Longstreet almost certainly could have made the attack earlier in the

Big Round Top as seen from the summit of adjacent Little Round Top at Gettysburg Battlefield.

Big Round Top in a photograph taken shortly after the battle from Little Round Top. Library of Congress Civil War Collection.

day, as General Lee expected. Had he attacked in the morning, the Confederates might have been able to occupy the higher ground south of Cemetery Ridge, from which to enfilade the Federal lines with artillery fire. The Second U.S. Sharpshooters, a small regiment of probably fewer than 250 men, managed to slow the Confederate attack on the extreme left flank of the III Corps. Troops from the Federal V Corps arrived just in time to defend Little Round Top and blunt Longstreet's attack. Although the III Corps was driven back with heavy casualties, the Federal line held and Longstreet failed to accomplish the breakthrough General Lee had anticipated.

In conjunction with Longstreet's attack, General Ewell was expected to make a demonstration at Culp's Hill and Cemetery Hill on the northern sector of the battlefield in order to prevent Meade from sending reinforcements to counter Longstreet's attack against the Federal left flank. Ewell was expected to make a concerted attack only if Longstreet succeeded in driving the Federals back. Concisely, Ewell did too little and was too late carrying out his assignment to have a meaningful impact on the outcome of

Opposite, top: At the base of Big Round Top some unburied corpses are visible in this photograph of an area known as the Slaughter Pen. Taken shortly after the fighting at Gettysburg, a man in an overcoat stands on a large rock at the left of the photograph. Library of Congress Civil War collection.

Opposite, bottom: The Slaughter Pen section at the base of Big Round Top was cleared in recent years. The large jutting rock in this view is the same one visible in the wartime photograph showing a man standing upon it.

6. 1863: The Year of Northern Ascendency

Longstreet's attack. Ewell finally did attack around dusk on July 2. He should have moved hours earlier. Ultimately, the fighting involving Ewell's corps on July 2 simply added to the casualty lists. Lee's plan for coordinated attacks along the Federal line in succession failed completely; thus, by nightfall of July 2 Meade held the upper hand at Gettysburg.

The Confederates had met with significant success by attacking during the first two days of fighting at Gettysburg, yet Lee had other options on the morning of July 3, 1863. General Longstreet again suggested his plan to skirt Meade's army and move to a new

This monument for the 1st Minnesota Infantry honors the famous sacrificial charge made by the regiment on that field on July 2, 1863.

The Federal line from Cemetery Ridge to the two Round Tops as viewed from the Pennsylvania Monument at Gettysburg.

defensive position near to or in Maryland. Lee, like Meade, could have also remained at Gettysburg to await an attack by the enemy, or he could have pulled back to the mountains west of Gettysburg to await developments. Lee chose to attack. His initial plan for the July 3 called for coordinated attacks by Ewell and Longstreet on opposite sectors of the battlefield.

Lee's plan was rendered obsolete before dawn on July 3 because General Meade ordered the Federal XII Corps to attack Ewell's troops at Culp's Hill. Federal artillery began shelling Ewell's troops in preparation for the attack at around 4:30 a.m.; Ewell's Confederates attacked in response to the shelling, upsetting General Lee's plan for the day. General Lee then decided to attack the center of Meade's line on Cemetery Ridge with Major General George Pickett's fresh I Corps division and a division and two brigades from A.P. Hill's III Corps, a force of over 12,000 infantrymen.

Just exactly what convinced General Lee that he could drive off the Federals with an attack against the middle of Cemetery Ridge remains a mystery. Anyone who has ever stood in the path of the Confederate attack made on July 3 could have seen that the ground there is an absolute killing field. It is open and flat from Cemetery Ridge to the edge of trees where the Confederate infantry started their advance and presented the Federals with a clear field of fire for miles from east to west and north to south.

General Lee ordered a massive bombardment upon the middle of Cemetery Ridge in preparation for his attack. The Confederates directed most of their artillery fire against

Located on the crest of Cemetery Ridge, the Bryan or Brian House, owned by a free black, was the headquarters of Brigadier General Alexander Hays who commanded a Federal II Corps division.

the focus of the attack on Cemetery Ridge. Perhaps as many as 180 guns with at least 22,000 rounds of ammunition were made available to pound the Federal positions, making this the greatest single bombardment in American history up to that time. Colonel Edward Porter Alexander, West Point Class of 1857, managed the bombardment for Longstreet. At around 1 p.m. the Confederate bombardment commenced and continued unabated for about two hours.[26] It was largely ineffective.

The fighting on Culp's Hill subsided before noon after a Federal countercharge pushed Johnson's Division of Ewell's Corps off the hill. There was a period of about four hours following Ewell's withdrawal and the start of the assault on Cemetery Ridge, which is known to history as Pickett's Charge. Meade had anticipated an attack on his center since the evening of July 2. The Federal II Corps would be the target of the main attack on July 3, as Meade had expected. The heavy shelling along Cemetery Ridge from 1 p.m. until Pickett's Charge commenced after 3 p.m. provided assurance that Lee was attacking there. Meade did not prepare for a counterattack. It is obvious from his posture that his overriding concern was to repel the anticipated attack rather than making an attack of his own. Meade did not even prepare to take the initiative. He demonstrated at Gettysburg that he was from the same overly-cautious pattern as General McClellan. He would never demonstrate an aptitude for aggressive tactical methods.

Pickett's Charge played out in much the way that General Longstreet had anticipated. The Confederates did manage to cross the open fields to reach the II Corps line on Cemetery Ridge, but they suffered heavy casualties getting there. The II Corps did not crumble as the XI Corps had at Chancellorsville and again on July 1. Pickett's Charge was repulsed without forcing Meade to rush in much support from the adjacent corps. The survivors from Pickett's Charge were fortunate to escape back to Confederate lines without being pursued or, for that matter, being battered much by the Federals watching them retreat. Federal soldiers later said they had little heart for shooting down the beaten rebels from behind. The commander of the 13th Vermont ordered his men not to shoot at the Pickett's men as they fled back to their lines.[27]

Meade was unprepared to follow immediately on the heels of the defeated Confederates as they scattered and made for their starting point on Seminary Ridge. An aggressive, confident commander in a similar situation would have prepared for the opportunity to counterattack Lee. General Hancock, who was wounded during Pickett's Charge, urged Meade in a message to use the V and VI Corps to go after the beaten Confederates. The VI Corps was the largest corps in the Army of the Potomac. Its 1st and 2nd Divisions had a total of thirty-four casualties, of which only three were killed, during the entire battle at Gettysburg. Obviously, the VI Corps was strong and fresh enough for making an attack, especially when compared to the battle-weary and depleted corps of Lee's army.

Meade, in fairness, did have justifiable reasons to be reluctant to counterattack after Pickett's Charge. For one thing, the attack would have to cross the same open killing ground to reach the Confederate lines. One Civil War writer of considerable merit opined that Meade had won decisively and "wisely chose to settle for that."[28] This viewpoint ignores the obvious fact that Meade had no intention of doing anything more than winning the battle. Meade was clearly thinking of survival first. To use a sports analogy, he was fighting not to lose rather than going for a knockout. In final analysis, Meade probably could and should have accomplished more than he did at Gettysburg. Meade, like many Northern generals in the East, had a little too much respect for and fear of the enemy.

Beyond the 3 inch ordnance rifle in the foreground is the open field crossed by Pickett's attacking Confederates on July 3 at Gettysburg.

As the survivors of Pickett's Charge straggled back to Seminary Ridge, Lee at last realized his army was not invincible. In his report for the battle, Lee spared nearly all of the details about his ill-fated attack on July 3. He praised the conduct and valor of his men, but he admitted that he may have asked more of them "than they were able to perform." After the repulse of Pickett's Charge, Lee immediately ordered preparations for meeting an enemy attack. Such a probability he naturally expected, for he likely would have attacked if the circumstances were reversed. In his battle report he expressed confidence in the continuing ability of his men "to cope successfully with the enemy."[29] He demonstrated that confidence by remaining on the field on July 4, essentially challenging Meade to attack.

The battle itself became a controversial topic for Southerners, particularly after the war. While Lee's tactics, especially the main attack on July 3, have been questioned and criticized, General Longstreet's role in the battle proved more contentious. Some of the criticism against Longstreet was justified. He was opposed to Lee's battle plan, and his performance seemed indifferent at Gettysburg. Nevertheless, the outcome of the war was not decided at Gettysburg, as some suggest. A Confederate victory there would not have likely caused the Union war effort to collapse. The legacy of Gettysburg is that it demonstrated the futility of Confederate hopes for carrying the war into Northern territory. At Gettysburg Lee's best effort to win a significant victory outside the South was defeated, with relative ease.

As the cavalry battle at Brandy Station marked the beginning of the ascendancy of the Federal cavalry, Gettysburg marked the end of Lee's dominance and the beginning of Northern ascendancy overall. Lee had taken an extreme risk by calling for a second invasion of Pennsylvania. Troops and resources that were needed in the fight against Grant at Vicksburg were wasted in the Gettysburg Campaign. Lee was responsible for his government's focus on the East and for the high-risk attempt to invade the North during the summer of 1863. Failure in Pennsylvania that summer accelerated the Confederacy's decline and brought about the opposite effect Lee had expected. In retrospect, the potential rewards of Lee's invasion were insufficient to justify the risk. Lee had not learned from his defeat at Antietam, and the Confederacy's chances of survival were diminished greatly because of it.

While the Battle of Gettysburg was being fought in Pennsylvania, the situation for General Pemberton at Vicksburg had reached a critical stage. By July 1 Pemberton knew that he would be compelled to surrender unless the siege could be lifted. His army was in no condition to withstand further attacks from Grant. On June 28, General Joseph Johnston finally moved toward Vicksburg with a view of enabling the city's defenders to escape. Johnston had given up hope of lifting the siege; his intention was to attack Grant's army to create a breach in the Federal lines sufficient for Pemberton's garrison to break out of Vicksburg. Johnston sent a message on July 3 to Pemberton informing him of his intention to attack on July 7. Before he received Johnston's message, Pemberton had initiated surrender talks with General Grant.

Pemberton surrendered Vicksburg to General Grant on July 4. Pemberton had

One of the numerous Union monuments at the Vicksburg Battlefield Park, this one depicts a soldier aiming a Burnside carbine.

consulted four of his division commanders and determined that his troops were in no condition to evacuate the city. His men were too exhausted to fight their way through the Federal lines and then make their escape. Pemberton should have evacuated Vicksburg in May before Grant's army attacked his defenses. General Johnston had essentially ordered him to evacuate the city and march to the northeast on May 17. The fall of Vicksburg followed a pattern of costly surrenders at Confederate strongholds resulting from poor command decisions.

General Grant offered to parole the Confederates rather than shipping them to camps as prisoners of war. The captured Confederates were expected to sign parole documents promising not to fight again until they were formally exchanged for paroled or captive Federals. "Several hundred refused to sign their paroles, preferring to be sent to the North as prisoners to being sent back to fight again." General Grant reported the following totals: "At Vicksburg 31,600 prisoners were surrendered, together with 172 cannon, about 60,000 muskets and a large amount of ammunition. The small arms of the enemy were far superior to the bulk of ours." Grant did not want the burden of feeding and transporting the captured rebels to a prison or a place where they could be exchanged. After signing their paroles, the Vicksburg garrison was marched out of town on July 11.[30]

On the same day that Vicksburg surrendered, Confederates led by Lieutenant General Theophilus H. Holmes attacked Helena, Arkansas, on the west bank of the Mississippi River. Holmes commanded a force of over 7,400 Confederates that included Major General Sterling Price, and John Marmaduke, Joseph Shelby and James Fagan, three brigadier generals associated with the fighting in Missouri. Major General Benjamin Prentiss, who had surrendered the Federal troops surrounded at the Hornet's Nest at Shiloh the previous April, commanded a Federal garrison of 4,129 men at Helena. The Navy gunboat U.S.S. *Tyler* also participated in the defense of Helena. At Helena Holmes doomed his "valiant army" to defeat by committing "his troops to a reckless, poorly conceived, and uncoordinated assault without proper reconnaissance and artillery support." Conversely, the Federal commanders managed the battle with "flexibility and boldness." Federal artillery supported by the *Tyler* pounded the attacking Confederates, inflicting severe losses. Holmes ordered a withdrawal well before noon, having been soundly beaten. Official Confederate casualty reports listed 173 killed, 687 wounded and 776 missing, but Prentiss reported that more than 400 Confederates were buried by his troops. Confederate casualties probably exceeded 2,000. Federal losses totaled fifty-seven killed, 127 wounded and thirty-six missing.[31]

The battle itself was an unfortunate, pointless sacrifice of lives. Holmes' movement against Helena was too late to have an impact on the outcome of the siege of Vicksburg, or, for that matter, any aspect of the war. It is included in this study because it is an example of the disproportionate losses that resulted when Civil War troops assaulted field works and fortifications, especially when the assault was fumbled or poorly directed. In this case the Confederates suffered the much heavier losses; later in the war, it would often be the Federals suffering in similar circumstances. The outcome of the Battle of Helena serves as a demonstration that the Confederates were not immune to defeat and disproportionate losses in battles involving the conditions that were often faced by Federal troops. During the course of the Civil War, Federal troops were required to attack forts and fieldworks much more often than their enemies. Casualty figures during the last two years of the war reflect this fact.

Meanwhile on the 4th of July at Gettysburg, General Lee was whipped, but he held his ground during Independence Day. He wasn't there to celebrate the happenings of 1776. He repeated the bluff he had played at Antietam the previous year and essentially dared Meade to attack. Should Meade have attacked on the 4th of July? At the least he should have been prepared to launch an attack that day. Lee was in an extremely dangerous situation, low on artillery ammunition, deep in enemy territory, having sustained massive casualties. General Longstreet later was quoted as saying he would have preferred that Meade attack that day because Hood and McLaws were not engaged on July 3, and he still had a "heavy force of artillery." But the Confederate artillery only had a supply of about five rounds per gun following Pickett's charge. Civil War writer Allan Nevins insightfully observed that if Meade had acted with the same "imprudence" as Lee and Jackson at Chancellorsville, "he might have routed the Confederates and ended the war."[32] General Meade, however, wasn't thinking about that at Gettysburg on the 4th of July.

General Meade was thinking "small" after the fighting ceased at Gettysburg. He allowed Lee to slip away, marching to the southwest toward Hagerstown, Maryland, and on to Williamsport on the Potomac River. Lee was indeed fortunate that Meade chose not to attack during his retreat. Confederate official losses totaled 20,451 of which 2,592 were listed as killed and 12,709 wounded. His actual losses were probably greater than 28,000. Only 5,150 of his soldiers were recorded as captured; however, records of Confederate prisoners of war "bear the names of 12,227 wounded and unwounded Confederates" captured by the Federals "at and about Gettysburg from July 1 to 5, inclusive." Also Meade later reported that "126 Confederate officers and 2,764 men were buried" by the Federals, not counting sixty-four Confederates buried by the Federal V Corps and those "buried by the" Federal XI and XII Corps. The number of known Confederate burials at Gettysburg exceeded the Confederate official report of killed by at least 300. Official Federal casualties totaled 23,049, including 3,155 killed and 14,529 wounded.[33] It seems that Confederate casualties were, sometimes at least, underreported, especially later in the war. Meade, with knowledge of Lee's heavy losses, should have appreciated his opportunity to destroy the Army of Northern Virginia as it retreated. Instead, he repeated McClellan's critical mistake following the Battle of Antietam: he allowed Lee's crippled army to escape back to Virginia.

Most of Lee's army reached Hagerstown by July 7 while Meade dawdled. A pontoon bridge across the Potomac at Williamsport, Maryland, was destroyed by Federal cavalry, and heavy rains rendered the river fords impassable. Thus, Lee and his army were stranded in southern Maryland, "penned up in a highly vulnerable position" at the mercy of Meade's approaching army. It was precisely the situation Lincoln and Halleck had hoped for and exhorted their generals to exploit. Lincoln pressed Halleck for action, and Halleck repeatedly urged Meade to destroy Lee's army. For example, on July 7 a message from Lincoln mentioned that Vicksburg had surrendered to General Grant. "Now," the message read, "if General Meade can complete his work ... by the literal or substantial destruction of Lee's army, the rebellion will be over." On the next day Halleck again urged Meade to take action, "If Lee's army is so divided by the river, the importance of attacking the part on this side is incalculable. Such an opportunity may never occur again."[34] Yet Meade failed to respond with urgency.

Lincoln and Halleck, even from the distance of Washington, could see that Meade was failing to press his opportunity to destroy Lee's army. The ordinary Federal soldiers in the field clearly saw it first hand and hoped for an attack before Lee could escape.

Lieutenant Colonel Thomas Wildes, who belonged to my paternal great grandfather's regiment, made the following observations in a letter written on July 6:

> We are doing good work here, harassing the rebels on their flank, cutting up their trains, and picking up their stragglers. There probably never was so complete a rout as Lee's army sustained. A train six miles long passed by on the Cumberland pike yesterday. It was terribly cut up by our cavalry and Pleasanton's. It will probably all be captured, or destroyed. Providence is favoring us with such copious rains. The Potomac has risen several feet.... The demoralization of Lee's army is something awful to witness, and if General Meade would press it hard, fully half of it would certainly be destroyed, or captured. Why he does not press forward is a mystery to us, who can see its hopeless condition here, as it passes by.

One Civil War writer observed that the captures of Lee's trains as mentioned by Colonel Wildes "demonstrated that if Meade had begun a rapid march on the 4th or 5th, Lee would probably have found surrender unavoidable."

Meade was too cautious in following Lee to the Potomac. He finally approached the Confederate defensive line, which ran nine miles from the Hagerstown area to near Falling Waters, by July 12. The fieldworks looked formidable from a distance, but actually they were "merely heaped earth covering a continuous line of piled rails." On the 12th, Meade consulted his generals again about whether to attack Lee's new defensive line north of the Potomac. Meade decided to examine the enemy fieldworks for himself on the 13th, wasting yet another day. On the 13th the Confederates managed to bridge the swollen Potomac River at Falling Waters, and that night Lee's army began withdrawing across the bridge and at a ford at Williamsport. The river was about chest deep at the ford and rising, but Ewell's corps had managed to cross over into Virginia by dawn of July 14. Longstreet's Corps had marched to the pontoon bridge and began to cross by daylight. Hill's Corps, bringing up the rear, was still marching for the bridge; it would be hours before the last Confederates could possibly get across the Potomac. Meade here had one last, best opportunity to destroy Lee's army. Yet again Meade refused to take the initiative. Federal cavalry finally did attack just as the last Confederate division was approaching the pontoon bridge. Confederate Brigadier General James J. Pettigrew, a brilliant scholar and promising officer who had just turned thirty-six on July 4, was mortally wounded during the cavalry foray. The Federal cavalry also managed to capture about 2,000 Confederates at Falling Waters. There is little reason to doubt that "a general of high courage and consummate skill" could have forced much of Lee's army to surrender at Falling Waters.[35]

President Lincoln was intensely distressed when he learned of Lee's escape. General in Chief Halleck informed Meade of the president's state of mind: "I need hardly to say to you that the escape of Lee's army without another battle has created great dissatisfaction in the mind of the president, and it will require an active and energetic pursuit on your part to remove the impression that it has not been sufficiently active heretofore." Meade replied within less than two hours that, basically, since the president didn't like his efforts, he felt "compelled most respectfully to ask to be immediately relieved from command of this army." The following is from a letter Lincoln wrote to General Meade that same day, July 14, to explain his dissatisfaction:

> You fought and beat the enemy at Gettysburg; and, of course, to say the least, his loss was as great as yours. He retreated; and you did not, as it seemed to me, pressingly pursue him; but a flood in the river detained him, till, by slow degrees you were again upon him. You had at least twenty thousand veteran troops directly with you, and as many more raw ones within

supporting distance, all in addition to those who fought with you at Gettysburg; it was not possible that he had received a single recruit; and yet you stood and let the flood run down, bridges be built, and the enemy move away at his leisure, without attacking him....

Again my dear general, I do not believe you appreciate the magnitude of the misfortune involved in Lee's escape. He was within your easy grasp, and to have closed upon him would, in connection with the other late successes (Vicksburg), have ended the war. As it is the war will be prolonged indefinitely. If you could not safely attack Lee last Monday, how can you possibly do so south of the river.... It would be unreasonable to expect, and I do not expect you can now effect much. Your golden opportunity is gone....

Abraham Lincoln probably penned this missive to vent his frustration. He filed the letter away and never sent it. In truth, part of the responsibility for Meade's failure belonged to Lincoln himself. He simply should have insisted that Meade attack before the Potomac receded enough to be crossed by the Confederates. He also should have ensured that reinforcements, which were available, were sent to Meade when he learned of the fighting at Gettysburg.

George G. Meade certainly deserves strong criticism for allowing Lee to escape back to Virginia. "It is impossible not to blame Meade for the failure," observed one historian regarding this incident. Nevertheless, Meade's reputation has not suffered significantly as a result. Civil War author Jeffry D. Wert offered a mitigating judgment of Meade by noting that "Lincoln's assessment" of the incident was "deeply flawed and clouded" by his hope for "another victory."[36] But Lincoln here wasn't simply looking for just a victory: he was anticipating an end to the war, a catastrophic blow to the Confederacy. Meade absolutely should have seen it that way as well. He failed to make every effort to take advantage of this one-time opportunity to shorten the war, perhaps even end it. Meade's generalship here is representative of the fecklessness of the Federal high command during the first thirty months of the war and thereby has contributed to the impression of Northern martial ineptitude.

Meanwhile the Federals won another significant victory out West. On July 9 the other Confederate fortress on the Mississippi at Port Hudson, Louisiana, surrendered. Major General Nathaniel Banks led a force of over 40,000 Federal troops against a Confederate garrison of about 7,500 men. In another Confederate blunder, the post was not evacuated in time, as was the case at Vicksburg, to save the garrison from capture. The prize proved very costly in Federal casualties as a result of ill-advised attacks on strong Confederate fortifications. However, the victory restored control of the Mississippi River to the Federals, thereby achieving Lincoln's intention of opening that river for navigation from the Northwestern farming region to the Gulf.

Although General Lee and his army had escaped back into Virginia, things everywhere were going against the Confederacy in July of 1863. In Tennessee, which had been in a condition of stalemate since January, the Federals finally got in motion. Major General William S. Rosecrans commanding the Federal Army of the Cumberland marched his army out of Murfreesboro, Tennessee, on June 24. Rosecrans had delayed his advance for months despite repeated urging from General in Chief Halleck to do something to take the heat off of Grant's operation against Vicksburg. Rosecrans had acted in much the same manner as McClellan did following the Battle of Antietam, which eventually led to McClellan's removal from command. Rosecrans for months had offered excuses and demanded supplies and reinforcements when ordered to take action. But once he got into motion, he quickly managed to drive General Braxton Bragg and his Confederate Army of Tennessee out of that state.

Bragg had positioned the Army of Tennessee north of the Duck River with a view of holding middle Tennessee with a strong defensive line. In fact, "Bragg was thinking only of defense" when Rosecrans made his move. Rosecrans arranged a feint against Bragg's strong defensive position at Shelbyville while he executed a turning movement around Bragg's right. At the cost of a small battle at Hoover's Gap, where the Confederates suffered heavier losses, Rosecrans managed to cause Bragg to abandon his defensive positions and retreat to Chattanooga. In a matter of days, Rosecrans had "completely outgeneraled" Bragg and at a cost of less than 600 casualties. On the night of June 30, Bragg began his retreat to Chattanooga, and the Federal effort to secure Chattanooga was finally on.[37]

After Lee's army escaped into Virginia, Meade, during the period of July 17 to 19, sent his army across the Potomac at Berlin and Harpers Ferry to follow. Meade remained supremely cautious, even concerned that "a part of Bragg's army" had "been sent to Virginia." But on July 23, Meade thought he had an opportunity to inflict considerable damage on the retreating Confederates. On the 23rd, Meade sent the Federal III Corps through Manassas Gap "in the hope of separating the force of the enemy and capturing such portions as had not reached the passes." Meade's III Corps led by Major General William French moved against part of Anderson's division from the Confederate I Corps. At Wapping Heights, near Linden Station, Virginia, the Federal III Corps spent the day leisurely skirmishing and probing the enemy on the mountainsides. French is hardly remembered as an efficient commander, and it showed on the 23rd. Union veterans remembered the action at Wapping Heights as more an attempt to avoid a fight than an actual battle. The Confederates, reinforced by Rodes' division of the Confederate II Corps, were forced off the heights during the afternoon. After dusk the Confederates withdrew. Meade reported the next day that "the enemy had again disappeared, declining battle…." Again Meade was too late to take advantage of an opportunity to cut off part of Lee's retreating army. Casualties indicated a desultory fight, 103 in total for the Federals and about 174 for the Confederates. Following the action at Manassas Gap, Meade turned away from the Shenandoah Valley to concentrate his forces at Warrenton and Warrenton Junction, Virginia, "for supplies and to establish a base of communications." Meade asked Halleck if he needed to occupy the Shenandoah Valley. On July 27, Halleck replied that "Lee's army is the objective point."[38] By then, Lee's army was well on its way to safety; soon a balance of power would prevail in Virginia for the remainder of the year.

In Tennessee, General Rosecrans occupied Tullahoma, as Bragg retreated to Chattanooga, and there he stayed for the next six weeks despite urging again from the president and General in Chief Halleck to advance on Chattanooga. Bragg anxiously awaited Rosecrans' next move. Anticipating an attempt by Rosecrans to capture Chattanooga from the north, he requested reinforcements to meet that threat. The Confederate high command agreed; General Longstreet and his corps were selected to assist Bragg. Meanwhile, General Burnside was ordered to advance on Knoxville, Tennessee, to liberate eastern Tennessee from Confederate occupation and to protect Rosecrans' left. On August 15, Burnside finally began his advance on Knoxville via Cumberland Gap. The next day Rosecrans commenced his campaign against Bragg and Chattanooga.

To his credit, Rosecrans again devised an efficient campaign to force Bragg to abandon Chattanooga without a large-scale battle. Instead of using the obvious approach to the town from the north, Rosecrans chose to cross the Tennessee River and operate against Chattanooga from the southwest. Once again Rosecrans used a feint to confuse

Bragg. He sent three infantry brigades and supporting cavalry to approach Chattanooga from the north to distract the Confederates away from his actual route. The tactic worked, as Bragg for weeks was immobilized while trying to determine where Rosecrans would appear in force. Finally in early September Bragg was certain that Rosecrans had moved most of his army south of Chattanooga. On September 7, Bragg, worried that Rosecrans would cut off his communications, abandoned Chattanooga without a fight. The Federals occupied the town on September 9.

Although Bragg pulled out of Chattanooga, he was receiving reinforcements. Within days his army would outnumber Rosecrans,' and he planned to spring a surprise on the Federals. He hoped to give the impression that he was retreating far into Georgia so that Rosecrans would follow without proper discretion. The route Rosecrans had selected to confront Bragg required him to divide his army into three dispersed forces. Bragg, with reinforcements, planned to pounce on the separated Federal commands and destroy them in succession.

For once, Rosecrans was reacting with an air of nonchalance rather than with his usual excessive caution. Rosecrans told Major General George Thomas, commander of the XIV Corps, that the Confederates were hurriedly retreating, perhaps to a fortified position farther south in Georgia. Rosecrans was anxious to strike the retreating Confederates before they could rally at that strong defensive position. General Thomas disagreed. He observed that Rosecrans' advance required the army to separate into three parts in difficult, mountainous terrain. George Thomas, a general also prone to excessive preparation, urged Rosecrans to concentrate his army at Chattanooga and then establish a supply base there as a safe launch point for the advance into Georgia. Communications between the Federal corps south of town were "tentative at best" and "nonexistent" between the left and right of the advance. Bragg was receiving reinforcements already, and Thomas was concerned that more Confederates might be on the way from Virginia, which, as it turned out, was correct.[39] In a rather uncharacteristic fashion, Rosecrans ignored the obvious perils of an advance into the mountains south of Chattanooga. He disregarded Thomas' advice and sent his army in pursuit of Bragg. The move provided the opportunity Bragg was hoping for, a chance to crush three isolated Federal corps before they could reunite.

By September 13, Rosecrans realized that Bragg wasn't actually retreating to fortifications at Rome, Georgia. Instead, Rosecrans realized that "every indication" demonstrated that Bragg "felt able" to give the Federals a battle near Chattanooga. Rosecrans asked for help from Burnside, noting that there was little doubt that the Confederates would soon "concentrate every available man in the Southwest against" his army. Rosecrans' tone revealed his concern, "It is highly desirable—I may say of utmost importance—that all of your cavalry should come to our relief as quickly as possible, and your infantry should march in this direction...." In his after-action report Rosecrans described the situation he faced on the 13th: "It was therefore a matter of life and death to effect the concentration of the Army."[40] On the 13th he finally realized that he had overextended his army. Indeed, Rosecrans was fortunate that the Confederates had bungled three opportunities to crush his isolated corps before he realized the extreme peril of his situation.

General Bragg again attempted to crush a Federal corps, this time Major General Thomas Crittenden's XXI Corps, on September 18. Bragg's troops again failed to accomplish the task, being late to arrive in position and then having difficulty in crossing Chickamauga Creek before dusk. Troops from Virginia were arriving to reinforce Bragg; Major

General John B. Hood with three brigades joined forces with Bragg's advance that day and managed to drive back Federal cavalry covering a bridge over Chickamauga Creek. Nevertheless, little was accomplished on the 18th, so the Confederate army crossed the creek during the night and prepared for an attack the next day.

The terrain south of Chattanooga along Chickamauga Creek was a poor choice for a place to fight a Civil War battle. The battlefield was mostly wooded, some of it quite densely. Only scattered areas cleared for farming provided much of a field of fire. Artillery was of limited use, and the guns were particularly vulnerable to capture. Neither army commander really knew much about the location of his enemy. Bragg and Rosecrans would have difficulty in maneuvering their troops and managing the battle. The situation overall favored Bragg because he would have superior numbers attacking in a place where Rosecrans could not shift his troops quickly in response. Also Rosecrans did not have time to prepare strong fieldworks to meet Bragg's attacks. The Federals were operating in enemy territory far from their supply source with a somewhat tenuous line of communications. These things considered, it was reasonable for the Confederates to expect to win the battle.

The serious fighting of the Battle of Chickamauga commenced on the morning of September 19, 1863, when a Federal brigade attacked some Confederate Cavalry near Jay's Mill on Rosecrans' left flank. Rosecrans had managed to gather his corps and make some preparations for a defensive stand. Neither commander was able to direct the battle with tactical savvy due to the nature of the battlefield. During the day on the 19th both commanders fed troops into the fray to counter enemy movements and reactions. Bragg was actually in position to split the Federal army, but, of course, he wasn't able to recognize his opportunity in the forested terrain. Later Bragg was criticized for repeatedly sending in piecemeal attacks rather than making a concentrated surge.

By dusk on September 19, the Confederates had pushed the Federal lines back and had almost managed a significant breakthrough at the center of Rosecrans' line. Rosecrans was fortunate to have had sufficient troops on hand at the opportune moment to launch a counterattack that thwarted the potential Confederate breakthrough. When the fighting sputtered out at nightfall, Bragg had received enough reinforcements, with more soon to arrive including General James Longstreet and the rest of his corps, to outnumber the Federals by perhaps 15,000 men. Federal casualties that day numbered approximately 7,000 compared to perhaps 9,000 for the Confederates. Overall, Bragg had at least three more fresh brigades available than Rosecrans did for the next day's fighting.[41] Bragg held the advantage after the first day of battle.

Bragg, of course, wanted to renew the fighting with the rising sun on September 20. His battle plan called for attacks on the Federal left, intending to force the Federal army away from its retreat route back to Chattanooga. Bragg ordered attacks in echelon, beginning with the division on the Confederate extreme right. Each Confederate division was to immediately launch an attack in concert with the unit adjacent on its own right. The attack was scheduled for dawn, at first light. Attacks along the entire Federal line would expectantly prevent Rosecrans from sending troops to strengthen his vital left flank. If the plan to smash the Federal left could succeed, Bragg expected to demolish Rosecrans' army in a trap formed by the ridges and heights south of Chattanooga.

Although it probably mattered little in the battle's outcome, the Confederate attack was late getting started. Bragg's orders failed to reach one of his corps commanders until nearly time for the attack; Bragg's dysfunctional command condition continued to blight his plans. At around 9:45 a.m., the initial Confederate attack was finally launched against the Federal extreme left. The Federal line initially held behind makeshift log breastworks. Then, at about 10:30 a.m., a remarkable command blunder by one of Rosecrans' generals provided the Confederates with a rare phenomenal opportunity to annihilate a Federal army.

Brigadier General Thomas J. Wood, West Point Class of 1845, had that same morning been severely reprimanded by General Rosecrans for not obeying an order to move his division. Shortly afterwards, a staff officer passing along the Federal line saw what he believed was a gap at the center and reported it to General George Thomas, commanding the Federal left. "A message from General Thomas" informed Rosecrans of the "gap" in the Federal center. Actually, there was no gap, but Rosecrans, acting on Thomas' message, ordered General Wood to "close up" on the division to his north. Wood complied with the order, likely because he had previously been excoriated for failing to obey orders. What General Wood should have done was send a message to Rosecrans, who was nearby, explaining that there was no gap and obedience to said order would, in effect, create an actual gap in the Federal line.

"By this unfortunate mistake," Rosecrans explained, "a gap was opened in the line of battle, of which the enemy took instant advantage, and striking Davis (the adjacent division commander) in flank and rear, as well as in front, threw his whole division in confusion." As Rosecrans observed, Wood's inexplicable action opened a portal for the enemy, in this case Longstreet's corps, to tear apart the Federal line of battle. It was Longstreet's good fortune to have ordered an advance at this propitious moment, and three of his divisions rushed in an opening a quarter mile wide separating the two halves of Rosecrans's army.

Longstreet's attacking corps caught other Federal units en route to reinforce Thomas on the far left and scattered them in a panicked flight. Soon most of the Federal line south of the breach crumbled, and about half of the Rosecrans' army fled toward Chattanooga. Rosecrans and two of his corps commanders, Crittenden and McCook, left the field with the routed troops. Longstreet and the rest of Bragg's army shifted their attention to where General George Thomas was making a stand on the Federal left. Thomas defended a slight eminence known to history as Horseshoe Ridge and adjacent Snodgrass Hill until darkness put an end to the fighting. Thomas' stand at Chickamauga earned him the sobriquet "The Rock of Chickamauga." With the benefit of some unexpected reinforcements, Thomas withstood twenty-five separate attacks by Longstreet's command alone. When Thomas finally withdrew on the night of September 20, he had withstood attacks from Bragg's entire army and still held. What Thomas accomplished at Chickamauga was extraordinary, one of the most impressive command feats of the entire war.[42]

General Wood's baffling decision to follow the mistaken order was the decisive factor in the battle's outcome. Wood's action appears to have been an unreasonable reaction to two previous reprimands for failing to obey orders. In January of 1864, Rosecrans addressed the issue of Wood's behavior, which he had largely overlooked in his report of the battle. Rosecrans explained the situation thusly: "When General Wood found there was no interval to close ... his plain duty as a division commander was to have reported that fact to the general commanding, who was not more than 600 yards from him, and asked further orders. His failure to do so was a grave mistake, showing want of military discretion." Wood must have understood that the purpose of the order was to close a gap,

A monument erected to honor Tennessee soldiers who fought for the Union on the Chickamauga Battlefield.

but his withdrawal from the battle line, while his skirmishers were engaging the enemy, instead "let the enemy in."

Strangely, it was Wood himself who had been reprimanded "for not occupying a position" a few days before the battle, and as a defense Wood had written a manuscript "upward of fifty pages" arguing that as a division commander he had used "sound discretion" in not exercising "blind obedience to orders" in that case. Perhaps Wood's resentment for being harshly criticized affected his command judgment at Chickamauga. On the other hand, perhaps General Rosecrans was right in his judgment of Wood's behavior: "his mean and unsoldierly defense of error shows him wrong both in head and heart."[43]

Wood's error at Chickamauga handed the Confederates their last great victory in the West on September 20. It is doubtful, however, that Rosecrans would have duplicated his Stones River victory at Chickamauga in any case. At best the Federals, if they had checked Bragg, would probably have withdrawn to Chattanooga to await reinforcements. The embarrassing Federal rout of at Chickamauga created urgency that otherwise wouldn't have existed, but the war's outcome was unaltered by the second bloodiest two days of fighting of the entire war. Confederate losses at Chickamauga totaled 18,454 killed, wounded and captured. Federal casualties of 16,179 killed, wounded and missing with "36 pieces of artillery" were also severe.[44] General Thomas' celebrated stand ensured that the Confederate triumph at Chickamauga was a Pyrrhic victory and ultimately fruitless.

In the weeks following the Battle of Gettysburg until the middle of September, the

Federal high command allowed the Confederacy a desperately needed breather "by diverting its attention to peripheral theaters." Troops were detached from Grant to invade Arkansas and capture its capital. The forces commanded by General Banks were selected for a Texas expedition. As a result of these peripheral operations, little was accomplished in the autumn of 1863, especially in Virginia. Meade always seemed to have a reason for not fighting Lee. General Halleck summed up the situation in Virginia during that period with the following remarks: "I am very certain that a large detachment from Lee's army has been sent west, and that Meade is greatly superior to him in numbers. Nevertheless, Meade seems unwilling to attack him without positive orders. To order a general to give battle against his own wishes and judgment is to assume the responsibility of a probable defeat. If a general is unwilling to fight, he is not likely to gain a victory. That army fights well when attacked, but all of its generals have been unwilling to attack, even very inferior numbers. It certainly is a very strange phenomenon."[45]

While Rosecrans was fighting the battle of Chickamauga, President Lincoln was suggesting to General Halleck that troops from the Army of the Potomac could be put to better use in the West. "If the enemy's 60,000," Lincoln wrote, "are sufficient to keep our 90,000 away from Richmond, why, by the same rule, may not 40,000 of ours keep their 60,000 away from Washington, leaving us 50,000 to put to some other use?" Lincoln reasoned further, "...I can perceive no fault in this statement, unless we admit we are not the equal of the enemy, man for man."

Halleck sent Lincoln's remarks to Meade that day, September 19, with this explanation of his reluctance to order him to attack Lee's army: "...unless directed to do so, I never attempt to direct a general when, where, or how to give battle. He must decide such matters for himself. No one can do it for him." Halleck went on to explain that Lee's army was the "object" of the Army of the Potomac, instead of Richmond. Halleck could have been more direct. He could have told Meade to immediately go on the offensive against Lee or expect to lose part of his army. Halleck, of course, never was wont to give orders and thus take responsibility for the results.

With Meade doing practically nothing in Virginia, the Federal high command transferred troops from the Army of the Potomac to reinforce Rosecrans at Chattanooga. On September 25, the Federal XI and XII Corps departed Virginia under the command of Major General Joseph Hooker. Hooker managed to get elements of these two corps to Bridgeport, Alabama, a short distance downriver from Chattanooga, in only six days. It was perhaps no coincidence that these two corps were selected to leave the Army of the Potomac. The XI Corps had a poor reputation due to its performance at Chancellorsville and Gettysburg, and the XII Corps was small and had not shared in all of the battles fought by the Army of the Potomac. On October 3, General Lee informed President Davis of the transfer, noting that an estimate for the strength of the two corps was "between 20,000 and 25,000 men." That estimate was close, as about 20,000 troops were sent with Hooker; however, Lee informed Davis that in his opinion the estimate was too high. Lee opined, "...they will probably not exceed 12,000. They are considered two of the smallest and most indifferent corps."[46] Lee obviously was referring to the poor reputation of the Federal XI Corps when he mentioned "indifferent."

After Lee learned that Meade's army had been reduced by the transfer of Hooker's detachment, he decided to go on the offensive and attempt a turning maneuver. Lee hoped to push Meade back to the north side of the Potomac River. Meade reacted by pulling back from the Rappahannock River to a strong position at Centerville, Virginia.

On October 14, 1863, while Meade's army was en route to Centerville, Confederate Lieutenant General A.P. Hill thought he saw an opportunity to crush the Federal II Corps as it marched along the Orange and Alexandria Railroad near Bristoe Station, Virginia. Hill launched an attack on the outnumbered Federals that afternoon.

The October battle at Bristoe Station is mentioned in this study not because of its significance in the war's outcome, which was minimal. The battle is relevant here instead because it is an example of fighting wherein the Federals, being on the defensive and in a good position, inflicted disproportionate losses on the Confederates. The results of this encounter demonstrate that the Southerners were not immune to the punishing results of attacks against strong defensive positions.

The Federal II Corps, commanded that day by Major General G.K. Warren, was in a vulnerable situation, practically beyond the reach of help from the rest of Meade's army. General Hill later reported that the Federal corps was "discovered resting," and he "determined that no time must be lost" in making an attack before the Federals could escape. When Hill's III Corps attacked at the station, Warren's troops sheltered along the railroad embankment and repulsed the Confederates with punishing volleys and supporting artillery fire. Hill admitted that the Federal position "was an exceedingly strong one, and covered by the direct and enfilading fire of batteries on the rising ground in rear." After checking Hill's attack, a brigade of Federals counterattacked briefly but returned to the railroad embankment. Before dusk the "entire strength of Gen. Robert E. Lee's Army of Northern Virginia had arrived, 40,000 strong" to go against the Federal II Corps. Nevertheless, heavily wooded sections of the field and the gloaming frustrated further Confederate attacks. The Federal II Corps escaped to join the rest of Meade's army at Centerville. The final result: 40,000 Confederates had allowed 9,000 Federals to inflict more than twice their casualties and thwart Lee's plan to advance against Meade. President Davis concisely observed, "There was a want of vigilance, by reason of which … the enemy got a position, giving great advantage to them." More often the roles were reversed during the war, as at Fredericksburg and later during the Overland Campaign.

"In conclusion," Hill explained, "I am convinced that I made the attack too hastily, and at the same time a delay of half an hour, and there would have been no enemy to attack. In that event I believe I should equally have blamed myself for not attacking at once." Lee is said to have surveyed the carnage on the following day and remarked to General Hill, "Well, well, general, bury these poor men and let us say no more about it." Confederate casualties on October 14 were 136 killed, 797 wounded, and 445 missing, 1,378 in total. Federal casualties totaled about 540.[47]

The Federal II Corps, having punished Hill's corps and escaped into the night, arrived with the rest of the Army of the Potomac at Centerville. Lee considered the defenses at Centerville too strong to attack, and his supply situation in that northerly region of Virginia was overly strained. Lee pulled back to a defensive line along the Rappahannock River, intending to hold that line as a winter encampment. Halleck continued to press Meade to fight Lee—somewhere. On October 18, he sent the following message to Meade expressing his frustration: "Lee is unquestionably bullying you. If you cannot ascertain his movements, I certainly cannot. If you pursue and fight him, I think you will find out where he is." Meade, a somewhat truculent fellow himself, didn't care for the tone of Halleck's suggestions. He replied, "…I must insist on being spared the infliction of such truisms in the guise of opinions as you have recently honored me with…."[48] Nevertheless,

Meade soon decided that it was time to attempt another advance toward Lee with the intention of getting a fight.

The Federal defeat at Chickamauga had elevated the situation at Chattanooga to a top priority for both sides in October. The town was firmly held by Rosecrans and his army, despite his defeat at nearby Chickamauga, and the Confederates desperately wanted it back. The challenge for the Federals was the extreme difficulty in getting rations and supplies there. For Bragg and the Confederates the problem was that the terrain about Chattanooga made the town easy to defend. As one Civil War writer observed, "Few cities or towns on the continent were both so intrinsically vulnerable to siege or offered topographical features so favorable to the defense as Chattanooga."[49] Bragg laid siege to the town from the southern outskirts while Lincoln and Halleck scrambled to find reinforcements for Rosecrans. Meanwhile the Federals holding Chattanooga were barely subsisting on very limited rations, and Rosecrans was not finding solutions to the challenges the Federals faced there.

Lincoln and his cabinet had lost confidence in Rosecrans after Chickamauga, and his apparent lack of command capacity in the battle's aftermath prompted a change of command. On October 16, 1863, Major General U.S. Grant received the following message from General in Chief Halleck: "You will immediately proceed to the Galt House, Louisville, Ky., where you will meet an officer from the War Department with your orders and instructions. You will take with you your staff, &c., for immediate operations in the field. Wait at Louisville for the officer of the War Department." Grant actually met with Secretary of War Edwin Stanton, who joined Grant on a train en route to Louisville. The orders Grant received appointed him to command of three Western armies: the Army of the

A view of Chattanooga from the heights of Lookout Mountain.

Cumberland, the Army of the Ohio and the Army of the Tennessee. These three armies were designated as "the Military Division of the Mississippi" with Grant "placed in command" with "headquarters in the field." Grant was offered the choice of leaving Rosecrans in command of the Army of the Cumberland or replacing him with Major General George H. Thomas. Grant chose Thomas to supersede Rosecrans, although Grant might have preferred someone else. So Grant was selected to fix the situation at Chattanooga, and on the 19th he sent the following orders to General Thomas: "Hold Chattanooga at all hazards. I will be there as soon as possible. Please inform me how long your present supplies will last, and the prospect for keeping them up." Thomas laconically answered that day; he informed Grant of his total rations in store and what was expected on the morrow. Then he closed his reply with this assurance: "I will hold the town till we starve."[50]

Grant reached Thomas' headquarters on October 23. He wasted little time before taking action to solve the supply problem at Chattanooga. Grant approved a plan developed by Brigadier General William F. "Baldy" Smith, who had recently assumed the duties of chief engineer for the Army of the Cumberland. Smith had determined that it was feasible to bridge the Tennessee River with pontoons at Brown's Ferry. Once a bridgehead could be established there, the Federals could send in enough troops to open a supply line from downstream. The operation to open the new supply line was launched well before dawn on October 27. A pontoon bridge was constructed at Brown's Ferry and makeshift breastworks were in place there by dusk on the 27th. On the next day, Major General Joseph Hooker led his XI Corps troops and a division from the XII Corps from the west to Brown's Ferry and nearby Wauhatchie. By nightfall of October 28 the Federals had secured a new supply line that was out of reach of the Confederate guns besieging Chattanooga.

All of this activity was accomplished with little interference from the Confederates until Hooker's force appeared marching in from the west. Bragg then assigned Longstreet the task of attacking Hooker and destroying the Federal bridgehead. Longstreet decided to attempt an unusual night attack at Wauhatchie. Longstreet chose to attack with only one division because "it was too late" for his other division to reach the attack launch point "before daylight, and the success of the affair depended entirely upon a night attack and surprise." Longstreet downplayed the affair, which was hard fought, reporting that his "object was merely to inflict such damage upon the enemy as might be accomplished by a surprise." By around 3 a.m. the Confederates began withdrawing, leaving Hooker's troops in control of the crossing.

When Longstreet's division withdrew, the Federals had finally opened a practicable supply route, which they dubbed as the "Cracker Line," capable of maintaining the ever growing host arrayed against Bragg at Chattanooga. A few days later Longstreet, Lieutenant General William Hardee and Major General John Breckinridge were ordered examine the area around Brown's Ferry to determine if they believed a "general battle" could drive the Federals back across the Tennessee and close the Cracker Line. Longstreet reported that "an attack was impracticable" because the only route to the battlefield was "entirely exposed to the enemy's batteries on the other side of the river." Apparently Longstreet did not feel that the Federal bridgehead was very important. He suggested that the "point was not essential to the enemy at Chattanooga" because the Federals had been getting supplies "at that place some six weeks without it." He summed up his opinion of the situation with the following remark: "We were trying to starve the enemy out by investing him on the only side from which he could not have gathered supplies."[51]

Obviously Longstreet did not apprehend how difficult it actually was to get supplies into Chattanooga during the siege.

Longstreet did not support and cooperate with Bragg as well as he did with General Lee when serving in Virginia. General Bragg suffered from poor relationships with many of his subordinate commanders, and in Longstreet he found yet another rival. In late October President Davis wanted something done about Burnside's occupation of Knoxville and eastern Tennessee. Burnside, with the Army of the Ohio and his IX Corps, had finally established a Federal presence in that region by capturing Cumberland Gap and Knoxville. Bragg was delighted to send Longstreet and his corps northward on a mission to recapture the area occupied by Burnside during the previous few months. On November 5, 1863, Longstreet left Bragg at Chattanooga to commence a forlorn mission in eastern Tennessee. The decision to separate Longstreet and his corps from Bragg has been recognized by historians as one of the Confederacy's prominent strategic mistakes.

Longstreet's departure left Bragg with about 40,000 men holding the heights above Chattanooga. Bragg's army occupied a strong defensive position; however, Grant was soon reinforced by troops led by Major General William T. Sherman, arriving from the west by mid–November. As Longstreet slowly moved towards Knoxville, Grant's force at Chattanooga swelled to at least 70,000 troops. Grant's "orders for battle were all prepared in advance of Sherman's arrival." In fact Grant had hoped to go on the offensive by November 21, but Sherman was late in reaching Chattanooga from Bridgeport, Alabama.[52]

On November 23, Grant ordered General Thomas to test the enemy lines beyond the town on a tree-shrouded hillock known as Orchard Knob. The Battle of Chattanooga commenced on the 23rd as Thomas secured that enemy position with his Army of the Cumberland. Grant's battle plan next called for Hooker to capture Lookout Mountain, if possible, and secure the area between the mountain and Missionary Ridge and Rossville Gap. Hooker commanded the troops transferred from the Army of the Potomac, and Grant (as General Lee also would have agreed) might have considered these two corps as rejects from the East. Grant gave the most important assignment to his friend, General Sherman. The Army of the Tennessee commanded by Sherman was tasked with turning the Confederate right on the northern edge of Missionary Ridge. As the fighting played out, Sherman's command performance was clearly the least effective. Thomas and the Army of the Cumberland unexpectedly accomplished the decisive breakthrough at the Confederate center on Missionary Ridge while Sherman fumbled his assignment against a single Confederate division commanded by Major General Patrick Cleburne at Tunnel Hill.

Hooker drove the Confederates off Lookout Mountain and on the 25th his troops carried Rossville Gap and attacked the southern slope of Missionary Ridge. But it was Thomas's Army of the Cumberland that won the admiration of the nation by scaling the steep side of Missionary Ridge against unfavorable odds and then driving Bragg and his army off the summit. Historian Allan Nevins called that charge "one of the most spectacular attacks of the kind in history." General Thomas actually had little to do with the inspiring deeds of his army that day. Grant had ordered him to only capture the rifle pits at the base of the ridge. When his troops overran the rifle pits, they soon continued to chase the Confederates up the sides of the ridge without orders. Thomas did not know, at the time, why his men continued to charge onward to the summit. The Federal breakthrough by the Army of the Cumberland made Cleburne's position at Tunnel Hill untenable, so Cleburne was obliged to withdraw and cover the rear of Bragg's routed army as it scrambled to the southeast to escape capture. The Battle of Chattanooga could be considered the prelude to an unraveling of the myth of Southern martial superiority. What happened at Missionary Ridge demonstrated that Confederate soldiers could be driven from a virtually impregnable position while defending their own territory, something that never happened on Northern soil.

Grant, of course, got the credit for the Federal victory at Chattanooga and Bragg got the blame for the Confederate defeat. Bragg was responsible for several faults that contributed to his defeat. He had not opposed President Davis's suggestion to send Longstreet away to Knoxville. As Grant observed, Bragg sent away "his ablest corps commander with over twenty thousand troops," and, just before the battle, he sent Simon Buckner's division off to reinforce Longstreet on the Knoxville operation. Bragg also erred by placing too much of his force in front of Missionary Ridge rather than at the top of the ridge, which Grant termed an "impregnable position." Equally important, Bragg's fortifications on Missionary Ridge had been improperly constructed, they were not built to provide the maximum field of fire down the slope of the ridge. Of these Confederate mistakes, the most detrimental was the weakening Bragg's army by detaching Longstreet and Buckner. "What sealed the Confederate fate" at Chattanooga, according to the author of a book about that battle, was the lack of a powerful reserve force available to "plug gaps along the ridge."[53] Had Longstreet remained with Bragg's army instead of marching off to Knoxville, Bragg could have had sufficient troops on hand to provide a ready reserve on Missionary Ridge. Defeat at Chattanooga, as was often the case during the war, resulted from an attempt by the Confederate high command to do too much with too little.

Grant's tactical management of the battle deserved criticism as well. Grant placed too much emphasis on Sherman's attack on the Confederate right at Tunnel Hill. Sherman mishandled that assignment, and Grant failed to adequately supervise that supposedly vital aspect of his battle plan. History has largely overlooked Sherman's mismanagement of his role in the fighting on November 25. However, author Peter Cozzens in his analysis of the battle observed that, "By any objective reckoning, Sherman handled the attack against Bragg's right," the crucial assignment in Grant's battle plan, "with a degree of incompetence that bordered on gross negligence."[54] Equally dubious was Grant's order for Thomas to seize the Confederate rifle pits at the foot of Missionary Ridge and then to await further orders. Once the Confederates were driven from the rifle pits, the attackers were soon subjected to a galling rifle fire from higher up on the ridge. Grant's order to occupy the rifle pits, when obeyed and accomplished, placed the Army of the Cumberland in a vulnerable situation with little benefit. The subsequent charge up Missionary Ridge by Thomas' army was partially the result of desperation to escape from a dangerously exposed position. Grant, in the years following the war, was often criticized by his own men for his seemingly callous disregard for their lives due to his tactical methods; the attack on Missionary Ridge did nothing to detract from that perception.

The irretrievable loss of Chattanooga was a signal to the Confederacy that its days were numbered. If Buell would have captured the town in 1862, the war might have been concluded with a Union victory by the close of 1863. Yet, once again, the Federals passed on an opportunity to shorten the war. Grant probably could have destroyed Bragg's army immediately following the battle on November 25 if he had pursued the routed Confederates with all his available forces. Instead, Grant did not make a full-fledged effort to catch Bragg's beaten army. The Federal high command had made a priority of assisting Burnside at Knoxville, so Grant detached General Sherman with his Army of the Tennessee and Granger's Reserve Corps to relieve Burnside. Hooker's troops followed the retreating Confederates from Missionary Ridge and caught up with them at Ringgold, Georgia, over a dozen miles southeast of Chattanooga. General Patrick Cleburne, who had repulsed Sherman's attack at Tunnel Hill, repeated that success, this time over Hooker, at a mountain pass near Ringgold on November 27. Cleburne's stand allowed Bragg's army to slip away from immediate threat, and Grant discontinued the chase. The invasion of Georgia would have to wait until after the New Year.

Federal losses in killed and wounded for the battles at Chattanooga were more than double those of the Confederates; however, the Confederates lost more than ten times as many men captured or missing. Federal losses totaled 743 killed, 4,722 wounded and 349 missing. The Confederates losses reported by Lieutenant General Hardee listed 361 killed, 2,180 wounded and 4,146 missing, a total of 6,687.[55] Being on the attack and subjected to artillery and musket fire out in the open in every action of the battle, the Federals were quite fortunate to have benefited from the breakthrough by the Army of the Cumberland. Federal losses probably would have been much greater otherwise. The Confederates had a marked advantage in holding a strong defensive position on higher ground; therefore, the Federal losses in killed and wounded were considerably higher, as was usually the case in such circumstances.

Longstreet decided to attack the Federals at Knoxville, and, after some delays for reconnaissance and to await reinforcements, he selected a redoubt called Fort Sanders at the northwest end of the Federal defenses as the focal point of his assault. Longstreet later explained why he made the dubious decision to attack Knoxville. He had heard several reports and rumors about fighting at Chattanooga, "the most authentic being from telegraph operators," so he determined that he had to "attack, and, if possible, get possession of Knoxville." Attacking Burnside at Knoxville, Longstreet believed, would prevent the Federals from overpowering Bragg. Initially the plan called for a heavy artillery barrage to precede the attack, but Longstreet decided that shelling the fort would preclude the advantage of surprise. The attack, scheduled for the 28th, was delayed so that sharpshooters could "advance at dark to within good rifle-range of the" fort. The advance of the Confederate sharpshooters succeeded, but the advance also gave away the intention to attack there. On the morning of the 29th Longstreet attempted to capture Knoxville by launching three Confederate brigades against the fort defended by 440 men, mostly from the 79th New York Infantry, and twelve cannons. The attack was, concisely, easily repulsed with remarkably one-sided losses for the Confederates. Longstreet's management of the assault, which was supposed to be against the weakest point of the Federal defenses, did absolutely nothing to enhance his reputation as an independent commander. Most of the attacking Confederates were unable to scale the fort's walls and "could not pass" the ditch fronting it. After probably about a half hour of slaughter, the attack was called off. When it was over, 129 Confederates had been killed, 458 wounded and 226 were captured or missing, a total of 813 casualties. Only eight Federals had been killed and five wounded at Fort Sanders, a ratio of sixty-two to one in favor of the Federals.[56] The brief fight at Fort Sanders demonstrated the extreme disadvantage incurred by troops attacking fortifications, something often required of Federal troops during the war.

After his defeat at Chattanooga, Bragg tendered his resignation on November 28. President Davis accepted Bragg's resignation two days later. On the day his troops were repulsed at Fort Sanders, Longstreet received a message from President Davis informing him of Bragg's rout at Chattanooga and ordering him to rejoin Bragg in Georgia.

With Sherman approaching Knoxville to reinforce Burnside, Longstreet and his generals concluded that their best course, and perhaps only alternative, would be to retreat into eastern Tennessee and go into winter quarters there. On December 4 and 5, Longstreet withdrew from Knoxville, marching northeastward toward Rogersville.

Burnside sent out Major General John Parke's infantry and a cavalry force led by Brigadier General James Shackelford to hound Longstreet as he withdrew into eastern Tennessee. By December 9 Shackelford had around 4,000 troops, cavalry and mounted infantry, at Bean's Station, less than twenty miles southwest of Longstreet's position. The place was an old settlement and stagecoach stop founded during Tennessee's pioneer days by Robert Bean, the son of Tennessee's first settler. Longstreet, aware that he greatly outnumbered Shackelford, turned back and maneuvered to isolate and capture the Federals at Bean's Station. My Grandmother Clara's father, as part of Shackelford's force, was there on December 14 when Longstreet attacked at Bean's Station. Shackelford's men were barricaded within a brick three-story hotel, built in 1813, that anchored the center of his line at Bean's Station. Brigadier General Bushrod Johnson, leading the Confederate attack on the hotel, reported that his men were "exposed to the fire of the Federals occupying the large hotel building at Bean's Station and firing through loop-holes cut in the wall of the second and third stories." One of Johnson's regiments sought cover by "lying on the ground," and when "that regiment subsequently arose to advance again on the hotel," its line was "marked out by the dead and wounded" struck by the "deliberate fire delivered with accuracy from the loop-holes of the hotel." By dusk, Longstreet's plan to trap Shackelford had unraveled, and the Federals managed to escape. When the shooting was over, the Confederate casualty list totaled 290, "considerably larger than the Union tally of 115." The Battle of Bean's Station was another failure for Longstreet and "the last engagement of any consequence" in his "ill-fated Knoxville Campaign."[57]

In November, while the situation in Tennessee was playing out in the Union's favor, "Lee and Meade probed and danced," as one historian described the events in Virginia that month. Early in November, Meade pushed back against Lee by attacking the Confederate bridgehead at Rappahannock Station on the north bank of the river. On November 7, 1863, Meade launched the war's first successful night attack at Rappahannock Station. Troops from the Federal VI Corps surprised the Confederates by approaching under the cover of a railroad embankment and then charging after nightfall. After an indecisive struggle, a second charge led by twenty-five-year-old Colonel Emory Upton overran the Confederate earthworks and captured the bridgehead. The loss of the bridgehead and 1,673 men captured was a disaster for the Confederates.[58] Lee decided to pull back south of the Rapidan River in response.

The Federals also made a successful crossing over the Rappahannock at Kelly's Ford on November 7, and Meade then advanced most of his army south of that river with the VI Corps on the right near Brandy Station and the II Corps on the left near Stevensburg. On the evening of November 21, Brigadier General Judson Kilpatrick, commanding the 3rd Cavalry Division, reported that General Lee had "but 36,000 men in his two corps." Kilpatrick added Pickett's division to this total and subtracted Lee's losses at Rappahannock Station and concluded that Lee's army numbered "39,000 men all told." Meade, with over 80,000 men, decided to go on the offensive. Lee's army was stretched thin across a front extending more than twenty miles, so Meade smelled an opportunity to slice between Lee's two corps and destroy each of them in detail. Meade turgidly explained his campaign plan with a gigantic sentence in a report dated December 7:

The plan I decided on was to cross the Rapidan at the lower fords, in three columns, and by a prompt movement seize the plank road and turnpike, advancing rapidly toward Orange Court-House, thus turning the enemy's works, and compelling him to give battle on ground not previously selected or prepared, and I indulged the hope that in the execution of this plan I should be enabled to fall on part of the enemy's forces before he could effect a concentration, and thus cripple him as to render more certain the success of the final struggle.

Meade's plan might have worked, except for one factor. The Army of the Potomac was a ponderous machine. Throughout the war, with various generals in command, the Army of the Potomac proved incapable of matching the speed and maneuverability of Lee's army. For Meade's plan to be successful, every assignment and evolution had to go off with precession and alacrity. That, of course, didn't happen.

Meade's first and most grievous mistake was selecting Major General William French to lead off the advance on November 26 with his III Corps. Historian Jeffry Wert singled out French as "unquestionably the army's worst corps commander." Meade's orders, issued on the 23rd but delayed until the 26th due to a storm, called for French to move his III Corps at 6 a.m. with the VI Corps to immediately follow behind. Rumors had it that French was drunk that day. In any case, his corps was late getting underway. As a result the VI Corps was stalled for hours while waiting for French's troops to break camp and take up the march. The delays caused by the III Corps "proved fatal" to Meade's plans for the 26th.[59]

On November 27, Lee reacted to the Federal advance. Three separate engagements were fought that day, all of them indecisive and limited. Lee's troops engaged the Federals at Payne's Farm on the northern sector, at Robertson's Tavern on the Orange Turnpike in the center and at New Hope Church along the Orange Plank Road at the southern sector of the opposing lines. The effect of these engagements was to buy time for Lee to prepare a strong defensive line and position his army behind it. Lee selected a ridgeline west of Mine Run that provided an open field of fire not unlike the Confederate position on Marye's Heights at Fredericksburg, and by the 28th his men had emplaced and manned strong fieldworks there.

Meade's operational plans had been completely thwarted by the 28th, not by General Lee but as a result of General French's incompetence and the inefficiency of the army's movements. There was now no opportunity to catch Lee outside of defensive works, and now Lee's army had concentrated. Nevertheless, Meade was not ready to quit. On the 28th, Meade prepared for an attack westward towards Mine Run, but a severe rain storm delayed the advance and hindered movement of his artillery. Meade learned from probes of the Confederate front that Lee's position west of the run was "extremely formidable." The 29th "was spent" probing Lee's defenses for a vulnerable place to attack; by dusk Meade had received reports that Lee's line could be assailed from the Federal extreme right. He also heard from General Warren that he had "taken a position which outflanked" Lee's defenses "from which there was no difficulty of assaulting and turning" the Confederate right flank. Meade decided to reinforce Warren and have him "make the main attack" at 8 a.m. Major General Sedgwick was ordered to attack the Confederate left with his VI Corps and the V Corps at 9 a.m., and the I and III Corps were assigned to make a demonstration at the center to distract the enemy commencing at 8 a.m.

On November 30, the Federal artillery opened fire at 8 a.m., and skirmishers from the Federal I and III Corps crossed Mine Run and drove in the Confederate skirmish line. Meade had things moving as planned when he received a message from General Warren advising him that the Confederate works on Warren's front were "so formidable" that he advised against attacking as Meade expected. Warren reported, "…the full light of the sun shows me that I cannot succeed." Without Warren's participation, Meade's battle plan stood no chance of success. Meade then realized that his "movement across the Rapidan was a failure." He made the following observations that reasonably accounted for his failure:

> I maintain my plan was a feasible one. Had the columns made the progress I anticipated, and affected a junction on the night of the 26th, at and near Roberson's Tavern, the advance the next day would either have passed the formidable position at Mine Run without opposition, or, had Ewell attempted to check that movement, he would have been overwhelmed before being re-enforced by Hill.
>
> Prisoners reported that Hill did not come up til the afternoon of the 27th, so that if the movements of the Third Corps had been prompt and vigorous … there is every reason to believe Ewell could have been overcome before the arrival of Hill. And after the enemy, through these culpable delays, had been permitted to concentrate on Mine Run, I have reason to believe, but for the unfortunate error of judgment of Major-General Warren, my original plan of attack in three columns would have been successful, or, at least, under the view I took of it, would certainly have been tried.[60]

Lee had probably escaped a disaster because of the torpid pace of the Federal advance, but he nevertheless recognized an opportunity to strike at Warren's position after Meade called off his attack. The Confederates were heavily outnumbered, but that had not mattered in previous battles Lee had won decisively. Not much happened from November 30 until December 1 except for some skirmishing that only added to the casualty lists, especially for the Federals probing the daunting Confederate fieldworks. Then on the night of December 1 Meade withdrew his army from Mine Run to fall back across the Rapidan. Meade's movement caught Lee by surprise; thus, the Federals managed to disengage before Lee could take advantage or even attempt his own offensive design. Casualties for the Mine Run Campaign for the Federals were recorded as 1,653 with 174 killed and 1,099 wounded. The cavalry corps accounted for 224 of these casualties. Confederate losses are, as usual, more difficult to determine with certainty. Major General Johnson reported the casualties in his division as 545 with 429 as wounded. A report for the Confederate II Corps listed a total of 601 killed and wounded.

The Army of the Potomac's performance during the Mine Run Campaign was typical. As General in Chief Halleck's quote cited previously in this chapter noted, the Army of the Potomac fought well when attacked. However, the Army of the Potomac nearly always failed to accomplish much when on the offensive. The Mine Run campaign demonstrates the flaws plaguing the Union's Eastern army throughout the war. McClellan had designed and built this army to overpower the Confederacy with brute force. It was a powerful yet cumbersome machine created to lay siege to the Confederate capital. When on the offensive, far too often the army's corps commanders suffered, just as at Mine Run, from inefficient staff work. Time and again this army's corps commanders failed to reach assigned positions on time to be successful, and they repeatedly failed to accomplish assigned objectives when there was reason to expect success.

Meade managed to get his army across the fords on the Rapidan and into winter camps around Culpeper and Brandy Station, Virginia, without much pressure from Lee. Winter brought an end to active campaigning in Virginia and Chattanooga as well. In the weeks ahead Lee's army would also settle into winter quarters not far south of Culpeper.

Longstreet and his corps would remain in eastern Tennessee for the winter. Until the coming of spring the attention of the Confederate high command would be dedicated to developing schemes to reclaim lost territory, dreams of an invasion of Kentucky, an advance from Mississippi and in Virginia. All of these ideas were little more than pipe dreams and would prove beyond the South's capability in the New Year.

The Confederacy was clearly losing the war in December of 1863. The two major Confederate victories in 1863 at Chancellorsville and Chickamauga were both sanguinary yet ultimately inconsequential. In each of these battles the Confederates had won only because of gross errors on the part of the Federals. The Confederate surrender at Vicksburg demonstrated that the Union was capable of mounting significant operations deep into the Confederacy with the expectation of success. Conversely, even General Lee would soon admit that the South was "not in a condition … to invade the enemy's country with a prospect of permanent benefit." The problem for the Confederacy, as one historian observed, was that "No one had figured out how to win the war." Confederate planning was succeeding, if at all, only at the operational level. There was no grand scheme to defeat the North. In effect, the Confederates were hoping to extend the war until the United States would be willing to quit. It was a poor choice for a strategy in a war where the main reason for fighting was all but eliminated anyway. The Confederacy, like most nations losing a war, was slow to recognize that continuing the fighting would not change the outcome.

At the close of 1863 the North had gained ascendancy over the Southern Confederacy, but a plethora of deficiencies and mistakes continued to plague the Federal war effort, lengthening the war and costing the lives of tens of thousands needlessly. The North had devised an effective strategy for winning the war; yet, decisions by the Federal high command, often made for political reasons, were counterproductive and actually benefited the enemy. After Grant's victory at Vicksburg, Lincoln chose to focus his attention on Texas rather than on Georgia and Mobile, Alabama, two objectives of far greater importance for closing out the war. Lincoln and Halleck proved incapable of forcing Meade to crush Lee's vulnerable army immediately after Gettysburg. Lincoln simply could not afford not to take advantage that single best opportunity to shorten the war, but he did fail to do so. Halleck was too slow in taking advantage of Rosecrans' success in capturing Chattanooga. Reinforcements should have been sent there immediately after Rosecrans had gained an advantage during his Tullahoma Campaign. Immediately following Grant's victory at Chattanooga, Lincoln should have given priority to crushing Bragg's demoralized army. Instead, part of Grant's force was sent to assist Burnside at Knoxville. These few ill-advised decisions alone effectively lengthened the war.

The North, despite significant lapses in 1862 and 1863, was finding its way to victory by the end of 1863. The Southern Confederacy continued to cling to an impractical strategy of defending too much territory and concentrating forces to counter the Federals at a few important points. The North had found a winning strategy and was prepared to initiate the final steps to victory. The war's outcome would be determined by the United States presidential and congressional elections in the year to come while the Confederacy's hope for survival lay in prolonging the war to exhaust the Union and force a negotiated settlement.

7

1864

The Decisive Year

The year 1864 began with comparatively sparse military activity. The winter was cold and snowy, and major operations in Virginia and Georgia would have to await the spring. The tyranny of time took a brief repose. Once the season for active campaigning commenced, however, the pace, intensity and significance of the fighting would make 1864 the decisive year of the war. It was a presidential election year, and a momentous election it would be. General George McClellan would be the Democratic Party's selection to challenge Lincoln. A significant wing of the Democrats in 1864, as was the case during the Vietnam War, opposed the war and wanted it ended promptly. McClellan would be expected to countenance a settlement to the war on terms unacceptable to the Lincoln Administration. Political necessity would dominate strategic applications; a timetable for Union success with a deadline in November would govern the pace of campaigns and operations as never before during the war.

The urgency created by political necessity in 1864 would result in altered strategic and tactical approaches, particularly for the Federals. Federal armies in the East and West would be constantly on the offensive, repeatedly making assaults against fieldworks and trenches, assaults that previous commanders would have declined to attempt. The result of these new tactics gave rise to a shift in the Federal casualty rate as compared to Confederate losses. According to a study of Civil War casualties, until 1864 "the aggregate of losses on each side was substantially the same." The tabulation for Confederate casualties is incomplete, so the "total loss of the Confederate armies in killed and mortally wounded will never be definitely known, and can only be stated in round numbers." But even with this limited statistical information it is believed that the Union suffered perhaps at least 60,000 more killed and wounded than the Confederacy by the war's conclusion. This increase in the casualty differential "occurred almost wholly in the campaigns of 1864–5."[1] Casualty figures are useful indicators of relative combat effectiveness or comparative efficiency in many cases. However, as already documented in this study, forces assaulting earthworks, trenches, forts and strong fieldworks in nearly every instance suffered disproportionate losses. Longstreet's attack on Fort Sanders at Knoxville and Sherman's attacks at Chickasaw Bayou are two demonstrative examples of this circumstance. It has been suggested that the Confederacy lost the war because of an "attack and die" approach to warfare. As the years 1864 and 1865 demonstrated, it was the Federal army that did more attacking and dying overall. In 1864 General Lee and General Johnston actually adopted a more defensive posture out of necessity while General Grant and General Sherman continually attacked out of political necessity.

The first Federal military operation of 1864 was, unsurprisingly, politically connected. President Lincoln was very interested in commencing reconstruction by the close of 1863, and in January of 1864 he sent John Hay, his personal secretary, to assist Major General Quincy Gillmore in a project intended to establish a pro-Union government in Florida. On January 13, 1864, President Lincoln wrote to Gillmore about Hay and his mission as follows: "I understand an effort is being made by some worthy gentlemen to reconstruct a loyal state government in Florida.... I have given Mr. Hay a commission of major and sent him to you ... to aid in the reconstruction.... I wish the thing done in the most speedy way possible, so that when done it will be within the range of the late proclamation on the subject." Gillmore sent a division led by Brigadier General Truman Seymour to Jacksonville on February 7. Gillmore had informed General in Chief Halleck of his intention to move into Florida on January 14. Halleck replied on the 22nd, "In regard to your proposed operation in Florida.... I attach very little importance to such expeditions. If successful they merely absorb our troops in garrisons to occupy the places, but have little or no influence upon the progress of the war." Nevertheless the movement into northern Florida went forward for political reasons and resulted in the first significant defeat for the Union of the year.

Seymour pushed out from Jacksonville with a force that included nine infantry regiments and four artillery batteries. Three infantry regiments in Seymour's force were African American units, two of them in Jayhawker Colonel James Montgomery's command composed of the 54th Massachusetts and the 1st North Carolina Volunteers. Seymour encountered Brigadier General Joseph Finegan, a hard-fighting Irish immigrant living in Florida, with his two Confederate brigades and a reserve near Ocean Pond on February 20, 1864. Seymour was soundly beaten because, according to him, "the disparity in numbers was too great and the defense too obstinate to permit of decisive results." Seymour fell back around dusk, "leaving upon the field five guns, and not a few dead and wounded." General Gillmore later commented that there was no "disparity in numbers" because Seymour had 5,500 men against what Finegan reported as "only about 5,000 men at that battle." Finegan reported his losses as 93 killed and 841 wounded. The report of Federal casualties listed a total of 1,861 with 203 killed and 1,152 wounded, about double the Confederate losses counting the missing.

Seymour had expressed his doubts about the objective of returning Florida to the Union before the battle. On February 11 he commented that "what has been said of the desire of Florida to come back is now a delusion." In the end, the Federals fell back to Jacksonville and occupied the town for the rest of the war.[2] Politics had been the major motivation for the Florida expedition, and political considerations would continue to influence the management of the war for the rest of the year.

Another politically-motivated operation was under way during the winter of 1863–1864 which became known to history as the Red River Campaign. President Lincoln wanted a strong Federal presence in Texas for political reasons rather than military necessity. Even before the war, New Englanders had hoped for an influx of Yankees settling in the cotton-growing regions of Texas to replace the slave plantation system and thereby provide an alternative source of the material for textile factories in the East. Another political consideration related to Mexico after French troops invading there had captured Mexico City in 1863. Because of the French incursion in Mexico, Lincoln realized that French troops in Mexico might either threaten Texas and Louisiana or somehow assist the Confederacy along the Rio Grande River. Lincoln also wanted an attempt to establish a reconstruction government in Louisiana, as was also attempted in the previously mentioned operation in northern Florida. There was yet another political factor motivating an advance via the Red River. It was believed that plenty of baled cotton was sitting in northwest Louisiana ready for the taking. New England mill operators wanted that cotton for their factories, not to mention traders and opportunists who stood to profit from bringing the material to market. These politically-related motivations trumped military priorities in the fall of 1863 and created stimulus for an invasion of northwestern Louisiana via the Red River.[3]

While the Red River Campaign was in the preparation stage, President Lincoln was taking steps to install a new supreme commander for the Federal war effort. He nominated Ulysses S. Grant for the highest rank ever held by a United States officer at that time—lieutenant general. Major General was the rank of then General in Chief Henry Halleck. George Washington and Winfield Scott, who held the grade by brevet, were the only two previous United States officers to hold that rank. On March 2, 1864, the Senate confirmed Grant's promotion. Lincoln had finally found a commander who would prosecute the war without reservations or restraint. Grant was not without his flaws and defects, but he possessed the necessary tools and temperament to deliver victory to the Union within the limited time frame available to Lincoln. He was, at the time, indispensable to the Union's war effort.

Grant received word of his promotion at his winter headquarters in Nashville on March 3, 1864. It was from Nashville on March 17 that he issued General Orders, No. 1, with the following statement: "I assume command of the armies of the United States, headquarters in the field, and until further notice will be with the Army of the Potomac. There will be an office, headquarters in Washington, to which all communications will be sent except those from the army where headquarters are at the date of their address."[4] Halleck would remain in Washington as the new chief of staff. It was a wise move by Grant, as Halleck would not have been of as much use anywhere else, especially as a field commander. Grant would leave the paperwork to Halleck while he went to the front to direct the fighting in Virginia.

Major General N.P. Banks commenced the ill-fated Red River Campaign early in March while Grant was in the process of assuming the duties of general in chief. The active part of this campaign started on March 12, 1864, when Brigadier General Andrew J. Smith landed at Simmesport on the Red River with 10,000 men from General William T. Sherman's command. Two days later Smith's force captured Fort DeRussy, Louisiana, and then on March 16 the Federals occupied Alexandria in central Louisiana. Once Banks arrived in Alexandria, the Federals went about the countryside "liberating" cotton bales as prizes for the gunboat sailors and holding elections for a reconstruction government in accordance with Lincoln's plan to restore Louisiana to the Union.

On March 15, 1864, Grant, from Nashville, having assumed the duties of general in chief, sent his instructions for the Red River operation to Banks. He told Banks that it was important to capture Shreveport as soon as possible so that General Smith's troops could be returned to Sherman. Grant further instructed Banks that if he could not capture Shreveport within the time specified by General Sherman, "you will send them back ... even if it leads to the abandonment of the main object of your expedition." Further, Grant discouraged Banks from attempting to capture more territory after getting to Shreveport. "I look upon the conquering the organized armies of the enemy," Grant explained, "as being of vastly more importance than the mere acquisition of territory." The crux of

Grant's instructions was that troops would be needed for operations east of the Mississippi soon; therefore, Banks had a very limited amount of time to accomplish his mission, which was of lesser strategic importance.[5]

After Grant retuned to Washington, he finalized his plans for the upcoming spring campaigns. Even before returning to Washington, Grant had decided to conduct simultaneous operations. He wanted the various departments operating in concert at different points against the Confederacy. From Washington he wrote a confidential letter explaining his plans for the critical spring campaigns of 1864 to General Sherman on April 4. He began his letter with the following short paragraph:

> It is my design, if the enemy keep quiet and allow me to take the initiative in the spring campaign, to work all parts of the army together and somewhat toward a common center. For your information I now write you my programme as at present determined upon.

He continued by explaining that Banks had been ordered "to finish up his present expedition against Shreveport with all dispatch" and then to return Sherman's troops. Banks would then collect 25,000 men with another 5,000 from Missouri and commence "operations against Mobile as soon as he can."

Grant then mentioned that Major General Benjamin Butler with 33,000 men was to "operate against Richmond from the south side of the James River." Grant himself would "stay with the Army of the Potomac, increased by Burnside's corps of not less than 25,000 effective men, and operate directly against Lee's army wherever it may be found." Major General Franz Sigel was to operate against the Virginia and Tennessee Railroad from the Department of West Virginia. As for General Sherman, Grant wanted him to "move against Johnston's army, to break it up and to get into the interior of the enemy's country as far as you can, inflicting all the damage you can against their war resources."

"From the expedition from the Department of West Virginia," Grant wrote, "I do not calculate on very great results, but it is the only way I can take troops from there." He nevertheless wanted Sigel to "move directly to his front" so as to inflict damage on the Confederacy or to draw troops from elsewhere to hold Sigel in check. Grant borrowed a phrase from President Lincoln to describe Sigel's role. Lincoln had agreed with Grant's plan for simultaneous movements against different points in the Confederacy, saying "Those not skinning can hold a leg." In regards to Sigel, Grant wrote, "if Sigel can't skin himself he can hold a leg whilst someone else skins." In his concise letter to Sherman, Grant had summarized the major campaigns he planned to commence in the spring of 1864. He intended to occupy and overwhelm the opposition on several fronts simultaneously and thereby prevent the Confederates from concentrating forces against a single Federal operation.[6]

Despite the urgency of the moment, Grant was waiting until May to commence the operations of Sherman, Butler, Sigel and the Army of the Potomac together synergistically. Weather, supplies, and troop movements weren't the only concerns for holding back. Many of the Union's veteran regiments had been given incentives to reenlist, including a month's leave to go home. Grant needed to wait for the veterans to return to their regiments before commencing his campaigns.

President Davis and his generals were also making plans for the spring resumption of hostilities that winter; they too wanted to take the initiative. Bragg, Longstreet, Johnston, Lee and even Hood prepared schemes that they believed would successfully alter the course of the war. From east Tennessee, Longstreet suggested mounting his force and then invading Kentucky from Abington, Virginia. His other suggestion involved uniting his forces with Johnston's and other troops from Mississippi and from Beauregard's department and then "making a campaign into Middle Tennessee." He believed "there can scarcely be a doubt but we can advance into Kentucky and hold that State if we are once united." Longstreet thought the movement into Kentucky promised "much greater results than any other without such difficult and complicated maneuvers as the move into Middle Tennessee ... and if entirely successful will put an end to the war." General Lee, apparently, had finally realized that attempts to invade Union territory could not succeed in the long term. There is little reason to doubt that Longstreet's plan would also have failed, and likely with worse results than previous Confederate attempts to invade Northern and Border States. General Bragg forwarded a plan for Johnston to combine forces with Polk, Beauregard and Longstreet to destroy the railroad between Nashville and Chattanooga. Then Johnston could "precipitate" his "main force upon Nashville, and capture that place" before the Federals could react and "fall back for its defense." Bragg stressed to Johnston "the great importance, not to say necessity, of reclaiming the provision country of Tennessee and Kentucky," and the opportunity to obtain recruits for his army there. General Hood wrote to President Davis on March 7 with the group's most sanguine outlook. Hood wanted to combine Longstreet's force with Polk's, Loring's and the troops in Georgia to create an army of 60,000 to 70,000 men, which he believed would be sufficient "to defeat and destroy all the Federals" south of the Ohio River. General Johnston was of the opinion "that the only practicable mode of assuming the offensive here seemed to me to be to wait for the enemy's advance, and if we beat him, follow into Middle Tennessee, it being easier to beat him in Georgia ... and the results of victory much greater." From this it can be concluded that Longstreet and Hood remained optimistic and suggested an offensive while Johnston had already committed to standing on the defensive until he could win a victory. None of the plans conceived by the Confederate high command that winter would come to fruition. One historian described the Confederate offensive proposals for 1864 as "nothing more than tactical and operational woolgathering." This observation certainly applied to General Longstreet's outlook, as he still believed at the time that the Confederacy could yet win the war within two years by going on the offensive.[7]

Nevertheless, the Confederates managed a significant victory in April by turning back the Federal advance against Shreveport. General N.P. Banks, who opposed the expedition in the first place, botched the Red River Campaign with a combination of poor management and bad luck. The star-crossed Banks, knowing that he had no time to waste, was delayed at Alexandria for days until the river raised enough for Union gunboats to resume following him upriver. Halleck had informed Banks that another Federal force commanded by Major General Frederick Steele would move overland from Little Rock, Arkansas, to cooperate "with all his available force." Steele, moving sluggishly, faced some resistance and supply difficulties while moving southward; he turned back without joining Banks in Louisiana. Halleck had warned Banks on March 15 to keep his forces concentrated on the march to Shreveport. "This is all important," Halleck wrote. "If you move in a weak column, the enemy will be certain to concentrate on you. It is the opinion here that your troops are too scattered by occupying too many unimportant points before the rebel force is broken." Halleck proved correct. Confederate Major General Richard Taylor, the son of former President Zachary Taylor, met the Federal lead advance near a hamlet called Mansfield on the road to Shreveport on April 8. Taylor managed to assemble 8,800 men against 7,000 Federals in action that day.

Banks had made the wrong choice for a route to march his troops from Grand Encore to Shreveport. The Federals advanced over the Old Stage Road away from naval gun support available along an alternative route beside the river. The advancing column was hobbled by about 1,000 wagons in a supply train moving over the narrow trace through wooded country. The advancing Federal column was strung out over twenty miles, so General Taylor was able to strike the head of the column with superior numbers before Banks could send up the bulk of his forces. The Federals were driven back to a second line, which was soon outflanked. Outnumbered and outflanked, the Federal second line collapsed into a disorganized rout. Taylor's Confederates, following on the heels of the routed Federals, overran the Federal cavalry supply train clogging the road and captured around 150 wagons. Brigadier General William Emory formed a third line with his division of the XIX Corps and checked Taylor's attack, despite a mass of fugitive Federals crashing through his ranks. After nightfall the Federals retreated about fifteen miles to the village of Pleasant Hill. At a cost of around 1,000 men killed and wounded Taylor had stopped Banks and inflicted 2,235 casualties. The attacking Confederates lost more killed and wounded, but the routed Federals lost 1,541 missing and twenty guns.

Both sides were reinforced during the night and prepared to renew the fighting. On the 9th Taylor attacked again near the village of Pleasant Hill with an additional 4,000 men from Arkansas and Missouri. Taylor's 12,100 men slightly outnumbered the 12,000 Banks had kept on the field while the remainder of his force withdrew to Natchitoches. Banks failed to align his brigades compactly, and Taylor's Confederates initially had success in driving back the Federal front lines. Fortunately for Banks and the Federals, hard-fighting Brigadier General Andrew J. Smith ordered a counterKcharge from the cover of woods on the edge of the battlefield. By sundown Taylor's men were on the verge of a complete rout, and Taylor ordered a withdrawal to avoid an obvious defeat. The Confederates were beaten worse than Banks realized, but most of his subordinate generals advised a retreat. From retrospect, Banks probably could have marched on to Shreveport successfully after the fighting at Pleasant Hill. Once again the attacking Confederates lost more men killed and wounded than the Federals. Total Confederate casualties were 1,626 with 426 captured. The Federals lost 150 killed, 844 wounded and 375 missing for a total of 1,369.[8]

Faced with a difficult supply situation and with a requirement to return Smith's troops to Sherman, General Banks opted to abandon the Red River operation as directed by General Grant. Banks waited for the Federal river fleet to turn back to Grand Encore and then retreated to Alexandria. At Alexandria the gunboats could not pass through shallows there because the river was lower than expected. A dam was needed in order to provide draft for the river fleet to pass beyond Alexandria, so Banks was further delayed in Alexandria until the fleet could pass the town. Fortunately for the Federals, Lieutenant Colonel Joseph Bailey, an Army engineer, designed a makeshift dam that raised the river level enough for the fleet to continue downstream. The Federals then resumed their withdrawal back to Simmesport, fighting pursuing Confederates in Louisiana at Mansura on May 16 and Yellow Bayou on May 18. Finally on May 20 the Federal army crossed the Atchafalaya River on a makeshift bridge conceived by the ingenious Lieutenant Colonel Bailey, and the remarkably futile Red River Campaign came to an end.

The Red River Campaign was just one of several poorly-executed military operations launched by both sides during the Civil War. It was, however, so ill-advised, pointless and mismanaged that it fit the antebellum Southern perception of Northern martial limitations particularly well. The politically-motivated operation was costly, accomplished practically nothing, and deprived General Sherman of the use of Smith's 10,000 veteran troops for his Atlanta Campaign for some time. Grant later observed that Banks did not get back in time to operate against Mobile, and, basically, 40,000 veteran troops were "paralyzed" as a result.[9] A combination of bad luck and time constraints imposed by a shift of operational priorities, not to mention Banks's very limited military capacity, doomed this campaign to fiasco status. The operation was planned before Grant assumed overall command; thus, the onus for it belongs to Lincoln and Halleck. General Banks was relieved of command at the close of the operation and replaced by Major General Edward R.S. Canby. Banks's career as a field commander was finally over; that was a boon for the Union.

The month of May in 1864 opened with a plethora of battles. General Grant intended to open the spring campaign with simultaneous operations, and during the first week of May that is exactly what happened. Besides Banks's Red River Campaign, two other operations incorporated into General Grant's plan for the spring of 1864 also failed miserably. The Bermuda Hundred Campaign was the most disappointing of the failed operations in Grant's spring offensive in 1864.

General Grant went to Fort Monroe to discuss with Major General Benjamin F. Butler his plans for the spring campaign in early April. Butler initially suggested that the Army of the Potomac should be combined with his Army of the James and sent against Richmond rather than confronting Lee and his Army of Northern Virginia on the Rapidan. Butler had heard from spies that Richmond and Petersburg were lightly defended and vulnerable. Grant nixed the idea. Grant explained, "The necessity for covering Washington with the Army of the Potomac and of covering your department with your army makes it impossible to unite these forces at the beginning of any move." Butler then suggested that he should land his reinforced army at Bermuda Hundred between the James and Appomattox Rivers and advance on Richmond from there. If Butler's could cut the rail lines south of Richmond, Lee's army would soon be short of supplies, and Grant could follow Lee to Richmond and join Butler in investing the Confederate capital. That idea was more to Grant's liking. Grant later suggested that Butler's idea was synonymous with his own. Butler's views, Grant wrote, "were very much such as I intended to direct, and as I did direct, in writing, before leaving." From Fort Monroe on April 2 Grant wrote his orders to Butler. Butler was to "deceive the enemy as to the real move to be made," then capture City Point near Petersburg. For troops, Butler was to collect 20,000 men to be reinforced with "10,000 men from South Carolina, under Major-General Gillmore," who would retain command of his men. Butler's army was "to operate on the south side of the James River" with Richmond as the "objective point." Once City Point was taken, Butler was ordered to concentrate his troops there and to fortify the place. Grant probably thought that a seasoned officer would benefit the amateurish Butler, so he sent Major General William "Baldy" Smith to "command the troops sent into the field" from Butler's department. Grant had recommended Smith for promotion against the preference of the Senate. Smith proved a major disappointment, and Grant later admitted the he "was not long in finding out that the objections to Smith's promotion were well founded."[10] Grant left all "the minor details" of the operation to Butler, a decision that was not at all well founded. This operation, like those of

Sherman and Sigel, was scheduled to commence simultaneously with Meade's advance against General Lee in early May.

It is beyond the scope of this study to narrate all the "details" of Butler's Bermuda Hundred Campaign, but a few facts about the general himself are pertinent. Benjamin Franklin Butler was possibly the most dichotomous, puzzling and provocative significant figure of the war. There is no doubt that Butler was intelligent, but his intellect did not translate into military command ability. Before the war he was a Northern Democrat. Remarkably, in 1860, as a delegate to the Democratic convention in Charleston, he voted fifty-seven times to nominate Jefferson Davis for President of the United States and then backed Kentuckian John Breckinridge in the 1860 election against Lincoln. Nevertheless, after the attack on Fort Sumter Butler backed the Union fully. In May of 1861, Butler became the first volunteer major general, having come to the aid of Washington a few days after the outbreak of hostilities as a brigadier general of Massachusetts militia. Although he was an antebellum Democrat supporting pro-slavery Southern politicians, he confiscated slaves as contraband when slave owners went within the Union lines. He had commanded the walkover amphibious landing on Hatteras Inlet and occupied New Orleans, following the Navy, by the spring of 1862. Evidently his attitude toward the South had made an abrupt turn because his behavior in New Orleans was such that he became one of the most odious Yankees ever to be despised by Southerners. He was removed from command at New Orleans, but being an important political figure, he was appointed to command of the Army of the James in 1863. From that point onward his military reputation took a decidedly downward turn. Somehow General Grant apparently came away from his first meeting with Butler with a "high opinion" of him in April of 1864, possibly because Butler had suggested the use of his Army of the James in step with Grant's own concept.[11] Ulysses S. Grant, as his record later as president would demonstrate, was a poor judge of character, and in this case he was a poor judge of Butler's leadership capacity. Even with Grant assigning veteran commanders to serve under Butler, the Bermuda Hundred Campaign would become a major disappointment for the Union.

General Butler commenced his movement up the James River with around 39,000 troops on May 4, 1864, the same day that the Army of the Potomac advanced against Lee. Butler had complied with Grant's instruction to mount a diversion by sending a small expedition on May 1 to West Point on the York River. At West Point Butler's men pretended to be preparing the place as a launch point for a movement up the Virginia Peninsula. On May 5 Butler disembarked a brigade of United States Colored Troops (U.S.C.T.) at City Point on the south bank of the James River across from Bermuda Hundred. City Point was a useful transportation station on the James. The Confederates had used the wharfs there as a shipping point for exchanged Federal prisoners of war, including my Great Grandfather James Earley, and it would serve the Federals as a supply hub for the remainder of the war. The rest of Butler's X and XVIII Corps troops not occupying points on the river landed at Bermuda Hundred by 8 p.m.[12]

To this point Butler's advance was unfolding with near perfection. Butler's army was within a few miles of Petersburg, which could have been taken easily. By capturing Petersburg, the Federals would have had control of the Southside, Weldon, and Norfolk & Petersburg railroads. All of these roads converged at Petersburg, closing them would deny communications between Richmond and the South. General Grant in his report dated July 22, 1865, stated that when he visited Butler at Fort Monroe he "pointed out the apparent importance of getting possession of Petersburg and destroying railroad communications as far south as possible." Grant, however, in his instructions directed Butler to make Richmond the "objective point of his operations."[13] From hindsight it is clear that Petersburg would have been the proper objective, at least initially, for Butler to capture. Unfortunately for the Federals, Butler did not accomplish much after May 5.

To his credit Butler made an offensive move the day after his troops landed by sending out a couple of brigades on a reconnaissance. Not much was accomplished, however. Then Butler's troops battled Major General George Pickett's Confederates near Walthall Junction on the 7th. That day the Petersburg defenses were manned by only 1,300 men and Richmond was protected by perhaps 5,000 Confederates. Nevertheless, Butler assigned most of his troops to digging defensive positions to protect his bridgehead at Bermuda Hundred. There was more fighting at Swift Creek and Chester Station as Confederate General Pierre G.T. Beauregard scrambled to piece together a force to defend Petersburg and Richmond. On May 9 General Gillmore and General Smith suggested to Butler in a note that a pontoon bridge could be "thrown across" the Appomattox River so that Petersburg could be captured and the railroads cut there. They further suggested that "all the work of cutting the road and perhaps capturing the city can be accomplished in one day." Butler replied to Gilmore and Smith that he regretted that "an infirmity of purpose" had led them to suggest a plan they had not mentioned when he was "personally present." Butler insisted that "our demonstrations should be toward Richmond, and I shall in no way order a crossing of the Appomattox for the purpose suggested in your note." From that point onward Gillmore and Smith withheld advice to Butler, which, of course, had an adverse affect on the operation. Butler continued his overly-cautious movements in the direction of Richmond, and digging trenches, while cavalry raids were sent out against railroads in the region. Meanwhile Beauregard had managed to gather around 20,000 reinforcements. By May 11 Butler had decided to make a "major demonstration" at Drewry's Bluff, about half way between Bermuda Hundred and Richmond. Butler, as usual having fieldworks dug, took four days to position some 18,600 Federals around Drewry's Bluff. Then on May 16 Beauregard attacked in a dense pre-dawn fog and drove back the Federal lines. The fog persisted throughout the morning and hampered both sides. In the afternoon Butler ordered a withdrawal back to the defenses at Bermuda Hundred. The Federal casualties totaled approximately 3,500 to 4,000, of which perhaps 1,400 were captured. Beauregard's losses came to 2,506 with only about 220 of that total being captured. The Federals were able to return to the Bermuda Hundred defensive line without much opposition by 9 p.m.[14] With that Butler's Bermuda Hundred plan fizzled out.

General Grant summed up Butler's situation henceforth with a concise observation he included in his report the following year. "He was forced back, or drew back," Grant wrote, "into his intrenchments between the forks of the James and Appomattox Rivers, the enemy intrenching strongly in his front.... His army, therefore, though in a position of great security, was completely shut off from further operations directly against Richmond as if it had been in a bottle strongly corked." Grant soon decided to take the XVIII Corps from Butler for use in his campaign against Lee because it would be of no use at Bermuda Hundred. Years later Grant wrote that he wished "to rectify all injustice that I may have done to individuals ... who were gallantly serving their country during the trying period of the war.... General Butler certainly gave his very earnest support to the war...." Unfortunately, Butler, who obtained his position because of his political station, was not a capable leader for such an important operation, and the war was therefore prolonged and many more lives were lost as a result of his failure as commander of the Bermuda Hundred Campaign.

It is not the objective of this study to offer alternative strategies or tactical solutions that might have succeeded in place of what happened historically. However, from hindsight it is clear that Grant wasted a tremendous opportunity with his handling of the Bermuda Hundred Campaign. Grant faced a difficult task as general in chief in finding an officer capable of accomplishing the objectives for the operation on the James River quickly, which Grant believed was vital for the purpose of breaking "the military power of the rebellion." Grant himself might have been the only general available to lead the campaign from the James River in May of 1864 who could be counted upon to succeed. Sherman was occupied with the Atlanta Campaign, Thomas was too slow for the job and other capable generals were occupied as corps commanders. Even so, there is no doubt that there were several officers available who could have been reassigned and who would have handled the campaign better than Butler did. Grant himself gave priority to the task of compelling "Lee to retreat or to so cripple him that he could not detach a large force to go north and still retain enough for the defense of Richmond." Clearly Grant's greatest priority was the destruction Lee's army, even "by mere attrition, if in no other way."[15] Yet the potential advantages of a movement against Richmond from the James were so compelling that Grant should have made that campaign his priority. Meade had already demonstrated that he was capable of preventing Lee from threatening Washington. Thus, Grant could have relied upon Meade with the three reconstituted corps of the Army of the Potomac to detain Lee along the Rapidan. If Grant could have combined the 39,000 troops available to Butler with the IX Corps and landed them at Bermuda Hundred, he would have had a force strong enough to capture Petersburg and Richmond and hold Richmond in the event that Lee moved south to challenge him. Meade and the Army of the Potomac could have in that case followed Lee to Richmond and then cooperated with Grant against Lee. The only real difference here from the historical record is that Grant placed his priority with the Army of the Potomac and an overland campaign rather than with the advance via the James River and Bermuda Hundred. History demonstrates that Grant made the wrong decision by settling for the Overland Campaign of 1864. It was a choice that was, doubtless, forced upon him by political necessity. He had to satisfy President Lincoln's requirement that Washington be kept safe from a Confederate incursion, and he needed to confront General Lee head to head in order to assure his place in history.

General Grant commenced his Overland Campaign early on the morning of May 4, 1864, with Major General George Meade in command of the Army of the Potomac. Meade, however, was subject to Grant's instructions. Grant had to decide how to best get at Lee from his winter camps around Brandy Station. He had two obvious choices: he could make a crossing of the Rapidan River above or below Lee's defensive line on that river. Grant decided on the downriver route which required the army to pass through the forbidding Wilderness region, a terrible place for the Federals to fight a battle. It was disadvantageous for the Federals because for many miles the Wilderness terrain was, with the exception of a few clearings, a dense second-growth forest of pine, cedar, scrub oak, dogwood and brambles that severely limited visibility and nearly eliminated the effective use of artillery. The thickly-wooded region was cut with rills, ravines and bogs that rendered maneuvering exceedingly difficult. These conditions strongly favored Lee by negating the Federals' advantage in artillery and numbers. Nevertheless, Grant selected the downriver route because utilizing it provided better supply options and allowed Meade to retain communications with Butler's army on the James River.[16] Grant and Meade hoped, and perhaps expected, that Lee would react slowly, as had happened during the Mine Run Campaign, and thus the Army of the Potomac would be enabled to pass beyond the Wilderness into more open country. Once there the Federals would be able to employ their advantages fully against Lee's army. Lee didn't allow that to happen.

As the Federal advance began, Meade erred by shifting most of his available cavalry away to occupy Confederate Major General J.E.B. Stuart's troopers near Fredericksburg as a ploy to protect his supply train. Major General Phillip Sheridan was then commanding Meade's cavalry, and he assigned the task of screening the Federal march through the Wilderness to his smallest cavalry division and least experienced division commander, Brigadier General James Wilson. With the inexperienced Wilson in charge, the Federal cavalry only tentatively scouted the Wilderness roadways. Wilson's inefficient cavalry patrols allowed Lee's II and III Corps to march undetected into position to challenge the Army of the Potomac in the Wilderness.[17] On the morning of May 5, Grant and Meade were faced with a confrontation deep in the Wilderness that neither of them should have wanted.

With the return of Longstreet's I Corps from Tennessee, Lee had perhaps as many as 75,000 officers and men to deploy against Grant. The Army of the Potomac numbered nearly 100,000 men at about the time that the battle occurred, and Burnside's IX Corps was over 19,000 strong. Thus, for the fight in the Wilderness Grant's force totaled nearly 120,000 soldiers counting all branches, staff and provost guards. Grant's numerical superiority was obviously significant; however, as Overland Campaign authority Gordon Rhea observed, numbers alone do not account for some valid comparative considerations. Although Grant's army greatly outnumbered Lee's, the Army of the Potomac, to a large extent, was manned by short-timers, conscripts and bounty men. Less than a third of the soldiers in IX Corps were experienced veterans. One estimate presumed that only about 70,000 men from Grant's army could be considered dependable enough to stand up against Lee's veterans. Conversely, Lee had no short-timers; his soldiers were required to serve until the war's conclusion. Unlike the Federal army, where recruits were usually assigned to newly formed regiments, Confederate draftees and recruits were usually assigned as replacements in veteran regiments. Even elite Federal regiments, when they obtained recruits, were getting men with little interest in soldering, as evidenced by the following lines from a letter written by a new recruit for the 2nd U.S. Sharpshooters:

> Within one year I am coming home for they will not want us any longer but them that go into the navey will have to stay their full term of Enlistment ... but we will be discharged just as soon As the war closes I am here for three years but expect to come home within one year for I think the war will close ... them that say into the navey will get their fingers burnt I guess....

The neophyte soldier who wrote these lines would be mortally wounded before the end of May, his short-term service not ending the way he had expected. For Grant and his army, the impending battle in Virginia's Wilderness also would not play out as expected.[18]

Major General Gouverneur Kemble Warren's V Corps troops collided with the Confederate II Corps along the Orange Turnpike around noon on May 5, 1864, and the Battle of the Wilderness began in earnest. General Warren ascended to command of a Federal corps partially as a result of his role in the Battle of Gettysburg. At Gettysburg Warren had discerned the importance of Little Round Top to the Federals, and a statue of him stands there today. Warren was born at Cold Spring, New York, site of the West Point Foundry across the Hudson River from the United States Military Academy. Headed by Gouveneur Kemble, the foundry received its first Federal contract in 1820, and during the Civil War it produced the famous Parrott rifled cannons for the government. At the age of sixteen Warren was appointed to West Point and was graduated second in the class of 1850. That Warren was an intelligent and able soldier there can be little doubt, but his handling of the V Corps at the Battle of the Wilderness left much to be desired.

Although the Army of the Potomac was still in transit through the Wilderness on May 5 and the IX Corps lagged behind, Grant and Meade ordered Warren to attack when the Confederate II Corps was discovered on the Orange Turnpike. By practically any analysis that was a mistake. Grant at that time was inexperienced with handling the Army of the Potomac. He was unfamiliar with its inefficiencies. He expected his corps commanders to move with alacrity and coordination. But none of the Federal corps commanders performed well in the Wilderness, and Burnside with his IX Corps, acting as an independent command, did nothing to enhance his reputation at the Wilderness either.

Some clarification for Meade's rush to attack is revealed in messages between him and Grant after sunrise on May 5. A message from Meade was received by Grant at 7:30 a.m. in which Meade mentioned that Confederates were forming a battle line along the Orange Turnpike. He informed Grant, "I have directed General Warren to attack them at once with his whole force." Meade was thinking that Lee was attempting to distract him with the activity on the turnpike. "I think the enemy is trying to delay our movement, and will not give battle," he wrote. Grant answered at 8:24 a.m. with the following: "If any

General Warren's monument on Little Round Top at Gettysburg National Battlefield.

opportunity presents itself to pitch into a part of Lee's army, do so without giving time for disposition." Meade soon answered, "Warren is making his disposition to attack, and Sedgwick to support him. Nothing immediate from the front. I think, still, Lee is simply making a demonstration to gain time. I shall, if such is the case, punish him. If he is disposed to fight this side of Mine Run at once, he shall be accommodated."[19] From these messages it appears that Meade was still thinking that Lee was seeking to move into his old fieldworks behind Mine Run, but Grant and Meade were spoiling for a fight even if it broke out in the Wilderness. This counterintuitive aggressiveness, in the tangle of the Wilderness, points to impatience rather than adaptability on Grant's part.

The fighting in the Wilderness on May 5 was intense but basically indecisive. Lee had ordered Lieutenant General Richard Ewell to move by the Orange Turnpike with his Confederate II Corps towards the Federal advance. Ewell was cautioned not to bring on a general engagement without consulting General Lee. Lieutenant General A.P. Hill marched his III Corps, accompanied by General Lee, on the Orange Plank Road, a couple of miles south of Ewell; the intersection with Brock Road was Hill's objective. Pressured by Meade, Warren finally attacked Ewell's dug-in rebels without appreciable results. The Federal VI Corps was slowly moving into position to link up with Warren's right flank during the morning hours. If the Federal VI Corps, commanded by Major General John Sedgwick, had moved quicker, Ewell's Corps would have been seriously threatened with destruction. As it played out, attacks by Warren's V Corps failed and only generated outsized losses compared to Ewell's II Corps, which was protected by fieldworks. Even veteran Federal brigades took a beating in Warren's attacks. The proud Iron Brigade, perhaps hardest-fighting unit in the Army of the Potomac, broke and fled from a rebel counterattack on May 5. It was the first time ever that the Iron Brigade had been driven from the field.[20] Hill's III Corps nearly reached the intersection of Brock Road and the Orange Plank Road before the Federal II Corps could secure it. Meade, learning that Hill's III Corps was nearing that intersection, dispatched Brigadier General George Getty's Second Division of the VI Corps, less one brigade, from reserve at nearby Wilderness Tavern to hold the intersection until the Federal II Corps could get there. Getty reached the intersection just in time to occupy it, and the Federal II Corps, led by Major General W.S. Hancock, soon arrived to support Getty. Meade then ordered Getty to attack while the Hancock's Corps was deploying. Here again, Meade conceded to his impatience. Meade could have waited for Hancock to deploy with a view of hitting Hill's right flank with his divisions marching in from the south on Brock Road. Getty attacked shortly after 4 p.m., but his available force was not sufficient to move Hill's Corps. Hancock then fed his corps into the fight along the Orange Plank Road in disjointed attacks that also lacked enough concentration to break Hill's lines. Darkness closed out the fighting with neither side losing or gaining much ground or advantage.

At 10:30 on the night of May 5, Meade sent a message to Grant concerning the plan for the following morning. Grant had given his orders for renewing the battle with 4:30 a.m. as the starting time for attacks against Hill's corps. Meade requested that the attacks be delayed until 6 o'clock. He also mentioned the important fact that Longstreet's Corps would be reinforcing Hill along the Orange Plank Road. Meade wrote, "It appears to be the general opinion among prisoners that Longstreet was not in the action to-day, though expected, and that his position was to be on their right or our left. His force is supposed to be about 12,000. He will probably attack Hancock to-morrow." Grant did not accept the delay until 6 o'clock. He directed Meade to commence the attacks at 5 a.m.; Grant believed that if he waited to attack until 6 o'clock, Lee would "take the initiative," which Grant wished "specially to avoid."

Meade had sent orders to General Hancock as follows: "You are required to renew the attack at 4.30 o'clock to-morrow morning, keeping a sharp lookout on your left. Your right will be relieved by an attack made at the same time by General Wadsworth's division and by two divisions from Burnside's corps." The plan for May 6 called for the main attack to be launched against Hill with the hope of destroying his corps before Longstreet could come up. As mentioned in Meade's message, Wadsworth and Burnside were to assist in the effort against Hill's command by attacking north of the Orange Plank Road while Hancock attacked with Getty's division supporting along and south of the road. Meade was unsure of where or when Longstreet would appear, so he stressed the importance of keeping a "sharp lookout" on Hancock's left. As the day's fighting unfolded, it was Hancock's left, which he had been specifically warned to watch, that proved vulnerable to a counterattack when Longstreet's Corps reached the battlefield.

Meade could not give orders to Burnside because his command was separate from the Army of the Potomac, so the following orders were sent from Grant by an aide to Burnside at 8 p.m. on May 5: "Lieutenant-General Grant desires that you start your two divisions at 2 a.m. to-morrow, punctually, for this place. (Wilderness Tavern) You will put them in position ... so as to close the gap between Warren and Hancock, connecting both. You will move from this position on the enemy beyond at 4:30 a.m., the time at which the Army of the Potomac moves."[21] From this we can see that Burnside was expected to "punctually" move his two divisions in place on Warren's left and then attack in conjunction with Hancock. It didn't happen that way. Burnside failed to fulfill his assignment on time and as planned.

The Federal attack against Hill's corps on the Orange Plank Road began as ordered at around 5 a.m. Hancock sent in three divisions from his II Corps, Wadsworth's Division from the V Corps and Getty's three brigades from his VI Corps division against Hill. The outnumbered Confederates, of course, reeled backward and were soon about to be engulfed by the Federal onslaught. Within less than an hour Hill's Corps had been beaten back in disorder. The dense vegetation in the Wilderness worked for and against the attacking Federals. It allowed the Federals to close with Hill's Confederates without taking heavy casualties on the approach, but it also slowed their advance and masked the overall desperate condition of Hill's Corps.

In one of the war's most dramatic moments, Longstreet's Corps strode onto the scene at the Widow Tapp's Farm clearing along the Orange Plank Road. Hill's Corps, as expected, had been defeated and might have soon been destroyed. The arrival of Longstreet's Corps immediately changed the course of the battle, nearly equalizing the numbers at the scene of the fighting. Meade and Grant had failed to finish Hill's Corps before Longstreet could intervene, and, worst yet, they had failed to prepare for Longstreet arrival on the battlefield.

Hancock's attack stalled when Longstreet's veterans deployed and counterattacked, along with some of Hill's rallied troops. By mid-morning a stalemate had developed as Longstreet's counterattack stalled in turn. During the morning, Longstreet was advised of an unguarded route around the Federal left flank, which Hancock had been urged to watch carefully. The unfinished roadbed of a railroad linking Fredericksburg with Orange Court House cut through the thick woods nearly perpendicular to where Hancock's force was battling Longstreet's counterattack. The unfinished railroad bed provided a swath through the woods that either side could have utilized to move around the enemy's flank undetected. Perhaps Hancock expected to smash Hill's Corps without resorting to a flank attack, because, although the Federals must have been aware of the roadbed, they made no attempt to make use of it or to effectively patrol it. Longstreet, having been informed of the unguarded path to Hancock's left flank, selected some available brigades and sent them via the roadbed to attack the Federals. Four Confederate brigades moved unseen along the roadbed and slipped into position at the exact location to unhinge Hancock's left flank. At around 11 a.m. the four Confederate brigades, masked by a ravine, managed to reach the rear of the Federal extreme left and attacked. Hancock explained what happened then, while sparing all the ugly details, as follows in his report the following winter: Longstreet's unexpected flank attack "struck the left of Mott's division, which in turn was forced back. Some confusion ensuing among the troops of that division, I endeavored to restore order and to reform my line of battle along the Orange Plank Road … but was unable to effect this, owing to the partial disorganization of the troops … when their formation was partially lost." In other words, Hancock was forced to "withdraw the troops from the wood … and to reform them in the breast-works along the Brock Road" where he had started his advance on the previous day.[22]

General Longstreet intended to keep up the pressure on the Federal left after his successful flank attack. He was, however, severely wounded by Confederate soldiers as he rode with his staff on the Orange Plank Road. The incident was much the same as what happened to General Thomas "Stonewall" Jackson at the nearby Chancellorsville Battlefield the previous year. With Longstreet thereby disabled, General Lee prepared another attack against Hancock's force, which had by then regrouped behind the fieldworks on the west side of the Brock Road.

Around 1:30 p.m. Burnside's IX Corps troops finally got into position to attack Longstreet's left flank and rear near the Widow Tapp Farm, west of the Brock Road. Burnside's trip from the Federal rear, commencing in the wee hours of May 6, had been something of an odyssey. He should have been in position to support Hancock's attack by 5 a.m. Only the 2nd and 3rd divisions of Burnside's four-division corps made it to the Tapp Farm area that afternoon. Burnside's 1st Division had gone to assist Hancock's fight, and his 4th Division did not accompany the movement to the battlefield. The IX Corps units that did reach the Tapp Farm met determined resistance from Lee's Confederates. Burnside's approach was detected, and Confederate units were shifted during a lull in the fighting to meet his attack. Ultimately, Burnside and his IX Corps had little impact on the outcome of the battle. Had Burnside reached his assigned positions on time, Hill's corps probably would have been destroyed and Grant might have achieved a victory as he had planned it.

Lee's final effort along the Orange Plank Road commenced shortly after 4 p.m. It had required some time for Lee to reorganize Longstreet's battle-weary divisions for yet another go at Hancock's command. The plan of yet another attack on the Federal left on May 6, this time going against troops sheltered by fieldworks, was certainly dubious. Here again, however, Lee had faith in the capabilities of his soldiers, and, it seems, significant doubts about the fighting abilities of his foes. By 6 p.m. Lee's attack had been thrown back with heavy Confederate losses. Brush caught fire and spread into the Federal fieldworks in an area south of the road intersection, and the Confederates briefly managed a near breakthrough there before Federal reinforcements drove them back. As evening loomed the south sector of the battlefield grew nearly silent, save for the cries and moans of the wounded and the distant thunder of renewed combat to the northwest.

The Wilderness near the Widow Tapp's Farm in a view taken before the vegetation sprouted. The Federal IX Corps was repulsed in the marshy woods here.

Just as the fighting on Hancock's front was ebbing, Ewell's II Corps troops launched a final attack against Meade's extreme right flank. Brigadier General John Brown Gordon, a brigade commander in Early's Division of the Confederate II Corps, suggested the attack to Ewell after discovering that the Federal VI Corps was exposed on its right flank. Ewell delayed the attack because General Early, Gordon's commander, convinced Ewell that "a column was threatening" Ewell's flank and Early believed that Burnside's corps was within supporting distance of the VI Corps. Ewell waited to approve the attack until he was convinced that it was safe to order it. Some controversy resulted from Ewell's decision because Gordon later claimed that he could have possibly created a disaster for Meade's entire right wing if he had been granted permission to attack sooner. Gordon even claimed that his attack was "the greatest opportunity ever presented to Lee's army." The attack commenced near sunset and managed to rout two VI Corps brigades before darkness closed out the fighting. Early suggested that although Gordon's attack, which Early directed, succeeded in capturing two Federal brigadier generals (Seymour and Shaler) and hundreds of soldiers, it was lucky for the Confederates that "darkness came to close" out the combat. Early believed that if Meade had thrown in more troops and discovered "the disorder" in the Confederate lines, he might have "availed himself" of an opportunity to create some serious mischief for Ewell that evening.[23] After nightfall neither army was able to accomplish anything further and the serious fighting on the Wilderness Battlefield was over.

Federal casualties at the Battle of the Wilderness were the third highest of all the battles during the Civil War. The Federals reported 17,666 total casualties of which 2,246 were listed as killed in action and 12,037 as wounded. Confederate casualties were never fully recorded; returns for only 112 of the 183 Confederate regiments engaged in the battle were found. It has been generally supposed that Confederate casualties for the Battle of the Wilderness totaled around 11,000 men. For much of the fighting in the Wilderness the Confederates were on the defensive, often behind fieldworks. The casualty figures would have been even more lopsided if Longstreet's corps had not attacked the Federal defenses along the Brock Road on the 6th. Another factor in the higher Federal casualties was the large number of inexperienced Federal soldiers seeing action for the first time in new regiments and as recruits in veteran units. However, Confederate casualty reports cannot be accepted as reliable. General Lee issued an order in May of 1863, and there could have been other similar directives, that affected the reporting of casualties. Lee's General Orders, No. 63, included the following mandate: "It is, therefore, ordered that in the future the reports of the wounded shall only include those whose injuries, in the opinion of the medical officers, render them unfit for duty." There is at least one Confederate report on record wherein the following caveat was included: "The wounded include only those disabled indefinitely."[24] This policy on casualty reporting should not have affected the list of those killed in action, although it demonstrates that Lee and the Confederates were reluctant to admit to their losses in battle for fear of encouraging the enemy.

The Battle of the Wilderness particularly belongs in this study because it demonstrates a pattern of circumstances in the Army of the Potomac that continued for the duration of the Overland Campaign. Poor staff work, sluggishness, indifference, inadequate cooperation and shortsightedness plagued the leadership of each corps of this army and the IX Corps. Somehow these deficiencies were never adequately addressed as the campaign progressed during the summer of 1864. Time and again General Grant devised tactics that should have won this battle—and other battles during the Overland Campaign—only to have his subordinate generals fail to find a way to implement them as planned.

Meade and the senior leadership of the Army of the Potomac commenced the Overland Campaign with characteristic miscalculations and oversights at the Battle of the Wilderness. Fighting in the Wilderness in the first place was a mistake accountable to both Grant and Meade. The terrain and road conditions in the Wilderness negated the substantial advantages in numbers and artillery that favored the Federals over Lee's Army of Northern Virginia. Meade did not use his cavalry effectively on May 4, and the limited cavalry he utilized as a scout for the Federal advance failed to detect Lee's presence in the Wilderness. Once the Confederate II Corps was encountered on the Orange Turnpike, Grant and Meade had three choices: the army could have attempted to move on to Spotsylvania, Meade could have hurried the VI Corps forward to cooperate with Warren's V Corps against the Confederates, or Meade could attack immediately and accept battle in the Wilderness. Grant and Meade, as a result of ill-advised impatience, chose the latter and attacked with the V Corps before the VI Corps was up. Meade ordered the attack without knowledge of the size and strength of the Confederate force Warren was facing on the Orange Turnpike, and Warren attacked before he could effectively organize a concerted effort, two more lapses compounding a poor decision by the army commander.

Staff and command lapses continued on May 6 in the Wilderness when Burnside and his IX Corps failed to reach the battlefield on time to cooperate effectively with the attack on Hill's Confederate III Corps along the Orange Plank Road. The IX Corps got moving on time to easily reach its assigned position as directed, but the route to the battlefield was clogged with wagons and artillery which substantially delayed its progress.

Poor staff work was accountable for the delay; someone from Meade's staff should have cooperated with Burnside's staff to check the condition of the road well before the movement was scheduled to commence. The failure of the IX Corps to hit the Confederates as planned probably saved Hill's III Corps from destruction early on May 6. Later that morning on the same front, Major General Winfield S. Hancock was surprised by an attack on his exposed left flank. Hancock had been admonished to watch his left flank closely in case Longstreet would arrive and strike it. He and his staff neglected to patrol an unfinished railroad cut that ran through the woods adjacent to his battle lines. Longstreet took advantage of the unguarded roadbed as an avenue to send four brigades undetected around Hancock's left. The ensuing Confederate surprise attack inflicted heavy casualties by enfilade and drove back Hancock's entire front, thereby shifting the initiative to the Confederates.

Yet another Federal oversight on May 6 enabled the Confederates to nearly turn the right flank of Sedgwick's VI Corps north of the Orange Turnpike. Ewell's Confederates managed to rout two Federal brigades after sunset on the 6th because Sedgwick did not secure his right flank effectively. An aggressive commander might have instead attacked the Confederate flank, but Sedgwick accomplished little and nearly allowed a disaster on his own flank.

General Lee fought the Battle of the Wilderness with characteristic desperation, taking risks that few army commanders would have found the courage to attempt. He made the correct choice in selecting the tangled forests of the Wilderness as his battleground. Lee was, however, slow in concentrating his army and getting it into position. Ewell's II Corps was sent to a vulnerable position and might have been destroyed if Grant and Meade had employed the Federal cavalry properly and discovered its presence in time to concentrate against it. Lee did nothing to prepare Hill's battered corps for an anticipated renewed attack during the night of May 5–6. Lee expected Longstreet's corps to arrive on the battlefield well before daylight, and when it didn't, Hill's front was easily driven back by Hancock's dawn attack on the 6th. Lee was very fortunate that Longstreet's corps reached the scene just as Hill's corps was disintegrating. The attack by Longstreet's and Hill's troops against the Federal defensive line on the Brock Road on May 6 was so dubious as to call into question Lee's justification for making it. Lee should have realized that such an attack, especially made by jaded troops without artillery support, had little, if any, chance of success. Overall, the Battle of the Wilderness does not rank as one of Lee's better showings as an army commander. He was, in fact, fortunate that the Federals were unable to implement Grant's tactics effectively.

By the morning of May 7, Grant had realized that continuing the fighting in the Wilderness would probably not yield a timely victory. Early that morning he sent Meade the following orders: "Make all preparations during the day for a night march, to take position at Spotsylvania Court-House with one army corps; at Todd's Tavern with one, and another near the intersection of Piney Branch and Spotsylvania Railroad with the road from Alsop's to Old Court-House." Grant later explained his reasoning for the move as follows: "My object in moving to Spotsylvania was two-fold: first, I did not want Lee to get back to Richmond in time to attempt to crush Butler before I could get there: second, I wanted to get between his army and Richmond if possible; and, if not, to draw him into the open field." Grant believed that it was "evident" that the fighting in the Wilderness had convinced the Confederates that they could not "maintain the contest in the open field," despite their advantage of position, and that Lee "would await an attack behind his works." Orders, therefore, were "at once issued for a movement" around Lee's right flank, tactics that became the theme of the Overland Campaign.[25] Grant, as he would demonstrate for the rest of the war, would not be intimidated by Lee. He was as audacious as Lee, and he understood that the days of disengaging and resting after a severe fight were, by necessity, finished.

While Grant was shifting his attention to Spotsylvania on May 7, Major General William Tecumseh Sherman launched his campaign against Atlanta from the Chattanooga vicinity as his role in Grant's concerted and interlinked effort to destroy the Confederacy. Sherman's task in Georgia was even more difficult and demanding than Meade's was in Virginia. Supplying his armies was the greatest challenge Sherman faced during his campaign. Sherman led three armies against General Joseph E. Johnston into Georgia. His supply link was a single rail line connecting his front with Louisville, Kentucky, a distance of over 320 miles. Protecting his supply and communications line against guerrillas and rebel cavalry raids was a daunting mission indeed. Sherman's invading force initially consisted of seven infantry corps totaling around 100,000 men assigned to the following armies: Major General James B. McPherson's Army of the Tennessee, 24,465 strong; Major General George H. Thomas's Army of the Cumberland, 60,733 strong; and Major General John M. Schofield's Army of the Ohio, 13,559 strong.[26] Although Sherman commanded nearly twice as many men as Johnston did, the road to Atlanta would require continuous fighting and many major battles and engagements lasting until September.

When Grant did not attack in the Wilderness on May 7, General Lee was remarkably alert to ongoing activity by the Federal cavalry south of the battlefield. Lee realized that Spotsylvania Court House needed to be "occupied by a portion of his army as a precaution for any option" Grant might be considering. Lee selected the Confederate I Corps, commanded by Major General Richard Anderson who replaced General Longstreet, to occupy Spotsylvania. Since the Federals held the Brock Road, the most direct route to Spotsylvania, a road was cut through the woods parallel to the Brock Road under the direction of Brigadier General William Pendleton, Lee's chief of artillery. This "Pendleton Road" connected the Confederate I Corps field works south of the unfinished railroad to the Catharpin Road which Anderson utilized to march his corps to the Shady Grove Church Road leading eastward to Spotsylvania Court House. Anderson got his troops on the road four hours ahead of schedule and marched them all night; thus, the Confederates arrived at Spotsylvania Court House before the Federal V Corps, in the vanguard, could secure the place.

The Federal movement to Spotsylvania was botched as a result of poor coordination, yet again. Federal cavalry should have secured the road to the Spotsylvania Court House crossroads. Instead of clearing the Brock Road to the crossroads, the cavalry rested at Todd's Tavern about five miles to the northwest, blocking the road and delaying the progress of the V Corps infantry. By the time the V Corps was nearing Spotsylvania Court House, the Confederate I Corps had arrived and was deploying on a ridge north of the village known to history as Laurel Hill. The Confederate position actually was not located on the farm known locally as Laurel Hill, which was farther north. Instead it was situated on high ground between the Spindle and Perry farms. Somehow this section of the battlefield acquired the name Laurel Hill nonetheless.[27]

Warren's V Corps finally got into position to attack the Confederate I Corps at the Spindle Farm on May 8 around 8 a.m., having been on the road since 9 p.m. on May 7. Warren's soldiers were weary after their all-night march from the Wilderness, but so were

Anderson's Confederate I Corps men. Warren did not waste time with an effort to probe the ridgeline where the Confederates were deploying. He also did not wait for all of his troops to deploy for a concentrated attack. Instead, he attacked piecemeal with brigades that morning. He failed to dent the enemy line.

At 1 p.m. Meade ordered Major General John Sedgwick to proceed with his VI Corps to "Spotsylvania Court House and join General Warren in a prompt and vigorous attack on the enemy now concentrating there. Use every exertion," Meade admonished, "to move with the utmost dispatch to get there." At 1:30 p.m. Meade informed Warren that "Sedgwick's whole corps" was on the way to join with Warren for an attack on his front, and Meade asked Warren to cooperate with Sedgwick for the attack. Apparently Warren possibly did not trust Sedgwick, who actually was senior to him, to be of much help. Warren angrily told Meade that he would not "cooperate with Sedgwick or anybody else."[28] Warren's insubordinate tone reflected the troublesome inability within the Army of the Potomac to concentrate on the task at hand with a reasonable show of cooperation with urgency. Repeatedly the senior leaders of that army failed to cooperate efficiently; Grant, simply put, could not depend on having his orders obeyed with the diligence and the zeal required to succeed against the Army of Northern Virginia.

While Warren was struggling with his assignment at the Spindle Farm, Grant was informing Chief of Staff Halleck, and thus Washington, of the situation as he saw it. "The army," Grant wrote, "commenced moving south at 9 p.m. yesterday.... It is not yet demonstrated what the enemy will do, but the best feeling prevails in this army, and I feel at present no apprehension for the result." Grant did not yet know that Lee was effectively moving to cut off his movement to the Spotsylvania crossroads. His immediate plan was to "form a junction with General Butler as early as possible," since the army had been unable to "inflict the heavy blow on Lee's army" that he had hoped for in the "fight at Old Wilderness." "My exact route to the James River," he conceded, "I have not yet definitely marked out." Unfortunately for his soldiers, Grant was "prepared to meet any enemy interposing" on the way to the James.[29] Grant's actions immediately following this report would prove costly to his army and his reputation as an army commander.

Lee managed to get his three corps entrenched north of Spotsylvania Court House before Grant could get at him in the open. The Federal attacks on May 8 were for more costly than effective and did not prevent Lee from concentrating his army to block Grant's movement. On May 9 both sides built fieldworks for protection as Meade used the day to rest his army and distribute ammunition. Skirmishing and sniping, however, continued on the 9th, and Major General John Sedgwick, the VI Corps commander, was killed that day, apparently by a long-distance shot from the rebel line.

The Federals probed the Confederate lines on the 9th and discovered that Lee was vulnerable to a flank attack on his far left. General Hancock moved three divisions from his II Corps into position for an attack by dusk on the 9th. Had he discovered the weakness sooner and attacked with his corps, the Federals probably would have driven Lee out of his fieldworks. General Grant decided not to push Hancock's corps against Lee's left on the morning of May 10. With the benefit of hindsight, it seems that Grant missed a good opportunity that morning by choosing to attack the main Confederate works seeking a soft spot instead of attacking Lee's lightly-guarded left flank.[30] This decision by Grant conforms to his principal perceived weakness as an army commander. Grant far too often resorted to frontal assaults against strong fortifications when other options were available. At Vicksburg, Chattanooga, the Wilderness and here again at Spotsylvania he ordered attacks against strong fortifications with little reason to expect success. Grant would continue to resort to this unreasonable tactical approach for the rest of the war.

On May 10 Grant ordered renewed assaults against the Confederate works rather than unleashing Hancock's corps against Lee's weak left flank. The best-remembered assault of that day was devised and led by twenty-four-year-old Colonel Emory Upton, commander of the Second Brigade, First Division, VI Corps. The young colonel formed the twelve regiments assigned for his attack into a line four regiments deep and three regiments wide to concentrate on a narrow section of the Confederate trenches east of the Brock Road. Emory's target was the western front of a salient called the "Mule Shoe" because it projected in a bulge at the point where the Confederate trenches angled southward. Ewell's Confederate II Corps troops manned the Mule Shoe defenses. The concealed launch point for Upton's attack was in a heavily wooded area only about 200 yards from the rebel trench line. At around 6:30 p.m. Upton's troops rushed out from the woods and overran the enemy trenches. The Confederates resisted fiercely at first

This monument located near Trophy Point at West Point honors Major General John Sedgwick who was killed by a sniper at Spotsylvania. The monument was cast from cannons captured by Sedgwick's VI Corps during the Civil War.

A side panel on the Sedgwick monument at West Point depicts the general's death scene. Tradition at West Point holds that a cadet who spins the general's spurs will have success in passing an academic test.

but were quickly overwhelmed and pushed back to a second defensive line. At about the same time another attack was launched on the Laurel Hill front by Brigadier General John H.H. Ward's First Brigade from the Third Division of the Federal II Corps. Ward himself was under reproach for apparent intoxication during the fighting on May 6, and he would soon be forced out of the service. Ward's regiments, nevertheless, also hit the rebel fieldworks with a very narrow front and also managed to penetrate them. Both of these partially-successful attacks ultimately failed because Federal corps commanders did not send in reinforcements at the moment the breakthrough occurred. Upton's attack impressed Grant, and he decided to attempt another attack on the Mule Shoe, this time with more than an entire infantry corps.

Grant waited another day to shift the II Corps in preparation for his massive attack against the apex of the Mule Shoe. The attack, mainly by Hancock's II Corps, was slated to commence at 4 a.m. on May 12 with perhaps as many as 20,000 infantrymen positioned to pitch in. At about 4:30 a.m. the attack got under way with a massive rectangle of regiments fifty ranks deep. Lee had ordered Ewell to move most of his artillery to the rear in case Grant decided to make another movement southward, so the Federal II Corps attack was not initiatively swept by heavy artillery fire this time. The vast horde of blue-uniformed Federals must have resembled an immense, gushing flashflood spewing out of the woods across the field from the Mule Shoe defenses. Very quickly the attackers swept over the earthworks, penetrating well into the Confederate lines, taking thousands of

These ruts and small mounds are all that now remains of the Confederate defensive line near the Bloody Angle at Spotsylvania Battlefield.

prisoners and dozens of colors. Then, things took a turn much for the worse for the Federals. This day, May 12, 1864, was destined to become perhaps the most gruesome day ever experienced anywhere by Americans soldiers in any war.

Once Hancock's men pierced the Mule Shoe salient, all order was lost. The troops mixed together promiscuously without regard to brigade, regiment or company. The attacking columns disintegrated into an unorganized mob, as officers were unable to maintain the momentum inside the rebel perimeter. Lee took advantage of the chaos and launched a counterattack that pushed the attackers back to the fieldworks at the edge of the Mule Shoe salient. One section of the Mule Shoe trenches just west of the apex came to be known as the Bloody Angle. All through the afternoon, with rain transforming the trenches into a morass, the two armies kept up a constant stream of musket and artillery fire that created an unimaginable scene of gore and horror. Corpses were pulverized and the surrounding vegetation was shredded by the crossfire of hundreds of thousands of rounds. A twenty-two-inch oak tree standing near the trenches was cut down by the hurricane of small arms fire. The Federals brought up ammunition by pack mules to keep up the constant volume of fire. Throughout the day and into the evening the Federal corps commanders were unable to reorganize their troops and continue the advance. The Federal VI joined in the attack on the Mule Shoe's western face around 6 a.m. without altering the stalemate. General Burnside was ordered to attack on his front southeast of the Mule Shoe. Somehow, despite the pandemonium in the Mule Shoe, Burnside's IX Corps had practically no impact on the outcome of the fighting. Throughout the day Lee's engineers worked to construct a second defensive line below the Mule Shoe to maintain a continuous front from west to east, and Lee shifted troops from quiet sectors to bolster the resistance at the Mule Shoe. After nightfall the Confederates used the cover of darkness to pull back to the new defensive line below the Mule Shoe; Lee had managed to save his army from a potential catastrophe.

Despite the enormous losses at the Wilderness and at Spotsylvania, Grant was sending sanguine reports to Washington. On May 11 he told General Halleck that the result of the fighting "to this time is much in our favor.... I think the loss of the enemy must be greater, we having taken over 4,000 prisoners in battle, while he has taken but few, except stragglers." He assured Halleck that he intended "to fight it out on this line if it takes all summer." Even after the terrible day at the Mule Shoe on the 12th, he suggested in another message to Halleck that the Confederates "seem to have found the last ditch." Grant kept looking for an opportunity to strike again at Spotsylvania, shifting troops to locations he believed to be vulnerable on the Confederate line. On May 18 Grant attempted yet another attack in the Mule Shoe salient and with Burnside's corps on the Federal left. These efforts were feeble yet costly in casualties. On the next day Lee sent his II Corps on a reconnaissance in force around the Federal right. At the Harris Farm, about a mile or so northeast of the main defensive line, Ewell's II Corps collided with a division of fresh troops just arrived from the Washington defenses. Most of the Federal troops were heavy artillery regiments being sent to the front to fight as infantry. The inexperienced heavy artillerymen managed to hold the Confederate II Corps until reinforcements arrived from the veteran Federal II and V Corps. Ewell was forced to retreat, although Federal casualties were reportedly over fifty percent higher than those of the Confederates. Apparently the green heavy artillerymen fired at other Federal units accidentally. Artillery commander Colonel Charles Wainwright observed that the Federal loss was "probably double what it would have been" if the officers in charge would have had more experience.[31] The fighting at Spotsylvania ended with the engagement at the Harris Farm.

The Federal casualties were the second highest of all the battles during the Civil War. This battle, however, lasted for nearly two weeks and was really a series of engagements at different points on a large front. Of the 18,399 total Federal casualties reported, 2,725 were listed as killed; and although Grant claimed that few Federals had been captured at Spotsylvania, the report listed 2,258 men as missing. Burnside's IX Corps, despite its minimal impact on the outcome of the battle, had 3,146 casualties listed in the report. These numbers reflect the devastating effect of repeated assaults, over open fields of fire, against trenches. Confederate losses were inexact, only estimated, but probably totaled at least 10,000. Lee admitted that his army's loss of artillery was "ascertained to have been twenty pieces."[32]

Grant had realized by May 20 that his best option was to move around Lee's right flank yet again. To many the Battle of Spotsylvania Court House was another tactical Federal defeat, but the battle ended in a draw and as a strategic setback for the Confederates. Lee wanted to drive the Federals back to the Potomac, in this he again failed. Still, Lee managed this battle on the defensive much better than the Meade and the Army of the Potomac managed their offensive tactics. Warren and Burnside completely failed overall. The attack on the Mule Shoe on May 12 got off to such a promising start that it is reasonable to blame indifferent leadership for its ultimate failure. Grant received criticism for doggedly resorting to costly frontal assaults against strong fieldworks, and this criticism was thoroughly justified. The loss of over 18,000 casualties for the sake of attrition would be viewed as unconscionable today, just as it was in 1864. Grant also deserves criticism for expecting too much from the Army of the Potomac. This campaign was unlike the Vicksburg Campaign, yet Grant fought as if he expected to maneuver against Lee as well as he had against Pemberton in Mississippi. Grant was failing in Virginia to adapt and to innovate for the demands of the theater. Equally prejudicial was his inability to address the inadequacies of his corps and divisional commanders. There is little in the historical record to indicate that Grant made any serious attempt to compel his generals to improve their performance or to appoint replacements to demonstrate that indifferent results would not be tolerated. Grant was, obviously, constrained by political considerations regarding his options in making changes in the command structure. Nevertheless, Grant can be criticized for a poor showing in such a vital and elevated executive position. These flaws continued to haunt the Federals for the duration of the Overland Campaign.

Although Grant was occupied with the Overland Campaign in May, his duties as overall commander of the Union armies required him to monitor the three other major operations under way that month in Georgia, the Shenandoah Valley region and at Bermuda Hundred. In Georgia, Major General William T. Sherman was battling Confederate General Joseph E. Johnston under circumstances similar to Grant's situation in Virginia. Johnston's army was almost constantly ensconced in strong positions that were impregnable to attack, thereby blocking Sherman's line of advance. At Rocky Face Ridge, near Dalton, Georgia, on May 8 and 9, Sherman demonstrated against the precipitous hillsides of that Confederate stronghold while sending a force on a turning movement through Snake Creek Gap to force Johnston to withdraw. Sherman's tactics worked, as Johnston fell back southward to Resaca, Georgia. Sherman's flanking tactics, commencing at Rocky Face Ridge, established a precedent for the Atlanta Campaign that continued until General Johnston was replaced in July.

Grant had planned a two-pronged operation for the Shenandoah Valley region in April. His plan called for one force to destroy the vital Confederate salt works at Saltville, Virginia, and to cripple the Virginia & Tennessee Railroad by destroying the railroad bridge over the New River near Dublin, Virginia. Major General Franz Sigel was ordered to simultaneously advance up the Shenandoah Valley with another force from Winchester to threaten the Virginia Central Railroad. Brigadier General George C. "Uncle George" Crook was in charge of the operation in southwest Virginia intended to make mischief on the salt works and railroad bridges. Grant had called Crook to his headquarters at Culpeper Court House, Virginia, to explain his intentions before the coordinated Federal operations began in early May. Crook returned to his command in West Virginia and commenced his march toward Dublin in late April.

The other half of Grant's two-pronged offensive in the Shenandoah was under the aegis of Major General Franz Sigel. His assignment was secured by the direction of President Lincoln, who valued Sigel's influence with the German-immigrant vote. Sigel's advancement to major general demonstrates that pandering to the immigrant vote is nothing new to American politicians; it was in full swing during the Civil War just as it is today. Sigel had been soundly defeated three times as a soldier in Germany, and his record in America was much the same. At the only battle during the war in which he had a role in a victory, Pea Ridge, he attempted to lead yet another retreat when the enemy was actually completely beaten. Sigel's appointment to command of the Department of West Virginia was not well received by the Americans serving under him. Colonel David Hunter Strother's diary entry reveals much about how Sigel was appraised by the army in the Shenandoah: "The Dutch vote must be secured at all hazards." The "sacrifice of West Virginia," he added, "is a small matter."³³

Sigel began his advance slowly up the Shenandoah Valley from Martinsburg on April 29. Sigel then cautiously moved up the Valley to reach Woodstock by May 11. Major General John C. Breckinridge had been sent by General Lee to protect the Shenandoah Valley from Sigel's incursion, and he gathered a force of more than 5,300 men, including the Virginia Military Institute (V.M.I.) Corps of Cadets, to oppose Sigel. Having not been reinforced by Crook, indeed not having heard from him since May 6, Sigel informed Washington that his "principal object in advancing up the Shenandoah Valley was to threaten Staunton, to divide the forces of Breckinridge, and to assist by these means General Crook, whose object is to destroy New River bridge." Sigel apparently was worried about the presence of Breckinridge, and he indicated that he had no intention of attacking Breckinridge in any case. "My forces are insufficient for offensive operations in this country," he suggested. He would, however, "resist" Breckinridge "at some convenient position" in the event that Breckinridge "should advance against us." Sigel believed, or at least later suggested, that he was outnumbered significantly by the rebels. Sigel's timid command execution contrasted starkly with the aggressive and determined efforts of Breckinridge. The Federal soldiers in the Shenandoah, already disadvantaged by operating in enemy territory, would be shackled with a commander whom they believed was incompetent and inferior to their enemy's general.

On May 14, Colonel Augustus Moor, commander of Sigel's 1st Brigade, was ordered to gather three infantry regiments, 1,000 cavalrymen and six pieces of artillery and "march to Mount Jackson to ascertain and feel the strength and position of the rebels ... reported to be on Rude's Hill." The cavalry pushed ahead to New Market, and Moor followed with the rest of his force and then deployed his infantry and artillery near the village. After dark the Confederates attacked but were repulsed, "losing 5 killed and many more wounded." Early on the morning of the 15th, Moor sent out patrols to locate the rebels. He learned that Breckinridge was advancing directly towards his position with a "heavy column of rebels."

Moor was reinforced by Major General Julius Stahel's cavalry on the morning of the 15th, and Stahel assumed command pending Sigel's arrival. The outnumbered Federals fell back to Manor's Hill, on the northern edge of New Market to await developments. Sigel reached the scene around noon as the Confederates, V.M.I. cadets included, prepared to launch their main attack.

Things began to deteriorate rapidly for the Federals after Sigel arrived. One of Moor's regiments, the 123rd Ohio Infantry, gave way as the Confederates bombarded Manor's Hill with thirteen guns. Sigel then ordered another withdrawal to Bushong's Hill, a little farther to the north of the town. Sigel had more troops, but some of his best regiments had been left far in the rear guarding his trains. His line on Bushong's Hill was vulnerable on each flank; and, although he commanded more men than Breckinridge, the Confederates outnumbered his men at the scene of combat by three to two. Breckinridge decided to press the issue and ordered his infantry to charge, and again the 123rd Ohio broke, causing other Federal units to follow to the rear. Yet somehow the Federals held fast on Bushong's Hill, and the course of the battle shifted temporarily.³⁴

The Confederate attack stalled, and Breckinridge then sent the V.M.I. cadets forward to fill a gap that had widened in the center of his battle line. The cadets charged up the slope of Bushong's Hill and fired a volley, sealing the gap in Breckinridge's line. Stahel, from the Federal left, sent his cavalry on a mounted charge that was checked by artillery fire and enfilading fire from rebel infantry in square formations. With the Confederate attack still stalled, Sigel attempted to mount a counterattack with his infantry. Sigel, it was said, gave the order and directions to attack in German, causing considerable confusion that required time to sort out. When the attack finally went forward, Breckinridge was ready.

The Federal infantry counterattack went off in confusion. The 1st West Virginia Infantry, in the center, went forward before the 34th Massachusetts Infantry, on the right, had heard the order to charge; and then, after a short advance, the 1st West Virginia turned and scattered to the rear. Soon only the 34th Massachusetts was confronting the rebels, and Colonel George Wells, the regiment's commander, "could not make a single man hear or heed" as he desperately tried to order the regiment to fall back. Wells, in the midst of a storm of musket fire and a violent thunderstorm's lightening and pouring rain, grabbed the color bearer and held him until the regiment stopped advancing. The 34th then "faced about and marched back" to its former position "in common time." While the 34th was being cut to pieces, "the artillery had limbered up and was moving off the field." Breckinridge's infantry, seeing the Federals falling back, charged without orders. This final Confederate push proved too much for the Federals; most of them took to their heels and fled northward on the Valley Pike.[35]

Sigel had left two infantry regiments and "quite a large body of cavalry" to guard his trains. When he had ordered Colonel Moor to make his reconnaissance on May 14, Sigel had withheld "Moor's two finest regiments" the 28th and 116th Ohio Infantries to guard his train. Sigel believed that the 116th Ohio was "poorly organized and 'entirely useless.'" But it was the 116th Ohio that arrived with bayonets fixed to clear the way "on the pike up to the battle-field through disgraceful fleeing masses of cavalry and straggling infantry." Captain Henry DuPont arrived from Mount Jackson with Battery B, 5th U.S. Artillery, supported by Colonel James Washburn and several companies of his 116th Ohio Infantry. Together these officers worked as a team to cover Sigel's disorderly retreat from New Market. DuPont positioned his guns in sections 500 yards apart to cover the Federal withdrawal. Each section fired until the rebels closed and then dashed well behind the other section to redeploy. By this process DuPont's battery bought precious time for Sigel and his beaten army to escape. Later, DuPont complained that he had taken the initiative by himself, without orders from Sigel, to shield the retreating army with his guns.[36]

Grant had not expected much from Sigel, but just when he began hoping "to hear of good work being done in the valley," General Halleck sent the following message to Grant: "Sigel is in full retreat on Strasburg. He will do nothing but run; never did anything else." Sigel certainly was the champion of the "masterful retreat"; but such expertise was out of demand by 1864, and Sigel was finished as a field commander henceforth. His leadership in the Shenandoah Valley had been a fiasco. He had again offended native-born soldiers under his command with his preferential treatment for his German and foreign immigrant comrades. The native-born soldiers had no confidence in his leadership; it showed in their performance at New Market. The 123rd Ohio Infantry, which broke twice during the battle, had an otherwise solid record as a dependable unit during the war. With the exception of the 34th Massachusetts, which Sigel apparently admired, most of the Federal infantry regiments had probably their worst performance of the war at New Market. This gives rise to the likelihood that these soldiers had doubts about Sigel's capabilities as a field commander and distrusted his decisions. Sigel certainly committed serious command errors at New Market. He left too many troops behind to protect his trains. The wagons should have been parked instead of being strung-out for miles on the pike. A portion of the trains had to be destroyed, in any case, to prevent capture by the rebels. Sigel fought the battle piecemeal and never managed to arrange a concentrated attack on the enemy. Breckinridge was thus allowed to pound portions of Sigel's force with greater numbers at the point of combat and then to repeat the process when Sigel brought up reinforcements. Breckinridge's victory at New Market was hard-earned, but it was virtually assured coming as it did against a general with Sigel's limitations. Nevertheless, despite all his faults as a leader and field commander, Sigel did not lack physical courage. He attempted, at considerable risk, to rally his men as they were being swept from the field. Colonel Wells, himself a brave soldier indeed, reported that Sigel sat his horse on the right of his 34th Massachusetts "during most of the engagement, and in the hottest of fire." "How he escaped," Wells wrote, "is a mystery to me."[37]

Casualties for Sigel's army at New Market totaled ninety-six killed, 520 wounded and 225 missing. Colonel Wells' 34th Massachusetts Infantry, which was hit especially hard by the Confederates, including the V.M.I. cadets, but fought courageously against desperate odds, lost twenty-eight killed, 174 wounded and nineteen missing; eleven of the wounded later died. Confederate losses came to forty-three killed, 474 wounded and three missing. As for the V.M.I. cadets, ten were killed and forty-seven were wounded. The battle is still remembered for the inspiring courage of the young cadets, who earned additional admiration for capturing a cannon at New Market.[38]

Fighting was ongoing at Resaca, Georgia, the same day, May 15, as the fiasco at New Market. Sherman, utilizing a somewhat elaborate plan conceived by Major General George Thomas, attempted to outflank General Joseph Johnston's Army of the Tennessee in order to destroy the Western & Atlantic Railroad at Resaca. Sherman expected the Confederates to withdraw when their communications line was disrupted, and he planned to use his own Federal Army of the Tennessee to strike the enemy flank at Resaca while the remainder of his force moved in from northern Georgia against the enemy rear. Had the plan worked to perfection, Sherman probably would have crushed Johnston's army and ended the Atlanta Campaign then and there.

Major General James B. McPherson, perhaps Sherman's most trusted subordinate, led the flanking movement to Resaca and was in position to fulfill his assignment. Instead of destroying the railroad as ordered, McPherson assumed a defensive stance and awaited Sherman's next move. As the situation played out, both armies concentrated around Resaca by May 13. On the 14th, Sherman pressed the Confederate lines with a series of attacks, and Johnston, in turn, launched a counterattack against the Federal left. Part of McPherson's army crossed the Oostanaula River on the 15th and threatened the railroad line in Johnston's rear. By the evening of May 15, Johnston, realizing that his position was once again turned, started his army moving southward to Calhoun, Georgia. The fighting around Resaca resulted in around 2,750 Federal casualties and perhaps 2,800 Confederate casualties.[39]

The attacks and counterattacks launched by each side at Resaca had no real chance of success. By this point in the war whenever a battle seemed imminent, the combatants would construct fieldworks for protection. Johnston, however, devised a clever plan to crush a part of Sherman's force as it marched in pursuit of the Confederates. On May 19, Johnston made the following announcement to his army: "Soldiers of the Army of Tennessee, you have displayed the highest quality of the soldier—firmness in combat.... I lead you to battle." Johnston by then had around 74,000 men to confront an approaching Federal separated wing numbering less than 35,000 troops. Yet when it seemed that the attack was about to commence, General Hood, according to Johnston, "was deceived by a false report that a heavy column of the enemy had turned" the Confederate right and was closing on Hood. Hood, concerned that the Federals might be getting behind him, "took a defensive position. When the mistake was discovered it was too late to resume the movement." Johnston's plan turned out to be another bungled opportunity, this time by the Confederates, that otherwise might have altered the outcome of the entire campaign.

President Davis had been calling for Johnston to attack the Federals, but Johnston, being outnumbered, fell back toward Atlanta and waited for an opportunity to exploit a mistake by Sherman. Davis had expressed his "disappointment" that Johnston had retreated. "I hope," Davis pronounced, "the re-enforcements sent will enable you to achieve important results." Johnston answered on May 21 with the following reply: "I have earnestly sought an opportunity to strike the enemy. The direction of the railroad to this point has enabled him to press me back by steadily moving to the left and by fortifying the moment he halted. He has made an assault upon his superior forces too hazardous...." Although both Davis and Lee believed that Johnston needed to attack Sherman to stop his advance, Johnston's only viable option was to stand on the defensive and to send cavalry raids against Sherman's vulnerable supply lines.[40] Johnston has been viewed by some historians as being too reliant on defensive tactics, both during the Peninsular Campaign in 1862 and here again during the Atlanta Campaign. However, a change to offensive tactics later in the campaign after Johnston was replaced proved ineffective and costly. Johnston has not always received the credit deserved for his generalship. Lee, who preferred offensive tactics, succeeded during the Seven Days Battles after replacing Johnston in 1862. His success against McClellan in 1862 does not translate as being likely to succeed in Johnston's situation during the Atlanta Campaign in 1864. Johnston handled the Atlanta Campaign as well as could be expected from any Civil War general.

Grant was not the kind of man to allow disappointment and difficulty to paralyze him. His plans, sent to the respective commanders in April, were not succeeding by mid–May. Banks had failed in Louisiana, and he had been unable to mount an effort against Mobile. Butler had failed to threaten Richmond or even capture Petersburg; instead, he was bottled up at Bermuda Hundred. Sigel had been sent reeling back to Cedar Creek in the Shenandoah Valley. Sherman had all he could handle in Georgia; his likelihood of success remained uncertain. Grant, himself, had been unable to get at Lee in open country; his Overland Campaign at this point had been a standoff. But Grant's fertile mind kept contriving new schemes to defeat Lee and his army in Virginia. On May 18, Grant sent orders to Meade for a new effort to catch Lee at a disadvantage. A Federal corps would be sent out from Meade's army as bait to pull Lee out of his fortifications. Grant later explained his idea as follows: "I believed that, if one corps of the army was exposed on the road to Richmond, and at a distance from the main army, Lee would endeavor to attack the exposed corps before reinforcements could come up; in which case the main army could follow Lee up and attack him before he had time to intrench."[41] Hancock's II Corps was selected as the bait to entice Lee to fight out in the open.

The Confederate high command was at this time seeking a means of dealing with Grant's and Butler's forces in Virginia. On May 18, General P.G.T. Beauregard suggested a plan to defeat Grant by sending "up 15,000 men to unite with Breckinridge and fall upon the enemy's flank with over 20,000 effectives, thus rendering Grant's defeat certain and decisive...." Beauregard would then proceed with reinforcements from Lee's army "to drive Butler from before Petersburg" thereby achieving by "such concentration" victories that otherwise seemed impossible. Beauregard observed that the two armies were "too far apart to achieve success," so he wanted Lee to fall back behind the Chickahominy "so as to draw" Grant into proximity where he could strike him and then quickly return to crush Butler at Bermuda Hundred. Lee wanted reinforcements to replace his losses at the Wilderness and Spotsylvania, and President Davis trusted Lee's "ability" too much "to adopt the opinion of any one at a distance," in other words, Beauregard. Davis informed General Bragg, his military adviser, that he believed 10,000 of Beauregard's troops could be spared to reinforce Lee. Davis noted that Lee's "correspondence" warranted "the belief that he" would defeat Grant without falling back to Richmond's environs. Davis told Beauregard on the 20th to send whatever men he could spare to reinforce Lee in his fight against Grant.[42]

Grant had learned by May 22 that Lee was not going to risk attacking the Federal II Corps as he had hoped, and Lee had moved to the North Anna River. From prisoners captured that day he deduced that Lee had been reinforced by Pickett's Division and probably other troops from the Richmond defenses. He surmised that Breckinridge, having whipped Sigel at New Market, was also joining Lee at the North Anna. He also knew that General Butler's operation at Bermuda Hundred was a failure. "Under these circumstances," Grant informed Halleck, "I think it advisable to have all of it (Butler's force) here except enough to keep a foothold at City Point."[43] To counter Lee's reinforcements, Grant was taking as much of Butler's force as he could to replace his own losses and retain his numerical advantage over Lee.

The Federals arrived at the North Anna on the afternoon of May 23, 1864. Immediately Grant sent the V Corps across the river, and a fight ensued. Grant nevertheless was confident that he could move to the south bank of the river without much interference, so he allowed Meade to send the entire V Corps across the river. That night he informed Halleck, "Everything looks exceedingly favorable for us."[44]

Grant's message to Halleck that night was overly optimistic. Lee actually had the advantage at the North Anna, and Grant did not seem to realize it. Lee had positioned his army so that the Federals could not concentrate without crossing the river in two places. Lee had the benefit of interior lines and could easily reinforce any portion of his line rapidly. On May 24 the Federals were twice repulsed in actions that accomplished nothing. An unauthorized attack by Brigadier General James H. Ledlie's IX Corps brigade that afternoon was particularly unfortunate and costly. Ledlie was said to have been intoxicated when he ordered the attack against a practically impregnable Confederate position. When the attack disintegrated into a rout, Ledlie joined in the running for cover rather than attempting to rally his soldiers. By evening of the 24th, Grant finally realized that his optimistic appraisal had been a mistake, and he admitted that a major assault would certainly "cause a slaughter ... that even a success would not justify." After more skirmishing on May 25, Grant informed Halleck that it was time to move once again around Lee's right flank. He would march the Army of the Potomac to the Pamunkey River, cross it at Hanovertown "to turn the enemy's right" and proceed southwesterly to get between Lee and Richmond.

Casualties, as usual difficult to determine for the Confederates at this point in the war, were probably nearly even at the North Anna. The Federal casualty list came to 2,623; Confederate casualties perhaps totaled over 2,500. Lee had an excellent opportunity on the North Anna to inflict a punishing blow on the Army of the Potomac, but, being ill, he failed to exploit his advantage. Grant continued his program of attrition but accomplished little else. He was pushing the Army of the Potomac relentlessly, hoping and perhaps expecting that the Confederates could not withstand the pressure. His report to Halleck on May 26 reveals no concern for his mounting losses. Instead, Grant gave the following appraisal of the situation: "Lee's army is really whipped. The prisoners we now take show it, and the action of his army shows it unmistakably. A battle with them outside of intrenchments cannot be had.... I may be mistaken, but I feel that our success over Lee's army is already insured." Grant's tactics at the North Anna were unexceptional, but his unrelenting pressure on the Confederates was the one sure method for ultimate success. As Lee was not assuming the offensive, Grant wisely saw no reason to remain at the North Anna. His movement to cross the Pamunkey, he later admitted, was not made with confidence of cutting Lee off from Richmond. He did, however, believe the movement would enable the Federal army to "reach the James River high up."[45] Grant would do whatever was required to defeat the Confederacy, but, in the mean time, he was managing the campaign according to the constraints imposed by Washington.

On May 18, while he was still at Spotsylvania, Halleck sent Grant the following message: "The Secretary of War directs me to say that the President will appoint General Hunter to Command the Department of West Virginia, if you desire it. Please answer as early as possible." Grant answered the following morning in a way that seems to suggest that anyone would be better in command than Sigel. "By all means," Grant replied, "I would say appoint General Hunter, or anyone else, to the command of West Virginia." That very day, May 19, Hunter was assigned to command in replacement of Sigel. Halleck asked for the "substance" of Grant's orders for General Hunter, and Grant replied on the 20th that he thought Hunter should advance to Staunton, which he believed was an important supply point for the Confederates, and then move on to Gordonsville or Charlottesville, providing that he did not "meet too much opposition." On May 25, from the North Anna, Grant updated his intentions for Hunter with the following message to Halleck: "If Hunter can possibly get to Charlottesville and Lynchburg, he should do so, living on the country. The railroads and canal should be destroyed beyond possibility of repair for weeks. Completing this he could find his way back to his original base, or from about Gordonsville join this army."[46]

Major General David Hunter was graduated from West Point with the class of 1822, just twenty years after the academy was founded. There was nothing about his career prior to the Civil War, or during the war for that matter, to demonstrate his qualification for high command. He had managed to befriend Lincoln in 1860; apparently Lincoln offered his name as a replacement for Sigel after the debacle at New Market. Although already nearly sixty-two, Hunter still had black hair and a swarthy complexion combined with an irascible personality, soon his soldiers were calling him "Black Dave." His subsequent conduct in the Shenandoah Valley demonstrated that the sobriquet was appropriate.

As soon as the Federals started for Staunton, the Confederates began scrambling to find a commander and enough troops to confront them. Breckinridge had returned to Lee's army, and Brigadier General John Imboden's cavalry brigade of 1,000 troopers and a single battery were all the Confederates that remained to oppose Hunter. Brigadier General William "Grumble" Jones had assumed command of the Department of Southwestern Virginia on May 23, and on May 30 Jones received this dispatch from General Lee: "Get all available forces you can and move at once to defend Valley; enemy said to be advancing by Mount Jackson and McDowell." Jones quickly gathered two infantry brigades, a dismounted cavalry brigade and a six-gun battery from far southwest Virginia and east Tennessee. These troops were rushed by rail transport to Lynchburg and onward to Staunton, arriving there by June 3. When Jones arrived on June 4, his reinforcements combined with Imboden's cavalry numbered around 5,600 men.[47]

Hunter marched his 8,500 troops southward on the Valley Turnpike, reaching New Market on May 30. At New Market the Federals found just how little respect and consideration the rebels, and the locals for that matter, had shown for their comrades killed in the battle there two weeks earlier. An officer from the 34th Massachusetts noted that he saw a pile of dead Federals dumped into a low spot and only partially covered with dirt. Heads, arms and legs in a nasty state of decomposition protruded out of this "festering mass." The Federals delayed long enough at New Market to properly inter their dead and then resumed the march toward Harrisonburg.[48]

At Harrisonburg, Hunter learned that Imboden had arrayed his cavalrymen in a good defensive position on the south bank of the North River at Mount Crawford. Hunter decided to bypass this impediment by detouring onto the Port Republic Road and then onto another road leading to Staunton. Hunter was delayed at Port Republic awaiting construction of a pontoon bridge over the North River. Hunter's troops bivouacked a mile south of Port Republic on the night of June 4, in a cold rain without tents. The Army of the Shenandoah marched out of camp early on the morning of June 5 with the rain still falling. About 6 a.m. at the junction of Port Republic Road and Staunton Road, the Federal cavalry vanguard encountered Imboden's cavalry pickets and began pushing the Confederate cavalry back. Hunter did not anticipate a serious battle that day on the Staunton Road, but Hunter and his new command were destined for a rumble with Grumble nevertheless at the tiny hamlet of Piedmont, Virginia.

William E. "Grumble" Jones, one Civil War author observed, was conceded to be as "caustic a personality" as anyone in the Confederate Army. Like many men of that time period, his appearance resembled what one would expect from an Old Testament prophet. Jones was born in 1824 in southwestern Virginia, and after schooling at Emory and Henry College and graduating twelfth in the West Point Class of 1848, he served in the Army until 1856. He resigned that year and returned as a hermit farmer to his native region with a reputation for being "embittered, complaining and suspicious." He raised a company of cavalry and joined the Confederate Army in 1861. While he was unkempt in appearance, he was a harsh disciplinarian and an excellent instructor. After being appointed colonel of his cavalry regiment, the men voted him out, probably due to his demanding methods and acerbic personality. He was nevertheless appointed colonel of another Confederate cavalry regiment and henceforth rendered outstanding service. Jones was promoted to brigadier general on Stonewall Jackson's recommendation in September 1862. In January 1863 General Lee received a report complaining about worthless artillery ammunition written by Jones. The report was forwarded and reached Chief of Ordinance Josiah Gorgas who replied: "...I am quite as much inclined to blame General Jones' artillerists as he is to blame my ammunition. Without wishing to detract from his skill as an officer, I may be allowed to state that he is known to be very apt to find fault." At the cavalry Battle of Brandy Station in 1863, Jones was credited with a key role in preventing a Confederate disaster.[49] He was a formidable adversary for Hunter and the Army of the Shenandoah on June 5, 1864.

Grumble Jones had barely arrived and assumed command of the Confederate

Army of the Valley District when he received an order from General Lee to fight and drive back Hunter "as quickly as possible" before Brigadier General George Crook could get to Staunton with substantial reinforcements for the Federals. General Crook had sent a message to his department commander on May 31 stating that he left Meadow Bluff, West Virginia, that day and expected to reach "Staunton in about six days." Jones marched his troops toward Piedmont while Hunter's cavalry was skirmishing with Imboden's Brigade on the morning of June 5. Jones selected a wooded area just north of Piedmont adjoining the west side of the Staunton Road to deploy his veteran infantry. His infantrymen quickly constructed breastworks of fence rails and dirt for protection perpendicular to the road. These hastily-built fieldworks were called "rail pens" or "bull pens" by the soldiers who had to attack them. Jones then sent Major R.H. Brewer's battalion forward to delay the Federals as his infantry deployed and prepared defenses.

Before mid-day the rebel cavalry had been pushed back to Jones' main defensive line, and here the senior Federal officers made a costly mistake. Hunter had not expected much resistance, and the rebel defensive line, shrouded in a wood, did not seem like too great an obstacle. So General Stahel ordered the Ringgold Cavalry Battalion to charge the Confederate left, and General Sullivan ordered his 1st Brigade to advance. The heavily outnumbered Federal cavalrymen drove back some rebel skirmishers but could not dent the fieldworks and withdrew. Colonel Augustus Moor, who was due that month for mustering out along with his 28th Ohio Infantry, commanded the 1st Brigade. Moor sent out skirmishers to fire at the fieldworks, and the rebels manning the bull pens held their fire. Instead of making an effort to probe the yet untested rebel defensive line, Moor held back his 28th Ohio and ordered three of the 1st Brigade's regiments to attack the woods where the cavalry had just been driven back. (One of the units from Moor's Brigade was actually the 1st Battalion of the 5th New York Heavy Artillery assigned as infantry. It will be described as a regiment in this account.) The attackers didn't stand a chance of success, being outnumbered by enemy troops sheltered by breastworks. Over 1,400 Confederates and guns from two batteries blasted the attacking regiments at close range. An enfilading fire hit the 18th Connecticut Infantry on the Federal right, and the New Englanders fell back in some disorder. The other two attacking regiments were then compelled to fall back in the face of concentrated enemy fire.[50]

Hunter then brought up Captain Henry DuPont, commanding his artillery brigade, to silence the Confederate artillery. DuPont's batteries soon dominated the field by systematically concentrating on each Confederate battery in turn until each of them withdrew or ceased firing. DuPont then targeted the Confederate defensive line in the woods and along the Staunton Road.

Hunter ordered another attack on the Confederate fieldworks after DuPont had managed to drive off the enemy's supporting artillery. General Sullivan reinforced Moor's 1st Brigade with a regiment from the 2nd Brigade, and Moor sent his 28th Ohio into the attacking formation as well this time. The 28th Ohio was a German regiment due to return to Cincinnati for mustering out. The regiment's three year enlistment term was nearly finished. The Germans went on the attack with the other regiments anyway, and, to their credit, fought as hard as any outfit on either side that day. The attack commenced at about 1 p.m. in a linear formation five regiments in length, too thin to smash through the Confederate fieldworks. Hunter decided to withhold the 2nd Brigade, less one regiment to reinforce Moor, because he feared a counterattack against his left. Thus, this second attack met the same fate as the first, only the losses were greater for the Federals this time. The 1st Brigade was nearly used up in this second piecemeal attack.

The three regiments attacking on the right soon fell back, leaving the two remaining regiments to face a concerted fire from the rail pens. The 116th Ohio, on the left of the attacking line, closed within yards of the breastworks and exchanged fire out in the open for several minutes before falling back to a rise that provided "slight cover." The Ohioans then went prone within short rifle range of the breastworks. To their right, the Germans of the 28th Ohio also went down on their bellies at the crest of the hill in front of the rail pens and exchanged fire with the sheltered rebels. As the Federal attack collapsed, the rebels rushed out from the cover of their rail pens in a determined counterattack, screaming "New Market, New Market!" to taunt the Federals. Soon, however, the Confederates returned to their protective fieldworks in the woods. Meanwhile, Colonel William Ely of the 18th Connecticut Infantry, "seeing an excellent opportunity to use cannon" on the Federal right, dispatched "an orderly" to request two howitzers. A section of two guns was soon deployed in a sheltered depression only 500 yards from the rebel fieldworks and opened fire, "knocking the rail pens in splinters amid great slaughter." When the rail pens were struck by artillery fire, the rebels would scatter. Then the Ohioans would "open fire on them the moment they showed themselves, the guns of the battery also saluting them at the same time with grape and canister." Jones allowed this battered section of his line to fall back to the shelter of bluffs in the rear, but he began shifting his troops to reinforce his left flank. This movement encouraged Hunter to make one more attack.[51] This time he would send in nearly all of his infantry, as he should have done in the first place. Hunter ordered Colonel Joseph Thoburn to strike the gap in Jones' line with his 2nd Brigade. Colonel Moor was ordered to assault the rail pens for a third time in conjunction with Thoburn's attack.

Colonel Thoburn used the cover of woods to mask the movement of his three

Federal troops marching at the base of this slope managed to break General Grumble Jones' defenses at the Battle of Piedmont, Virginia.

attacking regiments until they reached the cover provided by Crawford Run Ravine, nearly parallel to the road. By this method of approach Thoburn was enabled to get his troops into position and shifted into a line of battle facing the vulnerable area on the Confederate left, the object of his attack. Jones was informed of the approach of Thoburn's flanking movement during its transit, but he did not order an immediate response. When Jones finally saw Thoburn's regiments arrayed perpendicular to his line in the wood, it was too late to adjust. By then Moor was attacking the rail pens yet again, and Thoburn's flanking force charged out from the ravine, exposing Jones' line to enfilade from the right and rear.

Grumble Jones tried to react by sending his 60th Virginia Infantry and other troops to counter Thoburn's attack, but this time Moor's two Ohio regiments smashed through the rail pens. The Confederate line began to disintegrate from right to left with the Ohioans capturing hundreds of Confederates inside the rail pens. General Jones rode to the front and gathered some men who would follow him, but he was struck by a bullet in the forehead and instantly killed before he could accomplish anything. Onrushing Federals chased the surviving Confederates past the general's body and through the woods to the Middle River. The Federals did not immediately recognize Jones' body; he was dressed in a "dirty" gray suit without any insignia to identify him as even an officer.[52]

The rest of the Confederate narrative of the Battle of Piedmont is about retreat. Conversely for the Federals, Piedmont was revenge for New Market; and, as the rebels gave way, the Federals celebrated the most important Union victory in the Shenandoah Valley

This marker on the Piedmont Battlefield faces the position of the attacking Federals who killed General Jones nearby.

to that time. Hunter's army moved on and captured Staunton, an important rail and production town, for the first time during the war. The Shenandoah Valley was now wide open for occupation all the way to the vital supply depot and rail center at Lynchburg, Virginia. The Battle of Piedmont is usually overlooked or forgotten in Civil War studies. It was, however, the first meaningful victory for Grant's combined effort against the Confederacy that year. Piedmont prompted Lee to dispatch his II Corps into the Valley to protect Lynchburg. Hunter's victory also bolstered President Lincoln's political situation that summer.

Confederate casualties at Piedmont are probably inexact from any source. A good guess would be 600 killed and wounded and over 1,000 captured. Fox's book on regimental losses listed the Federal casualties at Piedmont as 130 killed and 650 wounded.[53] Jones had a very difficult assignment, and it showed at Piedmont. He arrived in the vicinity, took command of an army gathered from various locations and fought a battle the next day. He put in a creditable performance and displayed competence at Piedmont despite these disadvantages. The great superiority of the Federal artillery at Piedmont was a major factor in the outcome. Hunter was an improvement over Sigel, as demonstrated at Piedmont. He did, however, repeat the mistake of fighting the battle piecemeal, sending Moor on two forlorn attacks against the rail pens. He probably could have flanked Jones' fieldworks with a single attack, especially with such an artillery advantage. Hunter, as events would soon demonstrate, was no military mastermind.

The Atlanta Campaign and the Overland Campaign were both ongoing during this period without a satisfactory outcome for either side. In Georgia, C.S. General Joseph Johnston had blocked U.S. Major General William T. Sherman's route along the railroad by occupying Allatoona Pass, a position so strong that Sherman was unwilling to attack it. Sherman decided to outflank Allatoona Pass by sending his army in a southwesterly direction to a crossroads village called Dallas. From there Sherman hoped to march eastward to the railroad town of Marietta, about thirty miles from his objective at Atlanta. Unfortunately for Sherman, Johnston learned of the Federal movement and reacted by sending his entire army to fortify the ridges between the Federals and Marietta. By May 25, Sherman faced a situation quite similar to what Grant was facing in Virginia, an enemy army ensconced within strong fieldworks and unwilling to fight a standup battle in open country.

When Major General Joseph Hooker's corps found Confederate General John Hood's corps entrenched at New Hope Church on May 25, General Sherman impatiently ordered Hooker to attack. Hooker complied by sending a division to attack in a column of brigades through a dense forest of blackjack oak trees. The Confederates met Hooker's attack with massed artillery fire against the narrow brigade-wide attacking front, firing over 1,500 rounds of shell and canister in a few hours. Hooker's corps suffered over 1,600 casualties at New Hope Church and inflicted probably less than half as many on Hood's corps.[54]

Over the next few days both the Confederates and Federals made costly, ill-advised attacks on both ends of a long fortified front. On May 27, Sherman's army suffered a bloody repulse at Pickett's Mill on the Confederate right; and on May 28, the Confederates suffered the same fate at Dallas, Georgia, on Sherman's right. Sherman's army, attacking at two locations against earthworks, naturally suffered higher overall casualties. By the end of May, Sherman had abandoned his attempt to outflank Johnston southwest of the railroad. He occupied the now lightly-defended Allatoona Pass and marched his army back to the railroad. Johnston had no choice but to follow and repeat the process of blocking Sherman's path with his army behind earthworks.

Grant began moving the Army of the Potomac from the North Anna before dawn on May 27 on its way to Hanovertown on the Pamunkey River. Sheridan's Federal cavalry secured the crossings of the Pamunkey, and on the 28th Meade's army crossed on pontoon bridges to the south side. Lee had withdrawn his army a few miles southward to Atlee's Station on the Virginia Central Railroad. The Federals were now within twenty miles of Richmond and nearing the same battlefields fought two years prior between Lee and McClellan at Mechanicsville and Gaines's Mill. Grant and his army remained confident and with good reason. Grant was sending for the 16,000 troops of Major General William "Baldy" Smith's XVIII Corps from Butler's army to reinforce the Army of the Potomac. But somehow Grant's optimism proved misplaced in the week ahead as poor staff work, fatigue and bad luck combined to rob Grant of a decisive victory.

The next significant action of the Overland Campaign took place at another of the difficult-to-pronounce streams so common in that part of Virginia. Because Grant delayed to construct fieldworks to protect his bridgehead over the Pamunkey, Lee was able to shift troops from Atlee's Station to block Grant's path along Totopotomoy Creek. Lee's men quickly entrenched on the ridges overlooking the creek and stalled Grant's advance on May 29. On the next day, Lee ordered Major General Jubal A. Early to attack the Federal V Corps as a portion of it advanced near Bethesda Church on Grant's far left flank. Jubal Early had just replaced General Richard Ewell as commander of the Confederate II Corps, and his promotion to Lieutenant General would take effect on the following day, May 31.

Near Bethesda Church, Brigadier General Samuel Crawford, commanding the 3rd Division of Warren's V Corps, sent out Colonel Martin Hardin with his 1st Brigade to push Early's troops back, a job that proved considerably more difficult than Crawford anticipated. Confederate Major General Robert Rodes attacked with his division, pushing Hardin's brigade back to the Shady Grove Road where the V Corps was able to make a stand. Early asked for reinforcements from Lieutenant General Richard Anderson's nearby I Corps and sent for another division from his corps to continue the attack. The delay in bringing in additional troops gave Warren time to steady his V Corps and withstand a renewed rebel attack. Anderson never managed to shift troops to help Early; thus, the Federal V Corps stood its ground and inflicted probably double its losses on the attacking Confederates.

The Confederate attack at Bethesda Church demonstrated that Grant had been wrong when he suggested to Halleck on May 26 that a fight with Lee outside of trenches could not be had. Grant still hoped for a fight out in the open with Lee. He informed General Smith on the 30th that "movements of the enemy this evening on our left" (at Bethesda Church) indicated that Lee might go after Smith's XVIII Corps before it could rendezvous with the Army of the Potomac. Grant assured Smith that the enemy's movements would be very carefully watched, and he hoped Lee would attempt to move against Smith's corps. Smith was directed to move "up the south bank of the Pamunkey to New Castle" behind the rest of Meade's army.[55] Lee would not move to attack Smith, but Grant's orders to Smith would affect the outcome of the next major battle in the campaign.

Sheridan's cavalry had driven a Confederate cavalry force from a position along Matadequin Creek on the afternoon of May 30. The rebel cavalry retreated to the Cold Harbor crossroads that evening, and General Lee sent Major General Fitzhugh Lee, his nephew, to hold the crossroads with his division of cavalry until Hoke's division of 7,000 men could arrive from Beauregard's command. Sheridan followed the Confederate cavalry and renewed his attack on May 31 at Cold Harbor. His troopers fought Fitzhugh Lee's Division and part of Hoke's force as it arrived from Richmond, and by evening Sheridan's cavalry had possession of Cold Harbor and the crossroads there. But then Sheridan learned that Hoke's 2nd Brigade had reached Cold Harbor. Sheridan sent a message to Major General Humphreys, Meade's chief of staff, saying, "I do not feel able to hold this place ... with the heavy odds against me here, I do not think it prudent to hold on." Meade wanted to hold the crossroads at Cold Harbor, and he had ordered his VI Corps to march that night to Cold Harbor to attack Lee's right flank in the morning. At 1 a.m. on June 1, Sheridan replied to a dispatch from General Humphreys as follows: "I am in receipt of your dispatch to hold on to Cold Harbor, and will do so if possible." Then at 9 a.m. he informed Humphreys, "In obedience to your instructions I am holding Cold Harbor.... I have been very apprehensive, but General Wright (VI Corps) is now coming up."[56] Sheridan's efforts at the Cold Harbor crossroads had provided Grant with an opportunity to crush Lee's army or slip past it and invest Richmond.

On the afternoon of May 31, 1864, General Grant had within his grasp an opportunity to finally gain the upper hand against Lee. With possession of the Cold Harbor crossroads Grant could get his army between Lee and Richmond. Lee saw the need to block Grant at Cold Harbor, and he ordered General Anderson to move his I Corps to reinforce Hoke's division and the Confederate cavalry at Cold Harbor on the afternoon of May 31. Sheridan had been fortunate to hold at Cold Harbor, as we have seen, until the morning of June 1. For some unexplained reason, Grant did not order General Smith to march his XVIII Corps immediately to Sheridan's aid on May 31. Instead, Smith and his troops were at New Castle Ferry when a staff officer from Grant arrived "to say there had been a mistake," and that Smith should have been marching "to Cold Harbor instead of New Castle Ferry." Meade had pulled the Federal VI Corps (his most distant corps from Cold Harbor) from his right flank to make a night march to support Sheridan. Smith's corps was closer and could have arrived there quicker and less fatigued than the VI Corps, which had to march all night. Meade, having finally been given command of Smith's troops on June 1, sent orders to Smith at midday. The orders instructed Smith to cooperate with and "join in the attack" of the VI Corps at Cold Harbor. Meade explained the importance of making an attack as soon as possible: "The enemy have not long been in position about Cold Harbor, and it is of great importance to dislodge and, if possible, to rout him before he can intrench himself."[57] Meade's stress on getting into position before the Confederates could entrench was the key to winning the battle developing at Cold Harbor. This single factor, the late arrival of Smith's corps, very probably altered the outcome of the Overland Campaign. Small oversights like the failure in this case to communicate with Smith in a timely fashion proved extremely detrimental to Grant and extremely fortuitous to Lee in 1864.

The Confederates attacking to seize Cold Harbor on the morning of June 1 did not fight very well. They were easily repulsed by Sheridan's cavalrymen posted behind makeshift fieldworks. Anderson's men began digging in after their repulse. Had Smith arrived on May 31, the Federals probably would have had an opportunity to fight on more even terms instead of having to attack fieldworks yet again. But when Wright's VI Corps and Smith's troops finally attacked around 4:30 p.m., these men had to charge through a barrier of sharpened saplings and then against a line of trenches. The rebels at this point in the war had become experts at constructing fieldworks; they could do a day's worth of work in a few hours. Meade's opportunity for victory had evaporated because of the time lost in shifting troops to Cold Harbor. The Federal attacks at Cold Harbor on the afternoon and evening of June 1 failed to create a major breakthrough, as should have occurred if the VI Corps and XVIII Corps would have arrived sooner and attacked before the Confederates dug in. The Federals managed only limited gains against the Confederate earthworks on June 1, so Grant moved on to his next option.

Grant decided to concentrate his efforts against Lee's right, south of the Cold Harbor crossroads. As early as 3:30 p.m. on June 1, Meade informed Major General Winfield Hancock that he should make preparations to withdraw his II Corps from the Federal right. Grant's plan for dawn on June 2 called for Hancock's II Corps to hit Lee's right flank south of where the fighting was ongoing on June 1. The plan envisioned a massive attack by all of the Federal corps on a line extending from Bethesda Church to about a mile south of Cold Harbor. Hancock would march his II Corps during the night (a distance of about nine miles) and arrive south of Cold Harbor before daylight. The II Corps shift would extend the Federal line to the left of the VI Corps, and, if Grant guessed right, would place the II Corps in position to attack in an area where the Confederates had not yet had time to construct strong fieldworks. It was an excellent plan, provided everything went off as intended.

As usual for the Army of the Potomac, Grant's plan wasn't executed with anything resembling precision. Meade informed Hancock at 8:10 p.m. that he "must withdraw as soon as possible as we want you to move to the left. The route to take from Haw's Shop will be designated and guides furnished." Hancock replied that it would "take some time" to withdraw because his line was "very complicated and very close to the enemy." At 9 p.m., Meade told Hancock to make "every exertion to move promptly and reach Cold Harbor as soon as possible." Captain William Paine, Meade mentioned, would guide Hancock's column from Haw's Shop onward. Here yet another instance of inadequate staff work plagued Meade and Grant. Captain Paine led a division of the II Corps down a shortcut through the woods. The road narrowed until it became a path that could not accommodate the corps artillery. Clearly someone on Meade's staff, or Hancock's staff, should have determined the most efficient route to Cold Harbor sometime on the afternoon of June 1. That obviously didn't happen. Meade, still expecting the II Corps to reach Cold Harbor that night, sent Hancock his instructions for the next morning's operations at 11 p.m.: "On reaching Cold Harbor you will take a position on the left of the Sixth Corps and at once attack the enemy, endeavoring to turn his right flank and interpose between him and the Chickahominy." But Grant's plan, and any opportunity for a Federal victory at Cold Harbor, went awry during the wee hours of June 2. The vanguard of the II Corps did not reach Cold Harbor until after 6 a.m. Hancock later explained the reasons for his late arrival: "…the night was dark, the heat and dust oppressive, and the roads unknown. Still we should have reached Cold Harbor in good season had not Captain Paine unfortunately taken one of my divisions by a shortcut where artillery could not follow, and so thrown my command into great confusion."[58] When the II Corps finally did reach its assigned position early on June 2, it was in no condition to attack. It would be hours before Hancock could get his corps together and ready to fight. General Lee, having a shorter route by which to shift his forces, managed to cover the ground south of Cold Harbor before Hancock could get there. Fortuitous circumstances had once again favored General Lee.

The attack scheduled for dawn on June 2 was delayed until 5 p.m. because the II Corps was fatigued and was late arriving at Cold Harbor. Then Grant postponed the attack until June 3 at 4:30 a.m. The delay of the attack on June 2 probably had given Lee enough time to prepare his defenses well enough to repulse any attack by the Federals, but giving the Confederates all afternoon and night to dig in completely erased any chance of success for the attack on June 3. Grant simply should have realized that the opportunity for victory at Cold Harbor had been lost when the II Corps could not attack at dawn on June 2.

At 2 p.m., in any case, Meade sent this circular to his command: "The attack ordered for 5 p.m. this day is postponed to 4:30 a.m. to-morrow. Corps commanders will employ the interim in making examination of the ground in their fronts, and perfecting their arrangements for the assault." The battlefield terrain at Cold Harbor was a variegated mixture of woods, cleared fields, marshes, rills and swamps. It was exceptionally difficult to get a fix on the Confederate positions and dangerous to approach within close proximity of them. It is doubtful that Grant or Meade or anyone from their staffs reconnoitered the Confederate lines. Despite Meade's orders to examine the space between the opposing lines, it is probable that whatever scouting that was done was inadequate. Baldy Smith, an engineering officer by trade, was probably the corps commander with the best knowledge of the enemy works to be attacked. When he received Meade's order for the June 3 attack, he replied that an attack by his XVIII Corps "would simply be preposterous."[59]

The huge Federal attack on June 3 went off on time at 4:30 a.m. Grant had been sending much of his artillery back to the Washington defenses since the Battle of Spotsylvania because he felt that it was "a very burdensome luxury where it cannot be used." On June 1, Grant mentioned that another "forty pieces of artillery" were being sent back to Washington.[60] The artillery on hand for the Federals was primarily for defensive purposes; there was apparently no meaningful barrage preceding the attack in the pre-dawn hours of June 3.

An account of the fighting at Cold Harbor on June 3 could easily fill an entire volume with descriptions of horror and slaughter. Thousands of Federal soldiers were shot down or pulverized by artillery fire within the first twenty minutes of the assault. It was likely the worst killing field, for either side, of the entire war. Only on the southern portion of the battlefield did the Federals make a significant breakthrough, and even here it was quickly sealed as it happened in the only area where Lee had reserves posted. A Federal II Corps division in reserve should have gone forward to exploit the breakthrough but did not. A little farther north, Gibbon's II Corps Division ran into a swamp which split the division apart before reaching the Confederate lines. Apparently there had been little attempt on that front to examine the ground prior to the attack. The Federals suffered the most where they tried the hardest, but it mattered little. There was no chance for success. Confederate Brigadier General Evander Law had seen the slaughter at the Deep Cut at 2nd Bull Run and on Marye's Heights at Fredericksburg. Yet he had seen nothing in his many battles to exceed this slaughter. He precisely and succinctly described Cold Harbor with this comment: "It was not war; it was murder."

From hindsight Grant's decision to attack on June 3 seems, euphemistically, dubious, and there has been little in the interval to present an effective defense for it. Grant himself admitted that he regretted ordering it. It was unquestionably one of the worst command decisions of the war. Grant, having seen so many examples of heavy losses resulting from attacks against fortifications from Vicksburg to the North Anna, must have realized

Though now overgrown with tall trees, these Confederate trenches at Cold Harbor are still distinct.

that Cold Harbor would result in the same on June 3. Baldy Smith was correct, this time, when he characterized the attack at Cold Harbor as "simply an order to slaughter my best troops."[61] Grant should bear the onus for the debacle at Cold Harbor because he ordered the attack to proceed in the predawn hours of June 3. However, there is plenty of blame to be shared by Meade and his corps, division and brigade commanders. Meade was the army commander, and he should have visited the front to confer with his corps commanders concerning how they were going to ensure that the attacks would be successful. There is little to indicate that a sufficient assessment of the Confederate lines was undertaken during the relative calm on June 2. It would seem that surely some officer in the chain of command between Meade and the brigade level should have possessed the intelligence and moral courage to convince a leader that the attacks at Cold Harbor could not succeed. It is obvious that General Smith despised the order to attack on June 3, yet he did not present to Meade an adequate explanation for why the attack would fail. Concisely, something was terribly wrong with the command function in the Army of the Potomac in 1864, in particular.

The casualties at Cold Harbor were naturally very lopsided in favor of the Confederates. The official total for the Federals was 12,738; 1,745 were listed as killed in action. Probably more than half of the Federal losses were suffered during the first hour of fighting on June 3. Confederate casualties at Cold Harbor can only be estimated, ranging from a total of 3,000 to 5,000. Under Grant's direction the Army of the Potomac had since May 5 suffered over 50,000 casualties, about half the losses of that army during the course of the war to that point.[62] Lee deftly handled the task of shifting troops to respond to Grant's tactics, correctly anticipating where succeeding attacks would occur. Cold Harbor was a punishing and demoralizing debacle for the North. The statistics and outcome burnished the perception of Southern fighting prowess yet again, despite the fact that Lee and his army had benefited from all the advantages except manpower.

After the fighting at Cold Harbor tapered off, Grant consolidated his lines and prepared for his next offensive. While Grant lingered at Cold Harbor, Major General Benjamin Butler decided to launch an attempt to capture Petersburg, which was at the time lightly defended. Command of the operation was given to Major General Quincy Gilmore, who was best known for his success in reducing Fort Pulaski at Savannah, Georgia, in April 1862. Gilmore would have troops from his own X Corps, a division of U.S.C.T. from the XVIII Corps led by Brigadier General Edward Hinks, and a cavalry force led by Brigadier General August Kautz. On June 9, Gilmore's poorly coordinated effort to capture Petersburg ended in failure. Had Butler supplied a few more troops, the operation might have succeeded, as it should have in any case. The cost of capturing Petersburg would prove devastating in the months ahead.

Despite the fact that General Halleck had cautioned Grant that raids against Southern railroads were a waste of time, Grant, always looking to keep his troops occupied, ordered Major General Philip Sheridan to lead two of his cavalry divisions "on the morning of the 7th to Charlottesville and destroy the railroad bridge over the Rivanna, near that town." Then Sheridan was to "thoroughly destroy" the Virginia Central Railroad to Gordonsville and then continue the destruction back to Hanover Junction. Grant wanted the rails rendered useless, requiring complete replacement with new rails to repair the railroad. Word of Hunter's victory at Piedmont had reached Grant, so he anticipated having Hunter move east to rendezvous with Sheridan at Charlottesville to assist in the destruction of the railroad.[63]

Lee sent his cavalry under Major General Wade Hampton to intercept Sheridan and protect the Virginia Central Railroad. The two cavalry forces clashed at Trevilian Station east of Gordonsville on May 11. In a swirling, confusing fight, Sheridan's troopers bested the Confederates. Hampton withdrew to a position astride the road to Gordonsville near Trevilian Station. The cavalry battle had interrupted Sheridan's mission to destroy the railroad.

Hunter's army marched into Staunton on June 6, the day after his victory at Piedmont. On that day General Grant sent instructions to Hunter from Cold Harbor. Grant wrote, "The direction I would now give is ... you immediately turn east by the most practicable road until you strike the Lynchburg branch of the Virginia Central road. From there move eastward along the line of the road, destroying it completely and thoroughly until you join General Sheridan." Grant wanted Hunter to then follow Sheridan back to join the Army of the Potomac "by the route laid out in General Sheridan's instructions." On June 12, Chief of Staff Halleck informed Hunter that Grant was taking measures "to facilitate" the junction of Sheridan's cavalry and Hunter's army with the Army of the Potomac, so Hunter should have known Grant's intentions for him. General Crook had arrived at Staunton on June 8 after more than a week's march from the west, increasing Hunter's force to about 18,000 strong with thirty guns.[64] If Hunter had followed Grant's instructions and joined with Sheridan, it would have created a formidable strike force indeed.

Hunter, however, decided to march his army up the Shenandoah Valley to Lexington instead of heading southeast to Waynesboro and Charlottesville to join with Sheridan as instructed by Grant. Hunter delayed at Lexington long enough to burn most of the Virginia Military Institute and the home of former Virginia Governor John Letcher. He then left Lexington on June 15 heading for Lynchburg. By this time Hunter had been receiving reports that reinforcements were being sent from Richmond, that a Confederate force was at Rockfish Gap near Waynesboro and that Sheridan had been stopped at Trevilian Station. Sheridan, at Trevilian Station, heard that Hunter had turned toward Lynchburg and that reinforcements were being sent against Hunter. Sheridan then decided to terminate his mission to destroy the Virginia Central Railroad and return to the Army of the Potomac, since Hunter would not be able to assist him. Hunter's movement against Lynchburg would soon play out as yet another forlorn Federal mission.

The happenings west of Richmond did not escape General Lee's attention. General Braxton Bragg suggested to President Davis that something might be done to expel the Federals from the Shenandoah Valley. Bragg thought that Washington might be vulnerable to attack if the Valley could be reclaimed. Lee acknowledged the "advantage" of driving Hunter out of the Valley, but he recognized that it would require one corps from his army to accomplish the task. On June 12, Lee selected Lieutenant General Jubal Early and his II Corps for the task of reclaiming the Shenandoah Valley. Major General John Breckinridge, the victor of New Market, was also sent to Lynchburg along with 2,000 troops, reaching that place on June 16.[65]

Hunter finally reached Lynchburg's environs on June 17. His troops had to fight through delaying actions by the rebel cavalry, and then General Early, who had just reached Lynchburg, sent two infantry brigades to attack the approaching Federals. Hunter arrived on the scene around dusk and decided to suspend the attack on the city until morning. The soldiers and officers of Hunter's army wanted to press on into Lynchburg while the Confederates remained outnumbered, but Hunter had determined that it was "too late." During the night, the Confederates staged a ruse by having locomotives chug into town repeatedly to the cheers of soldiers pretending to be welcoming reinforcements. Hunter was unsure "as to whether General Lee had detached any considerable force for the relief of Lynchburg," so he waited until the next day to "settle the question."

On June 18 both Early and Hunter probed each other's lines during the morning. During the afternoon Early attacked Hunter's 1st Division at the center of his battle line. The Federals counterattacked, driving the Confederates back into their fieldworks. Hunter noted that the regiment that my Great Grandfather Earley served with managed to penetrate the enemy line: "one regiment (One hundred sixteenth Ohio) entered the works on the heels of the flying enemy...." (This fieldwork known as Fort Early still stands in Lynchburg.) But Hunter did not send any support for the breakthrough; the 116th Ohio was left isolated in the enemy fort and had to fight its way back to the Federal lines alone. Hunter had learned from captives that the veteran Confederate II Corps was facing him, and he decided to retreat. Somehow Hunter had come to the conclusion that Early had a force "at least double the numerical strength" of his own, and he also insisted that his troops had "scarcely enough ammunition left to sustain another well contested battle."[66]

After consulting with General Crook, Hunter made a controversial decision to retreat into West Virginia instead of withdrawing down the Shenandoah Valley. His decision left the Valley open to reoccupation by the Confederates and also left Washington vulnerable to a foray from Early's formidable force. Retreating via West Virginia was Hunter's safest course, but it rendered all of his efforts since taking command of the Department of West Virginia nugatory. Since Hunter had not destroyed the railroad in the direction of Charlottesville as Grant wanted, Early could use the railroad to move his army faster and thus cut off Hunter in the Valley. Hunter might have chosen a different retreat route to slow Early's advance toward Maryland. Instead, his retreat into West Virginia took his army out of the war for about a month.

The casualties at Lynchburg are difficult to determine. An estimate of the Confederate losses came to 500. Federal casualty reports spanned the period of May 26 until June 29, 1864, which included several skirmishes besides the fighting at Lynchburg. The total casualties for the Federals for this period came to 940 of which 577 applied to the infantry divisions that did much of the fighting at Lynchburg.[67]

Grant and the battered Army of the Potomac had remained in the trenches at Cold Harbor for over a week following the disastrous attacks on June 3. Grant decided to once again move around Lee's right flank, as he had done after every battle of the Overland Campaign. The next move would place the Army of the Potomac across the Chickahominy River just east of the Richmond defenses. But Grant decided to pass on an attempt to get another fight out of Lee there; instead, he would cross the wide James River and move against Petersburg. It was a good plan because the capture of Petersburg was practically tantamount to capturing Richmond itself. Taking Petersburg would isolate Richmond from its railroad supply lifelines, so the Confederate capital would soon have to be evacuated in that case.

Grant's plan to slip away from Lee at Cold Harbor and cross the James River undetected presented a number of difficulties. Grant began consolidating the details for making his army disappear from Cold Harbor and reappear at Petersburg after the failed assaults on June 3. Calculating the risks incident to the plan, Grant supposed that Lee would not sense the vulnerability of the Federal army as it marched to the James. Lee, he correctly assumed, would be much more concerned with preventing a Federal lunge at Richmond than with anything else. The movement to the James was complicated, requiring both logistical planning and a diversion to distract Lee. The shift to the James was, for once, a brilliant success, so now for the first time since the beginning of the Overland Campaign Grant succeeded in deceiving General Lee about his intentions. Lee lost track of the Army of the Potomac for two days; the Federals pulled out of the trenches at Cold Harbor on June 13 and were crossing the James River on June 14 before Lee knew where to react.

Everything appeared to be going in Grant's favor when the Army of the Potomac began crossing to the south bank of the James. On the afternoon of June 14, Grant informed Chief of Staff Halleck in Washington that the Confederates "showed no sign" of reacting to his movements, and he would have Petersburg "secured, if possible," before the Confederates could "get there in much force." President Lincoln seemed encouraged by the progress, and he sent a message the next morning telling Grant, "I begin to see it. You will succeed. God bless you all."[68]

Success was not as certain as Lincoln and Grant expected. For one thing, Grant depended once again on troops from General Butler reinforced by Major General Smith's XVIII Corps to take Petersburg. Smith was in charge of the operation designed to repeat the same procedure that had failed a week prior when Gilmore, Hinks and Kautz attacked Petersburg on June 9. This time General Hancock and his II Corps were ordered on June 15 to march to a position near Petersburg and await word from General Smith. Grant expected Hancock to be available to reinforce Smith if needed. Confederate General P.G.T. Beauregard commanded the defense of Petersburg with perhaps only 2,500 troops and some militia and irregulars on hand in the defenses. Placing Smith in command of such a vital operation was yet another oversight by Grant. After Cold Harbor, where

Smith's performance was uninspiring, Grant erred by failing to appoint someone with grit who was certain to appreciate the gravity of the assignment and sure to accomplish the mission. Smith had probably more than 16,000 troops in his force plus the II Corps was in position to assist. Hinks and Kautz were getting a second chance to capture the same enemy trenches and should have known what to expect. With all of his advantages, Smith was expected to secure Petersburg in one day. Only the incredible blundering of Smith and Kautz allowed the Confederates to hold the city until reinforcements arrived from Lee's army.

Smith was supposed to attack the Petersburg defenses at dawn on June 15 while Brigadier General August Kautz demonstrated with his cavalry south of the main attack. Instead of attacking at daylight as instructed, Smith began assailing the Confederate pickets around 9 a.m. Then he began probing the thinly-held trenches for the next few hours. For several more hours Smith delayed his attack before deciding to bombard one of the enemy redans. At around 7 p.m., Smith finally attacked with his infantry, overrunning several redans with his overwhelming numbers. By this time Kautz had abandoned his role and had withdrawn from the battle. By nightfall on June 15, the last great opportunity to capture Petersburg and shorten the war by many months was wasted. Lee would rush reinforcements into the defenses at Petersburg just in time to save it.

General Hancock, nearby with his Federal II Corps, could have had a decisive impact on the outcome of the attack on June 15. Smith sent a message to Hancock telling him that General Grant authorized him to have the II Corps hurry to assist in the capture of Petersburg. Smith explained that "heavy artillery fire" and "wide open spaces" had kept him from attacking during the day, but he suggested that a night attack in conjunction with the II Corps could succeed. At 5:25 p.m. on the 15th, Major General John Gibbon, a division commander in the II Corps, received a message from General Grant informing him that Smith had carried some of the "outer works" at Petersburg during the day. Gibbon was to use "all haste in getting up" because Smith might need assistance. Gibbon was to communicate the message to all the II Corps division commanders "and to General Hancock, and to push forward as rapidly as possible." But Hancock did not assist in the attacks on June 15. Smith sent a message to his boss, Major General Butler, at midnight saying he could do no more and that Hancock was "not yet up."

Grant did not seem to fault Hancock for not taking part in the fighting on June 15. He did mention, years later, that General Smith on June 15 "spent the day until after seven o'clock in the evening in reconnoitering what appeared to be empty works." That was about as strong a condemnation of Smith's performance as Grant was ever likely to offer. Grant also later wrote that if Hancock had received his orders for his role on the 15th, "Petersburg itself could have been carried without much loss." Grant deserved some of the onus for the failures on June 15 and what followed during the next few days at Petersburg. He should have assigned a more dependable officer to superintend such a vital operation, and he should have seen to it that Hancock and his II Corps would participate in the attacks on June 15. But General Meade perhaps summed up the real reason for the sorry performances on June 15 and the days that followed with the following observation: "Our men are tired and the attacks have not been made with the vigor and force which characterized our fighting in the Wilderness; if they had been I think we should have been more successful."[69]

Grant himself arrived at Petersburg on the morning of June 16, but the remarkably ineffectual Federal tactics continued. Instead of blocking Lee's route to reinforce

Petersburg from the north, Grant wasted most of the day on the 16th before launching renewed attacks against Petersburg's formidable defenses. Beauregard received just enough reinforcements to prevent an effective Federal breakthrough. So Grant resorted to the same sacrificial tactics that had failed in every battle since the Wilderness. The process was repeated on June 17 and 18 with the same result until Grant had added another 10,000 men to the casualty list. On June 18, the 1st Maine Heavy Artillery, fighting as infantry, participated in one of the attacks with the Federal II Corps. The outfit advanced farther than its supporting units that day but suffered 210 killed and 422 wounded of the 950 officers and men taken into the action. It was the heaviest loss suffered by any regiment during the course of the war.[70]

The Overland Campaign had ended with Grant in about the same location McClellan had managed to reach in 1862 at a fraction of the cost incurred by Grant. Some historians believe that Grant and Meade had realized the futility of frontal assaults against trenches by June of 1864. A passage from one Civil War study stated that "in the 1864 Virginia campaign Grant and Meade did not long continue" in the mistake of making repeated offensives against strong defensive positions.[71] The unsuccessful attempts to capture Petersburg resulted in a long siege which, of course, ended the campaign of maneuver that had featured so many Federal assaults against strong fieldworks. To suggest that Grant did not persist for too long with the seemingly irrational assaults on fieldworks and trenches is unconvincing. Perhaps when compared to the enormous losses incurred during World War I resulting from repeated offensives in trench warfare, Grant's losses don't seem so extravagant. However, when compared to McClellan's approach to warfare, Grant's methods seem wantonly dismissive of the cost in lives. Grant certainly deserves credit for devising a successful method of destroying the Confederacy, and his strategy was sound. The rub here is that his management of the war in Virginia was seriously flawed.

After four days of unsuccessful attacks on the Petersburg defenses, Grant realized he would have to resort to a siege at Petersburg, which was in effect a siege of Richmond as well. Nevertheless, Grant decided to make one further attempt to lure Lee out of his fortifications to do battle in the open. On June 20, Grant planned yet another raid against the railroads south of Petersburg. If these supply lines could be severed, the Confederates would be forced to do something about it. Lee might be forced to attack or even to abandon Petersburg and Richmond. Grant's plan called for the cavalry divisions of Brigadier General James Wilson and Brigadier General August Kautz to ride south of Petersburg to destroy as much as possible of the Weldon and Southside railroad lines, cutting off most of the food supplies and communications for Petersburg and Richmond. The plan also called for the II and VI Corps to march southwest to destroy the Weldon Railroad near Petersburg.

Chief of Staff Halleck had already stated his opposition to railroad raids as a waste of time and resources, and General Meade opposed this raid in particular. Yet here again Grant demonstrated that he was more than willing to proceed with high risk operations. This raid ultimately did not justify its cost. The cavalry managed to do significant damage to the Southside Railroad, but the raiders had to abandon their wagons and artillery on the return trip and were fortunate to make it back within the Federal lines. The Federal II Corps took a severe beating when it was ambushed by Confederates from Hill's Corps on its way to the Weldon Railroad, losing over 1,700 prisoners and abandoning its mission.[72] The fighting on June 22 involving the Federal II Corps at the Jerusalem Plank Road demonstrated how serious the morale problem affecting the Army of the Potomac was after weeks of continuous hard fighting and heavy casualties. Each corps of the Army of the Potomac needed a refit and time to recover; Grant had practically used up that army in a little over a month's time.

In Georgia on June 22, the same day that the Federal II Corps was whipped near Petersburg, troops from Sherman's army turned back an attack by Hood's Corps near Kolb's Farm. Hood suffered three times as many casualties as the Federals who fought behind makeshift fieldworks. If nothing else, the battle again demonstrated that it did not matter which side did the attacking against earthworks—the attackers almost always came out as the loser.[73] The fighting at Kolb's Farm, however, checked Sherman's attempt at a flanking movement around the Confederate left.

Johnston had been fighting against Sherman's invasion the only way he could—on the defensive. Hood's unauthorized attack at Kolb's Farm demonstrated that the Confederates had little hope in attempting offensive tactics against Sherman's superior numbers. But Sherman's supply line ran through Tennessee to Georgia. The Confederates did all they could to interrupt Sherman's communications, and Confederate Major General Nathan Bedford Forrest was positioned to threaten Sherman's supply line. A Federal force twice the size of Forrest's commanded by Brigadier General Samuel Sturgis went out from Memphis for the purpose of occupying Forrest so that he could not damage the railroads supplying Sherman's army. On June 10, 1864, Forrest defeated Sturgis' superior force decisively at Brice's Crossroads, about seventeen miles north of Tupelo, Mississippi. Forrest's victory at Brice's Crossroads was one of the most one-sided battles of the Civil War; the Confederates inflicted about five times as many casualties on Sturgis' force as they suffered. Sherman then replaced Sturgis with Major General Andrew Jackson Smith and increased his force to about 14,000 troops to go after Forrest. Sherman said he would order Smith to keep after Forrest "to the death," even if "it breaks the Treasury." At Tupelo on July 14, Forrest attacked Smith with a force of over 9,000 troops, but this time the Federals prevailed. Smith was "one of the most competent" commanders the Federals had; when the fighting was finished, Forrest's casualties came to approximately 1,326 while Smith's losses totaled 674.[74] Smith had not destroyed Forrest's force and his men had only wounded Forrest, but he had succeeded in the priority of his mission—he had kept the railroads supplying Sherman's army safe from Forrest's cavalry raids.

Despite the Army of the Potomac's succession of bloody failures resulting from attacks against strong Confederate fieldworks in Virginia, giving evidence of the folly of such tactics, Sherman opted for an attempt to break Johnston's strong position by frontal assault at Kennesaw Mountain on June 27. Sherman considered Kennesaw to be the crucial location to defeat Johnston and uncover Atlanta. His plan called for attacks against the middle of Johnston's line with a view of splitting the Confederate army and then pouring reinforcements into the breach. Following a massive bombardment commencing around 8 a.m. on the 27th, the Federals attacked at Pigeon Hill and shortly afterwards at Kennesaw Mountain. The attacks on the Kennesaw line went forward in densely packed columnar formations intended to punch through the enemy defenses. But the attacking columns, pushing through obstacles, soon lost their cohesion as they neared the Confederate earthworks. Neither of the Federal attacks managed to pierce the enemy line. After failing to achieve a breakthrough, the attacking Federals dug in adjacent to the Confederate earthworks. By the time the fighting subsided at Kennesaw Mountain, the Federals had lost three times as many men as the Confederates. Federal casualties totaled about 3,000; Confederate losses came to nearly 1,000 men.[75]

Fortunately for Sherman, Major General John M. Schofield's XXXIII Corps was demonstrating in support of the attacks on the 27th, and while Johnston's attention was fixed on the fighting around Kennesaw Mountain, Schofield managed to secure a route around the Confederate left. Thanks to Schofield's efforts on the 27th, Sherman was enabled to launch another turning movement and once again bypass an invincible Confederate defensive position.

Sherman commenced his flanking movement on July 2, hoping to get across the Chattahoochee River south of Marietta before Johnston could again block his path to Atlanta. Johnston anticipated the maneuver, so he abandoned his Kennesaw line and made another stand at Smyrna, Georgia. Sherman soon found a weakness in the Smyrna defensive line and managed to slip by Johnston's left flank yet again. Johnston always had an alternative prepared for each of Sherman's moves. This time Johnston fell back to the north bank of the Chattahoochee River to hold Sherman out of Atlanta. The defenses on the bank of the Chattahoochee had been built during a two week period and were especially formidable. Johnston knew that the Federals would have to cross the Chattahoochee in order to capture Atlanta, and he believed he could hold his line on the north bank of the river for some time.

Grant had failed to capture Petersburg in early June, which allowed Lee the luxury of allowing General Early and the Confederate II Corps to continue operating in the Shenandoah Valley. Lee had decided that the advantage of sending Early down the Valley outweighed the disadvantage of weakening his army defending Petersburg. If Early could threaten Washington, Grant would be expected to weaken his own force to send help to defend the capital.

Jubal Early was one of a few high-ranking officers on both sides of the conflict who, for whatever reason, never received fair recognition deserved for their abilities or accomplishments. Jubal Early graduated West Point in 1837, ranking eighteenth in a class of fifty. At West Point he consistently ranked near the top of his class in academics, but in conduct he ranked near the bottom. Of his West Point experience Early admitted, "I was not a very exemplary soldier.... I had very little taste for scrubbing brass and cared very little for the advancement to be obtained by the exercise of that most useful art." His personality certainly did nothing to enhance his popularity. Arbitrary, cynical, prejudiced, and "personally disagreeable" are terms that described his disposition. He was, however, a genuine soldier. A Confederate officer who knew Early well during the war wrote that after Stonewall Jackson's death none of Lee's lieutenants possessed more of the "essential qualities" of a commander than did Jubal Early.[76] After defeating Hunter at Lynchburg, Early moved down the Valley with his II Corps and some cavalry. He would lead the Confederacy's third invasion of Maryland and threaten Washington as never before since the War of 1812.

Lee's plan to reclaim the Valley, first suggested by General Bragg to President Davis in June, had succeeded; now the second objective of the plan, to invade Maryland and threaten Washington, was proving feasible. On July 9, Early demanded $200,000 from the mayor of Frederick, Maryland, or else his troops would torch the city. Early's threat wasn't empty, as he would later prove at Chambersburg, Pennsylvania. The Federal Government now faced the possibility that Early would continue his incursion to Baltimore or even Washington, perhaps with the same malignance Hunter had practiced in the Shenandoah Valley.

The man responsible for defending Maryland that July was Major General Lewis

Wallace as commanding general of the Middle Department from Baltimore, Maryland. Wallace, whose father was an erstwhile governor of Indiana, had served as an officer during the Mexican War, but his vocation was in law and politics. He is best known as the author of the novel *Ben Hur*, which became the basis of a series of movies in later years. At the outbreak of the Civil War, Wallace was appointed colonel of the 11th Indiana Infantry. He quickly rose to the rank of major general, but his performance at the Battle of Shiloh, where he was late arriving at the scene of the fighting, somewhat damaged his reputation. Wallace determined that he would make a stand near Frederick, Maryland, along the Monocacy River; there he could stand in Early's path to either Baltimore or to Washington, D.C.

Grant had sent a division from the VI Corps to Washington when General Early advanced down the Valley. On July 9, Wallace had these troops and a motley collection of militia, home guards, the Baltimore Battery and a small contingent of veteran cavalry. When Early's army reached the Monocacy on the morning of July 9, Wallace had a force of about 5,800 arrayed on the east bank of the river facing 14,000 or so Confederates intent on making mischief in Washington.

The outcome of the fighting on the Monocacy was never in doubt. Wallace did not have the benefit of extensive earthworks and plentiful artillery to augment his heavily outnumbered force, as the defenders at Petersburg did when the Federals were turned away there in June. The Confederates found a feasible ford to cross the river, and by late afternoon the Federals had been forced to withdraw or be overwhelmed. Early's troops had moved smartly to the attack and had efficiently seized the key positions on the battlefield. A significant portion of Wallace's force was composed of Maryland Home Guards and Ohio National Guard troops. The Ohio guardsmen were serving for only 100 days, and Wallace reported that these troops "straggled badly" while the veterans from the VI Corps "were not whipped" but "retired reluctantly" when ordered. Federal casualties were reported to be 123 killed, 603 wounded and 568 missing. Early reported his losses as "between 600 to 700"; however, his casualties might have been as great as 900. The number of killed and wounded might well have been about the same for each side.

On the following day President Lincoln informed General Grant that Wallace was "badly beaten yesterday at Monocacy," and that "100-days' men and invalids" would defend Washington. Lincoln continued by suggesting that Grant should hold Petersburg with a sufficient force "and bring the rest with you personally, and make a vigorous effort to destroy the enemy's force in this vicinity. I think there is really a fair chance to do this if the movement is prompt." Grant replied that day to Lincoln that he had sent an army corps (the VI Corps) and a division from the XIX Corps to reinforce Washington, and he suggested that these troops would "be able to compete" with Early's force. Grant declined Lincoln suggestion to "personally" lead the effort against Early, saying "it would have a bad effect for me to leave here." Grant believed that with Hunter returning from West Virginia, he had "great faith that the enemy will never be able to get back with much of his force." Lincoln had made the mistake of allowing Grant to decide for himself whether to take charge of the attempt to destroy Early's army at Washington. The destruction of Lee's II Corps certainly would have been a severe blow to the Confederacy and would have been worth the disadvantage of Grant's absence from Petersburg for a few weeks.[77]

After the fighting subsided along the Monocacy, Early sent part of his cavalry toward Baltimore. Brigadier General Bradley Johnson also was sent with around 1,500 cavalry for the purpose of freeing Confederate prisoners of war at Point Lookout prison camp where the Potomac River empties into Chesapeake Bay. Johnson's mission was aborted a few days later. Early turned toward Washington on July 10 with around 8,000 infantry and the remainder of his force. The march from the Monocacy to the outskirts of Washington was extremely enervating as a result of the hot and dry conditions along the way. Early later wrote that only about a third of his force "could have been carried into action" when they reached Fort Stevens a few miles north of the capital. Early spent the afternoon of the 11th probing the defensive line around Fort Stevens with the troops still able to fight after the difficult march. That night Early consulted with his senior commanders at the home of U.S. Postmaster General Francis P. Blair at Silver Spring, Maryland. Aware of significant Federal reinforcements arriving at Fort Stevens, Early and his generals had to choose between fight and flight. Early was concerned that his retreat route back across the Potomac might be blocked soon, but he decided to attempt an attack on Fort Stevens before retreating.

Early should have given up the hope of capturing Washington on the night of July 11. Instead he spent the day of July 12 skirmishing and wishing he could really attack. He later wrote, "I determined to remain in front of the fortifications during the 12th, and retire at night, as I was satisfied that to remain longer would cause the loss of my entire force."[78] The activities on the 12th only served to add names to the casualty lists. The advance on Washington had served its intended purpose. Two Federal army corps were sent to protect the capital, and the situation at Petersburg remained static. In final analysis, Lee's decision to send Early and the II Corps down the Valley succeeded despite uncertain odds. We will never know what would have happened had Grant acquiesced to Lincoln's call for him to go to Washington with sufficient forces to go after the raiding Confederate II Corps and destroy it. The Confederates slipped away from Washington on July 13 and crossed the Potomac into Virginia on the 14th and then rested at Leesburg.

The Federals followed Early's retreating force from Washington with bad intentions, but Early was able to make his escape probably more as a result of poor coordination and direction on the part of the Federal command than anything he did. The Federal VI Corps with Major General Wright in command along with Brigadier General William Emory's XIX Corps division could not catch the rebels on foot. General Hunter had reached Harpers Ferry on July 14, and he was directed to assist in the effort to destroy Early's army. That same day Halleck informed Hunter that Wright had been "placed by the President in supreme command of the forces operating in this expedition," regardless of the fact that Hunter was senior. A division from Hunter's army was within a few miles of the retreating Confederates but was "obliged to halt and allow the rebel army" to pass without much interference because "Wright did not proceed to Leesburg" until Early had escaped. Hunter's force alone could not block Early's retreat without support, but Hunter's chagrin at being replaced by a junior officer did nothing to help the situation. On July 17 Hunter sent the following revealing message to President Lincoln: "I again most earnestly request to be relieved from the command of this department. Your order, conveyed through General Halleck, has entirely destroyed my usefulness. When an officer is selected as the scapegoat to cover up the blunders of others, the interests of the country require that he should at once be relieved from command." Lincoln quickly answered with the following explanation: "The order you complain of was only nominally mine, and was framed, by those who really made it, with no thought of making you a scapegoat. It seemed to be General Grant's wish that the forces under General Wright and those under you should join and drive at the enemy, under General Wright. Wright had the larger part of the force, but you had the rank…. That is all of it. General Grant wishes you to remain in command of the department, and I do not wish to order otherwise."[79] That same day Early's army marched through Snicker's Gap and crossed the Shenandoah River. With the Shenandoah Valley straight ahead, Early's escape was virtually assured.

On the following day, July 18, Brigadier General George Crook, who was actively commanding the troops that Hunter had led on the retreat from Lynchburg, was directed by General Wright to follow the Confederates to the Shenandoah River and check on their whereabouts. Later that day Wright decided to cross part of Crook's command over the river at Island Ford near Snicker's Ferry. Around 2 p.m. Crook sent over Colonel Joseph Thoburn's division, another brigade of infantry and a motley collection of dismounted cavalry, probably around 3,250 men altogether, to secure a crossing over the Shenandoah. What followed that afternoon proved yet another Federal "egregious blunder" that "accomplished nothing" at the cost of hundreds of casualties.

Once Thoburn crossed to the west bank of the river, he learned from some captured rebel pickets that Early's "entire forces were encamped in the vicinity." The Confederates soon approached Thoburn's position with an overwhelming force of troops from Gordon's, Wharton's and Rodes' divisions. Crook saw the Confederates advancing toward Thoburn from the heights above the river, and he informed General Wright that his men should immediately return to the east bank. Wright assured him that he would send a division from the VI Corps across to support Thoburn. That never happened. Instead, when Wright saw how large the attacking Confederate force was, he declined to risk sending more troops across the river. Thoburn's men were left to fend for themselves against overwhelming odds with the Shenandoah River at their back.

Thoburn's regiments soon were holding a not-so-strong position along the riverbank. To make the situation worse for Thoburn, most of the dismounted cavalrymen who had crossed with him "fled ingloriously across the river at the first assault of the enemy." Some of them drowned during their panicked flight across the river when they missed the shallows of the fords. The rout of the cavalrymen placed Thoburn's right flank in peril, so he shifted the 116th Ohio from his left to his extreme right in hopes of checking an attack by Rodes' Division. Colonel James Washburn of the 116th Ohio was shot in his left eye as he led his regiment into the fight. The bullet passed through Washburn's head and exited behind his right ear, yet he somehow survived the seemingly-fatal wound. Two companies from the 116th drove Confederates from behind a stone wall along the riverbank while the rest of the regiment took a position behind the wall and opened fire on the enemy. Colonel Thoburn reported that the "attack was bravely met and the enemy driven back." Some of Thoburn's troops fled across the river late in the afternoon, but the 116th Ohio, 4th West Virginia, 12th West Virginia and remnants from other regiments "fought with unparalleled tenacity" against three Confederate assaults until darkness fell and they could withdraw across the river. Federal artillery massed on the east side of the river helped cover Thoburn's remaining troops as they withdrew across the river.

One Confederate involved in the battle could not remember being "engaged in a more sharp and obstinate affair" during the war. Yet the Battle of Snicker's Ferry, or Cool Spring to some, was but another unnecessary sacrifice of lives for no useful purpose. The onus for their sacrifice belonged to General Wright, yet nothing much came of it except for the bitterness of the Thoburn's men. Crook reported his losses as sixty-five killed, 301 wounded and fifty-six missing. Confederate casualties perhaps totaled 400 or more killed and wounded. Thoburn reported that the Confederate loss, "at their own estimate, was over 600 killed and wounded."[80]

On July 19, Hunter sent out his remaining cavalry and infantry that had just arrived at Harpers Ferry southward to Winchester in an effort to continue the push against Early. With the Federals still looking to cross the Shenandoah River in his front and with Brigadier General William Averell leading the Federal force southward against him from Harpers Ferry, Early decided to consolidate his forces near Strasburg, farther south in the Valley. Early also believed that his trains were vulnerable to Averell's approaching force. As Early moved south, Major General Stephen D. Ramseur marched his division to Winchester to cover Early's retreat. Early intended for Ramseur to assume a defensive posture at Winchester. Ramseur claimed that he had received reports that Averell's approaching force was small and could be captured if pressed. In any case, Ramseur decided to disregard his instructions and attack the approaching Federals at Rutherford's Farm a few miles north of Winchester on the afternoon of July 20.

Ramseur was only twenty-seven, and like George A. Custer, his contemporary at West Point, Ramseur had compiled an impressive combat record leading to rapid advancement and great expectations. At Rutherford's Farm his force outnumbered Averell's by nearly a third, but he was soundly beaten when his men panicked and, according to Ramseur, "ran off the field in a wild disorder." Facts indicate that Ramseur "failed to reconnoiter the ground before advancing," and he probably lost the battle because his left flank was exposed to attacking Federal cavalry and infantry. Ramseur's disordered division gathered at Fort Collier on the northern edge of Winchester, having lost four guns from the Amherst Battery and another 250 or so men captured. Confederate total casualties approached 500. Averell's infantry lost twenty-seven killed and 184 wounded; overall Federal casualties totaled perhaps less than 250. Major General Robert E. Rodes, Ramseur's "friend," wrote an exculpatory report several weeks later—only days before he was mortally wounded at the Battle of Winchester—to record his "belief that the cause of the disaster was the conduct of the men" who were "under the influence of panic." But Ramseur's soldiers blamed him for their defeat, claiming that Ramseur had "blundered terribly."[81] The Battle of Rutherford's Farm, regardless, demonstrates that Southern soldiers were at times defeated by a smaller enemy force—on Southern soil. The antebellum boast that one Southerner could whip five Yankees was debunked yet again in Virginia on July 20, 1864.

That same day, July 20, the Confederates in Georgia suffered another very costly defeat that resulted from what could be considered blunders. The first blunder was President Davis's decision to replace General Joseph E. Johnston as commander of the Army and Department of Tennessee. Davis shared a difficult relationship with Johnston despite the fact that he respected the general's abilities. But Johnston had been retreating ever since Sherman commenced the Atlanta Campaign, and Davis thought that Johnston should have held fast in the mountainous region north of Atlanta. He wanted a similar response to what General Lee had shown during the Seven Days fighting around Richmond in 1862. On July 17, Adjutant General Samuel Cooper, the Confederacy's senior general, had sent the following dispatch to Johnston: "Lieut. Gen. J.B. Hood has been commissioned to the temporary rank of general under the law of Congress. I am directed by the Secretary of War to inform you that as you have failed to arrest the advance of the enemy to the vicinity of Atlanta, far into the interior of Georgia, and express no confidence that you can defeat or repel him, you are hereby relieved from command of the

Army and Department of Tennessee, which you will immediately turn over to General Hood." Johnston complied, of course, with the order and replied to General Cooper with a dispatch of his own the next day. Johnston informed Cooper that his order had been obeyed and then asserted that his job in Georgia had been more difficult than Lee's was in Virginia. He pointed out to Cooper that Sherman had been forced to advance slower to Atlanta than Grant had advanced towards Richmond. He saw no point in expressing confidence to President Davis, and he ended his dispatch by reminding Cooper that confident "language by a military commander is not usually regarded as evidence of competency." In that final observation, Johnston might well have predicted the outcome of the change of command. Hood had perhaps recommended aggressive offensive tactics to Davis with confidence, but his leadership in replacement of Johnston would prove disastrous. Hood himself along with Generals Hardee and Stewart of Johnston's army had urged President Davis to retain Johnston in command until the fate of Atlanta was decided, but Davis, as he informed these men, only opted for the change of command because otherwise he would have had to continue a "policy that had proved disastrous."[82] In this case, at least, Davis's interference prompted something truly disastrous for the Confederacy.

Hood had a sound plan prepared for the fighting on July 20 at Peach Tree Creek, a short distance due north of Atlanta. Sherman's army was advancing on Atlanta in a wide arc and thus was vulnerable to a concentrated attack from Hood's position south of Peach Tree Creek. Hood planned to hit General George Thomas' Army of the Cumberland as it crossed Peach Tree Creek, knowing that the terrain would make it difficult for reinforcements to reach Thomas from the rest of Sherman's army. Hood intended to attack with two of his army corps, drive Thomas into a trap at the confluence of Peach Tree Creek and the Chattahoochee River, destroy Thomas' army and then attack the remainder of Sherman's army near Atlanta.

It was Hood's first experience as an army commander, and his plan fell apart from the start on July 20. The Confederate attacks were delayed until around 4 p.m.; by then the Federals had crossed the creek. When the Confederates finally did attack, the assault waves did not proceed according to Hood's plan and lacked coordination. The terrain, heavily wooded and cut with rills and ravines, was expected to hinder Federal movements, but instead it interfered with Hood's attacks. To further complicate Hood's situation, the main Confederate attack hit the one Federal division that had bothered to build fieldworks. One other factor disadvantaged Hood. General Thomas, commanding the Federals that day, was at his very best in just this sort of situation. Thomas was known as "the Rock of Chickamauga" because of his splendid stand at that battle. With Thomas in charge, the Federals held along the length of their battle line and launched a successful counterattack. Then at the critical stage of the battle when Hood needed to send in his reserves, he was forced to send troops to the eastern outskirts of Atlanta to block Federal Major General McPherson's Army of the Tennessee as it advanced and began shelling Atlanta. The day ended with Hood unable to gain any advantage over Thomas while suffering more than twice the Federal casualties. Confederate casualties totaled 4,796 at the Battle of Peach Tree Creek while the Federal losses came to only 1,779.[83]

Despite the setback at Peach Tree Creek, Hood opted for further offensive tactics— even though General Lee himself had been fighting a defensive war in Virginia. Hood devised a flanking attack to hit McPherson's army east of Atlanta at dawn on Friday, July 22. Hood's plan almost worked as intended, but here again, as was so often the case with the Federal Army of the Potomac, things didn't play out as designed. Lieutenant General William J. Hardee's Confederate corps was given the assignment for the flanking maneuver. Hardee was required to march his corps over fifteen miles during the night of July 21; when his troops reached the jumping off point on McPherson's left flank, it was approaching noon and his soldiers were exhausted. Fortunately for Sherman, McPherson had sent his reserve, the XVI Corps, to extend his left. If Hardee had launched his assault on time, possibly the outcome of the battle would have been different. The fighting on July 22, known to history as the Battle of Atlanta, was fierce, and the outcome was continually in doubt. General McPherson was shot and killed by Confederate skirmishers while riding with his staff to check his battle lines. McPherson was the only U.S. army commander killed in battle during the war. Major General John A. "Black Jack" Logan assumed command of the Army of the Tennessee in place of General McPherson at a critical point of the battle and led a counterattack that sealed the victory for the Federals.

At the Battle of Atlanta, Hood's 40,000 troops engaged 30,000 or so Federals mostly from the Army of the Tennessee. An estimated 3,240 Confederates were killed at this battle; an actual count of 2,200 bodies was made. Hood's losses totaled from 8,000 to perhaps as many as 10,000. Sherman reported his total casualties as 3,722.[84] The result of this battle was much like the fighting in Virginia where Grant attacked fieldworks and trenches and suffered higher casualties than the Confederates. At this battle Sherman was outnumbered and his army was not completely sheltered by strong fieldworks everywhere on the battlefield. Nevertheless, his army inflicted twice as many casualties as it suffered. The outcome demonstrated again that it didn't matter which side stood on the defensive, attacking fieldworks was a very costly battle tactic indeed.

Having had his attacks thwarted twice in three days, Hood backed into the strong fortifications around Atlanta, and Sherman devised a means of capturing the city without resorting to direct assaults against its defenses. Sherman intended to starve the Confederates out of Atlanta, if necessary, by cutting off all supply lines and railroads leading to it. Over the next several weeks Sherman would shift his troops to control the four vital railroads that converged at Atlanta. Hood would be left with three options: face a situation in Atlanta tantamount to a siege, fight to hold the railroads or withdraw.

Back in Virginia's Shenandoah Valley, Jubal Early, like General Hood, returned to the offensive. Lee could barely spare Early's troops from the defense of Petersburg; but after the Federal reaction to Early's raid in Maryland, ongoing operations in the Valley were given continuing priority. After the fighting at Rutherford's Farm, General Wright believed that Early would withdraw farther into the Valley or perhaps return to Lee's army at Petersburg. So Wright began retracing his path to Washington, and Early received a report form his cavalry about a large Federal force turning back. Early then decided to again advance down the Valley for another incursion into Maryland.

On July 17, General in Chief Halleck had sent a dispatch to General Hunter explaining Grant's intentions for Hunter's department. Halleck mentioned that Wright was to return to Washington as soon as he became confident that Early was retreating to Richmond. Hunter was directed to "pursue the enemy cautiously, even to Gordonsville"; failing that, Hunter was to cover Washington and make the valleys south of the B & O Railroad "a desert as high up as possible." Grant cautioned that he did not "mean that houses should be burned," but he wanted Hunter's troops "to eat out Virginia clear and clean as far as they go, so that crows flying over it for the balance of the season will have to carry their provender with them."

For several days Grant and Halleck were trying to decide what to do with Wright's VI Corps and Emory's XIX Corps division. On July 22, Grant informed Halleck that if Wright and Hunter could combine to push Early back and then destroy the "railroads from Charlottesville to Gordonsville, I would prefer that service to having them here." The following day, President Lincoln personally asked General Hunter about the situation in his department. "Are you able to take care of the enemy when he turns back upon you," Lincoln inquired, "as he probably will on finding that Wright has left?" Hunter quickly replied that his force was not strong enough to check Early if he returned with his entire force. However, Hunter did not expect Early to move northward because General Crook had information that Early had received orders to go back to Richmond. "I will take care," Hunter assured the president, "that no such movement of the enemy shall take us by surprise."[85]

Despite Hunter's assurances to the contrary, Jubal Early was turning back just as President Lincoln had predicted. On the morning of July 24, General Early marched his entire force, about 14,000 troops, toward Winchester. Neither Hunter nor Crook expected the move. Crook reacted with his 9,500 or so men by sending them south of Winchester to the nearby village of Kernstown, where General Stonewall Jackson had battled—and lost—to a Federal force in 1862. Crook expected to drive away the advancing Confederates. Crook was disappointed. His report on the subsequent battle at Kernstown, which resulted in 1,185 Federal casualties, filled only two small paragraphs. Crook reported that once again, as at Snicker's Ferry, the dismounted cavalry "broke to the rear the first fire." Averell's cavalry, which had performed well at Rutherford's Farm four days prior, failed to contribute much at Kernstown. Early was thus able to concentrate an overpowering force with a double envelopment against Crook's advanced infantry position. Crook was forced to retreat back to Bunker Hill north of Winchester. Some of the Federal teamsters "got stampeded" and abandoned their wagons during the retreat, but these were burned to keep them out of the hands of the enemy. The soldiers in Crook's 1st Division "were pretty sick of this sort of campaigning." One officer wrote years later that "this pursuit, in the Shenandoah, was incautious and reckless ... no campaign in the war was more disjointed, more fruitless and demoralizing." Early's casualties came to about half of Crook's at Kernstown.[86]

Crook's defeat at Kernstown enabled Early to move northward and continue his program of retribution. Crook retreated into Maryland by way of Sharpsburg and on to Harpers Ferry. The B & O Railroad was at Early's mercy at Martinsburg and was destroyed there. Early then set his sights on making mischief north of the Potomac. The Lincoln Administration, of course, needed an immediate solution to Early's continued raiding. During the following week Grant and Lincoln would meet to decide the fate of the Shenandoah Valley.

There was more fighting around Atlanta as the Confederate shift to offensive tactics continued to prove counterproductive there. After the Battle of Atlanta, General Sherman devised an operation to destroy Hood's sole surviving supply line, the Macon & Western Railroad. Sherman sent a two-pronged effort against the railroad. A cavalry force went out to the vicinity of Lovejoy's Station south of Atlanta while the Army of the Tennessee's infantry marched north and then west of the city to threaten the railroad. Sherman hoped to lure Hood out of the defenses surrounding Atlanta, and it worked.

On July 27, the Federal Army of the Tennessee marched on an arcing route around Atlanta to a country meeting house called Ezra Church. During the following morning, the Federals busied themselves with constructing fieldworks there. General Sherman commented that the speed and skill with which his men constructed these fieldworks was "wonderful" and "something new in the art of war." Hood sent four divisions out from the Atlanta defenses to stop Sherman's effort to reach the railroad. He instructed Lieutenant General Stephen D. Lee, commanding two divisions, and Lieutenant General Alexander Stewart, commanding the other two Confederate divisions, not to attack the Federals until July 29. Lee decided to disregard Hood's orders and attacked on the 28th near Ezra Church. Later in the afternoon Stewart arrived with his troops and joined in the attacks. Sherman succinctly described the outcome as follows: "...our men coolly and deliberately cut down his (Hood's) men, and, in spite of the efforts of the rebel officers, his ranks broke and fled.... These assaults occurred from noon until about 4 p.m., when the enemy disappeared, leaving his dead and wounded in our hands." When the battle at Ezra Church was over, Hood's army had lost over eight times as many men as Sherman's. Confederate casualties totaled perhaps 5,000 compared to 600 for the Federals. The Battle of Ezra Church has been largely overlooked, but Sherman's troops delivered a victory as one-sided as any achieved by the Confederacy during the war.

Conversely, Sherman's cavalry raid sent out against the Macon and Western Railroad during the same period was a dismal failure. Sherman remarked that "on the whole the cavalry raid is not deemed a success." Hood dispatched his cavalry led by Major General Joseph Wheeler to go after the Federal cavalry. Sherman had ordered his two cavalry forces to combine at Lovejoy's Station; however, the force commanded by Major General George Stoneman moved on to Macon and was overwhelmed by the enemy. At the time of Sherman's report on the operation, Stoneman's "mistake" was "yet unexplained."[87] This raid, like many others attempted by the Federals against railroads during the war, failed to reap benefits worthy of the cost.

While Sherman was making good progress overall in the Atlanta Campaign, General Grant in Virginia was producing a long list of failures. The fault wasn't with Grant's tactical planning, which was sound. Grant's troubles resulted mostly from the unexceptional command structure in the Army of the Potomac. No single operation during the war exhibited this handicap more than did the activities around Petersburg during the last few days of July 1864.

By the middle of July, the Federals had been stalled at Petersburg for a month, and Grant concluded that it was time "to do something in the way of offensive movement." The 48th Pennsylvania Infantry of Burnside's IX Corps had a complement of experienced miners, and Grant had experimented with undermining the enemy defenses at Vicksburg in May 1863. Grant allowed the Pennsylvanians to dig a shaft under the Confederate works at Elliott's Salient near Cemetery Hill on the outskirts of Petersburg. The mine shaft, continuing from within the Federal lines to beneath the Confederate works, was completed on July 23; Grant decided to prepare and launch an operation to explode the mine as a means to breach the enemy defenses and "carry Petersburg."

To improve the chances of success in conjunction with the mine explosion, Grant launched the Federal II Corps and Sheridan's cavalry north of the James River "to get as many of Lee's troops away from the south side of the James River as possible." On July 26, Grant sent Major General Hancock with his corps and two divisions of cavalry across the river at Deep Bottom via a pontoon bridge. The real purpose of the operation, other than drawing the Confederates away from Petersburg, was to "cut loose" the cavalry to "destroy as much as they could of the Virginia Central Railroad" while the II

Corps protected their rear and covered their eventual retreat to the crossing at Deep Bottom. This mission was another failure except that Lee sent four divisions north of the James to protect Richmond. Only 18,000 troops remained in the trenches at Petersburg, and Grant was ready to blast an opening with the gunpowder-packed mine shaft under Elliott's Salient.

Details for the attack following the mine explosion were complicated and exacting. On July 29, Hancock and Sheridan were recalled from Deep Bottom with the II Corps taking the place of the XVIII Corps within the Federal lines. The XVIII Corps, IX Corps and V Corps were assigned to participate in the attack on Elliott's Salient on July 30. Changes ordered by General Meade the day before the attack muddled the selection of the order of the attack. As a result, the weakest division commander, Brigadier General James Ledlie, was selected to lead the first, and thus most important, wave of the attack. General Burnside was given explicit instructions about how to conduct the attack: most important, he was told that the crest of the hill beyond the breach in the enemy line had to be "immediately gained," and the "troops were to be withdrawn" quickly if the assault proved unsuccessful.

The mine was scheduled to explode at 3:30 a.m. on July 30, but the lengthy fuse failed at a splice. The fuse was relit, and the mine finally exploded at around 4:40 a.m. A large crater in the Confederate line, perhaps nearly 200 feet long and twenty to thirty feet deep, resulted from the blast. After a delay of several minutes, Ledlie's division moved out. Instead of following Meade's instructions, Ledlie remained in a bombproof in the rear while his division went forward. From this inauspicious start the Federal effort deteriorated into a fiasco. Before long thousands of Federals were milling around in what became known to history as "the Crater" while the Confederates organized a counterattack. General Grant later succinctly described the "battle" with the following: "The effort was a stupendous failure ... all due to inefficiency on the part of the corps commander (Burnside) and the incompetency of the division commander (Ledlie) who was sent to lead the assault." Grant also stated that "Burnside seemed to have paid no attention whatever" to the instructions given by Meade.

Two days after the Crater disaster, Grant reported 450 killed, 2,000 wounded and 1,050 missing; Confederates losses perhaps came to 1,500. Grant voiced his disappointment with some unusual remarks to Chief of Staff Halleck: "It was the saddest affair I have witnessed in the war. Such an opportunity for carrying fortifications I have never seen and do not expect to have again.... I am constrained to believe that had instructions been promptly obeyed that Petersburg would have been carried ... without a loss of 300 men." The incredible inefficiency of the Army of the Potomac at the corps and staff level was never as vividly demonstrated as at Petersburg on July 30, 1864. Grant's and Meade's instructions had specified how the assault was to be conducted, and Meade had stressed to Burnside that the men should be withdrawn as soon and as safely as possible should something go wrong. Instead, Burnside's troops were trapped in the Crater and slaughtered for hours. On August 2, Grant requested a court of inquiry to study the causes and reasons for the failed assault on July 30 at Petersburg and to determine if any officer or officers were "censurable" for the failure.[88] Unfortunately for the Northern soldiers, efficiency within the Army of the Potomac was not soon forthcoming.

Since mid–July, General Grant had been calling for a unified command to deal with Early's incursions into Maryland. On July 18, he informed Halleck, and therefore the president, "I deem it absolutely necessary that the Departments of the Susquehanna,

West Virginia, and Washington be merged into one department and one head, who shall absolutely control the whole." Grant wanted to place Major General William Franklin in command of the proposed department. Franklin was a curious choice for such an important position because he was out of favor with the Lincoln Administration. Franklin had graduated at the top of the West Point Class of 1843 at the age of twenty; Grant, Franklin's classmate, finished twenty-first. Perhaps Grant respected Franklin's ability, and Franklin was not occupied with a vital job at the time. Halleck replied on the 21st that Franklin "would not give satisfaction." Lincoln had previously "ordered him to be tried for negligence and disobedience of orders." Grant informed the president on July 25 that it was "essential" to place a single commander in charge of the proposed merged departments. He explained that Franklin "was named because he was available," capable and trustworthy. The merged departments would be called a military division, and Grant suggested Major General George Meade as the new commander, since Franklin would not do.

Grant traveled to Fortress Monroe to meet with President Lincoln on July 31. Lee's decision to send his II Corps into the Shenandoah Valley had produced the desired affect; Lincoln and Grant were forced to prioritize the Valley at the expense of concentrating forces against Richmond, Atlanta and Mobile. At the meeting Grant and Lincoln considered whom to appoint as commander of the new military division to be employed against Early in the Valley. Lincoln did not want to reassign General Meade because he had been opposing calls from politicians to dismiss that general. Lincoln did not wish to appear to capitulate to those demands. General George McClellan was even mentioned for the assignment as a mechanism for keeping him out of politics, but, of course, he would not do either. Lincoln deferred to Grant for naming the new commander, with the exceptions of Franklin, Meade and McClellan.

It didn't take Grant long to make a decision. The day after his meeting with Lincoln, August 1, Grant wired Chief of Staff Halleck from City Point near Petersburg with the following: "I am sending General Sheridan for temporary duty whilst the enemy is being expelled from the border. Unless General Hunter is in the field in person, I want Sheridan put in command of all of the troops in the field, with instructions to put himself south of the enemy and follow him to the death." General Hunter remained in command of the Department of West Virginia, and, having seen for years the modus operandi in the East, President Lincoln sent the following message to General Grant on August 3:

> I have seen your dispatch in which you say "I want Sheridan put in command of all the troops in the field, with instructions to put himself south of the enemy, and follow him to the death. Wherever the enemy goes, let our troops go also." This, I think, is exactly right, as to how our forces should move. But please look over the despatches you may have received from here ... and discover, if you can, that there is any idea in the head of any one here of "putting our army *south* of the enemy," or of following him "to the *death*" in any direction. I repeat to you it will neither be done nor attempted unless you watch it every day, and hour, and force it.[89]

August of 1864 was a turning point in the war for the North and the South. Things would vastly improve for the North, and the situation would critically worsen for the South. Grant was subjecting Petersburg, and therefore Richmond, to siege; Sherman was succeeding daily in his campaign against Atlanta, and the Federals were finally providing ample resources to occupy and control the Shenandoah Valley. A little past noon on August 7, General in Chief Grant wired Sheridan, at Harpers Ferry, informing him that four departments, the Middle, Washington, Susquehanna, and Western Virginia, had "been formed into a military division called the Middle Division," and Sheridan had been assigned "to the temporary command." Grant further advised that Sheridan could "assume command without further authority."[90] Sheridan was a vast improvement over any of the previous Federal generals who had operated in the Valley, an officer who far excelled the blundering commanders who had been outclassed by General Stonewall Jackson in the Valley in 1862.

Sherman attempted to use Major General John Schofield's Army of the Ohio to sever the Macon & Western Railroad south of Atlanta on August 5. Schofield attacked at Utoy Creek on August 6 and drove the Confederates back to a stronger defensive line along the railroad. Sherman then wisely decided to refrain from further attacks against fortifications. Instead, he ordered up his siege artillery to pummel Atlanta commencing on August 9. The bombardment of Atlanta more than anything served to punish the civilian population of that city and not much else, but Sherman would soon devise a plan to finally force the Confederate army out.

While General Sheridan was assuming command of his new department at Harpers Ferry and consolidating his forces, Brigadier General Averell, after a disappointing performance at Kernstown in July, managed to surprise McCausland's cavalry at Moorefield, West Virginia, on August 7. Averell gained a success by routing the rebels and inflicting over 500 casualties and capturing four cannons and nearly 700 horses. Averell's losses were minimal, and his victory at Moorefield was a severe blow to Early's already weak cavalry arm.[91] The situation in the Valley was off to an auspicious start for the Federals in August.

Sheridan spent the month of August without attempting a serious offensive against Early. Sheridan's force now consisted of Hunter's Army of West Virginia, now designated as the VIII Corps, the VI Corps from the Army of the Potomac, a division and part of another division from the XIX Corps and two cavalry divisions from the Army of the Potomac. Sheridan with around 43,000 men greatly outnumbered Early's force, so General Lee sent an infantry division and cavalry division with a battalion of artillery from his army to the region within supporting distance of Early. These troops soon moved into the Valley to operate with Early.[92] Lee had deemed it worthwhile to defend the Valley and menace the border area and Washington at the risk of weakening his army defending Petersburg and Richmond. The strategic significance of the Shenandoah Valley had never been higher.

After Grant returned to the Army of the Potomac still besieging Petersburg, he again turned his attention to offensive operations. Grant knew in early August that General Lee had sent troops from Petersburg to reinforce General Jubal Early in the Shenandoah Valley. Grant essentially repeated his effort to draw Confederate troops north of the James by again sending Major General Hancock and his II Corps across the James at Deep Bottom. This time he sent the X Corps from the Army of the James to cooperate under Hancock's direction. The two combined Federal corps outnumbered the Confederate defenders near Deep Bottom 29,000 to 7,699. The operation seemed likely to deliver a sure victory for the Federals, but Hancock and his subordinates "threw away their opportunities one after another." The Federal commanders "day after day" fumbled their assignments, and General Hancock's reputation was justifiably tarnished in the aftermath. The fighting from August 13 to 20, 1864, is known as Second Deep Bottom or Fussell's Mill, where much of the hardest fighting occurred. In essence, the operation was a continuation of the kind of sloppy, bungling command performances by the officers charged with carrying out Grant's plans since the beginning of the Overland Campaign. The Federals had suffered 2,901 casualties compared to perhaps 1,500 Confederate casualties when the fighting was over.[93] It is difficult to determine whether the Confederate leadership should be acclaimed as praiseworthy or the Federal leadership was so dismal during this operation that the only a Federal defeat could have resulted.

General Lee sent a portion of his remaining force at Petersburg north of the James in response to the fighting at Fussell's Mill. This shift of forces allowed Grant to send out another raid against the Weldon Railroad, one of two vital supply lines for the Confederates at Petersburg and Richmond. Grant's objective for this operation was twofold. He wanted to sever the important Weldon Railroad line south of Petersburg. Perhaps more important, as he indicated to General Meade on August 17, was making "such demonstrations as will force Lee to withdraw a portion of his troops from the Valley, so that Sheridan can strike a blow against the balance." Following Grant's instructions, Meade informed Grant that he would order out the V Corps at 4 a.m. the following morning. Meade anticipated "no difficulty" for the V Corps to "make a lodgment on the railroad," but he thought the Confederates might be able to "interrupt" the effort to destroy the railroad. The ensuing operation proved much more difficult and costly than Grant or Meade anticipated. Fighting at Globe Tavern on August 19 cost the Federals nearly 2,600 men missing and probably captured, but by August 21 the "Confederate forces no longer could use the Weldon Railroad as a direct supply line into the city."[94]

Having blocked the Weldon Railroad at Globe Tavern, Grant wanted the tracks destroyed farther south. Major General Hancock's II Corps had returned from the Deep Bottom operation on August 21, so Hancock was assigned the task of destroying the railroad south of Globe Tavern with two of his divisions and assistance from a Federal cavalry division. Hancock's troops were physically fatigued from their march to Deep Bottom, fighting there, and then marching to the Weldon Railroad. Many, perhaps most, of these troops were by now suffering from combat fatigue as well. Nevertheless, Grant sent the II Corps to continue the destruction of the railroad southwards to Reams Station, which was accomplished by August 24.

Hancock's force was separated from potential support from the Federal V Corps at Globe Tavern by about five miles, so Confederate Lieutenant General A.P. Hill moved with his III Corps and two cavalry divisions against Federals at Reams Station on August 25. Hancock took refuge in some poorly-designed fieldworks near the station. Meade sent reinforcements to Reams Station, but these were sent by a circuitous route instead of the direct five mile hike from Globe Tavern. Many of Hancock's troops at this point were inexperienced recruits and sullen draftees who became demoralized during a fierce enemy bombardment late in the afternoon. Hill's Confederates managed a breakthrough in the center of the Federal line, and Hancock was unable to mount an effective counterattack. Several II Corps units refused to move forward when ordered. By nightfall Hancock's troops were abandoning Reams Station and retreating to the northeast with a loss of over 2,000 men captured or missing and over 700 more killed or wounded. Hill's Confederates suffered perhaps fewer than 800 casualties despite attacking fieldworks.

The reputation of General Hancock and his II Corps suffered after the fighting at Fussell's Mill and Reams Station. Hill and his troops won a clear tactical victory at Reams Station, and Hill's victory appeared remarkably easy. The greatest part of the blame for the Federal defeat belonged to General Hancock. He was aware of the fact that enemy troops were in force nearby; and when he realized that an enemy attack was probable, he chose to man the weak, inadequate fieldworks at Reams Station instead of withdrawing to Globe Tavern. Hancock arrived at Reams Station in time to strengthen and rearrange the fieldworks to meet a possible enemy attack. He chose not to do that. Hancock blamed his defeat at Reams Station on the performance of his men. The II Corps did, in fact, put up a sorry performance at Reams Station. The Overland Campaign and the fighting around Petersburg had seriously depleted the leaders and veterans of the II Corps. Hancock should have realized the reduced effectiveness of his corps. He apparently overlooked the condition of his corps and suffered because of it. General Meade bears a portion of the blame of the defeat as well. He overestimated the strength and capabilities of both Hancock and his II Corps. His decision to send reinforcement by a circuitous route rather than directly from Globe Tavern prevented their arrival in time to affect the outcome of the battle.[95] The Battle of Reams Station could have resulted in a punishing Federal victory similar to outcome of the battles at Peach Tree Creek and Ezra Church in Georgia. Instead, it was yet another in a series of remarkably poor showings by the Army of the Potomac in Virginia in 1864.

During most of August, Sherman's army remained stalled at Atlanta. On August 23, President Lincoln, seeing no favorable resolution to the war in the near future, wrote the following memorandum: "This morning, as for some days past, it seems exceedingly probable that this administration will not be re-elected." Lincoln asked his cabinet to sign it, placed in an envelope and then put it aside.[96] Sherman understood that something had to be done soon to capture Atlanta, as both he and Lincoln knew would be vital for getting Lincoln reelected. Sherman devised a plan to march most of his army away from the trenches besieging Atlanta and strike for the Macon & Western Railroad south of the city. Cutting that railroad supply line would eventually starve the Confederates out of Atlanta.

Hood upon learning that the Federals had abandoned their siege lines believed initially that Sherman had given up and withdrawn northward. By August 30, however, Hood had learned that the Federals were in force south of Atlanta and were threatening his vital railroad line around Jonesboro, Georgia. Two Confederate corps were dispatched from Atlanta under Lieutenant General William Hardee to deal with the Federals at Jonesboro while Hood remained at Atlanta with a single corps. Hardee attacked at Jonesboro on August 31 and was repulsed. Hood recalled one of his corps and left Hardee to defend the railroad with one corps against the bulk of Sherman's army. Hardee should have been crushed on September 1, but instead Sherman only managed to attack Hardee with a single corps. Hardee was driven back and withdrew to a new position near Lovejoy's Station, six miles south of Jonesboro. Once again the Confederates got the worst of the fighting at Jonesboro, suffering approximately 2,000 casualties compared to 1,149 Federal casualties. At 6 a.m. on September 3, 1864, Sherman wired General Halleck and summed up what happened next:

> In the night the enemy retreated south, and we have followed him to another of his well-chosen and hastily constructed lines, near Lovejoy's. Hood, at Atlanta, finding me on his road, the only one that could supply him, and between him and a considerable part of his army, blew up his magazines in Atlanta and left in the night-time, when the Twentieth Corps, General Slocum, took possession of the place. So Atlanta is ours and fairly won. I shall not push farther in this raid, but in a day or so will move to Atlanta and give my men some rest.

So the Atlanta Campaign was finally over. Sherman noted that "over 100 days of actual battle and skirmish" had passed during the campaign. The casualties were heavy on both sides. The Federals reported an aggregate total of 37,081 casualties for the period from May to September. The Confederate casualty list might have exceeded 35,000, with perhaps over 20,000 casualties during Hood's time in command.[97]

Confederate President Davis' decision to replace Johnston with Hood had possibly cost the Confederacy the war. General Grant seemed to think so. Grant later wrote of Johnston: "I think that his policy was the best one that could have been pursued by the whole South—protract the war, which was all that was necessary to enable them to gain recognition in the end." While Lee had succeeded in 1862 by attacking McClellan around Richmond, Hood had repeatedly attacked fieldworks rather than battling in the open field. He had been defeated and had lost far too many men as casualties. President Davis traveled to Georgia and nevertheless gave optimistic speeches despite the loss of Atlanta. At Macon Davis told the crowd, "What, through misfortune has befallen our arms from Decatur to Jonesboro, our cause is not lost." He predicted that Sherman would soon have to withdraw or face the same fate as Napoleon met in Russia. In another speech in South Carolina Davis approved Hood's strategy and opined that Hood would "soon have his hand on Sherman's line of communications."[98] Davis' decision-making, in this case, certainly, played out in favor of the North.

After the fall of Atlanta, the North again demonstrated a superior grasp of strategic planning. General Sherman began considering his options and ultimately convinced Grant to allow him to march an army through Georgia to Savannah. Sherman's decision to cut loose from his supply line and march part of his army to the sea was "strategy at its grandest" according to author Donald Stoker who taught Strategy and Policy at the Naval War College. Meanwhile, President Davis and the Confederate high command looked for a solution to the problem presented by the loss of Atlanta. Davis wanted Hood to dig in somewhere along the railroad between Atlanta and Chattanooga to induce Sherman to attack him. Hood instead decided to undertake an offensive against Nashville with a view of once again advancing to the Ohio River.[99] In effect Hood wanted to attempt another move into enemy territory, something that never had and never would succeed for the Confederacy. What had worked for Lee in Virginia in 1862 was not working for the Confederacy in 1864, and the Confederate high command was unequal to the task of finding an effective strategy to deal with the changing circumstances.

Major General Philip Sheridan, as noted previously, assumed command of the Middle Division, with responsibility for removing the rebel presence on the Maryland border and in the Shenandoah Valley, on August 7, 1864. Through the month of August Sheridan had not accomplished much and had not made any major mistakes. The days were passing without any meaningful impact in Sheridan's department. Something had to be done to check Early's threat to the B & O Railroad; Northern businessmen were concerned that coal would be in short supply by fall in the East if Early continued his raids against that railroad. On September 14, Grant decided to visit Sheridan again to urge some sort of action against Early. Early wasn't going away; President Davis had approved of General Lee's policy of using his troops in the Valley rather than sending reinforcements against Sherman in Georgia.

Sheridan finally found his opportunity to assume offensive operations against Early while Grant was visiting him at Charles Town, West Virginia. Sheridan had learned that Lee was recalling the reinforcements he had sent form Petersburg. Then on September 18 Sheridan learned that Early had sent a cavalry brigade and two infantry divisions northward towards Martinsburg to strike the B & O Railroad. Sheridan naturally realized he had an opportunity to crush the two Confederate divisions remaining at Winchester with his vastly superior force. He put his army in motion during the wee hours of September 19 to attack the remaining rebel force at Winchester.

The ensuing battle, known to history as Third Winchester or Opequon, proved much more difficult than Sheridan might have expected. Sheridan's army was composed of corps from three different armies. Since it included a corps from the Army of the Potomac, the VI Corps, the staff work was indifferent, as usual. Although the Federals got ready for action by 3 a.m., the VI Corps brought along supply wagons and ambulances contrary to orders into a long defile known locally as Berryville Canyon. As a result, the pathway to the battlefield was clogged for the two corps following the VI Corps into action.

The logjam in Berryville Canyon slowed Sheridan's attack long enough for General Early to recall two of his divisions from north of Winchester to join the single division defending the town. The slowly-developing Federal attack was held in check throughout the morning hours. The Confederates even managed to mount a counterattack as a result of another Federal blunder which opened a gap in center of the Federal line. By afternoon General Early thought that "a splendid victory had been gained." Sheridan was stalled, and the Confederates might have benefited by attempting to withdraw from Winchester while the Federals regrouped.

Sheridan then decided to use his VIII Corps, his reserve, to attack on the Federal right in the afternoon. He reportedly had intended to use the VIII Corps to seal the Confederate retreat route south of Winchester, but circumstances altered his plan. This modification proved the decisive factor in the outcome of the battle.

When the VIII Corps moved forward from reserve, the troops marched through Berryville Canyon, which was still clogged "with artillery caissons, ammunition wagons, ambulances, prisoners, wounded men" and the like. A soldier from the VIII Corps noted in his diary that General Sheridan met his regiment as it moved toward the fighting: "the Gen waved his hand and says 'go for 'em boys' ... which was heartily responded to.... Our command moved on to the field in the best order imaginable and about 2 O'clock became engaged."[100]

Early had stymied two Federal corps during the morning hours of September 19, but when Crook's VIII Corps arrived on the scene (the troops that Early had swept from the field at Kernstown less than two months prior) the situation changed dramatically. The VIII Corps managed to push back Early's left while the Federal cavalry, which outclassed Early's cavalry significantly, thundered in from north of Winchester to strike the Confederate rear. The Confederate lines gave way in what one rebel sergeant called "the most disorderly retreat I ever saw."

Early's operations since his arrival at Lynchburg in mid–June had "had a tremendous impact on the war in Virginia." He had drawn 30,000 Federal troops away from the operations against Petersburg and had threatened Washington. His defeat at Winchester, however, coupled with Hood's disastrous campaign in Georgia, accelerated the defeat of the Confederacy. Early can be faulted for his somewhat rash decision to send two divisions away from Winchester in the presence of an overwhelming enemy force, and perhaps he might have escaped from Winchester in a better condition than he ultimately did. But the Early was very critical of Sheridan's performance at Winchester and rightly so. Sheridan's force of about 40,000 troops was vastly superior to Early's 15,000 men, and at dawn on September 19 a large part of Early's force was still north of Winchester.

Colonel Joseph Thoburn's VIII Corps division pushed back General Early's Confederates here during the Third Battle of Winchester.

Sheridan did not manage the battle skillfully; the Federals should have crushed Ramseur's lone division defending Winchester, blocked Early's retreat route and then crushed the remainder of his force north of town. Despite winning the battle Sheridan's casualties in killed and wounded were over twice those of the Confederates. The Federals counted 697 killed, 3,983 wounded and 338 missing. Early's losses might have approached 4,000 in total with 226 reported as killed, 1,567 wounded and perhaps over 2,000 missing.[101]

Eric Wittenberg wrote an appraisal of Sheridan's abilities as a military leader. His assessment of Sheridan's role in this battle included the following observations: "Sheridan had tried to implement an unduly complicated battle plan that nearly led to the destruction of his army. Early's army had fought hard, and its execution was nearly flawless." Whatever the inadequacies of his staffers, Sheridan had unwisely chosen to funnel all of his infantry into Berryville Canyon. There were other routes to the field of battle that would have enabled the Federals to arrive on time to overpower Ramseur's Division before Early could intervene. It was the actions of General Crook and the Federal cavalry, rather than Sheridan's indifferent tactical applications, that won the battle at Winchester. Jubal Early's post-war criticism of Sheridan was justified. Early wrote, "A skilful and energetic commander … would have crushed Ramseur before any assistance could have reached him, and thus ensured the destruction of my whole force…. When I look back to this battle, I can but attribute my escape from utter annihilation to the incapacity of my opponent."[102]

On the day following the fight at Winchester, Early pulled up at Fisher's Hill, about four miles southwest of Strasburg, Virginia. It was a strong position; Fisher's Hill was considered as the Gibraltar of the Shenandoah Valley. Unfortunately for Early, he did not have enough men left to properly man the position. To make matters worse for the badly shaken Confederates, Early made perhaps the worst mistake of his career. He placed his infantry in the strongest positions and posted some dismounted cavalry on his far left flank which was the most vulnerable place in his defensive line. Early knew his cavalry was the weakest arm in his army. Apparently he did not expect an attack from that quarter, but General Crook had convinced Sheridan to allow his VIII Corps to again make a flanking attack against the Confederate left flank, as he had just done at Winchester. The tactic took Early by surprise at Fisher's Hill on September 22.

Early was hoping that Sheridan would hesitate to attack the strong position at Fisher's Hill and allow him to keep the Federals out of the upper part of the Valley until something could be done. But when Sheridan deployed two corps with the obvious intent of attacking, Early decided to withdraw to the gaps on the eastern edge of the Valley. He intended to wait to withdraw under the cover of darkness; instead, the Federal VIII Corps smashed the cavalry guarding the Confederate left flank before dusk. Crook's VIII Corps outflanked Early's infantry, and then the rebel line gave way into a rout.

Winchester and then Fisher's Hill were not the first major battles during the war where a Confederate army was driven from the field in confusion. But henceforth this sort of defeat would no longer be an exception. It would happen repeatedly in the following months, even General Lee would not be able to prevent it. The foregoing Confederate advantage in morale was deteriorating and would soon practically vanish. John Brown Gordon, then a major general and division commander in Early's corps, was critical of Early's leadership in the Valley. But Gordon himself was unable to hold a strong position on the right of the Confederate line at Fisher's Hill. His troops were flushed from the battlefield. He was unable to stem the route or perform any other form of magic to save the day. The tide had turned against the Confederacy, and no Southern commander would prove capable of resisting the continuum of defeat.

Now it was Jefferson Davis' and General Lee's turn to worry about the Shenandoah Valley. It had been an invasion route for the Confederates and an important source of forage and food for the Confederacy since 1861. Sheridan now controlled the lower Valley, and his presence threatened the Virginia Central Railroad linking the Valley's agricultural bounty to Richmond and the Army of Northern Virginia. Davis and the Confederate high command had tried to defend too much territory with too few men. This policy would continue in the Shenandoah Valley where Lee decided to send Kershaw's Division and some cavalry again to the Valley to help Early. On September 23, Lee sent the following message: "Kershaw's division, with battalion of infantry, has been ordered to re-enforce Early, and he has been directed to call out all the troops in the Valley. I have no other troops to send." Perhaps Lee should have made use of his limited resources where success would have been more likely.

On September 25, General Early informed Lee that his troops were "very much shattered" and "exhausted." He continued, "When Kershaw arrives I shall do the best I can, and hope I may be able to check the enemy, but I cannot but be apprehensive of the result." Lee replied on the 27th with the following: "I very much regret the reverses that have occurred to the army in the Valley, but trust they can be remedied. The arrival of Kershaw will add greatly to your strength…. I have given you all I can; you must use the resources you have so as to gain success. The enemy must be defeated, and I rely on you to do it."[103] The Confederacy could not afford another defeat with the presidential election at hand in the North; nevertheless, even with paltry reinforcements going back to the Valley another tactical offensive was in the offing there. Davis and Lee continued to push the offensive despite clear indications that their strategy was failing everywhere.

Another Confederate offensive, this one even more dubious than Hood's movement into Tennessee, commenced on the day Early was defeated at Winchester, September 19. Confederate Major General Sterling Price, a former governor of Missouri, would lead an expedition from Arkansas into Missouri with a view of occupying Missouri for several months and thereby drawing Federal troops into that state from east of the Mississippi River. If successful, Price's expedition would divert Federal troops that otherwise could had been used for operations in Tennessee or elsewhere east of the Mississippi. The Confederates hoped to recruit thousands of Missourians to their cause as Price moved through the state. Price's invading army "would be made up of all of the Missouri and Arkansas cavalry and mounted infantry now in Arkansas as well as one brigade of Louisiana cavalry, and would be self-sustaining largely by capturing arms, ammunition and food." Thomas Reynolds, the Confederate governor-in-exile for Missouri, would accompany the expedition, expecting to be inaugurated in the state capitol. Orders by direction of General E. Kirby Smith read as follows:

> Make Saint Louis the objective point of your movement, which, if rapidly made, will put you in possession of that place, its supplies, and military stores, and which will do more toward rallying Missouri to your standard than the possession of any other point. Should you be compelled to withdraw from the state, make your retreat through Kansas and the Indian Territory, sweeping that country of its mules, cattle and military supplies of all kinds. The division of General Fagan, the senior officer of your command, should be increased as soon as practicable.[104]

Sterling Price moved his somewhat rickety force northward out of Pocahontas, Arkansas, and into southeastern Missouri beginning on September 19. He decided to capture a small Union earthwork called Fort Davidson near Ironton, Missouri. Brigadier General Thomas Ewing, Jr., Major General William T. Sherman's brother-in-law, commanded Fort Davidson at Pilot Knob, Missouri. Price did not want to leave Ewing's force of over 1,000 Federal troops and Missouri State Militia behind as he moved toward St. Louis, so he ordered an assault on the earthwork. The small fort was commanded on both sides by Shepherd Mountain and Pilot Knob Mountain and was vulnerable to artillery bombardment from the mountaintops. Price's invading force numbered around 12,000 men, but perhaps 4,000 of them were unarmed and many were conscripts or recruits. On September 27, the Confederates attempted to storm the fort but were repulsed with heavy casualties. During the night Ewing and his men withdrew from the fort and escaped, ultimately making their way to Rolla, Missouri. A detail set off the powder in the fort's magazine to destroy the ammunition well before dawn. Ewing's stand at Pilot Knob had resulted in approximately 1,200 casualties in Price's army. Union losses totaled only 73 men at Fort Davidson.[105] Price's decision to assault the fort rather than attempting to shell it into submission proved costly in casualties and morale as his army continued its invasion of Missouri.

Price continued on to the outskirts of St. Louis with Fagan's Division. There he discovered that the city was fortified and too strongly defended to capture. So he headed west, as instructed, making Jefferson City, the state capital, his next objective. During its sojourn in Missouri, Price's army made mischief and plundered far and wide. Price declined to attack at Jefferson City, again, as at St. Louis, finding the place too well defended.

There was a brief interval between battles at Petersburg in September while Sheridan battled Early in the Valley and Sherman chased Hood around northern Georgia and into Alabama. But Grant would not give the rebels much of a reprieve, and in late September he unleashed another of his series of attacks north and south of the James River. As usual, Grant's plan was sound but its execution was feeble.

Corps from Major General Benjamin F. Butler's Army of the James crossed the James River at Aiken's Landing and Deep Bottom to launch attacks against Confederate Fort Harrison and New Market Heights at Chaffin's Bluff on September 29, 1864. The operation held great potential to breach Richmond's defenses and capture the Confederate capital. Troops from Butler's XVIII Corps managed to capture Fort Harrison but then accomplished little else. The X Corps attacked New Market Heights, sending about 13,000 troops, including several USCT regiments, against less than 2,000 Confederate defenders. Most of the Confederate defenders at New Market Heights were shifted to reinforce other Confederate forts farther north on the defensive line. The few remaining defenders at New Market Heights were overrun, but the attacking Federals lost heavily. Only perhaps fifty Confederates were lost in the fighting at New Market Heights; Federal casualties totaled 850.

General Lee reinforced the defensive line around Chaffin's Bluff with 10,000 troops and attempted to retake Fort Harrison on September 30. The assault was a complete failure, as over 1,200 Confederate soldiers "were needlessly shot down" without recapturing the fort. Total Federal casualties for the fighting at Chaffin's Bluff came to 3,300. The Confederate losses had been light until Lee ordered the attack on Fort Harrison. After the assault on September 30, Confederate casualties totaled around 1,700.[106]

Grant, having compelled Lee to rush 10,000 men north of the James, took advantage of the situation by sending troops from the V and IX Corps and a cavalry force to attack the Southside Railroad, the last western rail link for Petersburg. Confederate Lieutenant General A.P. Hill was in charge of the defense of Petersburg; he sent two divisions from his III Corps to meet the Federal movement. At the ensuing Battle of Peebles' Farm from September 30 to October 2, 1864, Hill managed to check the Federals and kept them from cutting the Southside Railroad. Federal casualties were double those of the Confederates. Despite another failure, Grant had extended the Confederate defensive lines, forcing Lee to stretch his defenses even thinner.

By October of 1864 the Confederacy was losing the conventional war rapidly; nevertheless, the Confederate high command continued to believe offensive operations would carry the day. In Georgia, General Hood sent a force in an attempt to capture an important Federal supply base at Allatoona. In fighting there on October 5 the Confederates got the worst of it and withdrew without success. Hood soon turned his attention to Tennessee, where he hoped to recapture Nashville and then move into Kentucky. In Missouri, Price continued his westward march through the state, moving toward Kansas City and the Kansas border. At this point the Southerners were much like an outmatched boxer summoning his last reserve of willpower to avoid a knockout. But the contest had been decided, and now the only way to win would be to have the enemy grow weary and quit. The Confederacy would have been better served by assuming a completely defensive posture that fall, giving ground but grinding down the enemy with heavy losses incurred by his compulsory offensive tactics. The South's lingering hubris would not abide that.

Jubal Early, having acquired reinforcements including Major General Joseph B. Kershaw's Division, again looked for an opportunity to strike Sheridan's army then camping near Strasburg, Virginia. Early chose an apposite time to hit his unsuspecting enemy. Sheridan intended to send much of his army back to Petersburg, believing that the Confederates were whipped in the Valley and the region had been damaged sufficiently to deny its customary use as a granary for the Confederacy. General Grant, however, wanted Sheridan to advance southward against Charlottesville and Gordonsville to sever the Virginia Central Railroad. Sheridan resisted the plan. He left the Valley for a conference in Washington on October 15, leaving his army with Major General Horatio Wright of the VI Corps in overall command. Early had moved back down the Valley to Fisher's Hill by October 13. On that day, Confederate artillery fired on a Federal VIII Corps camp at Cedar Creek just outside Strasburg. General Crook ordered out Colonel Joseph Thoburn's two brigades in response. Thoburn's First Brigade clashed with seven South Carolina regiments at Stickley's Farm just north of town and was driven back to the Federal camps. Early then fell back to Fisher's Hill, aware that Sheridan now knew that he had moved back down the Valley.

Sheridan, however, apparently decided that Early would not attack at Cedar Creek. As Civil War author Jeffry Wert observed, Sheridan probably "viewed the action of two days previous as little more than the final crowing of an old rooster." More concerned with the planned conference in Washington than with Early, Sheridan sent two cavalry divisions back from Front Royal to Cedar Creek with a message for Wright to be well prepared should Early somehow make an attack.

On October 15, when Sheridan headed for Washington, Early's Confederate Army of the Valley was at Fisher's Hill, only a few miles from the Federal Army of the Shenandoah's expansive encampment at Cedar Creek. Early understood that the optimal time to strike Sheridan and regain his reputation was at hand. General Lee expected Early to reverse the tide defeat in the Valley and then send part of his force back Petersburg. For most of the two previous years Lee had succeeded against the Yankees by taking extreme risk against long odds. Apparently he believed Early would do the same in the Shenandoah Valley in the fall of 1864. So Early and his generals planned what one Civil War writer called "a brilliantly conceived gamble unparalleled in the war."[107] If Early with his single corps could have whipped Sheridan with his three, this indeed would likely have been the greatest battlefield victory of the war. A huge Confederate victory that October might have cost Lincoln the presidential election in November. Perhaps the risk was a worthy gamble; from hindsight it is clear that the Confederates instead should have conserved their resources with a defensive strategy in an attempt to prolong the war.

After nightfall on October 18, the Early's infantrymen marched via a narrow pathway to positions along Cedar Creek adjacent to the Federal encampments. Tens of thousands of rebel soldiers managed to get there without raising an alarm. A Federal cavalry division was supposed to be posted on the outskirts of the encampments, but it wasn't.

In the predawn hours of October 19, 1864, a thick shroud of fog and mist wafted up from the bottoms along Cedar Creek; the fog blanketed the woods and hillsides and extended into the nearby camp of Colonel Joseph Thoburn's Federal VIII Corps division. Colonel Thomas Harris's 3rd Brigade had marched out of Thoburn's camp on a reconnaissance toward Fisher's Hill on the previous day and had not met any Confederates. Harris's brigade had only marched as far as Hupp's Hill, a short distance from their camp. Nevertheless, apparently Harris and those in command felt secure in their belief that Early was not going to attack soon. Lieutenant Colonel Thomas F. Wildes was commanding the 1st Brigade of Thoburn's 1st Division on the 19th. He was awakened sometime around 4 a.m.

and informed of suspicious sounds along the creek bank. Wildes aroused the three regiments of his brigade not on picket duty and posted them in the camp's fieldworks. He also sent Captain Hamilton Karr of his 116th Ohio to find the 3rd Brigade's Colonel Harris and warn him of an impending attack. Karr found Colonel Harris asleep in an ambulance a considerable distance behind his brigade. Karr informed Harris that the rebels were about to attack, but Harris answered with "That cannot be." Colonel Wildes himself rode to the 3rd Brigade's camp but "could do nothing with" the "sleepy fellows" there and returned to his own brigade.[108] Perhaps Harris and his men simply could not believe that their recent reconnaissance could have missed the enemy's approach. In any case, sometime shortly after 5:00 a.m. Kershaw's Division, having captured most of the Federal pickets along Cedar Creek, launched an attack on Thoburn's camp. At about the same time, Major General Gordon sent three divisions against the other Federal VIII Corps camps.

Harris's 3rd Brigade was assembling in its fieldworks when Kershaw's men broke through where a regiment had not yet reached its assigned position. A panic then spread through Harris's men, and they were very quickly swept away in disorder. All of Thoburn's regiments with the exception of the 116th Ohio and 123rd Ohio, with Lieutenant Colonel Wildes in command, were routed. Even so, the Ohioan's efforts were soon "doomed by the feeble performance of Harris's brigade."[109]

The situation was much the same at the camp of the 2nd Division of Crook's VIII Corps. Before long most of the VIII Corps was making for the rear; however, some of its troops fell in with the XIX Corps, which was strongly positioned athwart the Valley Pike behind the VIII Corps camps. Major General Horatio Wright, who presided over this debacle, later wrote that for "some unexplainable cause the troops forming this part of the line would not stand but broke under a scattering of fire."[110] Wright, who was clipped in the face by a bullet while leading the 116th and 123rd Ohio Infantries in a countercharge early in the battle, soon decided to order the XIX Corps to withdraw and form up on the right of the VI Corps. The Federals had been surprised by Early's attack and overwhelmed by superior numbers at the point of combat. Wright had been unable to concentrate his forces sufficiently to check the surging Confederate attack. By 10 o'clock it appeared that the Federals were destined for a drubbing.

The afternoon of October 19, 1864, witnessed the most remarkable turnaround of any battle during the course of the war. After smashing the smaller VIII Corps and pushing back the XIX Corps, the Confederate's momentum stalled late in the morning. The Federal VI Corps, having had time to prepare, fought the attacking rebels to a standstill by noon. General Early, and probably most of the Federals as well, believed that the Confederates had won the battle. A number of factors contributed to the turnaround at Cedar Creek, but the most important impact was the return of General Sheridan to his army during the critical phase of the battle.

General Sheridan had traveled to Winchester from Washington by special train on October 18 and had spent the night there. After receiving reports of fighting at the Federal encampments at Cedar Creek, Sheridan decided to return with haste to his army. Sometime around 10:30 a.m., Philip Sheridan arrived on the battlefield after his now famous ride from Winchester. Soon afterwards he found Generals Wright and Crook consulting, and then General Emory of the XIX Corps rode up to join the group. Emory reported that his corps was ready to begin covering the army's retreat. Sheridan would have none of that. Even though Sheridan could not have then known the condition of his army or its present situation, he immediately affirmed that the Federals would recover their encampments by nightfall.[111] Sheridan then began preparing his army for a shift to the offensive that ultimately changed the outcome of the battle from a stunning defeat to a complete victory.

Despite a considerable controversy concerning the reasons for the reversal of fortunes on the Confederate side, the facts about the afternoon of October 19, 1864, at Cedar Creek remain clear. Sheridan's cavalry was superior to Early's in almost every aspect, and it again, as it had at the battle at Winchester in September, played a major role in defeating the Confederates. Sheridan placed his cavalry on both flanks; in the middle he positioned the XIX Corps to the right of the VI Corps and counterattacked shortly after 4 p.m. The Federals pushed forward and eventually outflanked the troops led by General Gordon on the Confederate left. Yet again, as at Fisher's Hill, Gordon's men panicked and began to run. The Federal cavalry then launched a thundering charge on the Confederate flanks, and the whole Confederate line collapsed into a rout. The Federal cavalry chased the Southerners past Strasburg and beyond Fisher's Hill, capturing hundreds of prisoners and twenty-four Confederate cannons.

Jubal Early deserved some criticism for the way this battle played out, but he certainly got more than his share of censure for it through the years. His battle plan was similar to General Lyon's plan for the Battle of Wilson's Creek in that it was based on surprising the enemy in his camp, and it included a force detailed to cut off the enemy's retreat route. In Early's plan, Major General Lunsford Lomax's small cavalry division was assigned to move north of Cedar Creek on the Valley Pike to assail the enemy's rear; thus, Lomax's division was unavailable when it was most needed on the field of battle. Early, according to Civil War writer Jeffry Wert, should have occupied the Valley Pike north of Middletown on the northern sector of the battlefield so that his army could have

One of the few monuments on the Cedar Creek Battlefield.

Belle Grove Mansion on the Cedar Creek Battlefield. Confederate General Ramseur died here after the battle.

outflanked the retreating Federals. Maybe Early missed this opportunity in the fog of battle, real fog in this case, but so did General Gordon and Early's other subordinates—apparently. Early thought the Federals would withdraw to Winchester, and he stood his ground expecting to reap the benefits of his morning success. From hindsight it is clear that he should have pulled back to Fisher's Hill with the artillery and prisoners his troops had seized during the morning phase of the battle. Early's biggest mistake was in again underestimating Philip Sheridan. This man wasn't like the fellows General Stonewall Jackson had pushed around in the Shenandoah back in 1862, and his army was much stronger than the disjointed commands Jackson had defeated. Early should have known better, especially after his defeats at Winchester and Fisher's Hill.

The Federals suffered heavier casualties than the Confederates at Cedar Creek: 644 were killed, 3,430 were wounded and 1,591 went missing for a total of 5,665. Confederate losses might have been greater than what was reported, but the list came to 320 killed, 1,540 wounded and 1,050 missing. The loss of all the captured Federal guns and another twenty-three or twenty-four Confederate guns made this defeat exceedingly severe for Lee's Army of Northern Virginia.[112] The Federal's casualties were heavier because during the first phase of the battle they were surprised and outnumbered where the fighting occurred, and then during the afternoon they attacked over open ground while being subjected to heavy artillery and rifle fire.

Cedar Creek marked the third consecutive rout for Lee's II Corps in a month's time. Some historians consider the Confederate II Corps as the best troops in Lee's army and perhaps in the entire Confederate Army. Nevertheless, these defeats were no anomaly. Henceforth the Confederate armies in the East and West would continue to suffer this sort of crushing defeat until the end came.

In Missouri, General Sterling Price was finding that his incursion into that state had drawn a swarm of Federals in his direction. On October 19, his troops battled a heavily outnumbered Federal detachment led by Major General James G. Blunt at Lexington. Blunt managed to slow Price as his army moved westward toward Kansas City. A force of around 15,000 Kansas Militiamen was gathering along the Missouri border in northeast Kansas to protect the state from Price's impending invasion. These men did not want to leave the state and awaited Price's columns in the Kansas City area.

When Price reached the Kansas City, Missouri, vicinity, a series of engagements and battles were fought between October 21 and 23. There was fighting on the banks of the Little Blue River, at Independence, at Byram's Ford on the Big Blue River and a full-fledged battle at Westport, all near Kansas City. Price wanted to push through the city, cross the Missouri River and capture Fort Leavenworth; however, with enemy troops closing on his columns from different directions, Price had to turn southward instead. The fighting at Westport alone cost Price at least 1,500 casualties, and he was fortunate to escape from Kansas City with his army intact.[113]

Price and his army crossed the state line into Kansas several miles south of Kansas City. Price's troops immediately commenced foraging in an effort to systematically "destroy and confiscate" as much of the Kansas residents' property as possible. They burned haystacks, crops and barns and took household goods and clothing as well. But with Federal troops and militia on his heels, Price was restricted to the area near the state line for his men to plunder.[114] On the morning of October 25 the pursuing Federals caught Price's retreating horde at Trading Post, Kansas.

The vanguard of the Federal advance struck the rebel bivouac at Trading Post at first light on the 25th. Confederate units were posted on two mounds just north of the hamlet, but after a brief skirmish Price's troops withdrew southward. Price himself was farther south planning to capture the Federal post at Fort Scott, Kansas.

Later that morning, Price's wagon trains were stalled at a crossing of Mine Creek a few miles east of Mound City, Kansas. Two brigades from Major General Alfred Pleasonton's cavalry division arrived on the scene around mid-day. Lieutenant Colonel Frederick Benteen (best remembered for his part in Custer's debacle at the Little Bighorn) led one of the brigades composed of Iowa, Indiana and Missouri volunteer cavalry regiments. About 6,000 to 7,000 Confederates with eight guns faced perhaps 2,500 troopers in the two Federal cavalry brigades on the prairie north of the creek.

Although heavily outnumbered, the two Federal cavalry brigades charged the Confederate line, routed it and captured all of its artillery. Both sides fought on horseback, but Benteen's troopers had sabers, carbines and pistols while most of the rebels were armed as mounted infantry. Some of the Federals were armed with Henry rifles and others with Spencer repeaters, so the Federal cavalrymen held an edge in firepower. Remarkably, the fighting was over in as little as thirty minutes. The Confederates were swept from the field with apparent ease in what became known as the Battle of Mine Creek. Confederate generals William "Old Tige" Cabell and John S. Marmaduke were captured at Mine Creek along with at least 557 officers and men. Some 300 or more Confederates were killed and another 237 wounded as well. Federal casualties at Mine Creek numbered fifteen killed, 106 wounded and three missing.[115]

The Confederate defeat at Mine Creek is included in this study for two reasons. First, both sides fought the battle mounted, making this one of the largest cavalry battles of the war and perhaps the largest single cavalry charge of the war. Second, this battle provides yet another example of the failure of Southern arms while fighting on Northern soil. It was no mere coincidence that the Confederacy invariably was defeated when its troops ventured into Union states.

The pursuing Federals again clashed with Price's retreating columns on October 25

The main crossing over Mine Creek on the Fort Scott Road, Mine Creek Battlefield.

along the Little Osage River about eight miles south of Mine Creek and at a crossing of the Marmaton River a few miles east of Fort Scott. Price managed to continue his retreat into Missouri. When his troops stopped for a rest at Newtonia, Missouri, on October 28, Federal Major General James Blunt attacked with a smaller cavalry force. Confederate Brigadier General Joseph Shelby resisted with his division and troops from Major General James Fagan's division south of town. When Federal reinforcements arrived from Fort Scott, Shelby withdrew under the cover of darkness. Price was followed to the Arkansas River before the Federals gave up the chase. With his army disintegrating from desertion and sickness, Price crossed the Indian Territory into Texas. His incursion into Missouri had been unpleasant for Unionists in Missouri and Kansas, but it was a strategic failure. By the middle of December in Texas, Price had less than a third of the number of men remaining that had marched with him into Missouri in September.

The U.S. national election was drawing near at the end of October, so General Meade thought it was time for one final effort to cut the Southside Railroad at Petersburg, which would benefit Lincoln's election campaign. On October 27, Meade sent out three infantry corps and a cavalry force to the Boydton Plank Road near Hatcher's Run with the hope of getting the Federal II Corps past the Confederate works and onto the Southside Railroad. To prevent General Lee from concentrating his forces against this operation, Grant ordered a diversion by the Army of the James north of the James River in Henrico County. Although Meade sent out a powerful force for this operation, weather, terrain and the usual leadership deficiencies plaguing Meade's army combined to render an overall stalemate from the fighting along the Boydton Plank Road. The diversion north of the

James River, also on the 27th, was carried out by units from the XVIII and X Corps. The XVII Corps suffered heavy casualties needlessly despite the fact that its assignment was intended to simply distract the enemy. These operations on the 27th conformed to the ongoing foundering of the Army of the Potomac during the siege of Petersburg. Nearly all of Grant's offensive operations around Petersburg and north of the James ended much like the debacle at the Crater on July 30, 1864. The Federals got the worst of it and usually suffered much heavier casualties than the defending Confederates. Indifferent leadership played a significant role in the string of Federal setbacks during the siege of Petersburg. Better planning, coordination, staff work and corps-level leadership might well have rendered a different outcome in several of the operations and battles around Petersburg and Richmond in 1864.

After the fall of Atlanta, Grant and Sherman considered the next assignment for Sherman's army in Georgia. Sherman favored a march through Georgia to the Atlantic Coast. On September 20, Sherman sent a lengthy missive to General Grant that closed with the following observations: "The possession of the Savannah River is more than fatal to the possibility of Southern independence; they may stand the fall of Richmond, but not of all of Georgia.... If you can whip Lee and I can march to the Atlantic I think Uncle Abe will give us twenty days' leave of absence to see the young folks." By November Hood was on his path to Nashville, and Sherman had sent General George Thomas and reinforcements to Tennessee in order to deal with Hood. On November 1, Sherman sent a message to Grant informing him, "...I will destroy all the railroads of Georgia and do as much substantial damage as possible, reaching the sea-coast near one of the points hitherto indicated, trusting that General Thomas ... will be able in a very few days to assume the offensive." Grant replied on the following morning, "I say, then, go as you propose."[116] So by the first week of November, Sherman's scheme to impress upon the South that the war was lost, by operating at will deep in Confederate territory, was approved and about to be implemented.

There were many options and possibilities for the use of Federal armies in the West after the capture of Atlanta. Sherman's plan seemed risky at the time, but Sherman did not foresee much of a threat from Hood or any force the Confederates could send against him on his march to the sea. In the end, Sherman's march dovetailed with the operations that brought victory over the Confederacy the following spring. Here again, Federal strategy proved far superior to that of the Confederacy. Professor of Strategy Donald Stoker observed that "Strategic thinking in the South was almost nonexistent." On the other hand, he suggested that Sherman's plan "was strategy at its grandest."[117] Sherman's plan delivered a strike at the Southerner's will to carry on the war; his march through Georgia proved that the Confederacy could not protect the slave owner's property. Thus, the whole reason for succession was rendered void. Southern leadership failed to discern a means of destroying the North's will to continue the fight; this was demonstrated in the national election of 1864. The South, despite the belief in its martial superiority, had been proven incapable of protecting its own territory. The inferiority of Southern military strategy was fully on display in the fall of 1864.

For all intents and purposes, the outcome of the Civil War was decided on November 8, 1864, Election Day. Abraham Lincoln won that day by carrying all the loyal states with the exception of Delaware, Kentucky and New Jersey. The popular vote was closer, with General George McClellan getting around forty-five percent of the total. Unfortunately for the country, the rebel leadership was unwilling to face reality. The war would continue until the Confederacy was militarily crushed.

On November 14, 1864, Sherman turned his back on Hood's army and marched his 60,000 men out of Atlanta on his journey to the sea. Although Sherman had needed to convince Grant and the president of the merits of this operation, it proved one of the best strategic moves of the entire war. Sherman demonstrated that the Confederacy was incapable of preventing a Northern army from doing whatever it pleased. His army, as it moved through the Deep South, confiscated property at will. Henceforth it was clear that slavery could not be maintained anywhere in the South. The Southern motivation for the war, slavery, was effectively finished; Southern morale could now only decline.

As Sherman's army foraged its way across Georgia, creating a swath of devastation and all the while embarrassing the Confederate Government, Hood embarked on his forlorn and quixotic errand in Tennessee. Sherman had sent the IV and XXXIII Corps from Atlanta to reinforce General Thomas in the defense of Tennessee. These two corps, commanded by Major General John Schofield, were camping at Pulaski, Tennessee, as Hood moved into that state. As his first initiative, Hood planned to trap and destroy the two Federal corps south of the Duck River. Hood's invading army outnumbered Schofield's by perhaps 10,000 men, or about a third. Hood needed to seize Columbia, Tennessee, in order to block Schofield's route to Nashville and prevent his juncture with the Thomas' force there. Unfortunately for the Confederates, Hood had wasted time in Alabama before crossing into Tennessee. The delay gave Thomas time to consolidate his army at Nashville; thus, it was essential for Hood to destroy Schofield's command first and then move against Nashville.

Schofield unwisely remained at Pulaski until Hood's army had managed to march to a location nearly equidistant from Columbia. On November 22, Schofield broke camp at Pulaski and started for Nashville, knowing that Hood could possibly cut off his escape route via the Columbia Turnpike any day. The Federals barely reached Columbia before Hood's army arrived there and then entrenched south of town. On the night of November 27, Schofield retreated across the Duck River and destroyed the two bridges at Columbia. Hood sent most of his army ahead in an attempt to block the turnpike twelve miles north of Columbia at Spring Hill. Hood arranged a diversion to hold Schofield at Columbia while the bulk of his army got into position at Spring Hill. By November 29, Hood had every reason to believe that his plan to crush Schofield's two corps would soon be in play.

Things did not play out at Spring Hill as Hood anticipated. Schofield's Federals managed to reach and hold the crossroads at Spring Hill and then slip away under the cover of darkness to Franklin, eight miles farther north. What happened to frustrate Hood's plan was never adequately defined. An obvious breakdown of execution on the part of Hood's senior officers enabled Schofield to reach Franklin without fighting a breakout battle. Perhaps Hood's subordinates were insouciant in their approach to their assignments. Perhaps they were simply inefficient. Whatever the case, Hood and his generals fumbled an excellent opportunity to trap and probably crush Schofield's column at Spring Hill, Tennessee, on November 29. Hood's campaign in Tennessee demonstrated that Confederate forces were not immune to the sort of inefficiency that plagued the Federal Army of the Potomac during the Overland Campaign and the siege of Petersburg.

Schofield decided to make a stand at Franklin. He had requested a pontoon bridge from General Thomas at Nashville for a crossing over the Harpeth River at Franklin because the bridges were out there. The pontoon bridge had not arrived when Schofield reached Franklin, so Schofield, believing he would be unable to cross his wagon train over the Harpeth, put his troops to work constructing fieldworks on the southern edge of the town. With their backs to the river, the Federals could not afford a breach in their hastily-built fieldworks.

Hood, angry with his subordinates because the Federals had escaped from Spring Hill the previous day, found Schofield's troops stationary at last at Franklin on the afternoon of November 30. Hood was determined to attack, and he ordered his generals to attack without waiting for one of his corps to arrive from its assignment at Columbia. The strength of the opposing armies at Franklin was consequently about equal when Hood ordered an attack. The Federals had only hours to construct their fieldworks at Franklin, and the Harpeth River was blocking their retreat route. If the Confederates could punch through the Federal defenses at Franklin, most of Schofield's army would likely be destroyed. Hood had made the decisive attack on the Federal position at Gaines's Mill in 1862. That battle had made a hero of Hood, and he must have expected a similar result on November 30 at Franklin, Tennessee.

The Confederate attack at Franklin actually stood a very small chance of success. Assaults against earthworks and fortresses were routinely expected to require at least a two-to-one manpower advantage. Hood had roughly the same strength on hand as the Federals, and he lacked most of his artillery which was yet to arrive from Columbia. Hood's decision to attack at Franklin went unsupported by his key subordinates, and from hindsight his decision to attack was unreasonable. The outcome was another disproportionate beating for Hood's army.

A glaring mistake by a Federal division commander, nevertheless, handed the Confederates an opportunity to smash through the Federal center that day. Brigadier General George D. Wagner, an Indiana farmer and politician, posted two of his brigades about a quarter mile in front of the main Federal defensive line along the turnpike south of Franklin. Wagner was expected to withdraw when the Confederates approached in force. Instead, he ordered his men to hold in place when the Confederate main attack was launched near sunset on the 30th. Wagner's line was soon outflanked, and his troops were forced to run for the main Federal line or be overwhelmed. Wagner's fleeing troops prevented the Federal defenders from firing for fear of hitting their own men, so Hood's Confederates pursued them right into the Federal perimeter without taking heavy incoming fire. Part of a Federal regiment covering the perimeter at the turnpike gave way, and for a time it looked like Schofield's Federals were in danger of being crushed.

Schofield, however, was fortunate in that Colonel Emerson Opdycke's brigade was in position as a reserve directly behind the area where the Federal perimeter was endangered. Opdycke's seven regiments rushed into the breach along the turnpike, "carrying many stragglers back with them." According to Opdycke, the Confederates were "met this side of Carter's house by our charge, and at once put to rout with a loss of 394 prisoners, 19 of whom were officers, 1 a colonel, and 9 battle-flags." Hood's attacking formation was somewhat thin without a reserve available to exploit a breakthrough. After the Federals closed the breach along the turnpike, Hood's attacking force simply suffered heavy casualties in front of the Federal breastworks without accomplishing anything significant; nevertheless, Hood continued the attacks until well after dark.

Schofield reported losses of 189 killed, 1,033 wounded and 1,104 missing. The general observed "that more than half" of his losses "occurred in General Wagner's division of the Fourth Corps, which did not form part of the main line of defense." In other words, Federal casualties would have been considerably lighter if Wagner had moved into the main defensive line, as he should have, before being overwhelmed by the Confederate

This office on the Carter place at the Franklin Battlefield was riddled with bullets on all sides. A large bullet exit hole stands out above the windows on the door.

Monuments for the Confederate generals killed at Franklin were placed on a hill overlooking the battlefield. In the foreground stands Major General Patrick Cleburne's marker.

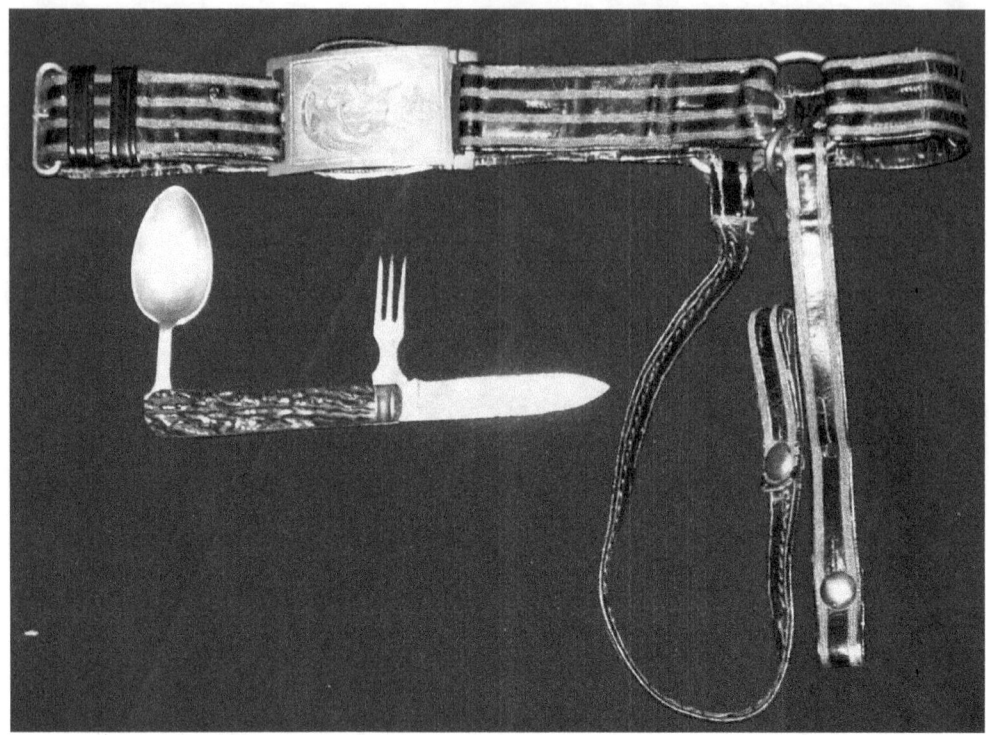

This sword belt and folding utensil belonged to General Cleburne. Cleburne was wearing this sword belt when he was killed.

attack. Hood's casualties probably totaled over 7,000, and six Confederate generals were killed or mortally wounded at Franklin, including the redoubtable Major General Patrick Cleburne. Information obtained after the battle documented 1,750 Confederate burials on the field at Franklin.

Schofield withdrew from Franklin, abandoning his wounded, under the cover of night and reached Nashville early on the morning of December 1. "I could not even rely upon getting up the ammunition necessary for another battle," Schofield explained. He believed that remaining at Franklin would "seriously hazard" the loss of his army.[118] Schofield's decision to retreat might not have been as necessary as he believed, but his management of the battle at Franklin was far superior to Hood's. Hood had practically crippled his army with unwise assaults against the strong Federal defenses at Franklin. Hood's tactics, even at this distance and time, seem rash, and his attacks were poorly executed. Essentially, Franklin was merely a continuation of the failed tactics Hood had employed during the Atlanta Campaign. Hood's methods served to speed the Confederacy on its progression to defeat.

Hood followed with his army to Nashville on the heels of Schofield, reaching Nashville's southern outskirts on the evening of December 1. He quickly established a defensive perimeter of fieldworks constructed in the hills below the city. Despite the worn, torn and frayed condition of his army and the fact that he was outnumbered, Hood hoped that Thomas would attack him and provide an opportunity for him to counterattack. In fairness to Hood, he had seen, first hand, General Lee win battles in Virginia against long odds.

The burial place for Confederates killed at Franklin, Tennessee. The bodies of the five slain Confederate generals were said to have been carried to the porch of the Carnton House visible in the background.

General Sherman, meanwhile, had marched his army across Georgia without a serious challenge. In fact, Sherman informed Grant that in all of his march through Georgia he had not been forced to "use anything but a skirmish line." By December 10, Sherman's host of over 60,000 had reached Savannah, Georgia. Sherman was faced with a difficult challenge in capturing the city, and he needed forage for his army's horses. The Confederates held the east bank of the Savannah River strongly enough to prevent Federal supply via that watercourse from the Navy on the coast. The Ogeechee River emptied into the Atlantic Ocean not far from Savannah, but Confederate Fort McAllister blocked access to the river from the sea. Fortunately for Sherman, the Confederates did not have sufficient manpower to defend both the city of Savannah and Fort McAllister. On December 13, Sherman sent Brigadier General William Hazen and his division against Fort McAllister. Hazen managed to capture the fort with an assault that lasted about fifteen minutes. With Fort McAllister captured, Sherman had access to supplies from the Navy which enabled him to besiege Savannah. His march to the sea had proved a compete success.

Events in December of 1864 compelled General in Chief Grant to make some momentous decisions that likely determined the duration of the war. At Nashville, Major General George Thomas was frustrating Grant by resisting Grant's instructions to immediately attack Hood before he could fortify. In Georgia, Sherman planned to besiege Savannah and then commence a campaign in the Carolinas. He expected to capture Savannah then "instantly to march to Columbia, S.C., thence to Raleigh," and then to join Grant in Virginia. Grant wanted Sherman to move his army by sea to reinforce the Federal forces operating against Petersburg and Richmond; he believed that defeating Lee was the most important task remaining to close out the war. On December 6, Grant sent a letter to Sherman mentioning that he had said all he could to force

Thomas to attack at Nashville. "Today, however," he wrote, "I could stand it no longer, and gave the order without any reserve." Still Thomas delayed. Grant then decided to replace Thomas with Major General John Logan, but the situation in Nashville played out before the change could be transacted. Sherman, making a case for his plan to campaign into the Carolinas, sent a message to General Halleck on December 13 with the following assessments: "The whole army is crazy to be turned loose in Carolina; and with the experience of the past thirty days I judge that a month's sojourn in South Carolina would make her less bellicose.... We have utterly destroyed over 200 miles of railroads, and consumed stores and provisions that were essential for Lee's and Hood's armies. A similar destruction of roads and resources hence to Raleigh would compel Lee to come out of his intrenched camp."[119] Grant was soon in agreement with Sherman and allowed the campaign into the Carolinas to proceed. Sherman, a better strategist than a tactician, had identified the more effective and rapid means of ending the war. His operations from Savannah onward virtually guaranteed a Federal victory and accelerated the Confederacy's collapse. Grant deserves credit for recognizing the merit of Sherman's plan and for adopting it. Davis and the Confederate high command, conversely, had helped enable Sherman's success by allowing Hood to proceed with his misadventure in Tennessee.

Hoping for reinforcements to augment his force at Nashville, Hood waited for Thomas to attack him rather than abandoning his forlorn mission in Tennessee. His army would have been of better use against Sherman in Georgia. Impatient for favorable results, he sent General Forrest with most of his cavalry and an infantry division southeast to strike Murfreesboro on December 2. This highly questionable initiative weakened his ability to resist the anticipated attack by Thomas and deprived Hood of much of his cavalry. Forrest declined to attack the large Federal camp at Murfreesboro, called Fortress Rosecrans, which was occupied a force larger than his own. On December 7, Major General Robert Milroy (who had been driven out of Winchester, Virginia, during the Gettysburg Campaign) sallied forth and drove Forrest's cavalry from the field. Forrest then prowled around Murfreesboro destroying railroad tracks for days after the battle but accomplishing little else. He would not make it back in time to be of any assistance to Hood at Nashville.

Major General George Thomas was under intense pressure to get his attack against Hood under way. General Grant was so anxious about the situation in Nashville that he decided to travel to Nashville himself. With Schofield's force and the Federal XVI Corps under Major General A.J. Smith on hand by December 1, Thomas fielded a force over twice the size of his adversary. Thomas intended to launch his attack on December 10, but a winter storm blanketed the region with a thick coating of ice on the 9th. This necessitated a further delay.

To his credit, Thomas devised a solid battle plan and attacked soon after the ice thawed in the hills south of Nashville. His battle plan called for a feint against the Confederate right to prevent Hood from shifting troops while the main attack was ongoing against the more vulnerable Confederate left flank. The Federal movement into attack position began at 4 a.m. on December 15, but heavy fog delayed the main attack until around 9 o'clock. By evening Hood's army had been driven back about two miles to a shortened second defensive line stretching between Shy's Hill near the Granny White Pike and Overton Hill on the Franklin Pike. Despite being driven into this compacted line, Hood stood his ground on the night of December 15. From hindsight it seems evident that he should have realized that his hope of counterattacking was lost; retreat was his best option.

Thomas repeated his tactics on December 16 with the main attack this time going against Shy's Hill on the Confederate left. A Federal artillery bombardment in the morning preceded a strong attack on Overton Hill. Hood's lines held during the morning, partially because Schofield failed to mount a serious attack against Shy's Hill until near dusk. Federal cavalry overlapped Hood's line on his extreme left and rear, and when Thomas finally ordered an assault on Shy's Hill the Confederate line gave way from left to right. The tardy attack coming from Schofield's command responsibility on the Federal right commenced too late to effectively destroy Hood's army. The Confederates managed to retreat after nightfall to Franklin and southward from there in the days following the battle.

Nashville was one of the worst defeats suffered by Confederate arms during the course of the war. It effectively took Hood's army out of the war and certified Federal control in the region. The Confederates estimated their casualties at 6,400 with thousands captured. Federal casualties were officially reported as 387 killed, 2,562 wounded and 112 missing for a total of 3,061.[120]

Hood, with the advantage of terrain, redoubts and earthworks, actually stood a reasonable chance of repulsing the Federals at Nashville. General Lee had repeatedly repulsed the Army of the Potomac at Spotsylvania, Cold Harbor and at Petersburg by relying on fieldworks to offset numbers. Hood had actually lost the battle on December 15 when his army was driven out of its original line of fortifications. He should have withdrawn after the first day of fighting. The Confederate defensive line on day two at Shy's Hill was faulty and thus vulnerable to attack. A lack of an available reserve on hand to close a breach and the lack of Forrest's cavalry were two important factors that also contributed to Hood's defeat on the 16th. The performance of Hood's army suggests that troop morale had been adversely affected by repeated defeats and a growing sense of despair. These factors in combination were enough to practically ensure a Confederate defeat. General Hood also did not benefit from luck or error on the part of his adversary at Nashville, as General Lee often did.

Savannah, Georgia, was evacuated on December 20, 1864, without forcing the Federals to fight for it. Lieutenant General William Hardee withdrew his troops from the city under the cover of darkness, unwilling to hazard the loss of the city's defenders who were desperately needed in the effort to oppose Sherman's forthcoming advance into South Carolina. Sherman sent a single sentence to President Lincoln on December 22: "I beg to present to you, as a Christmas gift, the city of Savannah, with 150 heavy guns and plenty of ammunition, and also about 25,000 bales of cotton."[121] Of course General Grant, Lincoln, and the Administration all wished that Sherman had also captured Hardee's defenders rather than having them escape. A siege of Savannah, however, would probably not have been worth its cost in lives and time. Thus, the capture of Savannah simply added another laurel to the list of Sherman's accomplishments without damaging the Confederacy to the fullest possible extent.

The Confederacy in December was, succinctly, falling apart. Confederate soldiers were deserting daily from units throughout the South and especially around Petersburg. Sherman was ready to march across South Carolina, and Major General Benjamin Butler was attempting to capture Fort Fisher on the North Carolina coast in order to close access to Wilmington, the Confederacy's last port still open to blockade runners. As is the case in many wars, the defeated refused to accept the obvious. The war would continue needlessly for months after the Federals were effectively eliminating the reasons for continued resistance. Wherever Federal soldiers were present the slaves were able to escape bondage, so the primary reason for Southern secession was being daily rendered void in many regions of the South. Henceforth, the South would never be able to retain the antebellum slave system. By December of 1864, the main motivation for the war had been swept aside. Morale no longer favored the rebels; the long lists of deserters confirmed this.

Despite the pervasive trend of success by Northern arms late in 1864, Major General Benjamin Butler (the senior volunteer major general in the Union army) had one more fiasco to administer before the year was over. On December 18, Butler set sail on a mission to capture Fort Fisher at the mouth of the Cape Fear River. It was an important mission for the purpose of isolating Wilmington, North Carolina, a real political plum for someone like Butler.

Apparently Butler concocted a scheme to pack an old steamer with explosives and then send it on a course for the fort where it would function as an enormous torpedo and blow up the fort. The steamer blew up at about 2 a.m. on the 24th without doing any damage to anything except itself. On Christmas Day, Butler landed his troops near the fort under the cover of naval gunfire support from sixty ships. Butler's troops then captured some rebels. They told him that Confederate reinforcements were on the way, and Butler started to worry. From General Grant's perspective, "Butler made a fearful mistake." Butler decided to forfeit the mission and return to the fleet, contrary to orders. Grant had instructed that any landing "would be of itself a great victory, and if one should be effected, the foothold must not be relinquished." Nevertheless, Butler's force re-embarked on the transports and arrived at Fortress Monroe on the 28th. Grant wired the president on that day with the following report: "The Wilmington expedition has proven a gross and culpable failure.... After the expedition sailed from Fort Monroe, three days of fine weather were squandered, during which the enemy was without a force to protect himself."[122] Grant fully realized that the mission had failed entirely as a result of the man in charge. Another commander would be selected, Butler would finally be shelved, and the fort would soon be captured. Fortunately for the Union, the days of tolerating inept leadership were closing out with the year 1864.

The United States accomplished in 1864 what could have been managed in 1862. In late December of 1864, the Confederacy was on the verge of collapse. The first half of the year had been rife with failures and heavy losses for the Federals that could have been avoided with better management. The same could be said of 1862 when poor decisions by President Lincoln and indecisive leadership from the Federal high command foiled a real possibility of defeating the Confederacy within months. Grant's Overland Campaign in 1864 has historically been viewed as wantonly wasteful of lives. Very true, although political pressure forced the unwise and ill-starred campaign on Grant, and indifferent corps-level leadership contributed greatly to its sanguinary outcome. The Union's penchant for appointing incompetent politically-connected generals also contributed significantly to prolonging the war and increasing Federal battle casualties. Benjamin Butler's farce at Bermuda Hundred is a prime example of the cost of prioritizing politics over military competence. Confederate military performance during 1864 under General Lee's direction was superior, though not quite flawless. General Johnston generalship during the Atlanta Campaign has historically been viewed with less admiration when compared to Lee in Virginia. Johnston, however, certainly did a credible job in Georgia, perhaps on par with Lee. But the outstanding feats of generalship by Lee and others could not compensate for the inadequate strategic planning of the Confederate high command. Grant and the Federal high command found and implemented a winning strategy in 1864; superior Federal strategy, more than any other circumstance or factor, provided the decisive advantage that led to a Federal victory in the Civil War. In 1864, the strategic combination of offensives on multiple fronts, blockading, raiding, Sherman's incursion in Georgia, and constant military pressure applied against the Confederate capital had finally produced the conditions that General Scott had anticipated with his Anaconda Plan in 1861.

The war's outcome was apparent in December of 1864 when Sherman occupied Savannah and prepared to march into South Carolina. Historically South Carolina had been preoccupied with secession, but now that state and the alliance it had spawned could not prevent an impending Federal occupation. Nevertheless, the Confederate high command would persist in its strategy of concentration, hoping for a long-shot victory over one Federal army at a time. The war would continue in the months ahead until the Federals would achieve the supremely difficult task of annihilating an entire enemy army. Only then would the war conclude.

8

1865

The Confederacy Collapses

Winter, with its accompanying ice, snow and mud in Virginia, was delaying the final blow against Richmond as the New Year arrived in 1865. Sherman's army, being farther south, managed to resume its progress into South Carolina despite the rain and mud there. With the Yankee presence now practically ubiquitous, the Southern people knew their experiment with secession was about to end. Clifford Dowdey in his study of the Confederacy observed that money, "that bloodless barometer of the people's spirits, showed the effect." The Confederate dollar in 1861 had been nearly equivalent to a gold dollar, but by the beginning of 1865 it required $60 in Confederate money in exchange for one gold dollar. Inflation was creating havoc. After Lincoln's election in November, Confederate currency commenced a steep decline, "and the bottom had dropped out by the first of the year."[1] Despondency had replaced the South's overconfidence and its advantage in motivation and morale; each day fewer men would answer the call to duty. Lincoln and his generals waited only the inevitably forthcoming conditions to end the war, as attrition had by then taken its toll.

The ongoing effort to secure the port of Wilmington had not been hampered by winter weather. Instead, it had been hampered by General Butler's fecklessness. Grant quickly arranged a replacement for Butler, the newly-promoted Major General Alfred Terry, and on January 6 another expedition sailed from Fortress Monroe for another joint operation with the Navy against Fort Fisher. The fort on the Cape Fear River passage to Wilmington became a priority for Grant and the Federal high command. Capturing Wilmington would close the last Confederate seaport. Nearly as important, Wilmington could function as a supply depot for Sherman's army as it moved through the Carolinas. The risky operation against Fort Fisher dovetailed with the overall Federal strategy implemented in 1864, and Grant deemed it worthy of its cost.

Fort Fisher fell to a combined attack by sailors, marines and army troops on January 15. Precise Naval gunfire support played a crucial role in assisting the Federal infantry by pummeling successive gun emplacements within the fort. Galusha Pennypacker, a twenty-year-old Pennsylvanian, emerged as the hero of Fort Fisher; he was promoted to brigadier general after the battle, which made him the youngest general officer ever appointed in the U.S. Army. The fort should have been easier to capture when General Butler attempted the feat in December. Its capture by General Terry less than a month later demonstrates the difference of competent leadership in determining the outcome of battles.

On January 19, 1865, General Robert E. Lee accepted the position of commander

8. 1865: The Confederacy Collapses

Trophy Point at West Point has many captured artillery pieces on display. This 150 pounder Armstrong cannon was captured at Fort Fisher.

in chief of all Confederate armies. That same day General Sherman issued orders for his advance into South Carolina. Heavy winter rains would trouble Sherman's army more than any strategic initiatives or directives coming from General Lee. Lee suggested to President Davis that the best impediment to Sherman's advance would be "the want of supplies." He ordered General Beauregard to "destroy or remove all provisions in his (Sherman's) route," and he noted that the Confederate armies would have to be concentrated to oppose Sherman.[2] Sherman, nevertheless, would find his trip through South Carolina more difficult than his famous March to the Sea in Georgia.

Grant knew that time was running out for the Confederate's hold on Richmond and Petersburg, but he nevertheless decided to attempt to cut Lee's supply line southwest of Petersburg on the Boydton Plank Road despite the potential cost of another severe battle. Grant later explained that he feared that Lee and his army would escape from its trap at Petersburg. "I knew he could move much more lightly and rapidly than I," he wrote, "and that, if he got the start, he would leave me behind so that we would have the same army to fight again farther south—and the war might be prolonged another year."[3] Hoping to keep Lee occupied, Grant sent out a cavalry division to Dinwiddie Court House on February 5 to disrupt Lee's supply route via the Boydton Plank Road. Major General George Meade sent out infantry support from the V Corps towards Dinwiddie, and two divisions from the II Corps were sent to the Hatcher's Run vicinity as additional support to prevent Lee from isolating the cavalry and V Corps.

Lee, seeing the Federal movements as a threat to the Southside Railroad, sent out troops in response. The Federals concentrated around Hatcher's Run for safety, and a battle erupted in the icy woods along the stream. Each side attacked and counterattacked without a significant result. By February 7, the fighting had fizzled out. Lee was forced to lengthen his defensive line to protect the Southside Railroad, but he had managed to hold the Boydton Plank Road supply route. As usual during the siege of Petersburg, the Federals suffered heavier casualties without accomplishing their objective.

In January and February, Sherman's army marched through South Carolina against light opposition. On February 17, Columbia, the state capital, surrendered to the Federals. The seemingly impregnable city of Charleston, the hotbed of secession, was evacuated on February 17; and the vital port of Wilmington was evacuated on February 21. Cities nearly as important to Southern morale as Richmond were falling like dominoes. Joseph Johnston, who was reappointed to command of all forces opposing Sherman, accepted that assignment on February 23, despite the fact that he believed it was too late to make a difference. General Lee placed a priority on saving the Confederate armies rather than challenging the Federals with battles over cities and territory. Lee suggested to President Davis that the "greatest calamity that could befall us is the destruction of our armies. If they can be maintained, we may recover from our reverses; but if lost we have no resource." Lee had few options remaining. He informed Davis that if Johnston could not halt Sherman south of the Roanoke River he would "unite with him in a blow against Sherman before the latter can join General Grant." He continued by informing Davis that such a move would "necessitate the abandonment of our position on the James River, for which contingency every preparation should be made."[4] The Confederate high command could not conceive any new strategic response to the steady wave of Federal successes. Lee was resorting to the same strategy employed by the Confederacy since the outbreak of war: he would concentrate his forces in an attempt to win a battle. The real difference being that now, with no other recourse, Lee was willing to give up territory, even Richmond, in exchange for a long-shot chance of defeating a Federal army.

While General Sherman's army was moving through the Carolinas, Major General Philip Sheridan chased the last significant Confederate force out of the Shenandoah Valley. Sheridan rode out of Winchester on February 27 with two cavalry divisions numbering about 10,000 in total to go against the 1,700 Confederates remaining in the Valley under General Jubal Early. After a skirmish at Mount Crawford, Early's band assembled and entrenched at Waynesboro near the Rockfish Gap exit from the Valley. Jubal Early attempted to make a stand there with his vastly outnumbered force on March 2 to "secure the removal of five pieces of artillery for which there were no horses" and to determine the object of Sheridan's advance up the Valley. Brigadier General George Armstrong Custer led an attack that dashed Early's small command to pieces, capturing nearly all of the Confederates with the exception of Early and his staff who escaped by riding "aside into the woods, and in that way escaped capture." Early once again had underestimated the Federals and again paid for his mistake at Waynesboro.

General Grant had ordered Sheridan in February to move on to Lynchburg to destroy the railroads there and then proceed southward to join Sherman in the Carolinas. Instead, Sheridan followed his own whim. He rode to the Richmond vicinity to rejoin the Army of the Potomac, expecting to "take part in the final struggle of the war." Sheridan wanted to be "in at the death" of the Confederacy rather than helping Sherman destroy Johnston's army in the Carolinas. As events played out, Sheridan ultimately was able to have a more decisive role in the final days of the war by "interpreting Grant's orders liberally."⁵ This sort of loose discipline is another example of the sort of command faults that plagued the Army of the Potomac throughout the course of the war.

Sherman's divided army continued its march into North Carolina, fighting at Wyse Fork, Monroe's Cross Roads and Averasboro, North Carolina, in March. On March 18, Johnston finally got his opportunity to attack Sherman's force on fairly equal terms. One wing of the Sherman's army was advanced perhaps a day's march beyond the other column when Johnston decided to give battle.

On March 19, Johnston held the advantage and could have probably defeated the advanced Federal column that day except for a delay in attacking. Federal reinforcements continued to stream in, and by the 20th the Federals greatly outnumbered Johnston's force in fighting that came to be known as the Battle of Bentonville. Major General Joseph Mower advanced against Johnston's left flank without orders on March 21 and nearly cut off the Confederate retreat route. Sherman later regretted not sending Mower reinforcements because doing so probably would have enabled him to crush Johnston's army that day. Johnston retreated during the night and had vacated the battlefield by the morning of March 22. Johnston's army, being on the attack, suffered heavier casualties than the Federals. Both Sherman and Johnston erred on the side of caution and forfeited an opportunity for a significant victory at Bentonville.

While Sherman was seizing control of the Carolinas, General Lee was becoming convinced that his best course of action was to abandon Richmond and join Johnston against Sherman. Jefferson Davis and the Confederate Government, however, would not allow the Lee to abandon the capital. So Lee sought an opportunity to send at least part of his army south to reinforce Johnston. He concluded that an attack on a vulnerable section of the Federal defensive line at Petersburg would force Grant to contract his line thereby enabling Lee to hold his own lines with fewer soldiers.

Early in March, Lee assigned Major General John B. Gordon, who had replaced General Early in command of the Confederate II Corps, the task of finding a weak spot in Grant's lines where an attack could achieve a breakthrough. Gordon, particularly in later years, was quite critical of General Early's conduct of operations in the Valley, especially at Cedar Creek. After nearly three weeks of observation, study and deliberation, Gordon concocted a scheme to attack Union Fort Stedman which stood across from and within easy rifle range of Colquitt's Salient on the Confederate defensive line around Petersburg. Gordon's plan called for a complicated pre-dawn attack which required coordination, surprise and abundant luck. Gordon asserted that Early would have won at Cedar Creek if he had only pressed the attack during the afternoon phase of that battle. Now he apparently believed that he could lead an attack that would capture Fort Stedman and crush an entire wing of Grant's army. Gordon convinced Lee that his plan could achieve Lee's objectives or even more, and Lee approved it. Lee provided Gordon with nearly half of the Confederate force protecting Petersburg and offered to commit even more men. Gordon then had his opportunity to demonstrate what he could accomplish by simply attacking the Yankees, as he had urged upon Early at Cedar Creek.

Gordon's attack commenced at 4 a.m. on March 25 in the pre-dawn darkness. Gordon had fifty axmen assigned to chop through the Federal abatis and defensive obstructions in front of the fort. With his II Corps and other troops augmented by General Lee, Gordon had four and a half divisions with which to attack, it was to be an all-out effort. Initially the attack was successful, catching the Federal pickets by surprise. Gordon managed to capture Fort Stedman and move against nearby Fort Haskell. But soon the Federal forces in the trenches around Petersburg began to stir. By 8 a.m., Gordon's attack had been contained at Fort Stedman, and Lee ordered a withdrawal. The one aspect Gordon may have neglected to consider came into play. His troops would have to cross the open ground between Colquitt's Salient and Fort Steadman under fire in broad daylight to escape capture. Many of Gordon's men refused to run the gauntlet of fire and surrendered to the Federals, about 1,900 Confederates were taken prisoner. Perhaps as many as 1,600 Confederates were killed and wounded that day, making Gordon's losses around 3,500 compared to around 1,000 Federal casualties of which about half were captured.[6]

Gordon's attack at Fort Stedman, with the troops that had fought at Cedar Creek, was a failure. He had failed to accomplish more than Early achieved with his attack at Cedar Creek and had suffered disproportionate losses. The Confederate armies were simply not performing as well late in 1864 and in 1865 as they had performed in 1863. Gordon or Longstreet or Hill or even Jackson couldn't have altered the course of the war as it trended in 1865.

General Grant issued orders for the final movements that resulted in the capture of Petersburg and Richmond on March 24 while Gordon was preparing his attack on Fort Stedman. Other operations were being carried out in March throughout the Confederacy. At Mobile, Alabama, Major General Edward R.S. Canby was positioning a Federal force to attack Spanish Fort and Fort Blakely. Another operation against Selma, Alabama, was launched by Brigadier General James H. Wilson on March 22. Wilson would successfully ride through that state and defeat the Confederacy's best cavalry commander, Lieutenant General Nathan Bedford Forrest. An army in the West was preparing to operate against the Trans-Mississippi under Major General John Pope, who had been fighting Indians in the Northwest. The Confederacy was being crushed on practically every corner of the South.

On March 29, Grant put his plan into effect. It was intended to keep Lee contained at Petersburg so that he could not unite with Johnston farther south. Sheridan, having returned to the Petersburg front in disregard of orders, was sent with 9,000 cavalrymen southwest of Petersburg to Dinwiddie Court House. His objective was to seize the Five Forks crossroads with a view of outflanking Lee's trenches at Petersburg, thus sealing his escape route from Petersburg. Sheridan was to destroy the Southside and Danville Railroads after reaching Dinwiddie. Grant ordered massive troop movements to prepare for a final large-scale effort to capture Petersburg. The movements initiated on the 29th were basically a continuation, on a larger scale, of previous efforts to force Lee out of his Petersburg defenses by either closing his supply lines or outflanking his defensive lines.

At first, as always during the long Petersburg siege, kismet seemed to favor Lee and the Confederates. Rains had turned the roads into quagmires and the rain intensified as the hours passed, making everything more difficult for the Federals. Although Lee actually wanted to evacuate Petersburg and Richmond, he reacted to the Federal movement with traditional alacrity and determination. Initially, the activities of March 29 very much resembled the feckless Federal efforts to get at the Southside Railroad during the fall and winter. But this time things would be different. Grant was not simply making some limited offensive to keep chipping away at Lee. He intended to finish Lee at Petersburg before Lee could unite with Johnston's army or before Johnston could join Lee at Petersburg.

From March 29 to 31, there was fighting at Lewis's Farm and along White Oak Road near Hatcher's Run, an area that already had been churned by intense fighting in the previous months. At the same time, Sheridan was fighting at Dinwiddie Court House in an attempt to move against the vital crossroads at Five Forks. Lee had sent his cavalry and then Major General George Pickett with five infantry brigades to Five Forks to repulse Sheridan. Sheridan found himself in some trouble facing Pickett's combined force but managed to hold at Dinwiddie. Pickett, realizing that he was exposed and could be isolated at Dinwiddie, moved his force to a defensive line at and around the Five Forks vicinity by the morning of April 1.

To his credit, Major General Gouverneur K. Warren recognized that Pickett's sizable force at Five Forks was practically isolated from the rest of Lee's army and might be destroyed if he could combine his V Corps with Sheridan and attack Pickett's left flank. On the evening of March 31, Warren sent a message to headquarters. Warren suggested, "…let me move down and attack the enemy at Dinwiddie on one side and Sheridan on the other…. I think we have a chance for an open field fight that should be made use of." By 10:45 p.m., Grant had made up his mind to reinforce Sheridan as Warren had offered. Grant informed Sheridan, "The Fifth Corps has been ordered to your support…. You will assume command of the whole force sent to operate with you and use it to the best of your ability to destroy the force which your command has fought so gallantly to-day."[7]

Sheridan didn't want Warren cooperating in his efforts at Five Forks, and he asked for a different infantry corps to support him. The locations of the sundry Federal infantry corps dictated that Grant had to send the V Corps to Five Forks, so Grant sent a staff officer to Sheridan allowing him to remove Warren from command "if his removal was necessary to success."[8]

The Battle of Five Forks developed slowly on April 1. Warren's V Corps was shifted, and the troop movements wasted time. During the interim, Pickett and his chief lieutenants were far to the rear enjoying a shad-bake near Hatcher's Run. This fish-feast consumed much of the afternoon; the Confederate commanders were absent when the Warren's V Corps struck the Confederate left flank and overlapped it. The Confederates manning the Five Forks defensive line faced Sheridan's attack with no overall commander on the scene. By the time Pickett reached the scene of the fighting, the Federals were driving the rebels from their fieldworks. Pickett managed to make a final stand and escape from the Federals, but his troops were routed with more than 5,000 men captured along with six guns and thirteen battleflags.[9]

Warren had acted bravely on the battlefield and his corps had played the decisive role in the Federal victory at Five Forks; nevertheless, Warren had provoked Sheridan's doubt before the battle and his wrath during the fighting. With the battle already won, Sheridan ordered Warren to relinquish command of the V Corps to Brigadier General Charles Griffin, one of Warren's division commanders. Sheridan's motives for removing Warren were later fully explained by him, but some of Sheridan's contemporaries believed that he did not want to share the credit for the victory at Five Forks with Warren. Warren was finally cleared of any misconduct by a court of inquiry many years after the war, but he never achieved the rank and status he deserved for his service during the war. The one glaring question arising from the controversy is: Why did Sheridan wait until the battle was won and nearly over before removing Warren? He had authority to remove Warren at any point he believed was necessary. It seemed a bit disingenuous to assert that the change was essential after the outcome of the battle had already been decided.

Grant kept his plans progressing without any interruption or delay after the fighting southwest of Petersburg. Grant had positioned the XXIV, II, VI and IX Corps in preparation for a huge assault on Petersburg while the fighting was ongoing in Dinwiddie County.

The final assault on the Petersburg defenses, involving the four Federal corps mentioned in the previous paragraph, was scheduled to commence at 4 a.m. on April 2 following the greatest artillery bombardment of the siege. It was about 4:40 a.m. before the Federal VI Corps went forward in a huge wedge-shaped formation that punched through A.P. Hill's Confederate III Corps defenses along the Boydton Plank Road about a mile northeast of Hatcher's Run. The Federal IX Corps attacked a little behind schedule at 5 a.m., hitting Confederate Fort Mahone and General Gordon's II Corps defenses. Two divisions from the Federal XXIV Corps broke through the Confederate defenses at the east bank of Hatcher's Run at around 7 a.m.; the Federal II Corps attacked the Confederate line west of Hatcher's Run, pushing the defenders back to Sutherland Station on the Southside Railroad.

Lieutenant General A.P. Hill, commanding the Confederate III Corps, rode to Lee's headquarters at the Turnbull House before dawn to confer with Lee. During the meeting, Hill learned that the Federal VI Corps had broken through his lines, so he rushed out of the house to find and rally his command. Federal soldiers were by then scattered within Hill's perimeter. Hill tried to capture two soldiers from the 138th Pennsylvania Infantry with a drawn pistol; instead, Hill was shot and killed by one of the Pennsylvanians. Hill was one of only three Confederate corps commanders killed in battle during the war.[10]

As the Federal attackers forged ahead following their breakthrough, two rebel forts stood in their path to Petersburg's inner defensive line, Fort Gregg and Fort Whitworth. General James Longstreet had returned from convalescing, and he was sending his troops into Petersburg's last line of defense that morning. Longstreet's role required him to hold that defensive line long enough for the Confederates to evacuate Petersburg. He needed a few more hours to move his troops into position. A small hodgepodge collection of rebel units assumed the task of holding two divisions of victorious Federals at bay at these two earthen forts, approximately 334 men in Fort Gregg commanded by Lieutenant Colonel James Duncan and 200 more in Fort Whitworth led by Brigadier General Nathaniel Harris. The soldiers in these earthworks answered the call of duty for an impossible task. The scenario was not unlike the Texas Alamo; the defenders would fight with the same grim determination that characterized the Alamo and reap nearly the same outcome.

Perhaps as many as 4,400 Federal soldiers charged the walls of Fort Gregg on the afternoon of April 2. My great-grandfather Earley was struck in the side by an exploding shell that day, apparently while advancing on Fort Gregg. He was one of the lucky ones, not seriously wounded. Major General John Gibbon, the XXIV Corps commander, reported that 122 Federals were killed and 592 wounded, most of them while attacking the two forts. Of the 334 soldiers defending Fort Gregg, 300 were killed or wounded and thirty-three men surrendered who were not hit. One rebel escaped Fort Gregg. North Carolina Corporal James Atkinson made a heroic dash, under fire as the fort was being overrun, into the Confederate inner line with a battle flag. Gibbon, who had commanded the famed Iron Brigade during its glory days, succinctly described the fighting with the following statements: "The enemy made a most desperate resistance, and it was not until Fort Gregg was almost entirely surrounded and our brave men had succeeded in climbing upon the parapet under a most murderous fire, that the place was finally taken by the last of several determined dashes with the bayonet.... This assault, certainly one of the most desperate of the war, succeeded by the obstinate courage of our troops, but at a fearful cost." Fourteen Federal soldiers earned the Medal of Honor for valor at Fort Gregg. These men accompanied General Gibbon to Washington, D.C., the following month to present captured Confederate flags in a ceremony there.[11]

The valor demonstrated by both sides at Fort Gregg was truly remarkable, but, for the Federals at least, the cost was excessive and probably unnecessary. Grant thought that the forts had to be carried that afternoon. From this distance it seems obvious that the forts were isolated and should have been bypassed. That was the tactical approach favored by General Douglas MacArthur during his Pacific campaigns in World War II. Grant has been justifiably criticized for wasting the lives of far too many of his soldiers. Fort Gregg stands as yet another example of why he was considered a butcher by many in his day.

It might have come as somewhat of a surprise to the Federal high command to see how easily Petersburg fell during the operations from March 30 through April 2, 1865. The Confederate defenders crumbled in a most uncharacteristic manner, but Lee still managed to escape with his army mostly intact under the cover of night. Management of that retreat, however, did not meet usual standards or even requirements. The Confederate high command was aware for several weeks of a high probability that Richmond and Petersburg would be forced to capitulate or else would require evacuation. Nevertheless, once the retreat went into effect, Lee was unable to feed his army. The retreat from Petersburg and Richmond was not simply inefficient, it was nearly chaotic.

Conversely, the Federal pursuit of Lee's army was superb. Some of the most prodigious marching of the entire war, by either side, was accomplished by the Federal infantry, the XXIV and XXV Corps, which managed in get behind Lee's army, in particular. The Federal army in the East never performed better than it did during the Appomattox Campaign.

Lee's army was under constant pressure from April 2 through April 9 when it was surrendered. Before the surrender of the Army of Northern Virginia, it was forced into seven more sizable actions or battles: Namozine Church, Amelia Springs, Sailor's Creek, Rice's Station, High Bridge, Cumberland Church and Appomattox Station, Virginia. By far the most devastating of these fights to the dismayed Confederates was the Battle of Sailor's Creek on April 6, 1865.

The Confederate defeat at Sailor's Creek resulted from a lapse by Lee's generals that allowed his retreating army to be split into three diverging segments in the presence of the enemy. Pursuing Federal forces attacked the divided Confederate forces effectively enough to prevent them from cooperating or consolidating. The Federal II Corps attacked Lieutenant General John Gordon's Confederate II Corps, which was acting as a rear guard for Lee's entire army and train, at the Lockett Farm. Lieutenant General Richard Ewell's corps of garrison troops was attacked by the Federal VI Corps at the Hillsman Farm. Sheridan's Federal cavalry attacked Lieutenant General Richard Anderson's small force at the Harper Farm. In all three of these engagements, each of which were fought within a distance of less than a mile or so from the others, the Federals scored an overwhelming victory.

A large number of Medals of Honor were awarded to Federal soldiers for capturing Confederate flags at Sailor's Creek. Private Samuel Eddy of the 37th Massachusetts Infantry earned his Medal of Honor in a different way. The story of his role in the battle was particularly interesting and included a remarkable coincidence. As the fighting was waning on April 6, John Bradley, the adjutant of Eddy's regiment, stepped forward to accept the sword of a Confederate colonel whom Bradley thought was surrendering his men. Instead of giving up his sword, the colonel attacked Bradley with his pistol and shot him in the thigh. As the two men wrestled, Eddy stepped up and shot the colonel dead with his Spencer repeating rifle. At that moment another Confederate soldier bayoneted Eddy, pinning him to the ground with the blade through his chest. Eddy managed to chamber another round and shoot his assailant. He then shoved aside the rebel's body and yanked the bayonet out of his chest. Having saved Bradley's life, Eddy crossed the flooding Sailor's Creek and walked back to the field hospital at the Hillsman House. In a remarkable happenstance, over a century later Park Historian Chris Calkins found the location near the creek where Eddy was wounded. He found Spencer cartridge cases and found Private Eddy's lead identification disk attached to a brass neck chain. Apparently these artifacts had lain untouched in the battlefield soil and revealed the location where Eddy performed his acts of gallantry over 100 years later.

The Battle of Sailor's Creek, "actually three separate engagements fought generally in one location, proved to be the beginning of the end for Lee's army." When the fighting was over at Sailor's Creek, Lee had lost about a fourth of his army; it was the worst defeat to that point for the Army of Northern Virginia. Perhaps more than 7,700 Confederates were casualties. Eight Confederate generals were captured including Lieutenant General Richard Ewell, Major General Joseph Kershaw, and Major General George W.C. Lee, the eldest son of General Robert E. Lee. The battle cost the Federal perhaps 1,148 casualties. Sheridan reported the day's events to Grant with the following: "I attacked them with two divisions of the Sixth Army Corps and routed them handsomely.... If the thing is pressed I think Lee will surrender." Grant clearly agreed. On the next day, Grant sent a message to Lee saying he regarded it to be his duty to shift the responsibility for "any further effusion of blood" by asking Lee to surrender his army.[12] Lee had reached the point of considering that suggestion enough to ask for terms.

Weighing Grant's suggestion was Lee's most important duty on the night of April 7. There was also a multitude of other duties and decisions requiring Lee's immediate attention as he directed the retreat of a deteriorating army. On April 8, Grant sent a message offering extremely generous terms: the Confederates would be paroled and ineligible to bear arms against the United States Government until exchanged. Lee replied that he did not believe he was quite ready to surrender, but he was willing to meet with Grant the following morning at 10 a.m. to discuss restoring peace.

Meanwhile, Federal cavalry captured four freight trains with food meant for Lee's army at Appomattox Station. The Federal II Corps and VI Corps were pressing in from northwest of Lee's camp near Appomattox Court House, and Federal cavalry and infantry were moving into position to block his escape south of the village. Grant told General Sheridan on the 8th, "I think Lee will surrender to-day.... We will push him until terms are agreed upon."

On April 9, Lee needed to fight his way out of a trap at Appomattox Court House. Grant sent a message informing Lee that his proposed meeting at 10 a.m. "could lead to no good." The South would have to lay down its arms to "hasten that most desirable event" of bringing peace to the country. Lee allowed General Gordon to attack on the morning of April 9 with his II Corps in an attempt to create an opening for the rest of Lee's army to follow and escape the trap at Appomattox. When Gordon reported to Lee that he was not making headway and would require reinforcements, Lee decided the right conditions for surrender had arrived. Lee sent word to Grant that he was ready to

A view of Appomattox Court House where Lee's army surrendered. The courthouse is on the left and the McLean House, where the surrender was negotiated, is on the right.

discuss surrender; he then requested "a suspension of hostilities pending the adjustment of the terms of the surrender" of his army.[13]

Lee did surrender his army at Appomattox Court House, Virginia, on April 9, 1865. With Lee's surrender, Ulysses S. Grant had accomplished more than any general on either side of the conflict: He had practically annihilated three Confederate armies during the course of the war. The annihilation of Lee's army while it was intact and in transit, even at this point in the war, was a supremely difficult task. Lee obviously appreciated the fact that Grant was capable and ready to destroy his army if he chose not to surrender.

The Civil War, of course, could have ended in a different way. As it played out, Lee chose to accept the reasonable path for his soldiers and country. He could have ordered his men to escape, disperse and then implement a guerrilla war rather than to submit to defeat. Lee understood that the motivation for secession had been completely and forever denied during the course of the war. So he wisely surrendered and told his soldiers that they had been forced to yield to the overwhelming odds against them. It was no disgrace, and clearly their cause was lost no matter which course he and his soldiers chose. He also probably felt that the North would and could afford to be magnanimous in victory.

Jefferson Davis assumed an irrational stance as Southern defeat became obvious. Davis opposed the surrender of Johnston's army and the other Confederate forces still under arms in April 1865. Johnston surrendered all of the Confederate forces remaining on the East Coast on April 26 contrary to Davis's wishes. Davis himself was captured on May 10 near Irwinville, Georgia, which removed this obstacle to the surrender of the remaining Confederate commands.

The defeat and surrender of Lee and his army at Appomattox was a fatal blow to the

The McLean House at Appomattox Court House, VA.

Confederacy. In early April, Spanish Fort and Fort Blakely, two vital Confederate forts defending Mobile, Alabama, surrendered, and the Confederate forces abandoned Mobile itself on April 12. By then the Federal cavalry raid led by Brigadier General James Wilson had captured the important ordnance production factories at Selma, Alabama, and the city of Montgomery, Alabama, the first capital of the Confederacy. The Confederate military capability had been in a steep decline since Atlanta fell; in 1865 the Confederate military response was virtually supine.

Without a president or supreme commander to surrender all military forces, the Confederates still operating west of the Appalachians struggled with deciding whether, where or to whom to surrender. The last major battle had already been fought, but one more small battle would erupt near Brownsville, Texas. On May 12, 1865, the colonel of a USCT regiment attacked a Confederate camp at Palmito Ranch with his regiment and a small cavalry force. On May 13, a Confederate cavalry force with six cannons in support attacked the Federals and drove them back to the coast. The victorious Confederate force, having won the last battle of the Civil War, disbanded later in May. General Edmund Kirby Smith surrendered his Trans-Mississippi Department in Galveston, Texas, on June 2, 1865. The final Confederate General and last Confederate command to surrender was Brigadier General Stand Watie who surrendered his band of Cherokees on June 23, 1865, at Doaksville, Indian Territory, in what is now Oklahoma.

By the fall of 1864, Federal forces were capable of roaming throughout the South, and the Confederate Government could not prevent it. Following Lincoln's reelection in November 1864, the South had no reasonable purpose for continuing the war. Nevertheless, it took several more months before the Southern leadership (with the notable

Despite such scenes as these mass graves at Andersonville Prison Camp, the nation was able to reunite with remarkable magnanimity in 1865.

exception of Jefferson Davis and others) would accept defeat. Lieutenant General Nathan Bedford Forrest certainly was one of the toughest and most determined rebels fighting for the Confederacy, but even he recognized the futility and irrationality of continuing to fight in 1865. Forrest urged his soldiers to lay down their arms and submit to Federal authority. He assured his men that the United States Government was manifesting "a spirit of magnanimity and liberality" which they should meet with "faithful compliance" to the terms of surrender. He further advised them to obey the laws because "the Government to which you have surrendered can afford to be and will be magnanimous."[14] The American Civil War ended with remarkable benevolence and restraint that enabled the country to be restored and renewed much sooner than what would have otherwise been anticipated. This fact was made possible by the wise counsel of President Lincoln who spoke these judicious words at his *Second Inaugural Address* in 1865: "With malice toward none, with charity for all, with firmness in the right as God gives us to see the right, let us strive on to finish the work we are in, to bind up the nation's wounds, to care for him who shall have borne the battle and for his widow and his orphan, to do all which may achieve and cherish a just and lasting peace among ourselves and with all nations."[15] It was with this mindset that Generals Grant and Sherman addressed their approach to the defeated Confederate armies as they surrendered. Here at the close of the Civil War, the Northern leadership managed to harness the best course of action required at that time. It was perhaps the greatest achievement by the leadership of either side during the entire course of the American Civil War.

9

Comparisons and Conclusions

The foregoing chapters of this book are intended as a concise account of the antebellum martial perceptions of the North and South, the genuine motivations of Northerners and Southerners for going to war and the larger battles and operations of the Civil War. Some of the smaller or lesser-known battles have been included because of their relevance as defined in the foreword. This concise analysis of the many battles and operations rendered in chronological order in the previous chapters provides the material for evaluation in this final chapter. The principal objective of this book is to compare the military capability and battle efficiency of the Confederate and Federal land forces. This final chapter is not a summary or epilogue; instead, it is a series of conclusions derived from the topics of the previous chapters with a view of evaluating the validity of the long-held notion of Southern martial superiority.

As explained in the foreword, this book is intended as a non-partisan appraisal of the military campaigns and operations of the Civil War. As many Civil War readers surely know, this has historically been a difficult subject to address without bias making its presence felt. Civil War magazine publisher and relic hunter Stephen Sylvia has commented on this aspect of Civil War writing. "Truth," Sylvia wrote, "was often a casualty of opinion, agenda, and ignorance. In short, it (Civil War history) was messy." Bias in Civil War writing began when the first shots were fired. Deliberate and unintentional bias continues to afflict Civil War writing today because, Sylvia observed, "as polarization continues, agendas, opinions, and ignorance will continue to result in errors." While researching for an article he intended to write about a Civil War cavalry battle, Sylvia discovered that some writing about the battle he had found, even in period reports, was inaccurate, as were maps of the battlefield. Over the years Sylvia had uncovered relics from the battlefield he was writing about in places that did not match the positions described in battle accounts and didn't find relics in places where his sources said the fighting had been. Additionally, landmarks and roadbeds were not where the maps in regimental histories indicated they should be.[1] Sylvia's remarks and findings demonstrate by example that fact has often been misrepresented as a result of bias through the years. The object of this study is to deliver conclusions free of agenda-driven distortion; opinion about the propriety of the historical figures involved herein is considered irrelevant.

First and foremost in comparing Confederate and Federal military prowess is to consider which side faced the greater challenge: that is, determining which side had the more difficult goal to accomplish. Given the assumption that the population of the South was at least equal (said to be superior by pre-war Southern elites) to the North in its fighting capability and equal in its willingness to fight, the North faced a much more difficult task in suppressing the rebellion and forcing the reunification of the country. The

Confederacy simply needed to exhaust the North's willingness to continue fighting to gain its independence. It wasn't necessary for the South to defeat the North or to even threaten Northern territory to gain its independence. Conversely, the North ultimately had to crush the Confederacy to compel the seceding states to return to the Union. Southern elites in the antebellum years realized that the North would have to undertake a terrible and onerous trial in order to sustain the Union. Even before the war began, Southerners believed the North might not be willing to contest the secession of their states. The North's war objective was demonstrably more challenging than the South's.

In order to crush the Southern rebellion and restore the Union, the United States military had to invade the seceded states after the shooting started at Fort Sumter. Invading the Confederacy required an aggressive or attacking mode of operation for the Federals, and attacking is more difficult than defending. All things being otherwise equal, the attacking force requires a numerical advantage or some sort of tactical advantage to be successful on the field of battle.

Besides invading the Confederacy, the Federals needed to establish an effective blockade of all Southern seaports, inlets and possible avenues for importation. It was an impossible task, but it was absolutely strategically necessary to declare and attempt to enforce a blockade. Without at least a partial blockade the Confederacy could have possibly gained foreign recognition, foreign assistance and possibly foreign allies. The blockade required complete naval superiority; there is no question as to the fact that the U.S. Navy completely outclassed its Confederate counterpart. The cost in manpower and resources for the naval blockade vastly increased the difficulty of the task of defeating the Confederacy.

The invading Federal armies could not campaign in the South without a secure supply line that had to be maintained and protected by a large allocation of manpower and resources. Supply is a constant preoccupation for invading armies. The allied advance into France and Germany during World War II serves as a ready example of how a successful advance can be crippled after supply lines are overextended. A ready, reliable and steady availability of ammunition, food and forage had to be sustained as the Federal armies operated on Southern soil. Troops that were needed at the front were continually assigned to protect railroads, supply trains and supply depots. The Federal advantage in manpower was diluted significantly because of the need to protect supply lines and to garrison occupied territory. It should be considered, although it is usually overlooked in Civil War histories, that the Confederacy was never able to successfully invade, occupy or even operate in Northern territory beyond attempting a few brief incursions. Obviously it was much more efficient for the Confederacy to assume a defensive stance whereby a greater percentage of available manpower could be employed in combat. While the North had a clear superiority in manpower and resources, much of that advantage was allocated to occupation garrisons and troops assigned to protect and deliver supplies in enemy territory.

A comparison of the strategic acumen of the Confederate and Federal high commands strongly indicates that the Federals demonstrated significantly superior strategic vision and superiority in the implementation of winning military strategies. During the first months of the war, General Winfield Scott conceived the template for overall Federal war strategy that ultimately delivered victory. The Northern press called Scott's proposal the Anaconda Plan and doubted its practicality. Scott did not have the opportunity implement his proposal, but it became the basis for the Federal strategy that eventually won the war. Major General George McClellan developed a comprehensive strategy that quite possibly would have won the war much sooner if the Lincoln Administration had allowed it to flourish. Historians routinely bash McClellan for his personality and leadership flaws and overlook the fact that his move to the James River could have succeeded if Lincoln would have allocated the resources that McClellan demanded. Historians also usually don't mention the fact that Grant's Overland Campaign in 1864 placed his army in practically the same position that McClellan reached in 1862 at a fraction of the cost in casualties that Grant incurred. McClellan certainly had his faults, but his strategic planning could have won the war by 1863 if the Lincoln Administration would have provided the same level of support that Grant received in 1864 and 1865.

The Confederate high command slavishly followed a strategy designed to protect as much territory as possible. While this is understandable because surrendering territory, even temporarily, could have allowed thousands of slaves to escape, this strategy required more than Southern resources could deliver. And, unless the Federals were willing to quit fighting, this strategy could not deliver victory. An erstwhile Civil War magazine editor summed up the fundamental problem with Confederate war strategy when he observed that General Robert E. Lee, the Confederacy's most influential general, knew "his strategic problem but never came close to solving it."[2] Those few words define the failing of Confederate war strategy as fully and comprehensively as an entire book chapter could. The Confederate reliance on concentration of forces did manage to win some battles; and it might have been enough to win against a lesser foe, but it wasn't sufficient or innovative enough to deliver victory against the North. Decisions by the Confederate high command in 1864, the crucial point in the war, led to swift defeat. Jefferson Davis replaced General Joseph Johnston with General John B. Hood in command of the Confederate Army of Tennessee on July 19, 1864. Hood proceeded to lose Atlanta and then destroy his army and the Confederacy's slim chances of winning the war. Davis's decision was designed to defeat Sherman in Georgia with offensive tactics of the sort utilized by Lee during the Seven Days' Battles in 1862. It proved to be an inopportune time to assume the offensive. Had Johnston managed with his defensive tactics to delay Sherman until after the Federal election in November of 1864, perhaps Lincoln would have lost the election. Had George McClellan won the election instead of Lincoln in 1864, the pressure for peace from Northern Democrats might have led to a war-ending settlement for the Confederacy rather than its eventual defeat the following spring. Overall, Confederate military strategy from the operational level to allocation of resources was counterproductive.

Comparing the capabilities of the armies, soldiers and officers of the North and South is the most complicated and nebulous assessment of this study. While preparing sources for this book, I interviewed National Battlefield Park historians, Civil War writers and Civil War experts. It was my impression that probably all of them seemed to give an unbiased assessment as to whether the Confederacy produced warriors superior to those of the North. From what I was able to gather, most of the experts were noncommittal: that is, the experts were either unable to give an explanation as to why one side would be superior or were of the belief that neither side was superior man for man. Perhaps the best answer to this comparison can be derived from a sports analogy. In comparing boxers, an adage says that a good big man will always beat a good smaller man. That is basically how the Civil War played out. The North was bigger, more powerful but less flexible and less agile. The South was leaner, more efficient in maneuver but lacked the size to compete with the North in a sustained contest. Essentially, the good big army defeated the good smaller army, as would be expected.

The Confederate armies had one distinct characteristic that differed significantly from the Federal armies: Confederate armies were comprised of a much higher percentage of native-born Americans than the Federal armies. Foreign-born soldiers accounted for about a fourth of the strength of the Federal armies during the Civil War. Germany and Ireland provided by far the largest percentage of foreign-born soldiers serving in the Federal armies. The results of a survey reported to the War Department on March 17, 1866, "based solely on the opinions expressed by the surgeons of boards of enrollment" who were asked which nationality "presents the greatest aptitude for military service" suggested that native-born Americans were best suited for war as compared to the immigrant inductees they had examined. According to the report, most of the surgeons suggested that "as a result of their experience that the physical, moral, and intellectual characteristics of the American gave him the precedence over other nations in respect to his fitness for war." Further, "the great majority of the surgeons" expressed the opinion that, "because of his physique, *élan*, and intelligence, the American was the best type of the soldier on this continent." From this survey of the doctors who examined recruits, substitutes and draftees during the war, it can be taken that native-born Americans, in their opinion, were better suited for war overall than the immigrants they examined. Federal units comprised entirely of foreign-born soldiers delivered a mixed record in combat during the Civil War. The performance of the principally German regiments at Chancellorsville was so poor that even General Lee decided that the corps in which those regiments served was indifferent. However, some German units earned an outstanding evaluation for gallantry and efficiency. The German 32nd Indiana Infantry was one such regiment. Then–Brigadier General Don C. Buell made note of the regiment's gallantry in a fight at Rowlett's Station, Kentucky, on December 17, 1861, and acknowledged it in general orders from his headquarters. The 32nd Indiana was recognized as one of Fox's "Fighting Regiments," having suffered 612 killed and wounded out of an enrollment of 1,283.[3] Be that as it may, the heavy reliance on immigrant troops in the Federal armies should not be considered as an advantage. There were documented problems relating to entirely foreign-born units in Federal service, language difficulties being one oft-mentioned problem. Then there is the case of the politically appointed immigrant generals, the career of Major General Franz Sigel being a case in point. The Confederate armies did not have to contend with the disadvantages of having multiple officers of the Sigel mold leading them.

To those who understand the making of a soldier, the level, quality and amount of training is the supreme consideration in evaluating the potential capability of troops. All things being otherwise relatively equal, troop training was and remains the single most important aspect in determining the combat efficiency and combat readiness of troops. The preceding statement seems to contradict the antebellum assumption that culture or heritage determines the potential fighting capability of warriors. Culture and heritage certainly do have an impact on the fighting man's morale, and troop morale is a critical factor in determining the outcome of battle. Even so, the defeat of the South in the Civil War demonstrated that morale or heritage or fighting aptitude, even in combination, were not enough to overcome the influence of training. As one military writer observed, "Union and Confederate troops performed well because of their soldiering skills" rather than because of some "innate fighting ability." Their fighting prowess was the result of the "drill, training, and discipline" they received in their transition from citizen to soldier.[4]

Instruction and basic training of Civil War soldiers "was far simpler and less rigorous" than what recruits experience now. In training camp or camp of instruction as it was called, recruits were drilled in the companies and regiments they would serve with for the duration of their enlistment. The nascent warriors were drilled incessantly for the period of time allotted for instruction before going to the field or campaign. Emphasis was placed on company and regimental drill; occasionally, if time permitted and if the officers were capable, brigade maneuvers were attempted and sometimes mock battles. One school of the soldier was apparently often curtailed—target practice. As one regimental historian recalled, "A system of target firing ... never amounted to much as we were never well supplied with ammunition." This practice seems to have been the norm in both armies. The recruits were drilled "in the manual and in the evolutions" of loading a musket, when time permitted.[5] The troops on both sides returned to drill and training after battles and marches during times, as during winter, when in camp. The repetitious drilling and marching and combat experience transformed recruits from all walks of life into efficient veteran soldiers. Men from the cities or farms or from the frontier eventually learned to be proficient soldiers. As a case in point, the British Army at that time was perhaps as good as or better than any army in the world, but probably very few British recruits had much, if any, firearms experience before going into the army. Nevertheless, these men were honed through training into excellent soldiers. The same was true of American volunteers—North and South.

The leadership in both armies was dominated by West Point graduates and Regular Army officers. Of the West Pointers, for years the North had a greater number of cadets who ranked near the top of their graduating class. In the antebellum years, cadets with the highest class ranking were assigned to the Corps of Engineers. Artillery was the branch selected for the next tier of cadets according to class ranking, followed by cavalry and last, for middling or lower ranked cadets, was the infantry. Conversely, today the highest ranked cadets usually choose to branch into the infantry, and considerable effort is made to get as many cadets as possible into combat arms. West Point cadets from the South often ranked in the lower half of their class at graduation in the antebellum years; thus, the nexus for many Southerners was service in the cavalry and infantry while many Northern West Point graduates were associated with technical proficiency and service in the engineers. A few examples of this pattern were Federal Civil War Generals William Franklin, Quincy Gilmore and James McPherson; all three of them graduated first in their class at West Point and branched as engineers. William "Baldy" Smith and Gouverneur K. Warren were two additional high ranking West Pointers who branched as engineers. That is not to say that the South did not produce cadets who graduated first in their class: two examples being Paul Hebert and George W.C. Lee. In any case, the point here is that the North produced more West Pointers with aptitude for technical fields or engineering while the South produced more graduates bound for cavalry or infantry duty. Writer Stephen Newton observed that "engineers often do not make the best field commanders," and the records of the officers mentioned above seems to validate Newton's perception.[6] Robert E. Lee graduated second in his West Point class and was commissioned as an engineer; however, Lee had a varied career that included a tour as superintendent of West Point and as a cavalry lieutenant colonel before the Civil War. Perhaps the experience gained by future Confederate commanders from service in the cavalry and infantry benefited the Confederacy during the war by providing officers better prepared and equipped for division, corps and army command. The author of a book on West Pointers in the Civil War suggested that the Army of the Potomac "fought as hard and as well as its Confederate counterpart" and was roughly equal in "military skill" to the Confederate Army of Northern Virginia; however, the Army of Northern Virginia "benefited from far superior brigade, division, corps, and army commanders."[7] One only has to compare Jackson, Longstreet, Hill and some of Lee's division commanders with Burnside, Franklin, Sickles, Howard and Sumner to reach the same conclusion.

Two additional factors that hobbled the Federal Army were far less of an issue for the Confederates. First, there was a superabundance of political generals in the Federal army who were totally unqualified and obviously unfit for command. Benjamin Butler, John Fremont and Nathaniel Banks were three prime examples of incompetent commanders who were appointed to command for political reasons. These men were appointed because President Lincoln was a political genius but a poor judge of military command potential. In effect, Lincoln was willing to make command capability a secondary consideration in his military appointments. Lincoln, for instance, wanted to pander to the immigrant vote, so he appointed Franz Sigel, Alexander Schimmelfennig, and Carl Schurtz to command rank. As for Schimmelfennig, Lincoln explained his appointment with: "there has got to be something done that will be unquestionably in the interest of the Dutch, and to that end I want Schimmelfennig appointed.... His name will make up for any difference there may be, and I'll take the risk of his coming out all right." The immigrant vote back then, even as is it does today, superseded the best interests of the Nation. Lincoln, perhaps believing that politics had to be prioritized in order to win the war, sacrificed many thousands of Northern soldiers' lives as a result of his penchant for appointing generals for political rather than practical reasons. Second, Federal manpower policy was simply irrational; it was as purely political as Lincoln's command appointments were. The states supplied new regiments to the Federal army, and the state governors desired and jealously guarded the political privilege of appointing colonels and regimental officers in those new units. General Sherman thought that this policy of sending new regiments to the field rather than sending recruits as replacements for losses in veteran regiments was the worst blunder committed by the North during the war. While this folly continued in the North for the duration of the war, the Confederates sent conscripts to veteran units and relied less on inexperienced, new regiments for their army.[8] The Confederacy also kept its soldiers for the war's duration while the North sent scores of veteran regiments home as their enlistments expired. The North's flawed method of supplying troops to the Federal Army resulted in heavier battle casualties than otherwise would have been the case. Ultimately, Federal manpower policy made winning the war significantly more difficult for the North.

The preceding chapters recounting the war itself demonstrate some observations that seem to be omitted in older Civil War histories and narratives. First, most of the major Confederate battle victories resulted from serious mistakes or blunders by Federal commanders. The implication here is that the war was prolonged and the Confederate armies were made to appear more efficient because of the unforced mistakes of Federal generals. The common soldier in the Federal army suffered in reputation because of the decisions made by a string of inferior army commanders. As one writer noted, "too many factors beyond a soldier's control dictated the success or failure of a battle. Decisions made by higher-level officers ... directly affected an army's success."[9] The Federal defeats at 1st and 2nd Bull Run, Jackson's Valley Campaign, Fredericksburg, Chancellorsville and Chickamauga all resulted from poor generalship or egregious error.

Next, the Overland Campaign in 1864 was a poorly-managed, unnecessary waste of lives and resources. Instead of plodding through the series of battles in May and June, Grant should have supervised the Bermuda Hundred expedition with a force sufficient for the task while leaving Meade with most of the Army of the Potomac to occupy Lee north of Richmond. As it was, the "absence of a strong cohort of corps and division commanders in the Army of the Potomac contributed as much to the Overland campaign's stalemate as did the increasing power of fieldworks."[10] Here again Grant was ultimately responsible for the poor corps and division level leadership in Meade's army, which he supervised during that campaign. Some historians consider Grant to be the best general of the Civil War. That may be true, but Grant was a poor judge of character and ability. It was his responsibility to weed out inefficient corps and division commanders under his supervision. He allowed generals to retain their commands when it was obvious that someone else needed to supplant them for the efficiency of the army. Grant also fixated on objectives when it was unnecessary. The repeated assaults on impregnable positions during the Overland Campaign and the attack on Fort Gregg are two cases in point. Grant found a way to win the war according to Lincoln's parameters, but his methods proved more costly and inefficient than was necessary.

Finally, there is no algoristic solution to determine whether the Southerner was a better warrior than the Yankee or the man who served in the Federal armies during the Civil War. There have been attempts to use mathematics to compare fighting efficiency or other factors pertaining to the capabilities of the Confederate and Federal armies. However, there were a multitude of variables that cannot be calculated that affected the statistics of the war. The battles covered in the previous chapters are sufficient to enable the reader to determine if the soldiers of one side were actually superior.

A National Battlefield Park historian with whom I discussed the object of this book made an observation that was both obvious and cogent. He said that the Confederacy did more with less. That implies that the Confederate Army was more efficient overall than the Federal Army. From the record of Lee's Army of Northern Virginia that appears convincing. But perhaps a better, more accurate assertion would be to say that the Federal Army did more with more. Lee's army was absolutely more maneuverable than the Army of the Potomac, and it operated without the restrictions and encumbrances that disadvantaged all of the Federal armies. Lee's army also had better leadership from the brigade to corps level as well. Despite these disadvantages the Federals eventually, ploddingly, managed to overcome Lee's army by attrition if not finesse. Ultimately, wars are decided by substance rather than style: in the end the Union accomplished its goals and the Confederacy did not. The Federal and Confederate armies were basically equal in training, the single most important deciding factor in military capability. Had the Southerners truly been superior man for man as they often avowed during the antebellum years, the Confederacy would be expected to win the war.

Comparisons of military performance require consideration of a multitude of crucial factors. For example, Stonewall Jackson's Valley Campaign in 1862 usually is viewed as superior to Early's Valley Campaign in 1864. Jackson won most of his battles and accomplished Lee's strategic goals. However, Jackson, as noted historian Gary Gallagher observed, "fought against much weaker foes.... Early labored under more difficult circumstances." Historians have considered Jackson's performance in the valley as brilliant.

Nevertheless, Jackson probably would not have beaten Sheridan in 1864 either; Sheridan "had the ability and numbers to vanquish any opponent laboring under the handicaps imposed on Early." Despite the fact that Early failed in the Valley in 1864, Early's efforts "measure up well against Jackson's," according to Gallagher.[11] No doubt many through the years believed that Jackson would have managed the campaign in 1864 better, perhaps successfully. Gallagher has doubts. The point here is that the situation was markedly different in 1862 than it was in 1864 in the Shenandoah Valley, yet Jackson has been esteemed for his success against lesser competition and probably would not have had success in Early's place two years later. The fact is that important variables were often ignored, overlooked or not taken into account in previous Civil War histories and studies.

Through the years the Confederate soldier has retained the aura of fighting prowess and *élan* that has traditionally gone unnoticed, or perhaps ignored, in Union soldiers. One of the most important and enduring reasons for this ongoing trend is that a great many Confederate soldiers loathed their enemies and remained determined to restrain admiration of any kind for them, even after the war. On the other hand, the victorious Union soldiers often respected their foes. Robert E. Lee became a hero nationwide while Yankees were hated for generations in the South. Confederate soldiers commenced discounting their foes before the war, and after First Bull Run this attitude "continued to flourish till the end of the war."[12] For Union soldiers, the honor of their service and nation was measured by how fierce their enemies were. What honor is found in beating a weakling or an inept foe? Having won the war, the Federals were able to feel some compassion for their defeated countrymen. Southerners lost the war, so they found mitigating excuses for their defeat. Southerners retained their bitterness and resentment for decades or lifetimes. Naturally, writers and historians with Southern heritage were exposed to this tradition during their breeding. It is a small wonder that the myth of the lost cause has persisted in Civil War writing.

The Union soldiers certainly deserve better than what history has bestowed. A single sentence from Donald Stoker's book on Civil War strategy sheds some light on yet another reason why Confederate soldiers compare favorably in the history books. Stoker noted that some Federal generals did not expect as much from their soldiers as Confederate generals did from theirs. "The Union troops," Stoker wrote, "certainly were up to the task, but too often they were lions led by lambs."[13] There was a greater sense of desperation in the Confederacy that gave an edge in morale to the South through much of the war until it was obvious that their cause was lost.

A final comparison of the wartime performance of Confederate and Federal troops should include this opinion from a partisan but certifiably qualified observer. General Ulysses S. Grant mentioned the respect shown to General Lee and his army in the North during the war. Grant noted that Lee's "praise was sounded throughout the entire North after every action he was engaged in," and such admiration "was calculated to give him the entire confidence of his troops and to make him feared by his antagonists." This one-sided rendering of the war continued through the war years and afterwards. Grant once expressed an opinion about the comparison of Confederate and Federal troops that resonates with authenticity. He wrote, "The troops on both sides were American, and united they need not fear any foreign foe. It is possible that the Southern man started in with a little more dash than his Northern brother, but he was correspondingly less enduring."[14] The Confederate soldiers did perhaps demonstrate more dash simply because of an advantage in morale, particularly early in the war. Confederate soldiers fought well enough to exact a strong measure of respect from the Federals. However, despite the fact that they were defeated by the Federals, Southerners were loath to give the respect due to their erstwhile foes. They made a case for the belief that the war was an unequal contest. From the foregoing chapters of this book it should be apparent that the Civil War was a much more equal contest than what Americans have been traditionally led to believe. The Confederates absolutely demonstrated admirable fighting qualities during the Civil War and could have won the war. The Federals could have won the war much sooner with better leadership. Ultimately, the South did not possess superior military capability. Otherwise the Confederacy would have won the war. The North faced the more difficult and onerous task and admirably accomplished it. Americans can be thankful that our Civil War ended in the benign manner that it did. Both sides deserve our admiration for the valor, determination, endurance and military savvy demonstrated by our forebearers.

Chapter Notes

Preface

1. Charlton Heston, *In the Arena: An Autobiography* (New York: Simon & Schuster, 1995), p. 120.
2. William H. Humphrey to John Gould, March 24, 1893, letter, Dartmouth College Library, copy from Antietam National Battlefield Library.
3. D. Clayton James, *The Years of McArthur, Volume II 1941–1945* (Boston: Houghton Mifflin Company, 1975), p. 686.
4. David Brion Davis, *Inhuman Bondage: The Rise and Fall of Slavery in the New World* (New York: Oxford University Press, Inc., 2006), p.305.

Chapter 1

1. Mark D. Okey, *The Justice of Our Cause: A History of the Okey Family in the War of Rebellion 1861–1865* (Mark D. Okey, 1999), p. 8.
2. John D. McKenzie, *Uncertain Glory: Lee's Generalship Re-Examined* (New York: Hippocrene Books, Inc., 1997), p. 31.
3. Michael C. C. Adams, *Fighting for Defeat: Union Military Failure in the East 1861–1865* (Lincoln, NE: University of Nebraska Press, 1992), p. 81.
4. Henry Woodhead, ed. *Echoes of Glory: Arms and Equipment of the Confederacy* (Alexandria, VA: Time-Life Books, 1991), p. 27.
5. Kevin Phillips, *The Cousins' Wars: Religion, Politics, & the Triumph of Anglo-America* (New York: Basic Books, 1999), pp. 350–51.
6. William R. Taylor, *Cavalier and Yankee: The Old South and American National Character* (New York: George Baziller, 1961), p. 210.
7. Phillips, p. 153.
8. Charles Powers Smith, *Yankees & God* (New York: Hermitage House, 1954), p. 3.
9. Phillips, p. 133.
10. Ibid., pp. xii, 26.
11. Ibid., p. 351, Adams, pp. 4–6.
12. Taylor, pp. 329–332.
13. Phillips. pp. 409–456.
14. Ulysses S. Grant, *Personal Memoirs* (New York: The Modern Library, 1999), p.18.
15. Taylor, p. 238.
16. Ibid.
17. Carter Smith, *Presidents: Every Question Answered* (Irvington, NY: Hylas Publishing, 2004), pp. 82, 300, 317, James Webb, *Born Fighting: How the Scots-Irish Shaped America* (New York: Broadway Books, 2004), pp. 202–03, Wayne Wei-siang Hsieh, *West Pointers and the Civil War: The Old Army in War and Peace* (Chapel Hill, NC: The University of North Carolina Press, 2009), pp. 94–95.
18. William Y. W. Ripley, *Vermont Riflemen in the War for the Union, 1861 to 1865: A History of Company F First United States Sharpshooters* (Rutland, VT: Tuttle & Co. Printers, 1883), pp. 3–5, Bruce Catton, *American Heritage: The Civil War*, ed. James M. McPherson and Noah Andre Trudeau (New York: Tess Press, 2009), pp. 338–57.
19. Henry Woodhead, ed., *Echoes of Glory: Arms and Equipment of the Union* (Alexandria, VA: Time-Life Books, 1991), p. 296.
20. *The New York Times*, 1 May 1861, p. 4.
21. Brent Nosworthy, *The Bloody Crucible of Courage: Fighting Methods and Combat Experience of the Civil War* (New York: Carroll & Graf, 2003), p. 154.
22. Grady McWhiney and Perry Jamieson, *Attack & Die: Civil War Military Tactics and the Southern Heritage* (Tuscaloosa, AL: The University of Alabama Press, 1982), p. 178, Webb, *Born Fighting*, p. 180, James Webb, "Why You Need to Know the Scots-Irish," *Parade Magazine*, 3 October 2004, p. 5.
23. Gerald L. Earley, *The Second United States Sharpshooters in the Civil War: A History and Roster* (Jefferson, NC: McFarland & Company, Inc., Publishers, 2009), p. 1.

Chapter 2

1. David Brion Davis, p. 89.
2. Kenneth M. Stampp, *The Peculiar Institution Slavery in the Ante-Bellum South* (New York: Vintage Books, 1989), p. 18.
3. David Brion Davis, pp. 104–06.
4. Clifford Dowdey, *A History of the Confederacy, 1832–1865* (New York: Barnes & Noble Books, 1992), pp. 16–24.
5. David Brion Davis, p. 209.
6. Thomas Streissguth, ed., *The Civil War: The South* (San Diego, CA: Greenhaven Press, Inc., 2001), p. 48.
7. David Brion Davis, p. 266.

8. Stampp, pp. 30, 33. 425.
9. *Ibid.*, p. 338.
10. James McPherson, *What They Fought For* (Baton Rouge: Louisiana State University Press, 1994), p. 36.
11. Joseph Glatthaar, *General Lee's Army from Victory to Collapse* (New York: Free Press, 2008), pp. 32–41.
12. McPherson, *What They Fought For*, p. 32.
13. James M. McPherson, *For Cause and Comrades: Why Men Fought in the Civil War* (New York: Oxford University Press, 1997), p. 11.
14. McPherson, *What They Fought For*, p. 32.
15. William F. Fox, *Regimental Losses in the American Civil War, 1861-1865* (Albany, NY: Albany Publishing, 1889), p. 63.
16. James M. Dazell, *Private Dazell* (Cincinnati, OH: Robert Clarke & Co., 1887), pp. 94, 174.
17. McPherson, *What They Fought For*, p. 56.
18. Glatthaar, *Lee's Army*, p. 40.
19. *Ibid.*, p. 203.
20. David Hackett Fischer, *Albion's Seed: Four British Folkways in America* (New York: Oxford University Press, 1989), p. 860.
21. Glatthaar, *Lee's Army*, p. 150.
22. Edward H. Bonekemper III, *The Myth of the Lost Cause: Why the South Fought the Civil War and Why the North Won* (Washington, D.C.: Regnery Publishing, 2005) p. 40, Glatthaar, *Lee's Army*, p. 468, Joseph Glatthaar, *Soldiers in the Army of Northern Virginia: A Statistical Portrait of Troops Who Served Under Robert E. Lee* (Chapel Hill, NC: University of North Carolina Press, 2011), pp. 161, 164–65.
23. U.S. War Department, *The War of the Rebellion: A Compilation of the Official Records of the Union and Confederate Armies* (Washington, D.C.: U.S. Government Printing Office, 1880–1901), Series III/V, p. 771, hereafter cited as OR. All references are to Series I unless otherwise noted, Webb, *Born Fighting*, p. 225.
24. Glatthaar, *Lee's Army*, pp. 63, 95.

Chapter 3

1. William Davis, *Brother Against Brother* (Alexandria, VA: Time-Life Books, 1983), pp. 119, 128–30.
2. OR, Series IV/I, pp. 5–11.
3. Dowdey, *History*, P. 78.
4. Robert Cowley and Thomas Guinzburg, ed. *West Point: Two Centuries of Honor and Tradition* (New York: Warner Books, 2002), pp. 34–35.
5. John S. Bowman, ed. *The Civil War Almanac* (New York: Bison Books, 1983), pp. 325–26.
6. Adams, p. 50, Geoffery Perret, "Anaconda: The Plan That Never Was," *North & South*, Vol. 6, No. 4, May 2003, p. 37.
7. Allan Nevins, *The War for the Union: The Improvised War, 1861–1862* (New York: Charles Scribner's Sons, 1959), pp. 96–97.
8. Streissguth, pp. 16–17.
9. Herman Hattaway and Richard E. Beringer, *Jefferson Davis, Confederate President* (Lawrence: The University Press of Kansas, 2002), p. 43, OR, Series IV/I, pp. 117, 126–131, Carter Smith, *Presidents*, pp. 319–322.
10. Hattaway and Beringer, p. 64, Streissguth, p. 16.
11. Davis, *Brother*, pp. 140, 160.
12. OR, Series III/I, pp. 67–70.
13. Nevins, *Improvised War*, p. 74.
14. Ethan Rafuse, *Robert E. Lee and the Fall of the Confederacy, 1863-1865* (New York: Roman & Littlefield Publishers, Inc., 2008), p. 9, Hattaway and Beringer, pp. 108–09.
15. Glatthaar *Lee's Army*, p. xiv, McWhiney and Jamieson, pp. 6–7, Richard M. McMurry, *Two Great Rebel Armies An Essay In Confederate Military History* (Chapel Hill, NC: University of North Carolina Press, 1989), pp. 58–59.
16. Ezra Warner, *Generals in Blue Lives of the Union Commanders* (Baton Rouge: Louisiana State University Press, 2006), pp. 67–68, OR, IV, pp. 1344, 65.
17. OR, IV, p. 85.
18. OR, Series III/I, p. 83.
19. Warner, *Generals in Blue*, pp. 429–30.
20. Stephen W. Sears, "Winfield Scott and the Coming of the War," *North and South*, Vol. 10, No. 4, January 2008, pp. 36–37, Perret, p. 38.
21. Sears, "Scott," p. 36, Rafuse, *Lee*, p. 5, David Nevin, *The Road to Shiloh Early Battles in the West* (Alexandria, VA: Time-Life Books, 1983), p. 52, Larry J. Daniel, *Shiloh The Battle That Changed the Civil War* (New York: Touchstone, 1997), p. 18.
22. OR, Series IV/I, pp. 11–15.
23. Nevins, *Improvised War*, pp. 130–33.
24. T. J. Stiles, *Jesse James Last Rebel of the Civil War* (New York: Vintage Books, 2002), pp 11–12, 38, Nevin, *Shiloh*, pp. 12–13.
25. OR, Series III/I, p. 83, Nevin, *Shiloh*, p. 12.
26. Nevin, *Shiloh*, pp. 13–16.
27. Benson J. Lossing, *Mathew Brady's Illustrated History of the Civil War, 1861-1865* (New York: Gramercy Books, 1994), p. 512, Frederick Phisterer, *Statistical Record of the Armies of the United States* (New York: The Blue & The Gray Press), p. 4, Frederick H. Dyer, *A Compendium of the War of the Rebellion* (Des Moines, IA: Dyer Publishing, 1908), III, pp. 1712–1716.
28. Douglas Southall Freeman, *Lee's Lieutenants Volume One Manassas to Malvern Hill* (New York: Charles Scribner's Sons, 1946), p. xxiv.
29. Nevins, *Improvised War*, p. 108.
30. Hattaway and Beringer, p. 61, McMurry, pp. 98–99.
31. William C. Davis, *First Blood Fort Sumter to First Bull Run* (Alexandria, VA: Time-Life Books, 1983), pp. 56–57.
32. John Grant, James M. Lynch and Ronald H. Bailey, *West Point The First 200 Years* (Guilford, CT: The Globe Pequot Press, 2002), pp. 18–19, Cowley and Guinzburg, p. 53.
33. McWhiney and Jamieson, pp. 146–147, John F. Marszalek *Commander of All Lincoln's Armies A*

Life of General Henry W. Halleck (Cambridge, MA: Harvard University Press, 2004), pp. 22–23.

34. Frances H. Kennedy, ed. *The Civil War Battle Guide Second Edition* (New York: Houghton Mifflin Company, 1998), p. 6.

35. Stephen W. Sears, *George B. McClellan The Young Napoleon* (New York: Ticknor & Fields, 1988), p. 84, Dowdey, *Lee* (Boston: Little Brown and Company, 1965), pp. 162–165.

36. Nevins, *Improvised War*, pp. 140–42.

37. Davis, *First Blood*, pp. 89–92, Sears, *McClellan*, p. 91, Lossing, p. 64, Kennedy, p. 106.

38. OR, II, p. 743.

39. OR, II, p. 993.

40. Dowdey, *Lee*, p. 170.

41. Ezra J. Warner, *Generals in Gray Lives of the Confederate Commanders* (Baton Rouge: University of Louisiana Press, 2002), pp. 181, 193–94, Kennedy, pp. 9–10.

42. Davis, *First Blood*, pp. 85, 92.

43. Clayton R. Newell, *Lee vs. McClellan The First Campaign* (Washington, D.C.: Regnery Publishing, Inc., 1996), pp. 171–72, 223.

44. Sears, "Scott," p. 36.

45. Perret, p. 39, Sears, "Scott," p. 40.

46. Davis, *First Blood*, pp. 110–13.

47. Ibid., pp. 58, 93–95, David Detzer, *Donnybrook The Battle of Bull Run, 1861* (New York: Harcourt, Inc., 2004), pp. 93–94, OR, II, p. 167.

48. OR, II, pp. 168, 178–79.

49. Ibid., pp. 311, 314, Warner, *Generals in Blue*, p. 514.

50. Henry P. Elliott, "First Manassas," Blue and Gray, XXXVII, #5, 2011, p. 21, OR, II, pp. 330–31.

51. Davis, *First Blood*, PP. 122–23.

52. Elliot, pp. 21–13.

53. OR, II, pp. 346–48.

54. Detzer, p. 86.

55. Nevins, *Improvised War*, pp. 221–22.

56. OR, II, pp. 327, 570.

57. Detzer, p. 431.

58. Ibid., 199.

59. Hattaway and Beringer, p. 93.

60. Hsieh, pp. 116, 130, 133.

Chapter 4

1. Nevins *Improvised War*, pp. 132–34, OR, IV, p. 378.

2. Nevin, *Shiloh*, pp. 12–17.

3. Jay Monaghan, *Civil War On The Western Border 1854–1865* (Lincoln, NE: University of Nebraska Press, 1955), pp. 141, 146, 151.

4. Ibid., pp. 151–53.

5. Ibid., pp. 156–58.

6. OR, III, p. 58, Monaghan, pp. 160–63.

7. OR, III, p. 96.

8. Bruce Catton, *The American Heritage Picture History of the Civil War*, ed. Richard M. Ketchum (New York: American Heritage/Bonanza Books, 1960), p. 88.

9. Monaghan, p. 157.

10. Richard W. Hatcher III and William Garrett Piston, ed. *Kansans at Wilson's Creek: Soldier's Letters from the Campaign for Southwest Missouri* (Springfield, MO: Wilson's Creek National Battlefield Foundation, 1993), Hans Christian Adamson, *Rebellion in Missouri: Nathaniel Lyon and His Army of the West* (Philadelphia, PA: Chilton Company, 1961), p. 32.

11. Edwin C. Bearss, *The Battle of Wilson's Creek* (Bozeman, MT: George Washington Carver Birthplace District Association, 1975), pp. 51–79.

12. Bearss, pp. 82–85, 161, Nosworthy, pp. 5–8, William Garrett Piston and Richard W. Hatcher III, *Wilson's Creek: The Second Battle of the Civil War and the Men Who Fought It* (Chapel Hill, NC: The University of North Carolina Press, 2000), pp. 218–19, OR, III, pp. 72–73.

13. Piston and Hatcher, p. 256, OR, III, pp. 87–88.

14. OR, III, p. 67, Earl J. Hess, Richard W. Hatcher III, William Garrett Piston and William L. Shea, *Wilson's Creek, Pea Ridge, and Prairie Grove: A Battlefield Guide, with a Section on Wire Road* (Lincoln, NE: University of Nebraska Press, 2006), pp. 70–71, Bearss, p. 116.

15. OR, III, pp. 74, 119.

16. Ibid., p. 64.

17. Piston and Hatcher, pp. 260–61, OR, III, pp. 68, 72, 119.

18. OR, III, pp. 65–72.

19. Fox, *Losses*, pp. 62, 417.

20. Hess, Hatcher, Piston and Shea, p. 50.

21. OR, III, pp. 63–64, 98, Christian B. Keller, *Chancellorsville and the Germans: Nativism, Ethnicity, and Civil War Memory* (New York: Fordham University Press, 2007), p. 24.

22. OR, III, pp. 72, 107, Bearss, pp. 162, 164, Adamson, p. 289.

23. Monaghan, pp. 189–94.

24. Donald Stoker, *The Grand Design Strategy and the U.S. Civil War* (New York: Oxford University Press, 2010), p. 48.

25. Warner, *Generals in Gray*, pp. 242–43, 160.

26. Shelby Foot, *The Civil War A Narrative: Fort Sumter to Kernstown: First Blood—The Thing Gets Underway* (New York: Random House, 1958), pp. 87–88, Hattaway and Beringer, p. 106.

27. OR, IV, pp. 193–94, Stoker, p. 51.

28. OR, VII, p. 922, Warner, *Generals in Gray*, p. 38.

29. Webb, *Born Fighting*, p. 228, Dyer, pp. 1189–1212.

30. Peter M. Chaitin, *The Coastal War: Chesapeake Bay to Rio Grande* (Alexandria, VA: Time-Life Books, 1984), p. 17, Stoker, p. 69.

31. Ronald H. Bailey, *Forward to Richmond: McClellan's Peninsular Campaign* (Alexandria, VA: Time-Life Books, 1983), pp. 39–52, Byron Farwell, *Ball's Bluff: A Small Battle and Its Long Shadow* (McLean, VA: EPM Publishing, Inc., 1990), pp. 134–35.

32. Stephen W. Sears, ed. *The Civil War Papers of George B. McClellan: Selected Correspondence,*

1860–1865 (New York: Ticknor & Fields, 1989), p. 81.
33. Warner, *Generals in Blue*, pp. 290–91, Nevins, *Improvised War*, pp. 270–73.
34. Marszalek, pp. 5–6, 22–23, Warner, *Generals in Blue*, pp. 195–96.
35. Warner, *Generals in Blue*, p. 51.
36. Allan Nevins, *War for the Union, Volume II—War Becomes Revolution, 1862–1863* (New York: Konecky & Konecky, 1960), pp. 11–12.
37. Gabor S. Boritt, ed. *Why the Confederacy Lost* (New York: Oxford University Press, 1992), p. 21.

Chapter 5

1. Nevins, *War Becomes Revolution*, pp. 14–17.
2. Bowman, pp. 79–80.
3. James M. Perry, *Touched with Fire: Five Presidents and the Civil War Battles That Made Them* (New York: Public Affairs, 2003), pp. 59–87. OR, VII, pp. 29, 55–57.
4. OR, VII, p. 78.
5. Eric Ethier, "Folly at Mill Springs," *America's Civil War*, November 2015, pp. 46–51, OR, VII, pp. 81–82, 108.
6. OR, VII, p. 108.
7. Daniel, pp. 16–20.
8. Grant, pp. 147–48.
9. OR, VII, pp. 863–64.
10. OR, VI, p. 825.
11. Nevin, *Shiloh*, pp. 78–79, OR, VII, pp. 613–24.
12. OR, VI, p. 826.
13. Nevin, *Shiloh*, p. 101.
14. Alvin M. Josephy Jr., *War On the Frontier* (Alexandria, VA: Time-Life Books, 1986), pp. 23–26, OR, IX, pp. 487, 493.
15. OR, IX, p. 520.
16. Warner, *Generals in Gray*, pp. 117, 276–77.
17. Josephy, pp. 27–28, Warner, *Generals in Blue*, pp. 363–64, OR, IX, p. 646.
18. OR, Series IV, I, pp. 853–859.
19. OR, IX, pp. 533–35, 542.
20. Warner, *Generals in Gray*, pp. 314–15, Josephy, p. 138.
21. Warner, *Generals in Blue*, pp. 107–08.
22. William L. Shea and Earl J. Hess, *Pea Ridge Civil War Campaign in the West* (Chapel Hill, NC: The University of North Carolina Press, 1992), pp. 46–50.
23. *Ibid.*, pp. 68–82, 270–71.
24. *Ibid.*, pp. 88–94.
25. *Ibid.*, pp. 95–101, OR, VIII, pp. 207–08.
26. Shea and Hess, pp. 151–57, 179.
27. *Ibid.*, pp. 104, 110–11.
28. *Ibid.*, pp. 135–44.
29. *Ibid.*, pp. 216–17, 230.
30. Kennedy, p. 37, Shea and Hess, pp. 239, 255, 271.
31. OR, VIII, p. 598, Shea and Hess, pp. 256–58.
32. OR, VIII, pp. 282, 284.
33. Daniel, pp. 92, 98.
34. *Ibid.*, pp. 72–75, OR, X/2, pp. 28–29, 44.
35. OR, VI, p. 826.
36. OR, X/1, p. 89, OR, X/2, p. 94.
37. OR, X/1, pp. 278–79.
38. Nevin, *Shiloh*, pp. 136–37, OR, X/1, p. 279.
39. Daniel, pp. 145, 236–37.
40. Nevin, *Shiloh*, p. 150.
41. OR, X/1, p. 262, Nevin, *Shiloh*, p. 152.
42. Grant, pp. 193, 195.
43. *Ibid.*, pp. 201.
44. Nevins, *War Becomes Revolution*, p. 123.
45. *Ibid.*
46. OR, XII/1, pp. 554, 708.
47. OR, XII/1, pp. 643–49.
48. Champ Clark *Decoying the Yanks* (Alexandria, VA: Time-Life Books, 1984), p. 153.
49. OR, XII/1, pp. 664, 782.
50. *Ibid.*, pp. 690, 718.
51. OR, XII/3, p. 847.
52. *Ibid.*, pp. 910, 913.
53. OR, XI/1, pp. 28, 31–32.
54. *Ibid.*
55. Jeffry Wert, *The Sword of Lincoln: The Army of the Potomac* (New York: Simon & Schuster, 2005), p. 85.
56. OR, XI/1, pp. 762, 942, 991.
57. *Ibid.*, pp. 52–53.
58. Ethan S. Rafuse, "Culture and Cavalry, Discourse and Reality: Some Observations on the War in the East," *North & South*, Vol. 10, No. 4, January 2008, pp. 74–80.
59. Stephen Sears, *To the Gates of Richmond: The Peninsula Campaign* (New York: Ticknor and Fields, 1992), pp. 183–89, OR, XI/1, p. 51.
60. OR, XI/1, p. 51.
61. Sears, *Richmond*, p. 195.
62. Stoker, p. 63, Wert, *Sword*, p. 94.
63. Sears, *Richmond*, pp. 201–209, OR, XI/2, p. 39.
64. Ethan S. Rafuse, *McClellan's War: The Failure of Moderation in the Struggle for the Union* (Bloomington, IN: Indiana University Press, 2005), p. 221.
65. Dowdey, p. 196.
66. OR, XI/2, p. 41, Sears, *Richmond*, p. 249.
67. Kennedy, p. 97.
68. OR, XI/1, p. 63.
69. *Ibid.*, p. 65.
70. OR, XI/2, p. 495.
71. Sears, *Richmond*, pp. 335, 338.
72. Herman Hattaway and Archer Jones, *How the North Won: A Military History of the Civil War* (Chicago: University of Illinois Press, 1983), p. 200.
73. Sears, *Richmond*, p. 343, OR, XI/2, p. 37, Time-Life Books, ed, *Lee Takes Command: From Seven Days to Second Bull Run* (Alexandria, VA: Time-Life Books, 1984), p. 75.
74. OR, XI/2, p. 497.
75. OR, XI/3, p. 313, Wert, *Sword*, pp. 126–27.
76. Grant, pp. 200–02, Nevins, *War Becomes Revolution*, p. 153.
77. Lossing, p. 512.
78. OR, XI/1, pp. 80–83.
79. *Ibid.*, pp. 77–78.

80. Edward J. Stackpole, *From Cedar Mountain to Antietam, August-September 1862* (Harrisburg, PA: The Stackpole Company, 1959), pp. 60-61.
81. OR, XII/2, p. 146, 151.
82. Stackpole, p. 75, OR, XII/2, p. 139.
83. Rafuse, *Lee*, P. 17.
84. OR, XII/3, p. 576.
85. C. A. Stevens, *Berdan's United States Sharpshooters in the Army of the Potomac, 1861-1865* (Dayton, OH: Morningside Bookshop, 1984), p. 179.
86. Alan T. Nolan, *The Iron Brigade: A Military History* (Bloomington, IN: Indiana University Press, 1994), pp. 89-96, John Hennessy, *Return to Bull Run: The Campaign and Battle of Second Manassas* (New York: Simon and Schuster, 1993), pp. 192-93.
87. OR, XXII/2, p. 260, *Lee Takes Command*, p. 158, Fox, p. 191.
88. Wert, *Sword*, p. 136.
89. *Lee Takes Command*, p. 167, Kennedy, p. 111, OR, XII/2, p. 262.
90. OR, XIX/2, pp. 590-92.
91. OR, XIX/2, pp. 603-04.
92. Wert, *Sword*, p. 147.
93. Lossing, p. 512.
94. OR, XIX/2, pp. 281-82.
95. Stephen W. Sears, *Landscape Turned Red: The Battle of Antietam* (New Haven, CT: Ticknor & Fields, 1983), pp. 88-89, Ronald H. Bailey, *The Bloodiest Day: The Battle of Antietam* (Alexandria, VA: Time-Life Books, 1984), p. 30.
96. Sears, *Landscape*, p. 143.
97. OR, XIX/1, p. 29, OR, XIX/2, p. 281, Sears, *Landscape*, p. 153.
98. OR, LI/1, p. 839, XIX/2, p. 307, XIX/1, p. 30.
99. OR, XIX/1, p. 30.
100. Jubal Anderson Early, *Narrative of the War Between the States* (1912; rpt. New York: Da Capo Press, 1989), p. 149.
101. Sears, *Landscape*, p. 302, John M. Priest, *Antietam: The Soldiers' Battle* (New York: Oxford University Press, 1989), p. 343.
102. Sears, *Landscape*, p. 313.
103. OR, XIX/2, p. 280.
104. OR, XVI/2, p. 9.
105. Stoker, pp. 197, 204.
106. OR, XVI/2, pp. 627, 637.
107. OR, XVI/1, pp. 1036, 1094, Kennedy, p. 127.
108. OR, XVII/1, pp. 78, 126, Stoker, p. 199.
109. OR, XVI/2, p. 858, XVII/2, p. 714.
110. Grant, p. 112.
111. OR, XVII/1, pp. 176, 381.
112. OR, XVI/2, pp. 621, 627, 631, 637, 639, 642.
113. OR, XIX/2, pp. 417, 485, 496-97.
114. Ibid., pp. 553, 579.
115. Grant, p. 224.
116. Peter Cozzens, *The Battle of Stones River: No Better Place to Die* (Chicago: University of Illinois University Press, 1991), p. 30.
117. OR, XX/2, pp. 102, 117-18.
118. Wert, *Sword*, pp. 188-89, Stoker, pp. 216-17.
119. OR, XXI, p. 129, Fox, p. 118.
120. OR, XXI, pp. 142, 562.
121. Ibid., pp. 953-54.
122. Stoker, p. 219, OR, XXI, pp. 807, 868.
123. OR, XX/2, pp. 218-19, Kennedy, p. 152.
124. OR, XX/1, pp. 577, 583, 587-88, 593.
125. Ibid., p. 215, Hattaway and Jones, p. 322.
126. Grant, p. 226.
127. Ibid., pp. 229-30.
128. OR, XVII/1, pp. 602, 606-08. 625, Jerry Korn, *War on the Mississippi: Grant's Vicksburg Campaign* (Alexandria, VA: Time-Life Books, 1985), pp. 63-67, Grant, p. 232.

Chapter 6

1. OR, XX/1, p. 186, Cozzens, *Stones River*, p. 207.
2. OR, LII/2, pp. 398-99.
3. Warner, *Generals in Blue*, p. 235.
4. William K. Goolrick, *Rebels Resurgent Fredericksburg to Chancellorsville* (Alexandria, VA: Time-Life Books, 1985), pp. 110-11.
5. Stephen W. Sears, *Chancellorsville* (New York: Houghton Mifflin Company, 1996), pp. ix, 445.
6. Ibid., pp. 131-32.
7. OR, XXXV/2, pp. 756-57, 759.
8. Sears, *Chancellorsville*, pp. 232, 264, Goolrick, pp. 126-28.
9. Sears, *Chancellorsville*, pp. 269-70, John F. Krumwiede, "The 'Burning Shame' of Chancellorsville," *America's Civil War*, May 2001, pp. 26-27, OR, XXIX/2, p. 769.
10. Simon Van Akin, Jr., "Who Captured the 23rd Georgia," *National Tribune*, 20 October 1889.
11. OR, XXV/2, pp. 438, 412.
12. Sears, *Chancellorsville*, pp. 286, 366, 440-42.
13. Grant, p. 256.
14. Kennedy, pp. 154-73, Grant, pp. 265, 269, 275, Korn, *War*, p. 123.
15. Duane Schultz, *The Most Glorious Fourth: Vicksburg and Gettysburg, July 4, 1863* (New York: W. W. Horton & Company, 2002), p. 103, OR, XXIV/3, pp. 887-88, 890.
16. Korn, *War*, p. 132.
17. Boston Publishing Company, ed. *Above and Beyond: A History of the Medal of Honor from the Civil War to Vietnam* (Boston, MA: Boston Publishing Company, 1985), p. 37.
18. OR, XXV/2, p. 790. Dowdey, *History*, pp. 260-61.
19. Sears, *Chancellorsville*, p. 449.
20. OR, XXVII/2, p. 167, Champ Clark, *Gettysburg, the Confederate High Tide* (Alexandria, VA: Time-Life Books, 1985), p. 25.
21. Warner, *Generals in Blue*, pp.315-16.
22. Gary Kross, "The XI Corps at Gettysburg July 1, 1863," *Blue and Gray Magazine*, December 2001, p. 16.
23. Clark, *Gettysburg*, p. 60, Wert, *Sword*, p. 281, Kross, pp. 50-51.
24. Early, p. 270.
25. Clark, p. 129.
26. Earley, *Sharpshooters*, p. 133, Schultz, p. 333, OR, XXCII/1, p. 181, Wert, *Sword*, p. 300.

27. OR, XXVII/2, pp. 308–09.
28. Grant, pp. 303, 306.
29. Gregory J. W. Urwin, "A Very Disastrous Defeat," *North & South*, December 2002, p. 37.
30. Allan Nevins, *The War for the Union, Volume III: The Organized War, 1863–1864*. (New York: Konecky & Konecky, 1971), p. 112.
31. OR, XXVII/2, p. 346, XXVII/1, pp. 119–20, 187.
32. Nevins, *Organized War*, pp. 112–113, OR, XXVII/1, pp. 83, 85.
33. Thomas F. Wildes, *Record of the One Hundred and Sixteenth Regiment Ohio Infantry Volunteers in the War of the Rebellion* (Sandusky, OH: I. F. Mack & Bro. Printers, 1884), p. 62, Nevins, *Organized War*, pp. 112, 114–15.
34. OR, XXVII/1, p. 93, Paul M. Angle and Earl Schenck Miers, ed. *The Living Lincoln* (New York: Barnes & Noble, 1992), p. 565 Nevins, *Organized War*, p. 115, Wert, *Sword*, p. 309.
35. Peter Cozzens, *The Battle of Chickamauga: This Terrible Sound* (Chicago: University of Illinois Press, 1992), pp. 117–18, Jerry Korn, *The Fight for Chattanooga* (Alexandria, VA: Time-Life Books, 1985), p. 30.
36. OR, XXVII/1, pp. 96, 99, 101–02, Fred R. Ray, *Shock Troops of the Confederacy: The Sharpshooter Battalions of the Army of Northern Virginia* (Ashville, NC: CFS Press, 2006), pp. 75–77, Stevens, pp. 349–50.
37. Cozzens, *Chickamauga*, p. 63.
38. OR, XXX/3, p. 618, XXX/1, p. 54.
39. Cozzens, *Chickamauga*, p. 294.
40. Korn, *The Fight*, pp. 55–68, OR, XXX/1, p. 50.
41. OR, XXX/1, pp. 103–04.
42. Korn, *The Fight*, p. 73, OR, XXX/1, p. 59.
43. Stoker, p. 312, OR, XXIX/2, p. 277.
44. OR, XXIX/2, pp. 206–07, 796.
45. J. Michael Miller, "The Battles of Bristoe Station," *Blue & Gray Magazine*, Vol. XXVI, #2, 2009, pp. 43–50, OR, XXIX/1, pp. 426–28, Kennedy, p. 254.
46. OR, XXIX/2, p. 346.
47. Peter Cozzens, *The Shipwreck of Their Hopes* (Chicago: University of Illinois Press, 1994), p, 11,
48. Korn, *The Fight*, OR, XXX/4, pp, 404, 479.
49. OR, XXX/1, p. 218.
50. Stoker, p. 329, Grant, p. 334, Korn, *The Fight*, p. 118.
51. Nevins, *Organized War*, p. 209, Grant, p. 351, Korn, *The Fight*, p. 143, Cozzens, *The Shipwreck*, p. 390.
52. Cozzens, *The Shipwreck*, p. 391.
53. OR, XXXI/2, pp. 88, 684.
54. Korn, *The Fight*, pp. 113–15, Kennedy, p. 249, OR, XXXI/1, pp. 461, 476.
55. Lowell Harrison, "Battle Beyond Knoxville," *Civil War Times Illustrated*, May 1987, pp. 21, 46–47, OR, XXX/1, p. 535.
56. Stoker, p. 316, Gregory Jaynes, *The Killing Ground: Wilderness to Cold Harbor* (Alexandria, VA: Time-Life Books, 1986), p. 33, Kennedy, p. 255.
57. Chris Howland, "Misfire at Mine Run," *America's Civil War*, January 2005, pp. 50–53, OR, XXIX/2, p. 476, XXIX/1, pp. 13–15, Wert, *Sword*, p. 320, Jaynes, p. 29.
58. OR, XXIX/1, pp. 15–19.
59. *Ibid.*, pp. 686, 838, 847.
60. OR, XXXII/2, p. 667, Stoker, p. 330.

Chapter 7

1. Fox, *Losses*, p. 555.
2. OR, XXXV/1, pp. 278–91, 298, 333.
3. Josephy, pp. 46–47, Kennedy, p. 265.
4. OR, XXXII/3, p. 82.
5. Josephy, pp. 51–54, Kennedy, pp. 265–67, OR, XXXIV/2, pp. 610–11.
6. OR, XXXII/3, pp. 245–46, Stoker, p. 353.
7. OR, XXXII/3, pp. 639–40, 614–15, 607, 618, 628, Stoker, p. 342.
8. Grant, p. 380, OR, XXXIV/2, p. 610, Kennedy, pp. 267–72, Josephy, pp. 51–65.
9. Grant, p. 379.
10. Herbert M. Schiller, "The Bermuda Hundred Campaign," *Blue & Gray Magazine*, Vol. XXXI, #1, 2014, p. 7, OR, XXXIII, p. 795, Grant, p. 376.
11. Warner, *Generals in Blue*, pp. 60–61, Schiller, p. 7.
12. Schiller, p. 8.
13. OR, XXXIV/1, p. 14.
14. Schiller, pp. 20, 26, 28, 44, 46, OR, XXXVI/2, p. 35, William C. Davis, *Death in the Trenches: Grant at Petersburg* (Alexandria, VA: Time-Life Books, 1986), p. 28.
15. OR, XXXIV/1, pp. 17, 14–15, Grant, p. 386–87.
16. Gordon C. Rhea, *The Battle of the Wilderness, May 5–6, 1864* (Baton Rouge: Louisiana State University Press, 1994), pp. 49–55.
17. *Ibid.*, pp. 91–93, Gordon C. Rhea, "The Overland Campaign of 1864," *North & South*, June 2004, p. 15.
18. Rhea, *Wilderness*, pp. 34–35, Wert, *Sword*, p. 335, Joseph Barton to his wife, March 30, 1864, letter, copy from the United States Army Military History Institute.
19. OR, XXXVI/2, pp. 403–04.
20. Jeffry D. Wert, *A Brotherhood of Valor: The Common Soldiers of the Stonewall Brigade, C.S.A. and the Iron Brigade, U.S.A.* (New York: Simon & Schuster, 1999), p. 292.
21. OR, XXXVI/2, pp. 405, 412, 425.
22. OR, XXXVI/1, p. 323.
23. Early, pp. 348–50, Rhea, *Wilderness*, p. 428.
24. OR, XXXVI/1, p. 133, Fox, pp. 541, 559, Rhea, *Wilderness*, p. 440.
25. OR, XXXVI/2, p. 481, XXXVIII/1, p. 8. Grant, p. 423.
26. OR, Ronald H. Bailey, *Battles for Atlanta: Sherman Moves East* (Alexandria, VA: Time-Life Books, 1989), p. 31.
27. Gregory A. Mertz, "General Gouverneur K. Warren and the Fighting at Laurel Hill During the Battle of Spotsylvania Court House, May 1864," *Blue & Gray Magazine*, Vol. XXI, #4, 2004, pp. 5–11.

28. OR, XXXVI/2, pp. 545, 541, Mertz, p. 48.
29. OR, XXXVI/2, p.526.
30. Jaynes, pp. 48–49.
31. OR, XXXVI/2, pp. 627, 652, Chris Mackowski and Kristopher D. White, "Maneuver and Mud: The Battle of Spotsylvania Court House, May 13–20, 1864," *Blue & Gray Magazine*, Vol. XXVII, #6, 2011, p. 49.
32. OR, XXXVI/1, p. 149, Jaynes, pp. 105, 118.
33. Thomas A Lewis, *The Shenandoah in Flames: The Valley Campaign of 1864* (Alexandria, VA: Time-Life Books, 1987), p. 24.
34. OR, XXXVII/1, pp. 446–47, 79–80, Lewis, *Shenandoah*, pp. 31–34.
35. Lewis, *Shenandoah*, pp. 34–37, OR, XXXVII/1, pp. 84–85.
36. Wildes, p. 87, Scott C. Patchan, *The Forgotten Fury: The Battle of Piedmont* (Fredericksburg, VA: Sergeant Kirkland's Museum and Historical Society, Inc., 1996), p. 98, William C. Davis, *The Battle of New Market* (Garden City, NY: Doubleday & Company, Inc., 1975), p. 24, OR, XXXVII/1, p. 80, Lewis, *Shenandoah*, p. 37.
37. Grant, pp. 383–84, Wildes, pp. 87–88, OR, XXXVII/1, pp. 85–86.
38. Lewis, *Shenandoah*, pp. 37–39, Fox, p. 171.
39. Kennedy, p. 331.
40. OR, XXXVIII/4, pp. 728, 725, 736, Bailey, *Atlanta*, pp. 48–49, Stoker, pp. 356–57.
41. Grant, p. 441.
42. OR, XXXVI/2, pp. 1021–22, LI/2, pp. 945, 952.
43. OR, XXXVI/3, p. 77.
44. Ibid., pp. 114, 119–20.
45. Ibid., p. 206, Kennedy, pp. 287–89, Grant, p. 447.
46. OR, XXXVII/1, pp. 485, 492, 500, 536.
47. Ibid., pp. 747, 750, Scott C. Patchan, "Piedmont: The Forgotten Battle," *North & South*, April 2003, p. 64.
48. Lewis, *Shenandoah*, pp. 41–42.
49. Ibid., p. 43, Gerald L. Earley, *I Belonged to the 116th: A Narrative of the 116th Ohio Volunteer Infantry During the Civil War* (Bowie, MD: Heritage Books, 2004), p. 23, OR, XXI, p. 747, Patchan, "Forgotten Battle," p. 63.
50. Patchan, "Forgotten Battle," pp. 67–70, OR, XXXVII/1, p. 561, Earley, *the 116th*, pp. 80–83.
51. Patchan, "Forgotten Battle," pp. 71–72, Wildes, pp. 93–94, OR, XXXVII/1, p. 117.
52. Earley, *the 116th*, p. 86, Lewis, *Shenandoah*, pp. 48–50.
53. Lewis, *Shenandoah*, p. 49, Fox, p. 547.
54. Bailey, *Atlanta*, pp. 50–53.
55. Earnest B. Furgurson, *Not War But Murder: Cold Harbor 1864* (New York: Vintage Books, 2000), p. 71, OR, XXXVI/3, p. 371.
56. Ibid., pp. 411, 469–70.
57. OR, XXXVI/1, p. 999.
58. OR, XXXVI/3, pp. 440–42, XXXVI/1, p. 344.
59. OR, XXXVI/3, pp. 479, 505.
60. Grant, p. 441, OR, XXXVI/3, p. 472.
61. Jaynes, pp. 158, 156.
62. OR, XXXVI/1, p. 180, Furgurson, p. 278, Kennedy, p. 294, Jaynes, p. 169.
63. OR, XXXVI/3, p. 629.
64. OR, XXXVII/1, pp. 598, 626, Lewis, *Shenandoah*, p. 51.
65. OR, LI/2, p. 1003, Lewis, *Shenandoah*, pp. 52, 59.
66. OR, XXXVII/1, pp. 99–100.
67. Ibid., p. 106, Lewis, *Shenandoah*, p. 61.
68. OR, XL/2, pp. 18–19, 47.
69. Ibid., pp. 59, 63, 83, 117, Grant, pp. 472, 474.
70. Fox, *Losses*, p. 125.
71. Hattaway and Archer, pp. 692–94.
72. Davis, *Death*, pp. 53–57, OR, XXXVI/3, p. 114, Wert, *Sword*, p. 377.
73. Bailey, *Atlanta*, pp. 64–65.
74. Kennedy, pp. 344–50, Warner, *Generals in Blue*, 455.
75. Kennedy, pp. 336–39.
76. Thomas A. Lewis, *The Guns of Cedar Creek* (New York: Dell Publishing, 1991), pp. 8–9, Early, p. xviii.
77. Kennedy, pp. 305–08, OR, XXXVII/1, pp. 191–92, 202, 348, XXXVII/2, pp. 155–56.
78. Kennedy, pp. 308–09, Early, pp. 391–94.
79. OR, XXXVII/2, pp. 316, 365, Wildes, p. 127.
80. Jonathan A. Noyalas, "Tempest at Cool Spring," *Civil War Times*, August 2016, pp. 52–59, OR, XXXVII/1, pp. 287, 291–92.
81. Scott C. Patchan, "The Shenandoah Valley July 1864," *Blue & Gray Magazine*, summer 2006, pp. 15–22, Kennedy, p. 309, OR, XXXVII/1, pp. 353–54.
82. OR, XXXVIII/5, pp. 885, 888.
83. Hattaway and Jones, p. 609.
84. Ibid., OR, XXXVIII/1, p. 75.
85. OR, XXXVII/2, pp. 966, 414, 423.
86. Kennedy, pp. 310–12, OR, XXXVII/1, pp. 290, 286, Wildes, pp. 145–46.
87. OR, XXXVIII/1, pp. 77–78, Bailey, *Atlanta*, pp. 132–36.
88. Grant, pp. 479, 482–83, OR, LI/1, pp. 18–19, 47, Davis, *Death*, pp. 70, 89.
89. OR, XXXVII/2, pp. 374, 408, 433, 558, Wert, *Sword*, p. 11, Angle and Miers, p. 612.
90. OR, XLIII/1, p. 719.
91. Lewis, *Shenandoah*, p. 91.
92. Jeffry D. Wert, *From Winchester to Cedar Creek: The Shenandoah Campaign of 1864* (Mechanicsburg, PA: Stackpole Books, 1997), pp. 22, 33–34.
93. Bryce A. Suderow, "Nothing But a Miracle Could Save Us: Second Deep Bottom, Virginia, August 14–20, 1864," *North & South*, Vol. 4, #2, January 2001, pp. 12, 31.
94. OR, XLII/2, pp. 244–45, Chris Calkins, "The Battle of Weldon Railroad (or Globe Tavern), August 18–19 & 21, 1864," *Blue & Gray Magazine*, winter 2007, pp. 20, 23.
95. Bruce M. Venter, "Hancock the (Not So) Superb: The Second Battle of Reams Station August 25, 1864," *Blue & Gray Magazine*, winter 2007, pp. 49–50.
96. Angle & Miers, p. 616.

97. Kennedy, pp. 342–43, OR, XXXVIII/5, p. 777, XXXVIII/1, pp. 84–85, Bailey, *Atlanta*, pp. 154–55.
98. Grant, p. 500, Stoker, pp. 378–79, Lynda Lasswell Christ, Barbara J. Rozerk, and Kenneth H. Williams eds. *The Papers of Jefferson Davis Vol. II* (Baton Rouge: Louisiana State University Press, 2003), pp. 61, 85.
99. Stoker, pp. 380–81.
100. Early, p. 423, Wildes, p. 169, Commissary Sergeant William T. Patterson, Diary, July-October 1862, Ohio Historical Society, Entry of September 19, 1864.
101. Scott C. Patchan, "Opequon Creek: The Third Battle of Winchester, Sept., 19, 1864," *Blue & Gray Magazine*, Vol. XXVII, #2, 2010, pp. 6, 49–50.
102. Eric J. Wittenberg, *Little Phil: A Reassessment of the Civil War Leadership of Gen. Philip H. Sheridan* (Washington, D.C.: Potomac Books, Inc., 2002), p. 64, Early, pp. 427–28.
103. OR, XLIII/1, pp. 557–59.
104. Lumir F. Buresh, *October 25th and the Battle of Mine Creek*, ed. Dan L. Smith (Kansas City, MO: The Lowell Press, 1977), p. 28, OR, XLI/1, p. 729.
105. Scott B. Sallee, "Missouri! One Last Time: Sterling Price's 1864 Missouri Expedition 'A Just and Holy Cause,'" *Blue & Gray Magazine*, June 1991, pp. 14, 18.
106. Kennedy, pp. 362–68, Davis, *Death*, pp. 142–50.
107. Wert, *From Winchester*, pp. 172, 175, Lewis, *Shenandoah*, p. 141.
108. Earley, *The 116th*, pp. 172–73, Wildes, p. 203.
109. Lewis, *Cedar Creek*, p. 186.
110. OR, XLIII/1, p. 161.
111. Lewis, *Cedar Creek*, p. 240.
112. Lewis, *Shenandoah*, pp. 157–58, Wert, *From Winchester*, pp. 246–47.
113. Sallee, p. 57.
114. Buresh, p. 62.
115. *Ibid.*, pp. 216, 221, 224, 233.
116. OR, XXXIX/2, p. 411, XXXIX/3, pp. 577, 594.
117. Stoker, pp. 411, 381.
118. OR, XLV/1, pp. 241, 343–44, Kennedy, pp. 395–96.
119. OR, XLIV, pp. 728, 637, 702.
120. David Nevin, *Sherman's March: Atlanta to the Sea* (Alexandria, VA: Time-Life Books, 1986), p. 144, OR, XLV/1, p. 105.
121. OR, XLIV, p. 783.
122. Grant, pp. 524–27.

Chapter 8

1. Dowdey, *History*, p. 359, Jerry Korn, *Pursuit to Appomattox: The Last Battles* (Alexandria, VA: Time-Life Books, 1987), p17.
2. OR, LIII, p. 412.
3. Grant, p. 542.
4. OR, LIII, pp. 419, 413.
5. Early, pp. 462–63.
6. Earley, *The 116th*, p. 195, Wittenberg, pp. 98–99.
7. Korn, *Pursuit*, p. 39.
8. OR, XLVI/3, pp. 365, 381.
9. Grant, p. 553.
10. Korn, *pursuit*, pp. 87–91.
11. John J. Fox, III, *The Confederate Alamo Bloodbath at Petersburg's Fort Gregg on April 2, 1865* (Winchester, VA: Angle Valley Press, 2010), pp. 38–39, Fox, *Losses*, p. 571.
12. Fox, *Alamo*, pp. 187–89, 225–26, 229, 251–52, OR, XLVI/1, p. 1174.
13. Chris Calkins, "From Sailor's Creek to Cumberland Church, April 6–7, 1865," *Blue & Gray Magazine*, Vol. XXXI, #3, 2015, pp. 26, 39, Kennedy, p. 427, OR, XLVI/3, pp. 610, 619.
14. OR, XLVI/3, pp. 641–42, 664.
15. Kennedy, p. 437.

Chapter 9

1. Stephen Sylvia, "Publisher's Forum, History: Where Lies the Truth?," *North South Trader's Civil War*, Vol. 38, No. 3, 2014, p. 18.
2. Stephen H. Newton, William G. Piston, Keith Poulter, Gregory J. W. Urwin, and Stephen E. Woodworth, "The Most Overrated Generals," *North & South*, December 2009, p. 19.
3. Fox, *Losses*, pp. 63, 349, OR, Series III, V, p. 771, VII, p. 15.
4. Mark A. Weitz, "Drill, Training, and the Combat Performance of the Civil War Soldier: Dispelling the Myth of the Poor Soldier, Great Fighter," *The Journal of Military History*, 62 (April 1998), 263–90.
5. James I. Robertson, Jr., *Soldiers Blue and Gray* (Columbia, SC: University of South Carolina Press, 1988), pp. 48–49, 275, Ames M. Judson, *History of the Eighty-Third Regiment Pennsylvania Volunteers* (Dayton, OH: Morningside, 1986), p. 12.
6. Newton, Piston, Poulter, Urwin and Woodworth, p. 15.
7. Hsieh, p. 133.
8. Carl Sandburg, *Abraham Lincoln: The Prairie Years and the War Years, One-Volume Edition* (New York: Galahad Books, 1993), p. 354, Hsieh, pp. 160, 170.
9. Weitz, p. 283.
10. Hsieh, p. 187.
11. Gary Gallagher, "'Stonewall' and 'Old Jube' in the Valley," *Civil War Times*, December 2014, pp. 18–20.
12. Bell Irvin Wiley, *The Life of Johnny Reb: The Common Soldier of the Confederacy* (Baton Rouge: Louisiana State University Press, 1988), p. 313.
13. Stoker, p. 193.
14. Grant, pp. 471, 192.

Bibliography

Adams, Michael C. C. *Fighting for Defeat: Union Military Failure in the East 1861–1865.* Lincoln: University of Nebraska Press, 1992.

Adamson, Hans Christian. *Rebellion in Missouri: Nathaniel Lyon and His Army of the West.* Philadelphia, PA: Chilton Company, 1961.

Allen, Felicity. *Jefferson Davis: Unconquerable Heart.* Columbia: University of Missouri Press, 1999.

Angle, Paul M., and Earl Schenck Miers, eds. *The Living Lincoln.* New York: Barnes & Noble, 1992.

Bailey, Ronald H. *Battles for Atlanta: Sherman Moves East.* Alexandria, VA: Time-Life Books, 1989.

_____. *The Bloodiest Day: The Battle of Antietam.* Alexandria, VA: Time-Life Books, 1984.

_____. *Forward to Richmond: McClelland's Peninsular Campaign.* Alexandria, VA: Time-Life Books, 1983.

Barton, Joseph. Letter to his wife, March 30, 1864.

Bearss, Edwin C. *The Battle of Wilson's Creek.* Bozeman, MT: George Washington Carver Birthplace District Association, 1975.

Bonekemper, Edward H., III. *The Myth of the Lost Cause: Why the South Fought the Civil War and Why the North Won.* Washington, D.C.: Regnery Publishing, 2005.

Boritt, Gabor S., ed. *Why the Confederacy Lost.* New York: Oxford University Press, 1992.

Boston Publishing Company, ed. *Above and Beyond: A history of the Medal of Honor from the Civil War to Vietnam.* Boston, MA: Boston Publishing Company, 1985.

Bowman, John S., ed. *The Civil War Almanac.* New York: Bison Books, 1983.

Buresh, Lumir F. *October 25th and the Battle of Mine Creek.* Ed. Dan L. Smith. Kansas City, MO: The Lowell Press, 1977.

Calkins, Chris. "The Battle of Weldon Railroad (or Globe Tavern) August 18–19, 1864." *Blue & Gray Magazine,* winter 2007.

_____. "From Sailor's Creek to Cumberland Church April 6–7, 1865." *Blue & Gray Magazine,* Vol. XXXI, #3, 2015.

Catton, Bruce. *The American Heritage Picture History of the Civil War.* Ed. Richard M. Ketchum. New York: American Heritage/Bonanza Books, 1960.

_____. *American Heritage: The Civil War.* Eds. James M. McPherson and Noah Andrew Trudeau. New York: Tess Press, 2009.

Chaitin, Peter M. *The Coastal War: Chesapeake Bay to Rio Grande.* Alexandria, VA: Time-Life Books, 1984.

Christ, Lynda Lasswell, Barbara J. Rozerk, and Kenneth H. Williams, eds. *The Papers of Jefferson Davis, Vol. II.* Baton Rouge: Louisiana State University Press, 2003.

Clark, Champ. *Decoying the Yanks.* Alexandria, VA: Time-Life Books, 1984.

_____. *Gettysburg: The Confederate High Tide.* Alexandria, VA: Time-Life Books, 1985.

Cowley, Robert, and Thomas Guinzburg, eds. *West Point: Two Centuries of Honor and Tradition.* New York: Warner Books, 2002.

Cozzens, Peter. *The Battle of Chickamauga: This Terrible Sound.* Chicago: University of Illinois Press, 1992.

_____. *The Battle of Stones River: No Better Place to Die.* Chicago: University of Illinois Press, 1991.

_____. "Fire on the Mountain." *Civil War Times,* October 1997.

_____. *The Shipwreck of Their Hopes.* Chicago: University of Illinois Press, 1994.

Dalzell, James M. *Private Dalzell.* Cincinnati, OH: Robert Clarke & Co., 1887.

Daniel, Larry J. *Shiloh: The Battle That Changed the War.* New York: Touchstone, 1997.

Davis, David Brion. *Inhuman Bondage: The Rise and Fall of Slavery in the New World.* New York: Oxford University Press, 2006.

Davis, William C. *The Battle of New Market.* Garden City, NY: Doubleday, 1975.

_____. *Brother Against Brother.* Alexandria, VA: Time-Life Books, 1983.

_____. *Death in the Trenches: Grant at Petersburg.* Alexandria, VA: Time-Life Books, 1986.

_____. *First Blood: Fort Sumter to First Bull Run.* Alexandria, VA: Time-Life Books, 1983.

Detzer, David. *Donnybrook: The Battle of Bull Run, 1861.* New York: Harcourt, 2004.

Dowdey, Clifford. *A History of the Confederacy 1832–1865* New York: Barnes & Noble, 1992.

_____. *Lee.* Boston: Little, Brown, 1965.

Dyer, Frederick H. *A Compendium of the War of the Rebellion.* 3 vols. Des Moines, IA: Dyer Publishing, 1908.

Earley, Gerald L. *I Belonged to the 116th: A Narrative of the 116th Ohio Volunteer Infantry during the Civil War.* Bowie, MD: Heritage Books, 2004.

_____. *The Second United States Sharpshooters in the Civil War: A History and Roster*. Jefferson, NC: McFarland, 2009.

Early, Jubal Anderson. *A Narrative of the War Between the States*. New York: Da Capo Press, 1912; rpt. 1989.

Ecelbarger, Gary. *Black Jack Logan: An Extraordinary Life in Peace and War*. Guilford, CT: The Lyon Press, 2005.

Elliott, Henry P. "First Manassas." *Blue and Gray*, XXXVIII, #5, 2011.

Ethier, Eric. "Folly At Mill Springs," *America's Civil War*, November 2015.

Farwell, Byron. *Ball's Bluff: A Small Battle and its Long Shadow*. McLean, VA: EPM, 1990.

Fischer, David Hackett. *Albion's Seed: Four British Folkways in America*. New York: Oxford University Press, 1989.

Foot, Shelby. *The Civil War: A Narrative Fort Sumter to Kernstown: First Blood—The Thing Gets Underway*. New York: Random House, 1958.

Fox, John J., III. *The Confederate Alamo: Bloodbath at Petersburg's Fort Gregg on April 2, 1865*. Winchester, VA: Angle Valley Press, 2010.

Fox, William F. *Regimental Losses in the American Civil War 1861–1865*. Albany, NY: Albany Publishing, 1889.

Freeman, Douglas Southall. *Lee's Lieutenants: Volume One, Manassas to Malvern Hill*. New York: Charles Scribner's Sons, 1946.

Furgurson, Ernest B. *Not War But Murder: Cold Harbor 1864*. New York: Vintage Books, 2000.

Gallagher, Gary. "'Stonewall Jackson' and 'Old Jube' in the Valley." *Civil War Times*, December 2014.

Glatthaar, Joseph. *General Lee's Army: From Victory to Collapse*. New York: Free Press, 2008.

_____. *Soldiers in the Army of Northern Virginia: A Statistical Portrait of Troops who Served Under Robert E. Lee*. Chapel Hill: University of North Carolina Press, 2011.

Goolrick, William K. *Rebels Resurgent: Fredericksburg to Chancellorsville*. Alexandria, VA: Time-Life Books, 1985.

Grant, John, James M. Lynch, and Ronald H. Bailey. *West Point: The First 200 Years*. Guilford, CT: The Globe Pequot Press, 2002.

Grant, Ulysses S. *Personal Memoirs*. New York: The Modern Library, 1999.

Harrison, Lowell. "Battle Beyond Knoxville." *Civil War: Times Illustrated*, May 1987.

Hatcher, Richard W. III, and William Garrett Piston, eds. *Kansans at Wilson's Creek: Soldier's Letters from the Campaign for Southwest Missouri* Springfield, MO: Wilson's Creek National Battlefield Founddation, 1993.

Hattaway, Herman, and Archer Jones. *How the North Won: A Military History of the Civil War*. Chicago: University of Illinois Press, 1983.

Hattaway, Herman, and Richard E. Beringer. *Jefferson Davis, Confederate President*. Lawrence: University Press of Kansas, 2002.

Hennessy, John. *Return to Bull Run: The Campaign and Battle of Second Manassas*. New York: Simon & Schuster, 1993.

Hess, Earl J., Richard W. Hatcher, III, William Garrett Piston, and William L. Shea. *Wilson's Creek, Pea Ridge, and Prairie Grove: A Battle-Field Guide, with a Section on Wire Road*. Lincoln: University of Nebraska Press, 2006.

Heston, Charlton. *In the Arena: An Autobiography*. New York: Simon & Schuster, 1995.

Howland, Chris. "Misfire at Mine Run." *America's Civil War*, January 2015.

Hsieh, Wayne Wei-siang. *West Pointers and the Civil War: The Old Army in War and Peace*. Chapel Hill: University of North Carolina Press, 2009.

Humphrey, William H. Letter to John Gould, March 24, 1893.

James, D. Clayton. *The Years of McArthur, Volume II 1941–1945*. Boston: Houghton Mifflin Company, 1975.

Jaynes, Gregory. *The Killing Ground: Wilderness to Cold Harbor*. Alexandria, VA: Time-Life Books, 1986.

Josephy, Alvin M., Jr. *War on the Frontier*. Alexandria, VA: Time-Life Books, 1986.

Judson, Ames M. *History of the Eighty-Third Regiment Pennsylvania Volunteers*. Dayton, OH: Morningside, 1986.

Keller, Christian B. *Chancellorsville and the Germans: Nativism, Ethnicity, and Civil War Memory*. New York: Fordham University Press, 2007.

Kennedy, Frances H., ed. *The Civil War Battlefield Guide, Second Edition*. New York: Houghton Mifflin Company, 1998.

Korn, Jerry. *The Fight for Chattanooga*. Alexandria, VA: Time-Life Books, 1985,

_____. *Pursuit to Appomattox: The Last Battles*. Alexandria, VA: Time-Life Books, 1987.

_____. *War on the Mississippi: Grant's Vicksburg Campaign*. Alexandria, VA: Time-Life Books, 1985.

Kross, Gary. "The XI Corps at Gettysburg July 1, 1863." *Blue & Gray Magazine*, December 2001.

Krumwiede, John F. "The 'Burning Shame' of Chancellorsville." *America's Civil War*, May 2001.

Lewis, Thomas A. *The Guns of Cedar Creek*. New York: Dell Publishing, 1991.

_____. *The Shenandoah in Flames: The Valley Campaign of 1864*. Alexandria, VA: Time-Life Books, 1987.

Little, David Eicher. *Dixie Betrayed: How the South Lost the Civil War*. New York: Brown, 2006.

Lossing, Benson J. *Mathew Brady's Illustrated History of the Civil War, 1861–1865*. New York: Gramercy Books, 1994.

Mackowski, Chris, and Kristopher D. White. "Maneuver and Mud: The Battle of Spotsylvania Court House May 13–20, 1864." *Blue & Gray Magazine*. Vol. XXVII, #6, 2011.

Marszalek, *Commander of All Lincoln's Armies: A Life of General Henry W. Halleck*. Cambridge: Harvard University Press, 2004.

McKenzie, John D. *Uncertain Glory: Lee's Generalship Re-examined*. New York: Hippocrene, 1997.

McMurry, Richard M. *Two Great Rebel Armies: An Essay in Confederate Military History.* Chapel Hill: University of North Carolina Press, 1989.

McPherson, James M. *For Cause and Comrades: Why Men Fought in the Civil War.* New York: Oxford University Press, 1997.

_____. *What They Fought For.* Baton Rouge: Louisiana State University Press, 1994.

McWhiney, Grady, and Perry Jamison. *Attack & Die: Civil War Military Tactics and the Southern Heritage.* Tuscaloosa: University of Alabama Press, 1982.

Mertz, Gregory A. "General Gouverneur K. Warren and the Fighting at Laurel Hill During the Battle of Spotsylvania Court House, May 1862." *Blue & Gray Magazine*, Vol. XXI, #4, 2004.

Miller, J. Michael. "The Battles of Bristoe Station." *Blue & Gray Magazine*, Vol. XXVI, #2, 2009.

Monaghan, Jay. *Civil War on the Western Border 1854–1865.* Lincoln: University of Nebraska Press, 1955.

Nevin, David. *The Road to Shiloh: Early Battles in the West.* Alexandria, VA: Time-Life Books, 1983.

_____. *Sherman's March: Atlanta to the Sea.* Alexandria, VA: Time-Life Books, 1986.

Nevins, Allan. *The War for the Union: The Improvised War 1861–1862.* New York: Charles Scribner's Sons, 1959.

_____. *The War for the Union: Volume II, War Becomes Revolution, 1862–1863.* New York: Konecky & Konecky, 1960.

_____. *The War for the Union: Volume III, The Organized War, 1863–1864.* New York: Konecky & Konecky, 1971.

New York Times, 1 May 1861, p. 4.

Newell, Clayton D. *Lee vs. McClellan: The First Campaign.* Washington, D.C.: Regnery, 1996.

Newton, Stephen H., William G. Piston, Keith Poulter, Gregory G. W. Urwin, and Stephen E. Woodworth. "The Most Overrated Generals." *North & South*, December 2009.

Nolan, Alan T. *The Iron Brigade: A Military History.* Bloomington: Indiana University Press, 1994.

Nosworthy, Brent. *The Bloody Crucible of Courage: Fighting Methods and Combat Experience in the Civil War.* New York: Carroll & Graf, 2003.

Noyalas, Jonathan A. "Tempest At Cool Spring." *Civil War Times*, August 2016.

Okey, Mark D. *The Justice of Our Cause: A History of the Okey Family in the War of the Rebellion 1861–1865.* Mark D. Okey, 1999.

Patchan, Scott C. *The Forgotten Fury: The Battle of Piedmont.* Fredericksburg, VA: Sergeant Kirkland's Museum and Historical Society, 1996.

_____. "Opequon Creek The Third Battle of Winchester, Sept., 19, 1864." *Blue & Gray Magazine*, Vol. XXVII, #2, 2010, pp. 49–50.

_____. "Piedmont the Forgotten Battle." *North & South*, April 2003.

_____. "The Shenandoah Valley July 1864." *Blue & Gray Magazine*, Summer 2006.

Patterson, Commissary Sergeant William T. Diary July-October 1864. Ohio Historical Society, Entry of September 19, 1864.

Perret, Geoffrey. "Anaconda The Plan That Never Was." *North & South*, Vol. 6, No. 4, May 2003.

Perry, James M. *Touched with Fire: Five Presidents and the Civil War Battles That Made Them.* New York: Public Affairs, 2003.

Phillips, Kevin. *The Cousins' Wars: Religion, Politics & The Triumph of Anglo-America.* New York: Basic Books, 1999.

Phisterer, Frederick. *Statistical Record of the Armies of the United States.* New York: The Blue and the Gray Press.

Piston, William Garrett, and Richard W. Hatcher, III. *Wilson's Creek: The Second Battle of the Civil War and the Men Who Fought It.* Chapel Hill: University of North Carolina Press, 2000.

Priest, John M. *Antietam: The Soldiers' Battle.* New York: Oxford University Press, 1989.

Rafuse, Ethan. "Culture and Cavalry, Discourse and Reality: Some Observations on the War in the East." *North & South*, Vol. 10, No. 4. January 2008.

_____. *McClellan's War: The Failure of Moderation in the Struggle for the Union.* Bloomington: Indiana University Press, 2005.

_____. *Robert E. Lee and the Fall of the Confederacy, 1863–1865.* New York: Roman & Littlefield, 2008.

Ray, Fred L. *Shock Troops of the Confederacy: The Sharpshooter Battalions of the Army of Northern Virginia.* Ashville, NC: CFS Press, 2006.

Rhea, Gordon C. *The Battle of the Wilderness, May 5–6, 1864.* Baton Rouge: Louisiana State University Press, 1994.

_____. "The Overland Campaign of 1864." *North & South*, June 2004.

Ripley, William Y. W. *Vermont Riflemen in the War for the Union, 1861–1865: A History of Company F First United States Sharpshooters.* Rutland, VT: Tuttle & Co., 1883.

Robertson, James I., Jr. *Soldiers Blue and Gray.* Columbia: University of South Carolina Press, 1988.

Sallee, Scott B. "Missouri! One Last Time Sterling Price's 1864 Missouri Expedition 'A Just and Holy Cause,'" *Blue & Gray Magazine*, June 1991.

Sandburg, Carl. *Abraham Lincoln: The Prairie Years and the War Years.* New York: Galahad Books, 1993.

Schiller, Herbert M. "The Bermuda Hundred Campaign." *Blue & Gray Magazine*, Vol. XXXI, #1, 2014.

Schultz, Duane. *The Most Glorious Fourth: Vicksburg and Gettysburg, July 4, 1863.* New York: Horton, 2002.

Sears, Stephen W. *Chancellorsville.* New York: Houghton Mifflin, 1996.

_____, ed. *The Civil War Papers of George B. McClellan: Selected Correspondence, 1860–1865.* New York: Ticknor & Fields, 1989.

_____. *George B. McClellan The Young Napoleon.* New York: Ticknor & Fields, 1988.

_____. *Landscape Turned Red: The Battle of Antietam.* New Haven, CT: Ticknor & Fields, 1983.

_____. *To the Gates of Richmond: The Peninsula Campaign.* New York: Ticknor & Fields, 1992.

_____. "Winfield Scott and the Coming of the War." *North & South*, Vol. 10, No. 4, January 2008.

Shea, William L., and Earl J. Hess. *Pea Ridge: Civil War Campaign in the West.* Chapel Hill: University of North Carolina Press, 1992.

Smith, Carter. *Presidents: Every Question Answered.* Irvington, New York: Hylas Publishing, 2009.

Smith, Charles Powers. *Yankees & God.* New York: Hermitage House, 1954.

Stackpole, Edward J. *From Cedar Mountain to Antietam August–September 1862.* Harrisburg, PA: The Stackpole Company, 1959.

Stampp, Kenneth M. *The Peculiar Institution: Slavery in the Antebellum South.* New York: Vintage Books, 1989.

Stevens, C. A. *Berdan's United States Sharpshooters in the Army of the Potomac: 1861–1865.* Dayton, OH: Morningside Bookshop, 1984.

Stiles, T. J. *Jesse James: Last Rebel of the Civil War.* New York: Vintage Books, 2002.

Stoker, Donald. *The Grand Design: Strategy in the U.S. Civil War.* New York: Oxford University Press, 2010.

Streissguth, Thomas, ed. *The Civil War: The South.* San Diego, CA: Greenhaven, 2001.

Suderow, Bryce A. "Nothing But a Miracle Could Save Us Second Deep Bottom, Virginia, August 14–20, 1864." *North & South*, Vol. 4, #2, January 2001.

Sylvia, Stephen. "Publisher's Forum, History: Where Lies the Truth?." *North South Trader's Civil War*, Vol. 38 No. 3, 2014.

Taylor, William R. *Cavalier and Yankee: The Old South and American National Character.* New York: George Braziller, 1961.

Time-Life Books, ed. *Lee Takes Command: From Seven Days to Second Bull Run.* Alexandria, VA: Time-Life Books, 1984.

Urwin, Gregory J. W. "A Very Disastrous Defeat." *North & South* December 2002.

U.S. War Department. *The War of the Rebellion: A Compilation of the Official Records of the Union and Confederate Armies.* 128 vols. Washington, D.C.: U.S. Government Printing Office, 1880–1901.

Van Akin, Simon, Jr. "Who Captured the 23rd GA." *National Tribune*, 20 October 1889.

Venter, Bruce M. "Hancock the (Not So) Superb The Second Battle of Reams Station August 25, 1864." *Blue & Gray Magazine*, winter 2007.

Warner, Ezra J. *Generals in Blue: Lives of the Union Commanders.* Baton Rouge: University of Louisiana Press, 2006.

_____. *Generals in Gray: Lives of the Confederate Commanders.* Baton Rouge: University of Louisiana Press, 2002.

Webb, James. *Born Fighting: How the Scots-Irish Shaped America.* New York: Broadway Books, 2004.

_____. "Why You Need to Know the Scotts-Irish," *Parade Magazine*, 3 October 2004, p. 5.

Weitz, Mark A. "Drill, Training, and the Combat Performance of the Civil War Soldier: Dispelling the Myth of the Poor Soldier, Great Fighter." *The Journal of Military History* 62 (April 1998), 263–90.

Wert, Jeffry D. *A Brotherhood of Valor: The Common Soldiers of the Stone-Wall Brigade, C.S.A. and the Iron Brigade, U.S.A.* New York: Simon & Schuster, 1999.

_____. *From Winchester to Cedar Creek: The Shenandoah Campaign of 1864.* Mechanicsburg, PA: Stackpole Books, 1997.

_____. *The Sword of Lincoln: The Army of the Potomac.* New York: Simon & Schuster, 2005.

Wildes, Thomas F. *Record of the One Hundred and Sixteenth Regiment: Ohio Volunteer Infantry in the War of the Rebellion.* Sandusky, OH: I. F. Mack & Bro., 1884.

Wiley, Bell Irvin. *The Life of Johnny Reb: The Common Soldier of the Confederacy.* Baton Rouge: Louisiana State University Press, 1988.

Wittenburg, Eric J. *Little Phil: A Reassessment of the Civil War Leadership of Gen. Philip H. Sheridan.* Washington, D.C.: Potomac, 2002.

Woodhead, Henry, ed. *Echoes of Glory: Arms and Equipment of the Confederacy.* Alexandria, VA: Time-Life Books, 1991.

_____. *Echoes of Glory: Arms and Equipment of the Union.* Alexandria, VA: Time-Life Books, 1991.

Index

Alexander, Brig. Gen. Edward P. 162
Anaconda Plan 27, 35, 267, 281
Anderson, Lt. Gen. Richard 141, 203, 221–222
Antietam, Battle of 112–17, 136, 151, 155, 166. 168
Appomattox Court House, surrender at 276–78
Arkansas troops: CSA: Mounted Rifles: 2nd 49-50, 75
Army of Northern Virginia 17–18, 29–30, 104, 113, 116–17, 139, 175, 191, 201, 204, 249, 255, 276, 285–86
Army of the Potomac 10, 79, 91, 96–98, 100, 101–2, 107, 110, 112, 124, 126, 128–29, 136, 139–40, 142, 146, 153–55, 162, 174–75, 178, 182–83, 187–88, 191–92, 194–98, 201, 204, 209, 214–15, 221, 223, 225–28, 230–31, 238, 240–41, 243, 258, 265, 271, 285–86
Ashboth, Brig. Gen. Alexander 77–78
Atkinson, Corp. James 274
Atlanta, Battle of 238–39
Averell, Brig. Gen. William 139, 236, 243

B & O Railroad 34, 238, 246
Bailey, Brig. Gen. Joseph 190
Baker, Col. Edward 60
Ball's Bluff, Battle of 60–61
Banks, Maj. Gen. Nathaniel 87–90, 103–4, 168, 187–91, 213, 285
Barnard, Maj. Gen. John G. 38, 95, 130
Bean's Station, Battle of 181
Beatty, Col. Samuel 131, 133
Beauregard, Gen. Pierre G.T. 36–41, 43, 68, 82–83, 85, 92–93, 118, 193, 213–14, 228, 229, 269
Benjamin, Sec. Judah P. 68–69, 79
Benteen, Lt. Col. Frederick 256
Bentonville, Battle of 271
Bethesda Church, Battle of 221
Big Black River Bridge, Battle of 149–50
Blair, Francis P, Jr. 46
Blenker, Brig. Gen. Louis 88
Blunt, Maj. Gen. James 126, 255, 257

Bragg, Gen. Braxton 68–69, 72, 79–80, 85, 118–21, 123, 125–26, 130–32, 134, 168–71, 173, 176–80, 189, 214, 227, 232
Brawner's Farm, Battle of 106, 109
Breckenridge, Maj. Gen. John 132, 177, 192, 210–12, 214
Brice's Crossroads, Battle of 231
Bristoe Station, Battle of 175
Buchanan, Pres. James 9–10
Buckingham, Brig. Gen. Catharinus 124
Buckner, Lt. Gen. Simon 46, 59
Buell, Maj. Gen. Don C. 63–64, 66–67, 80, 101, 118–19, 122–23, 125, 137, 179, 283
Buford, Brig. Gen. John 153
Bull Run, 1st Battle of 33, 35–45, 50, 60, 86, 108, 286–87
Bull Run, 2nd Battle of 107–9, 116, 224, 286
Burnside, Maj. Gen. Ambrose 65, 79, 103, 115, 124–26, 128–30, 135, 139, 145, 170, 178, 180–81, 184, 198–99, 207, 241, 285
Butler, Maj. Gen. Benjamin 60, 188, 191–94, 202, 204, 213, 226, 229, 265–66, 268, 285

Cameron, Sec. Simon 24
Canby, Maj. Gen. Edward R.S. 26, 69–70, 191, 272
Carnifex Ferry, Battle of 34
Carr, Col. Eugene 74–76, 79
Carson, Col. Christopher (Kit) 70
Carthage, Battle of 47, 77
Casey, Brig. Gen. Silas 91
Cedar Creek, Battle of 252–55, 271
Cedar Mountain, Battle of 104
Chaffin's Bluff, Battle of 251
Champion's Hill, Battle of 149
Chancellorsville, Battle of 141–47, 151, 154–55, 157, 174, 184, 199, 286
Chantilly, Battle of 109
Chase, Sec. Salmon P. 35
Chattanooga, Battle of 178–180, 204
Cheat Mountain, Battle of 34–35
Chickamauga, Battle of 171–74, 176, 184, 286
Chickasaw Bluffs, Battle of 134–35, 185

Chivington, Maj. John 71–72
Cleburne, Maj. Gen. Patrick 178, 180, 261–62
Cold Harbor, Battle of 222–26, 265
Colorado Troops: Infantry (1st) 71
Connecticut Troops: Infantry (18th) 217–18
Cooper, Gen. Samuel 236–37
Corinth, Battle of 121–22, 134
Couch, Maj. Gen. Darius 145
Cozzens, Peter 179
Crater, Battle of 240–41, 258
Craven, Joseph F. 110
Crawford, Maj. Gen. Samuel 104, 221
Crittenden, Maj. Gen. George B. 66–67
Crittenden, Maj. Gen. Thomas L. 130, 172
Crook, Maj. Gen. George 209, 217, 226–27, 235, 239, 248–49, 252–53
Cross Keys, Battle of 88–89
Curtis, Maj. Gen. Samuel 72–76, 78–79
Custer, Brig. Gen. George A. 236, 270

Dalzell, James 16
Davis, David Brion 3
Davis, Pres. Jefferson 16, 20–21, 24–25, 30, 35, 44–45, 58–59, 67–69, 72, 80, 89, 109, 116–17, 125, 136, 138, 150–51, 174–75, 178–80, 188–89, 192, 213–14, 227, 232, 236–37, 246, 249–50, 264, 269–71, 277, 279, 282
Davis, Brig. Gen. Jefferson C. 76, 172
Dodge, Maj. Gen. Grenville M. 74, 79
Douglass, Frederick 14
Dowdey, Clifford 13, 268
Drewry's Bluff, Battle of 193
Dug Springs, action at 47
Duncan, Lt. Col. James 274
DuPont, Capt. Henry 211, 217

Earley, James 110, 152, 192, 227, 274
Early, Lt. Gen. Jubal A. 36, 115, 152, 154–55, 200, 221, 227, 232–

301

34, 236, 238–39, 241–43, 246–55, 270–71, 286–87
Eddy, Pvt. Samuel 275–76
Ely, Col. William 218
Emerson, Ralph W. 8
Emory, Brig. Gen. William H. 190, 253
Evans, Col. Nathan 39, 60–61
Ewell, Lt. Gen. Richard 36, 87–89, 106, 152, 154–55, 157–58, 160–62, 183, 197, 200, 206, 208, 221, 276
Ewing, Brig. Gen. Thomas 250
Ezra Church, Battle of 239–40, 245

Fagan, Maj. Gen. James F. 250, 257
Fallen Timbers, action at 84
Featheringill, Clara 5
Finegan, Brig. Gen. Joseph 186
Fisher, David H. 17
Fisher's Hill, Battle of 248–49, 254–55
Five Forks, Battle of 272–73
Foote, Flag. Off. Andrew H. 67–69
Forrest, Lt. Gen. Nathan B. 84, 125, 135, 231, 264, 272, 279
Fort Craig 69–70
Fort Davidson 250
Fort Donelson, Battle of 68–69, 80–81, 90, 99, 111, 135
Fort Early 227
Fort Fisher, Battle of 265, 268–69
Fort Gregg, Battle of 274–75, 286
Fort Harrison, action at 251
Fort Haskell 271
Fort Henry, capture of 67–69, 135
Fort Leavenworth 46, 256
Fort McAllister, Battle of 263
Fort Pulaski 79, 135, 226
Fort Sanders, Battle of 180, 185
Fort Scott 56, 256–57
Fort Stedman, Battle of 271–72
Fort Stevens, Battle of 234
Fort Sumter 13, 16–17, 23–25, 29, 59
Fort Union 71
Fort Whitworth 274
Franklin, Maj. Gen. William 100, 111–12, 242, 284–85
Franklin, Battle of 260–63
Fredericksburg, Battle of 128–29, 135, 155, 175, 224, 286
Freeman, Douglas S. 29
Fremont, Maj. Gen. John C. 47–48, 56, 58, 63, 77, 87–89, 103, 285
French, Maj. Gen. William 169, 182
Fussel's Mill, Battle of 243–44

Gaines's Mill, Battle of 95–96, 108, 221
Gallagher, Gary 286–87
Garfield, Maj. Gen. James A. 66
Garnett, Brig. Gen. Robert S. 33
Georgia troops: Infantry (18th) 95, 112; (23rd) 142; (49th) 109
Getty, Brig. Gen. George 197

Gettysburg, Battle of 153–66, 168, 173–74, 184, 195
Gibbon, Maj. Gen. John 106, 229, 274–75
Gilmore, Maj. Gen. Quincy 186, 191, 193, 226, 228, 284
Glendale, Battle of 97
Globe Tavern, Battle of 244
Glorieta Pass, Battle of 71
Gordon, Maj. Gen. John B. 154, 200, 249, 254–55, 271–72, 276
Gorgas, Brig. Gen. Josiah 216
Grant, Lt. Gen. Ulysses 8, 31, 58, 67–68, 81, 83–85, 94, 99, 101, 118, 120–22, 125, 130, 134–35, 139–40, 147–52, 164–65–66, 174, 176–79, 184, 187–88, 190–98, 201–6, 208–9, 211, 213–15, 221–26, 228–30, 232–35, 238–44, 246, 251–52, 258–59, 263–73, 275–77, 279, 282, 286–87
Green, Col. Thomas 70
Greer, Col. Elkanah 52–53
Gregg, Brig. Gen. John 148–49
Grider, Col. Benjamin 133
Grierson, Brig. Gen. Benjamin H. 148
Griffin, Brig. Gen. Charles 40, 273

Hale, Com. S.F. 19, 27
Halleck, Maj. Gen. Henry W. 30–31, 63–64, 67, 72–73, 80–81, 85, 100–5, 110–12, 117–20, 123–26, 128–30, 137, 152, 155, 166–69, 174–75, 176, 183–84, 186–87, 189, 191, 204, 208, 211, 214–15, 221, 226, 230, 234, 238–39, 241, 264
Hampton, Maj. Gen. Wade 36, 39, 226
Hancock, Maj. Gen. Winfield S. 155, 162. 197–99, 202, 214, 223, 228–29, 240–41, 243–45
Hardee, Lt. Gen. William J. 68, 177, 237–38, 245, 265
Harpers Ferry, Battle of 112
Harris, Gov. Isham 82, 120
Harris, Brig. Gen. Nathaniel 274
Harris, Col. Thomas 252–53
Hatch, Brig. Gen. John P. 106
Hatcher's Run, Battle of 270
Hattaway, Herman 129
Hays, Brig. Gen. Alexander 161
Hazen, Brig. Gen. William 263
Hebert, Col. Louis 75–76, 78
Hebert, Paul 284
Heintzman, Maj. Gen. Samuel 99
Helena, Battle of 165
Herron, Brig. Gen Francis 126
Heston, Charlton 1
Hill, Lt. Gen. Ambrose P. 103, 144, 175, 183, 197–98, 244, 251, death of, 274, 285
Hill, Lt. Gen. Daniel H. 91, 111
Hindman, Maj. Gen. Thomas 126
Hinks, Brig. Gen. Edward 226, 228–29
Holms, Lt. Gen. Theophilus 39, 138, 165

Hood, Gen. John B. 95, 151, 166, 171, 188–89, 213, 231, 236–39, 245–47, 250–51, 258–60, 263–65, 282
Hooker, Maj. Gen. Joseph 98, 113, 139–42, 144–47, 151–53, 174, 177–78
Hoover's Gap, Battle of 169
Howard, Maj. Gen. Oliver O. 142–43, 146, 154, 285
Huger, Maj. Gen. Benjamin 92
Humphrey, Capt. William 2–3
Humphreys, Maj. Gen. Andrew A. 222
Hunt, Brig. Gen. Henry 10
Hunter, Maj. Gen. David 39, 215–18, 220, 226–27, 232, 234–35, 239, 242

Illinois troops: Cavalry (3rd) 74; Infantry (23rd) 56; (35th) 74; (36th) 75
Imboden, Brig. Gen. John 216
Indiana troops: Infantry (7th) 33; (9th) 33; (11th) 233; (19th) 106; (27th) 109; (32nd) 283
Iowa troops: Artillery (1st Iowa Battery) 74; Cavalry (3rd) 74; Infantry (4th) 74
Island No. 10, 69, 72, 80, 84, 99, 103
Iuka, Battle of 120–21

Jackson, Pres. Andrew 9
Jackson, Gov. Claiborne F. 28–28, 46
Jackson, Lt. Gen. Thomas 17, 31, 36–37, 86–90, 92–93, 103–9, 141–47, 157, 199, 232, 239, 243, 285–87
Jackson, Battle of 148–49
Jefferson, Pres. Thomas 9, 30
Johnson, Brig. Gen. Bradley 233
Johnson, Brig. Gen. Bushrod 181
Johnston, Gen. Albert S. 27, 58–59, 67–68, 72, 80–82, 85, 86
Johnston, Gen. Joseph 18, 33, 36–40, 79, 86–87, 90–91, 125, 138, 148–50, 164–65, 185, 188–89, 203, 209, 212–13, 220–21, 231–32, 236–37, 246, 266, 270–72, 277, 282
Jones, Archer 129
Jones, William 59, 130–31, 181
Jones, Brig. Gen. William E. 215–20
Jonesboro, Battle of 245

Kansas troops: Infantry (1st) 46, 48–49; (2nd) 46, 48, 51–52
Karr, Capt. Hamilton 253
Kautz, Brig. Gen. Augustus 226, 228–30
Kearney, Maj. Gen. Phillip 98, 108–9
Kelly's Ford, Battle of 139–40
Kennesaw Mountain, Battle of 231

Index

Kentucky troops: Infantry (4th) 66; (11th) 59, 131, 133
Kernstown, Battle of 239, 247
Kershaw, Maj. Gen. Joseph B. 36, 249, 276
Keys, Maj. Gen. Erasmus D. 99–100
King, Brig. Gen. Rufus 106
Knoxville, Siege of 180
Kolb's Farm, Battle of 231

Law, Brig. Gen. Evander M. 224
Lawler, Brig. Gen. Michael 149
Ledlie, Brig. Gen. James H. 214, 241
Lee, Maj. Gen. Fitzhugh 139, 221
Lee, Major Gen. George W.C. 276, 284
Lee, Gen. Robert E. 7, 21, 27, 33–35, 72, 89, 91, 93–99, 102–13, 115–18, 122, 124, 129, 136, 138–43, 146–47, 150–52, 154–58, 160–68, 174–75, 178, 181–85, 188–89, 191–97, 199, 201–4, 206–10, 213–17, 221–223, 225–28, 232, 236–37, 241, 243–44, 246, 249–52, 257–58, 265–77, 282–84, 287
Lee, Lt. Gen. Stephen D. 135, 240
Lexington, Battle of 56–58, 60
Lincoln, Pres. Abraham 7–9, 17, 19–21. 23–24, 26–29, 36, 44, 56, 58–60, 63–65, 67, 79, 87–88, 90. 98–103, 110, 116, 118–19, 122–26, 128–30, 134, 136, 138–39, 152, 166–69, 174, 176, 184–88, 191–92, 209, 215, 220, 228, 233–35, 239, 242, 245, 252, 258, 265–66, 279, 282, 285–86
Little, Brig. Gen. Henry 120
Logan, Maj. Gen. John A. 238, 264
Longstreet Lt. Gen. James 36, 91, 105–8, 110–111, 117, 139, 155–58, 160–63, 166, 169, 171–72, 177–81, 184, 188–89, 198–99, 202–3, 272, 274, 285
Loring, Brig. Gen. William W. 34
Louisiana troops: Infantry (3rd) 50, 152
Lynchburg, Battle of 227–28, 232
Lyon, Brig. Gen. Nathaniel 46–52, 54, 72, 254

MacArthur, Gen. Douglas 3, 275
Magoffin, Gov. Beriah 19, 24, 27–28, 45–47, 58–59
Magruder, Maj. Gen. John B. 96
Mahan, Prof. Denis H. 31–32, 63
Maine troops: Heavy Artillery (1st) 230
Malvern Hill, Battle of 97–98, 129
Mansfield, Battle of 190
Marmaduke, Brig. Gen. John S. 46, 165, 256
Marshall, Brig. Gen. Humphrey 66
Massachusetts troops: Infantry (34th) 211–12, 216; (37th) 275 (54th) 186

McClellan, Maj. Gen. George B. 27, 30–34, 45, 61–63, 65, 79, 85–87, 89–105, 110–13, 115–18, 122–24, 129–30, 134, 136, 144, 146, 153, 162, 168, 183, 185, 213, 221, 230, 242, 246, 258, 282
McClernand, Maj. Gen. John 134, 150
McCulloch, Brig. Gen. Ben 46–48, 52, 54–55, 72–76, 78
McDowell, Maj. Gen. Irvin 27, 33, 35–36–41, 43, 88, 90, 94, 103
McIntosh, Brig. Gen. James M. 50, 74–76, 78
McPherson, Maj. Gen. James B. 212, 238, 284
Meade, Maj. Gen. George G. 153, 155–56, 158, 160–63, 166–69, 174–76, 181–83, 192, 194–98, 200–2, 204, 213–14, 223–25, 229–30, 241–42, 244, 257, 286
Mechanicsville, Battle of 93–94, 221–22
Middle Creek, Battle of 66, 68
Mill Springs, Battle of 66–68
Milroy, Maj. Gen. Robert 87, 152, 264
Mine Creek, Battle of 256–57
Mine Run Campaign 181–83
Missouri troops: Infantry (1st) 46, 48–49; (2nd) 52; (3rd) 46, 48, 53; (5th) 46, 48; (11th) 121
Mitchel, Maj. Gen. Ormsby M. 101, 118
Mobile, AL, surrender of 278
Monocacy, Battle of 233
Montgomery, Col. James 186
Moor, Col. Augustus 210–11, 217–19
Moorefield, Battle of 243
Morgan, Brig. Gen. George W. 118
Morton, Gov. O.P. 123
Mower, Maj. Gen. Joseph 271
Mulligan, Col. James 56, 58

Nashville, Battle of 264–65
Nevins, Allan 166, 178
New Hope Church, Battle of 220
New Market, Battle of 210–212, 215–16
New York troops: Heavy Artillery (5th) 217; Infantry (5th) 108; (10th) 108; (11th) 40; (14th) 40; (79th) 180
Newton, Stephen 284
North Anna, Battle of 214–15, 224
North Carolina troops: Infantry (18th) 144

Oak Grove, Battle of 92
Ocean Pond, Battle of 186
Ohio troops: Infantry (14th) 33; (19th) 131, 133; (27th) 121; (28th) 211, 217–18; (77th) 84; (116th) 16, 110, 167, 211, 218, 227, 235, 253; (123rd) 210–11, 253
Opdycke, Colonel Emerson 260

Opequon/3rd Winchester, Battle of 247–49, 254
Ord, Maj. Gen. Edward O.C. 120
Osterhaus, Maj. Gen. Peter J. 74

Paine, Capt. William 223
Palmito Ranch, action at 278
Parke, Maj. Gen. John 181
Patterson, Maj. Gen. Robert 33, 36–38, 43
Paul, Col. Gabriel 71
Payne's Farm, action at 182
Pea Ridge, Battle of 50, 73–80, 90, 134, 209
Peabody, Col. Everett 56, 58
Peach Tree Creek, Battle of 237, 245
Pelham, Maj. John 140
Pemberton, Lt. Gen. John C. 134, 148–50, 164–65, 209
Pender, Brig. Gen. Dorsey 117
Pendleton, Brig. Gen. William 203
Pennypacker, Brig. Gen. Galusha 268
Pennsylvania troops: Cavalry (Ringgold Battalion) 110, 217; Infantry (48th) 240; (138th) 274
Perryville, Battle of 119–20, 122
Petersburg, actions and battles of 226, 228–31, 234, 251, 265, 270, 272, 274–75
Philippi, Battle of 32
Phillips, Kevin 7
Pickett, Maj. Gen. George 273
Pickett's Charge 162–63, 166
Pickett's Mill, Battle of 220
Piedmont, Battle of 217–220, 226
Pierce, Pres. Franklin 9–10, 21, 26
Pike, Brig. Gen. Albert 74, 76
Pilot Knob, Battle of 250
Pipe Creek 155
Pleasant Hill, Battle of 190
Plummer, Capt. Joseph 49–50
Polk, Lt. Gen. Leonidas 58–59, 69, 189
Pope, Maj. Gen. John 56, 72, 84, 103–9, 272
Port Gibson, Battle of 148
Port Hudson, Siege of 168
Port Republic, Battle of 89
Porter, Admiral David D. 148
Porter, Maj. Gen. Fitz John 93, 96, 98–99
Post, Col. Henry 106
Prairie Grove, Battle of 126–27
Prentiss, Brig. Gen. Benjamin 81–83, 165
Price, Maj. Gen. Sterling 46–49, 52–54, 56, 58, 72–73, 75–76, 78, 118, 120–21, 165, 250–51, 255–57

Rafuse, Ethan 92
Ramseur, Maj. Gen. Stephen 236, 255
Rappahannock Station, Battle of 181
Raymond, Battle of 148

Ream's Station, Battle of 244–45
Reno, Maj. Gen. Jesse 108–9; death of 111
Resaca, Battle of 212
Reynolds, Maj. Gen. John 153–54
Ricketts, Brig. Gen. James 40
Ripley, Lt. Col. William 10
Rocky Face Ridge, Battle of 209
Rodes, Maj. Gen. Robert 221, 236
Rogers, Col. William 121
Rosecrans, Maj. Gen. William S. 33, 120–23, 125–26, 130–32, 134, 138, 168–73, 176–77, 184
Ruggles, Brig. Gen. Daniel 69, 81
Rutherford's Farm, Battle of 236, 238–39

Sailor's Creek, Battle of 275
Schimmelfennig, Col. Alexander 285
Schofield, Maj. Gen. John 55, 126, 232, 243, 259–60, 263–65
Schurz, Maj. Gen. Carl 143, 285
Scott, Lt. Gen. Winfield 9, 18, 22, 26–27, 33, 35–38, 43–45, 61–63, 65, 100, 187, 267, 281
Scurry, Col. William R. 71–72
Sears, Stephen 140
Sedgwick, Maj. Gen. John 144–46, 182, 197, 202, 204–6
Seven Pines, Battle of 91
Seymour, Brig. Gen. Truman 186, 200
Shackelford, Brig. Gen. James 181
Shelby, Brig. Gen. Joseph 165, 257
Sheridan, Maj. Gen. Phillip 119, 195, 221–222, 226–27, 240–44, 246–48, 251–55, 270, 272–73, 276, 287
Sherman, Maj. Gen. William T. 31, 36, 81, 84–85, 124, 134–35, 148, 178–79, 181, 188, 191–92, 194, 203, 209, 212–13, 220, 231–32, 236, 238–40, 242–43, 245–51, 258–59, 263–65, 267, 269–71, 279, 285
Shields, Brig. Gen. James 88–89
Shiloh, Battle of 81–85, 90, 118, 137, 165, 233
Sibley, Brig. Gen. Henry H. 69–71
Sickles, Maj. Gen. Daniel 156–57, 285
Sigel, Maj. Gen. Franz 46–51, 53–55, 77–78, 88, 103, 107, 143, 188, 192, 209–12, 214–15, 283, 285
Slocum, Maj. Gen. Henry 155, 245
Slough, Col. John P. 71

Smith, Brig. Gen. Andrew J. 187, 190, 231, 264
Smith, General Edmond K. 118, 120, 250, 278
Smith, Maj. Gen. William F. 177, 191, 193, 221–22, 224–25, 228–29, 284
Snicker's Ferry, Battle of 235–36, 239
South Mountain, Battle of 111–12, 116
Spotsylvania, Battle of 203–8, 224, 265
Stahel, Maj. Gen. Julius 210, 217
Stanton, Sec. Edwin 98, 101, 176
Stewart, Lt. Gen. Alexander 237
Stickley's Farm, Battle of 252
Stoker, Donald 246, 258, 287
Stoneman, Maj. Gen. George 140–41, 146–47, 240
Stones River, Battle of 5, 50, 130–34, 138
Strother, Col David H. 209–10
Stuart, Maj. Gen. James E.B. 36–37, 91, 93, 144–45, 155, 195
Sturgis, Maj. Gen. Samuel 46, 53–55, 231
Sumner, Maj. Gen. Edwin V. 96, 99, 285
Sylvia, Stephen 280

Taliaferro, Brig. Gen. William 106
Taylor, Maj. Gen. Richard 189–90
Taylor, Pres Zachary 9, 20, 72, 189
Terry, Maj. Gen. Alfred 268
Texas troops: Infantry (2nd) 121
Thoburn, Col. Joseph 218–19, 235–36, 248
Thomas, Maj. Gen. George H. 37, 66–67, 170–72, 177–79, 194, 212, 237, 258–59, 263–65
Toombs, Sec. Robert 23–25
Totopotomoy Creek, Battle of 221
Totten, Capt. James 53
Trading Post, action at 256
Trevilian Station, Battle of 226
Tupelo, Battle of 231
Tyler, Brig. Gen. Daniel 38–39
Tyler, Brig. Gen. Erastus 89

United States Sharpshooters: (1st), 10, 142 (2nd), 106, 142, 158, 195
United States troops: Artillery (Battery B 5th) 211; Cavalry (1st) 70; (3rd) 70; Infantry (5th) 70–71; (7th) 70; (10th) 70

Upton, Brig. Gen. Emory 181, 205
Urbanna Plan 79, 85

Valverde Ford, Battle of 70
Van Cleve, Brig. Gen. Horatio 131
Van Dorn, Maj. Gen Earl 72–80, 118, 120–22, 134–35
Vermont troops: Infantry (13th) 162
Vicksburg, siege and battle of 50, 140, 149–52, 164–66, 168, 184, 204, 224, 240
Virginia Military Institute Cadets 210, 212
Virginia troops: Infantry (60th) 219

Wagner, Brig. Gen. George 260
Wainwright, Col. Charles 208
Waite, Brig. Gen. Stand 278
Wallace, Maj. Gen. Lewis 85, 232–33
Wapping Heights, action at 169
Ward, Brig. Gen. John H.H. 206
Warren, Maj. Gen. Gouverneur K. 175, 182–83, 195–97, 201, 204, 273, 284
Washburn, Col. James 211, 235
Waynesboro, Battle of 270
Wells, Col. George 211–12
Wert, Jeffry 108, 168, 182, 252, 254
West Point 20, 30–32, 61–62, 92, 196, 205–6, 232, 269, 284
West Virginia troops: Infantry (1st) 211; (3rd) 87; (4th) 235; (12th) 235
Westport, Battle of 256
Wilderness, Battle of 196–202, 204, 208
Wildes, Lt. Col. Thomas F. 167, 252–53
Williams, Brig. Gen. Alpheus 104
Wilson, Brig. Gen. James 195, 230, 272, 278
Wilson's Creek, Battle of 48–56, 70, 72, 77, 107, 254
Winchester, 2nd Battle of 152
Wittenberg, Eric 248
Wood, Brig. Gen. Thomas J. 172–73
Wright, Maj. Gen. Horatio 234–35, 238, 252–53

Yamashita, Gen. Tomoyuki 3

Zollicoffer, Brig. Gen. Felix 66

www.ingramcontent.com/pod-product-compliance
Lightning Source LLC
Chambersburg PA
CBHW060336010526
44117CB00017B/2846